OXFORD WORLD'S CLASSICS

MADAME BOVARY

GUSTAVE FLAUBERT was born in 1821 in Rouen, where his father was chief surgeon at the hospital. From 1840 to 1844 he studied law in Paris, but gave up that career for writing, and set up house at Croisset in 1846 with his mother and niece. Notwithstanding his attachment to them (and to a number of other women), his art was the centre of Flaubert's existence, and he devoted his life to it. His first published novel, *Madame Bovary*, appeared in 1856 in serial form, and involved Flaubert in a trial for irreligion and immorality. On his acquittal the book enjoyed a *succès de scandale*, and its author's reputation was established.

Flaubert has been considered a realist. It is true that he took enormous trouble over the documentation of his novels—his next, *Salammbô* (1862), involved a trip to North Africa to gather local colour. But Flaubert's true obsession was with style and form, in which he continually sought perfection, recasting and reading aloud draft after draft.

While enjoying a brilliant social life as a literary celebrity, he completed a second version of *L'Éducation sentimentale* in 1869. *La Tentation de Saint Antoine* was published in 1874 and *Trois contes* in 1877. Flaubert died in 1880, leaving his last work, *Bouvard et Pécuchet*, to be published the following year.

TERENCE CAVE is a Fellow of St John's College, Oxford.

MARK OVERSTALL taught French at Winchester College.

OXFORD WORLD'S CLASSICS

*For over 100 years Oxford World's Classics have brought
readers closer to the world's great literature. Now with over 700
titles—from the 4,000-year-old myths of Mesopotamia to the
twentieth century's greatest novels—the series makes available
lesser-known as well as celebrated writing.*

*The pocket-sized hardbacks of the early years contained
introductions by Virginia Woolf, T. S. Eliot, Graham Greene,
and other literary figures which enriched the experience of reading.
Today the series is recognized for its fine scholarship and
reliability in texts that span world literature, drama and poetry,
religion, philosophy and politics. Each edition includes perceptive
commentary and essential background information to meet the
changing needs of readers.*

OXFORD WORLD'S CLASSICS

GUSTAVE FLAUBERT

Madame Bovary
Life in a Country Town

Translated by
GERARD HOPKINS

With an Introduction by
TERENCE CAVE
and Notes by
MARK OVERSTALL

OXFORD
UNIVERSITY PRESS

OXFORD
UNIVERSITY PRESS

Great Clarendon Street, Oxford OX2 6DP

Oxford University Press is a department of the University of Oxford.
It furthers the University's objective of excellence in research, scholarship,
and education by publishing worldwide in

Oxford New York

Athens Auckland Bangkok Bogotá Buenos Aires Calcutta
Cape Town Chennai Dar es Salaam Delhi Florence Hong Kong Istanbul
Karachi Kuala Lumpur Madrid Melbourne Mexico City Mumbai
Nairobi Paris São Paulo Singapore Taipei Tokyo Toronto Warsaw

and associated companies in Berlin Ibadan

Oxford is a registered trade mark of Oxford University Press
in the UK and in certain other countries

Published in the United States
by Oxford University Press Inc., New York

Introduction, Select Bibliography, and Chronology
© Terence Cave 1981, 1994
Notes © Mark Overstall 1981
Revised translation © Oxford University Press, 1981

The moral rights of the author have been asserted

Database right Oxford University Press (maker)

First published as a World's Classics paperback 1981
Reissued as an Oxford World's Classics paperback 1998

British Library Cataloguing in Publication Data

Data available

Library of Congress Cataloging in Publication Data

Data available

ISBN 0-19-283399-5

7 9 10 8

Typeset in Ehrhardt
by RefineCatch Limited, Bungay, Suffolk
Printed in Great Britain by
Clays Ltd, St Ives plc

CONTENTS

Introduction   vii

Select Bibliography   xxi

A Chronology of Gustave Flaubert   xxiii

MADAME BOVARY

PART I   I

PART II   61

PART III   211

Explanatory Notes   325

Mark Overstall died as this book was going to press. The editors acknowledge with gratitude his generous and invaluable help with all aspects of the enterprise.

INTRODUCTION

In September 1851, when the first pages of *Madame Bovary* were drafted, Flaubert was thirty and had published nothing. He had, however, written a great deal: short stories on more or less exotic subjects, semi-autobiographical narratives, a novel called *L'Éducation sentimentale* (not to be confused with the novel published in 1869 under that title), and the first draft of *La Tentation de Saint Antoine*, a grotesque fantasy in dialogue form. All in all, these works reveal a decided preference for the extravagant and the bizarre, although *L'Éducation sentimentale* is already a notable exception. While travelling in the Near East in 1850, he had had three new projects in mind: *Une nuit de Don Juan*, *Anubis*, and a novel about a 'young girl who dies a virgin and mystic after living with her father and mother in a small provincial town' (letter of 14 November 1850).

It was this third subject which was to be taken up. Flaubert preserved the provincial setting and characters, together with something of the interplay between the mystical and the erotic, but invented a new heroine who would make the story, as he put it, more 'entertaining' for the reader. Despite this concession, the writing of *Madame Bovary* was for Flaubert both an exercise and an experiment. From the outset, his letters speak of the atrocious stylistic difficulties the subject presented, and although there were moments of optimism and enthusiasm, his most characteristic feeling was one of disgust for the sheer banality of his materials. He viewed the whole enterprise as training ('gymnastics') for a later novel which would suit his own tastes and what he believed to be his own talents. The nearest he came to this ideal was *Salammbô*: a magnificent novel in its own way, but one which would hardly be read except by historians of literature, had *Madame Bovary* never been written.

The story of Flaubert's fanatical self-mortification during the five years of composition, although a highly readable one, might well seem to be just another of those colourful portraits of the artist which contribute nothing of real value to the understanding of the work itself. Yet it is always instructive to see a writer reaching the height of his powers by denying himself the very resources he feels most tempted to exploit. And in this instance one can go further.

The absence of what Flaubert cut out in writing *Madame Bovary* arguably creates the most important part of the effect of the novel: it determines both the angle from which the action is viewed and the precise sense in which that action is tragic.

The pertinence of this way of looking at *Madame Bovary* – as an exercise in amputation – will, however, become clearer after a brief account of the experimental character of the novel. What was new about *Madame Bovary* in the 1850s? As a portrait of 'life in a country town' it owes something to Balzac, who used provincial settings in many of his novels; Balzac's *Physiologie du mariage* anticipates Flaubert's anatomy of a marriage doomed to failure from the outset by inexperience and illusion; and the theme of lost illusions, the subject of another of Balzac's novels, is a commonplace of French Romantic literature. Furthermore, a number of the motifs used in *Madame Bovary* had already appeared in Flaubert's own earlier writings (*Passion et vertu*, for example). Thus the general conception of the novel's plot, subject, and characters could hardly be called experimental. What was exceptional for the mid-nineteenth century was the rigour with which Flaubert restricted himself to the petty details of everyday life, avoiding high drama and grand moral dilemmas. While writing the first half of the novel, he referred more than once in his letters to the problems of making an almost event-less narrative interesting:

What worries me in my book is the element of *entertainment*. That side is weak; there is not enough action. I maintain, however, that *ideas* are action. It is more difficult to hold the reader's interest with them, I know, but if the style is right it can be done. I now have fifty pages in a row without a single event. (letter of 15 January 1853)

By 'ideas', Flaubert seems to mean something like 'psychology': not explicit psychological analysis, of which there is very little in *Madame Bovary*, but the gradual accumulation of apparently trivial responses which finally, after long preparation, leads to the outbreak of 'action' in the conventional sense: 'I think that this is rather characteristic of life itself. The sexual act may last only a minute, though it has been anticipated for months' (letter of 25 June 1853).

These aspects of the experiment allow *Madame Bovary* to be classed as a realist novel in the strict, historical sense of the term. It was in fact in the 1850s in France that 'realism' became a fashionable term of literary criticism and literary history. Brought into prominence by the controversial experiments of the painter Gustave Courbet in the unadorned representation of mundane objects, it was subsequently adopted by a not very distinguished group of anti-idealist and socially progressivist writers; in 1858, it was applied retrospectively by Taine, in an important essay, to the novels of Balzac. Baudelaire detested the more literal forms of realism as a denial of the aesthetic imagination: he believed that the artist's task was to seek the conjunction of a precise, immediate representation of phenomena with the maximum degree of imaginative penetration (his *Salon* of 1859 provides a lucid series of essays on this topic). Flaubert's view was remarkably similar, although it should be remembered that *Madame Bovary* was begun before realism became a burning issue. Thus his *boutade* 'I undertook this novel in hatred of realism' (in a letter of 1856) should be understood as a reaction against a local variant of realism; it is clear from many references in the letters that he saw his own task as the aesthetic transformation of mundane and vulgar reality.

This is indeed another of the principal senses in which Flaubert thought of *Madame Bovary* as an experiment:

It is perhaps absurd to want to give prose the rhythm of verse (keeping it distinctly prose, however), and to write of ordinary life as one writes history or epic (but without falsifying the subject) . . . But on the other hand it is perhaps a great experiment, and very original. (letter of 27 March 1853)

Four years later, Sainte-Beuve was to make much the same point in his review of the finished novel: 'One precious quality distinguishes M. Gustave Flaubert from the other more or less exact observers who in our time pride themselves on conscientiously reproducing reality, and nothing but reality, and who occasionally succeed: he has *style*.'

Flaubert's conception of a prose which was flawlessly elegant in its colours and rhythms, without being either flowery or bombastic, and which might succeed in fusing the vulgar with the poetic, could well be considered in relation to the contemporary emergence of the prose poem: Baudelaire's first experiments in this new genre date from the 1850s. But it is in a rather different context that Flaubert's cultivation of style makes its greatest impact on the novel. It is the counterpart of what is perhaps the most significant experiment of all: the suppression of the author as a source of reflections and judgements external to the narrative. At the earliest stages of composition, Flaubert speaks almost exclusively of the difficulty of stringing sentences together. In January 1852, he sketches a more general theory of style, defining it in a much quoted phrase as 'an absolute manner of seeing things'. Three weeks later, the decision to eliminate the authorial presence is explicit: 'I do not want my book to contain a *single* subjective reaction, nor a *single* reflection by the author.' By December 1852, the absence of the author has become a special kind of presence: 'An author in his book must be like God in the universe, present everywhere and visible nowhere.' Flaubert will return to this point again and again. It has two aspects: rejection of first-person-singular, quasi-autobiographical narrative; and the exclusion of a moral discourse imposed from 'outside'. What Flaubert calls style – the aesthetic point of view – guarantees the moral autonomy of the novel.

Madame Bovary is not the first novel in which the narrative is presented without authorial commentary: the epistolary form of *Les Liaisons dangereuses*, to cite one example at random, has the same effect. And there are some apparent lapses. The narrator does appear briefly in the unexplained 'we' of the opening chapter, and the perfect tense is used here and there to imply a connection between the fictions of the novel and the real world ('nothing has changed in Yonville . . .'; 'He has just received the Legion of Honour'). Then there are general observations and aphorisms ('One should never touch idols: the gilt may come off on one's hands'), and occasional uses of morally loaded vocabulary. But these intermittent instances do not add up to a consistent authorial presence, and in other respects a strict economy is maintained in order to ensure that the reader will not be conscious of a voice telling him how to interpret the story. The reader must, in the end, accept full responsibility for what he makes of it.

Flaubert's attempt to use the technique of non-intervention systematically in all his mature novels marks the beginning of a new and fruitful development in the history of the genre. The major innovations of novelists as different as Zola, Henry James, Gide, Woolf, Faulkner, and Alain Robbe-Grillet all have to do with the displacement of the author from the narrative scene. In retrospect,

Flaubert's ideal of a 'book about nothing' (letter of 16 January 1852) with its implied suppression of plot (exciting adventures), character (interesting, large-as-life people), and even theme (love, adultery, ambition, art) as anything other than a pretext, may indeed seem remarkably close to the calling in question of standard conventions of the novel by the French 'new novelists' of the 1950s and 1960s.

The most celebrated and wide-ranging of Flaubert's techniques for 'showing' rather than 'telling' is a persistent use of irony, which he himself saw as innovative. Speaking of the conversation between Emma and Léon in Part Two, Chapter II, he remarks:

It is something that could be taken seriously, and yet I fully intend it as grotesque. This will be the first time, I think, that a book makes fun of its leading lady and its leading man. The irony does not detract from the pathetic aspect, but rather intensifies it. In my third part, which will be full of farcical things, I want my readers to weep. (letter of 9 October 1852)

Ironic narrative, as well as the analogous mixing of comedy and pathos, has a long history in which Ariosto and Cervantes are major landmarks: *Don Quixote* was one of Flaubert's favourite novels. Oddly enough, he was scornful of Stendhal's *Le Rouge et le noir*, which has some of the same characteristics. But the use of irony in *Madame Bovary* is highly distinctive. It is not simply a means of making fun of the characters by inflating and then deflating them. Only the crudest of misreadings would maintain that in *Madame Bovary* Flaubert is uniformly destructive of his characters. Nor does his irony consist in an alternation of contrasting tones or registers: he aimed at, and achieved, an extraordinary consistency of style. Within this uniform medium, there are infinite nuances of irony, covering the whole spectrum from caricature (the officials at the agricultural show, Homais and Bournisien arguing beside the corpse) to an acutely tragic sense of the discrepancy between Emma's dreams and the real world.

Irony, as used by Flaubert, is thus a medium which creates a dual vision. In the 'honeymoon' episode of Part Three, Chapter III, for example, a delicate equilibrium is maintained between the fresh immediacy of sounds, flavours, light and shade, sensations of all kinds, and the undercurrent of indications that Léon and Emma inflate their experience and turn it into a Romantic cliché. It is essential to avoid reducing this perpetual changing of angle to a fixed interpretation of character and action. The reader who is not disconcerted by the shift from the schoolroom scene of the opening chapter to the moments Charles spends looking out of his window in Rouen, or to his dawn arrival at Rouault's farm, has already grasped the sense of Flaubert's method. The key here, I think, is to recognize that the novel invites us to share not the mental responses of the characters but the physical surface of the world – real or imagined – through which they move. The intensity of this world is preserved in scene after scene, regardless of the extent to which its value, as assessed by the character, is undermined. The principle is maintained even in the dialogue passages: utterances so evidently banal nevertheless emerge, in Flaubert's prose, elegant in sound and rhythm: 'My characters are completely commonplace, but they have to speak in a literary style, and the politeness of the language takes away so much picturesqueness from their way of expressing themselves!' (letter of 19 September 1852). The immaculate evenness of style both creates the irony by which the world is seen so often as false and petty, and presents that same world as a thing of extraordinary beauty. No other novelist has ever preserved the fineness of that balance.

'I have dissected myself to the quick, with total honesty, at moments which were not in the least amusing' (letter of 6 June 1853). This remark epitomizes the dual vision of Flaubert's novels, the fusion of sensibility with the sharpest irony. It is also an example of the way Flaubert's imagination draws on medicine – and, more precisely, on surgery – as a source of metaphor both in his letters and his fiction. That he was the son of a celebrated doctor, that as a child he surreptitiously looked through the windows of his father's mortuary, and that he was considered not bright enough to become a doctor himself, is sufficient to give scope to anyone who wants to speculate on his psyche: Sartre's vast, unfinished study *L'Idiot de la famille* takes this theme as its starting-point. What is perhaps more pertinent here is simply the observation that, in *Madame Bovary*, the inadequate husband is also an inadequate doctor. Two hundred years previously, in Molière's comedy, the caricaturing of doctors as pedants and charlatans called in question no fundamental beliefs. But in the mid-nineteenth century, when the progress of medical science and the transformation of society had already made the doctor a figure no less prestigious than the priest, Charles's impotence is more pathetic and more alarming. The point here is not that Flaubert is portraying contemporary attitudes to medical science (although he is no doubt doing that, too), but that, as a metaphor, medical incompetence goes deep.

At the metaphorical level, it needs little reflection to discern that the figure of the doctor is one variant of the figure of the artist: the remark quoted above, which refers to the sense in which Flaubert felt himself to be incorporating his personal experience into his novel, already suggests that the equivalence came naturally to him. But, before pursuing this and other equivalences, a more general point needs to be made. Flaubert's excision of the authorial presence from his novels – itself a kind of surgical operation – is accompanied by another form of invisibility. Aesthetically self-conscious novelists are inclined, at some point in their career, to make writing (or another art) the principal subject of a novel. Balzac's fiction is full of artists, geniuses, journalists, inventors, and the like; Henry James's *Roderick Hudson*, and a number of his short stories, enable him to analyse overtly the problems of the American artist; in Gide's *Les Faux-monnayeurs*, one of the characters is writing a novel called *Les Faux-monnayeurs;* and Proust's *A la recherche du temps perdu* proves, in the end, to be an aesthetic odyssey. But none of Flaubert's mature novels place such a figure at the centre of the stage. His only extended experiment in this mode was the 1845 (as opposed to the 1869) *L'Éducation sentimentale*, and it is worth looking at this text briefly in order to see why the experiment was not repeated.

Henry and Jules, the two central characters, begin with idealistic visions of becoming great artists and lovers. Henry has a passionate affair, runs away with his mistress (a married woman who in some respects anticipates Emma Bovary), gets bored, and ends up as a successful but banal man of the world. Jules fails in love, is disillusioned with life, and turns to art as the only medium through which the powers of the imagination can be brought to fruition. The novel already illustrates a theme which will recur in the mature works, namely, that the attempt to make the real world conform to the world of the imagination is a fundamental error which can only end in disaster (*Madame Bovary*) or emotional bankruptcy (*L'Éducation sentimentale* of 1869). But Jules is a special case, since his

abandonment of the world in favour of a hermit-like existence dedicated to art is the pretext for an overt exposition of the view of art
Flaubert was to adopt in the years to come. The novel ends, in fact,
with a substantial piece of aesthetic theory, attributed to Jules, but
representing the nearest Flaubert was ever to come to a credo. The
fact that the experiment was not to be repeated is no doubt due to
the perception that the artist's solution is, paradoxically enough,
death to the novel. There is literally nothing to say about Jules once
he has assumed his pose as high priest of the imagination. Minor
figures in the later novels provide a parody of art at its most banal –
Binet and his napkin rings; Pellerin, the painter turned photog-
rapher, in the 1869 *Éducation sentimentale*. Otherwise, the portrait of
Flaubert as an artist can only be constructed from his letters.

The excision, however, leaves its traces, and the most visible of
these is the way Flaubert exploits in his narrative works themes
which appear elsewhere as metaphors of the writer's condition. Next
to the image of the doctor, one may here place that of the writer as a
monk or hermit, enjoying 'debauches of the imagination' which are
more intense than any lived experience: Jules's meditations on this
theme recur in the correspondence and are mirrored in the scenarios
of *La Tentation de Saint Antoine* and, in miniature, in *La Légende de
Saint Julien l'Hospitalier*. The association of abstinence with sexual
desire is fundamental to this group of themes. In a letter of 24 April
1852, Flaubert speaks thus of his writing:

I am leading an austere life, stripped of all external pleasure, and am
sustained only by a kind of permanent frenzy, which sometimes makes me
weep tears of impotence but never abates. I love my work with a love that is
frantic and perverted, as an ascetic loves the hair shirt that scratches his belly.

Equivocations between sexual and religious longings dominate
Emma's sensibility from convent to death-bed, and the pattern will
reappear in *Salammbô*, *Trois contes*, and even *Bouvard et Pécuchet*.

In the correspondence, Flaubert insistently, even obsessively,
refers to sex in relation to writing. Metaphors of potency and impotence are frequent. Rather less frequent, but no less striking, are his
fantasies of self-castration. In a letter of 27 December 1852 he speaks
of the shock he received when he read Balzac's *Louis Lambert*:

At the end, the hero wants to castrate himself, in a kind of mystical
madness. During my wretchedness in Paris, when I was nineteen, I had

that same wish . . . later I spent two entire years without touching a woman. (Last year, when I told you about my idea of entering a monastery, it was my old leaven rising in me again.) There comes a moment when one needs to make oneself suffer, needs to loathe one's flesh, to fling mud in its face, so hideous does it seem. Without my love of form, I would perhaps have been a great mystic.

Louis Lambert, it should be added, is a genius whose mental (and physical) powers come to nothing.

The presentation of sex in the novels is much less sensational. It is usually left to the reader's imagination, as in the consummation of Emma's affair with Rodolphe, or the famous episode of the cab-ride with Léon. Indirection is Flaubert's most characteristic technique in this respect. One of the most sensual passages in the book is a description of Emma in full bloom at the height of her affair with Rodolphe, and elsewhere much of the powerful erotic effect is conveyed through reference to other pleasures and other sensations – the sound of melted snow dripping on Emma's tightly stretched parasol, the falling of ripe fruit and the scuttling of nocturnal beasts in the garden where she makes love with Rodolphe.

It is clear, then, that in *Madame Bovary* the 'debauches of the imagination' are achieved by a practice of veiling, suppression, and transference. From this it follows that sexual implications may be present in episodes which are not ostensibly erotic. It is at this point that we may return to Charles's double incompetence. The operation on Hippolyte's club-foot, which occurs at the very centre of the novel, is directly implicated in Emma's erotic motivation. She has begun to grow tired of Rodolphe, and her fantasy of Charles's fame as a surgeon momentarily arouses in her a sexual response. But his pathetic failure finishes him in her eyes, and she returns to Rodolphe with a renewed and blatantly physical passion. The turning-point takes the form of a scene in which Emma watches Charles pacing up and down the room while from outside come the terrible screams of Hippolyte as he undergoes amputation.

I would emphasize that these remarks are not designed to assert the idiotic theory that what *Madame Bovary* is 'really' about is Flaubert's fears of castration or impotence. I merely wish to point to the fact that these different echoes of the writer and his exercise permeate all of Flaubert's work. Whether they are linked in his subconscious is not in question here. The narrative is demonstrably fabricated from materials which, in Jules's meditations, or in the scarcely less fictional drama of the correspondence, are figures of the writer's problems.

The examples considered so far already suggest that the displacement of these materials from one side of the fence to the other may often take the form of an inversion. Charles's botched surgery is, in one sense, at the opposite end of the scale from Flaubert's accomplished stitching together of sentences to form a perfectly seamless textual body. But one can go further than this and say that the failure of the characters is a necessary condition of the artist's success. The world of Flaubert's novels is notoriously one in which all values are eroded, all dreams deflated. The only way for its inhabitants to achieve success is to remain immaculately and aggressively banal. Imagination is a disease which will infallibly cripple or kill unless one learns, like Henry, to immunize oneself against it. Emma enacts this predicament by attempting to apply to the real world an imaginative sensibility which can only be productive, according to Flaubert's logic, in the realm of art. Indeed, her error – the attempt to live life as if it were a novel is one which is peculiarly visible to a novelist who has learnt Jules's lesson, and thus eminently suited, as Jules's story is not, to be the subject of a novel. Emma's experiments are doomed to disaster, one might say, because she fails to recognize that she *is* a character in a novel; the fact that the writer and reader know she is provides the ultimate grounding for the novel's ironic perspective. What is loss for the character is gain for the novelist; *Madame Bovary* is the apotheosis of the mastered imagination, its subject the tragedy of imagination dissipated and broken on the wheel of reality. The pathos is all the greater because the subject is, in its basic essentials, a 'realist' subject: Emma perceives the triviality of everyday reality, but can't escape from it; the writer can.

At the point where Léon begins to tire of his vacuous relationship with Emma, Binet says to him:

'The trouble with you is that you don't know how to relax.'
'And what's the best way of doing that?'
'If I were you, I should invest in a lathe.'
'But I don't know how to work a lathe.'
'I hadn't thought of that,' said the other, stroking his chin with a mingled air of contempt and satisfaction.

The exchange could almost be a burlesque passage between a travestied author and his even less well endowed character.

It is in this sense, above all, that the view of *Madame Bovary* as an exercise, of what Flaubert denied himself in order to write the novel, has its furthest reach. Like Cervantes, he uses at one remove all the materials and devices of the 'conventional' novel. The actual elopement of the 1845 *Éducation sentimentale* is replaced in *Madame Bovary* by an imagined elopement; Emma's dreams, although shown to be both precarious and dangerous, none the less bring into the novel the kind of exotic fantasies the writer and the reader hanker after; the pleasures of sex, the drama of death, the conversion of heroine into saint, are enacted for us in one form or another. The novel must work at that level – the level of conventional response – if its irony is to bite deep. It is as if Flaubert were out to beat the commonplace at its own game. The reader must sympathize with, identify with Emma, who is after all as seductive as a good novel, in order to grasp the point about the inauthenticity of such identification. But conversely, once the magic has begun to work, the reader is drawn deeper and deeper into a demonstration of the procedures by which we fictionalize our lives, or mistake the fictional for the real. When Flaubert had written about half of his novel, he described what he was engaged in as 'a work of criticism, or rather of anatomy' (letter of 2 January 1854). The remark is true in more than one sense, but the sense we are concerned with here is the literary one: *Madame Bovary* as an exercise in literary criticism.

Novels can only produce their effect by making things interesting. Their materials, viewed dispassionately, are always commonplace. They deal endlessly in the same currency – quests, embraces, duels, suicides – while building upon it constantly changing imaginative structures. *Madame Bovary* is of course no exception: and, more than most novels, it reveals how the process works. Sexual desire and its consummation, as an unadorned commonplace, appears as unendingly repetitious, the nadir of all commonplaces: 'As the charm of novelty slipped from her like a dress, Rodolphe saw nothing but the naked horror of an eternal monotony of passion, always with the same face, always speaking the same words.' In order to be made interesting, it has constantly to be dressed up, refined on, deferred, transposed into sentimental poetry or romantic novels; the transaction itself must be disguised and displaced. So, too, in

Emma's dealings with Lheureux, the circulation of bills of exchange, the naked and banal truth of commerce, supports an ever-growing superstructure of fantasies: Emma uses paper money to furnish the world of her imagination. And, most strikingly of all, language becomes in the mouth of the characters a grossly inflated or counterfeit currency. There is hardly a single oral utterance in the whole book which is not banal or inauthentic. The characters speak in double quotation marks: their dialogues are presented to us not as instances of communication but as examples of the kind of things people conventionally say. The same effect is conveyed outside the dialogue proper by the use of italics indicating that a phrase is an *idée reçue* (Flaubert's project for a *Dictionnaire des idées reçues* developed as he was writing *Madame Bovary*). Language is shown to be doubly inauthentic in that it both exceeds and falls short of reality; it creates a world of its own, and is inadequate for the real world. The text actually makes both inauthenticities explicit, lest the reader should fail to infer them from the action: 'Human language is like a cracked kettle on which we beat out tunes for bears to dance to, when all the time we are longing to move the stars to pity'; 'feelings are endlessly extended by language, as though forced through a metal-press.'

Once the reader has noticed these themes, it is impossible for him not to notice also that the transaction between novels and their readers is itself inflationary. A novel provides indications which the reader interprets and supplements according to the directives of his own desire. It is a paper currency specifically designed to replace the real thing. From this point of view, *Madame Bovary* may be regarded as a showcase exhibiting the mechanisms of inflation. Emma is seen attaching to an accidentally discovered cigar case an imaginary narrative which gives it value and interest for her; Léon and Emma reread their pasts to make them conform to their present desires; Charles, finally, interprets the whole story as an illustration of the workings of fate. This last example is particularly instructive. The invocation of fate as an explanation of events is revealed explicitly as an *idée reçue* when Rodolphe inserts it into his letter to Emma; when Charles reproduces it, in his terminal conversation with Rodolphe, it is again marked as a commonplace ('And then, for the first and last time in his life, he uttered a deep thought'). But above all, Charles's attempt to make sense of what has happened to him strikes us as pathetic and ironic because he has never, throughout the novel, read or interpreted anything correctly. Just as the volumes of the medical dictionary he keeps in his consulting room remain uncut; just as he fails to understand the story of *Lucia di Lammermoor*; so, too, in his dealings with Emma, he proves totally incapable of reading her and the all too patent story of her adultery. When his discovery of Emma's letters finally gives him no other way out, he explains the story for himself, and thus disposes of it, by the most banal of all interpretations.

The point might still seem to go beyond the evidence were these semi-implicit examples not supported by the recurrence throughout the novel of the theme of reading as such. Again and again, the text insists on the extent to which the characters draw on books in their desire to make sense of their experience. Emma's reading at the convent is presented as determining her misreading of life; she and Léon constantly fictionalize their relationship; Emma's fantasies of elopement with Rodolphe are episodes from an imaginary novel; and in the scene at the opera which forms a prelude to her renewed relationship with Léon, she herself becomes conscious of that essential confusion between the real and the fictional from which she suffers. By portraying Emma as a reader, the novel deflates not only her false expectations, but also the reader's: when she reads Balzac and George Sand, 'seeking in their pages satisfaction by proxy for all her longings', when she becomes momentarily aware of 'the triviality of those passions which art paints so much larger than life', the rug is jerked from beneath the reader's feet. What he is looking for is just as inauthentic as what the characters are looking for.

One might say, then, that *Madame Bovary* repeats with steadily diminishing returns the experiencing of a commonplace. Emma sets out 'to discover what it was that people in real life meant by such words as "bliss", "passion" and "intoxication" – words, all of them, which she had thought so fine when she read them in books'; the outcome will be that she discovers in adultery all the platitudes of marriage. As *Madame Bovary* moves towards its consummations, it describes an inverse movement, the movement of a critic uncovering the procedures by which readers inflate a text.

When Emma, having just arrived at Yonville, meets Léon at the Golden Lion, they talk about reading. For Léon, this means above all becoming identified with the characters, and finding in the book an image of one's own feelings. Emma likes exciting stories, and hates '*low* heroes and lukewarm sentiments of the sort one finds in real life'. And Léon caps this by claiming that reading compensates for the disillusionments of life by the portrayal of superior characters and feelings. This dialogue, which is the one Flaubert singles out as an example of a new use of irony, is an awful warning to the would-be reader of *Madame Bovary*. There are many ways of misreading the novel, and most of them are itemized here. Another arises from taking too literally Flaubert's claim that 'My poor Bovary, without a doubt, is suffering and weeping at this very hour in twenty villages of France' (letter of 14 August 1853): he would have been amused to hear that, not long after his death, the villagers of Ry in Normandy believed their village was the model for Yonville and 'Bovarized' it to the point of exhibiting pears from a tree planted by Charles Bovary. Yet another type of misreading is represented by Henry James's surprise at the low intelligence of Flaubert's characters: the nuances of stupidity make as great a claim on the intelligence of writer and reader as the finesse of Charlotte Verver or Lambert Strether. The best solution, perhaps, is to recognize that *Madame Bovary* is a novel constructed with a high degree of self-consciousness by a novelist who is always ahead of his reader; and then to explore, sentence by sentence and episode by episode, the ways in which its elegant, amusing, and sensuous surface produces a mirage of tragedy.

TERENCE CAVE

SELECT BIBLIOGRAPHY

Two editions of the French text of *Madame Bovary* may be recommended:

(i) ed. Mark Overstall (London, Harrap, 1979), introduction and notes in English

(ii) ed. Claudine Gothot-Mersch (Paris, Garnier, 1971), the standard French critical edition

Readers who have enjoyed *Madame Bovary* should go on to try *L'Éducation sentimentale*, *Trois contes*, and perhaps *Bouvard et Pécuchet*; all are available in paperback English translations. *Salammbô* and *La Tentation de Saint Antoine* are for addicts.

A selection of Flaubert's letters is presented in Francis Steegmuller's *The Letters of Gustave Flaubert 1830–1857* (Cambridge, Mass., and London, Harvard University Press, 1980); it is from this translation that most of the passages quoted above in the Introduction have been taken. The most up-to-date and informative biography of Flaubert is Herbert Lottmann's *Flaubert: a Biography* (London, Methuen, 1989).

Three essays on Flaubert by Henry James, first published in 1876, 1893 and 1902, provide a good starting-point for critical reading on Flaubert and an interesting picture of the development of James's ideas. The whole of the substantial 1902 essay, originally an introduction to a translation of *Madame Bovary*, and sections of the other two relevant to this novel, may be found in *Henry James: The Critical Muse. Selected Literary Criticism* (Penguin, 1987). Among more recent studies in English, the following (in chronological order of publication) are recommended:

Thorlby, Anthony, *Gustave Flaubert and the Art of Realism* (London, Bowes and Bowes, 1956)

Ullman, Stephen, *Style in the French Novel* (Oxford, Blackwell, 1960)

Fairlie, Alison, *Flaubert: Madame Bovary* (London, Edward Arnold, 1962)

Levin, Harry, *The Gates of Horn: a Study of Five French Realists* (New York, Oxford University Press, 1963)

Bart, B. F., *Madame Bovary and the Critics: a Collection of Essays* (New York University Press, 1966)

Brombert, Victor, *The Novels of Flaubert: a Study of Themes and Techniques* (Princeton University Press, 1966)

Steegmuller, Francis, *Flaubert and Madame Bovary* (revised edition) (London and Melbourne, Macmillan, 1968)

Sherrington, R. J., *Three Novels by Flaubert* (Oxford University Press, 1970)

Nadeau, Maurice, *The Greatness of Flaubert*, translated by Barbara Bray (London, The Alcove Press, 1972)

Culler, Jonathan, *Flaubert: the Uses of Uncertainty* (London, Paul Elek, 1974)

Tanner, Tony, *Adultery in the Novel: Contract and Transgression* (Baltimore and London, The Johns Hopkins University Press, 1979)

Lowe, Margaret, *Towards the Real Flaubert* (Oxford, Clarendon Press, 1984)

Knight, Diana, *Flaubert's Characters* (Cambridge University Press, 1989)

Roe, David, *Gustave Flaubert* (London, Macmillan, 1989)

Heath, Stephen, *Gustave Flaubert: Madame Bovary* (Cambridge University Press, 1992)

A CHRONOLOGY OF GUSTAVE FLAUBERT

1821   12 December: born in Rouen, where his father is chief surgeon at the Hôtel-Dieu.

1836   While at school in Rouen, writes several stories. On holiday at Trouville, falls in love with Elisa Foucault, a woman of twenty-six, who shortly afterwards marries Maurice Schlésinger. The image of Elisa Schlésinger recurs in a number of Flaubert's writings: in particular, she is said to be the model for Madame Arnoux in *L'Éducation sentimentale*.

1837   More stories. One of these, *Une leçon d'histoire naturelle, genre Commis*, is published in a local journal; another, *Passion et vertu*, anticipates the story of *Madame Bovary* in certain respects.

1838   *Mémoires d'un fou*, an autobiographical narrative; *Loys XI*, a five-act play.

1839   Completes *Smarh*, a semi-dramatic fantasy which may be considered an embryonic version of *La Tentation de Saint Antoine*.

1842   *Novembre*, another autobiographical narrative. Passes his first law examination.

1843   Begins the first version of *L'Éducation sentimentale*. Fails his second law examination.

1844   Has a form of epileptic seizure. Gives up law.

1845   *L'Éducation sentimentale* (first version) completed.

1846   Flaubert's father and sister die. He sets up house at Croisset, near Rouen, with his mother and niece. Meets Louise Colet in Paris; she becomes his mistress.

1847   *Par les champs et par les grèves*, impressions of his travels in Brittany with his literary friend Maxime Du Camp.

1848   Together with Louis Bouilhet (another literary friend) and Maxime Du Camp, witnesses the 1848 uprising in Paris; he will later draw on these memories for scenes in *L'Éducation sentimentale*. Begins *La Tentation de Saint Antoine* (first version).

1849   Reads *La Tentation* aloud to Bouilhet and Du Camp, who consider it a failure. Leaves for a tour of the Near East with Du Camp.

1851   Returns to Croisset. 19 September: begins writing *Madame Bovary*.

1852   While working on *Madame Bovary*, recalls his earlier project for a *Dictionnaire des idées reçues*.

1854   End of affair with Louise Colet.

1856   *Madame Bovary* completed and published in serial form in *La Revue de Paris* (from 1 October). Begins to revise *La Tentation*.

1856–7 Fragments of *La Tentation* published in *L'Artiste*.

1857   Flaubert and *La Revue de Paris* prosecuted for irreligion and immorality; acquitted. The trial attracts a great deal of attention and makes *Madame Bovary* (now published as a complete novel) a *succès de scandale*. Begins work on *Salammbô*.

1858   Visits North Africa to gather material for *Salammbô*.

1862   *Salammbô* completed and published: an enormous success. Flaubert by now a famous literary figure.

1864   Begins work on *L'Éducation sentimentale*. In the course of the next five years gathers material for his novel, and at the same time enjoys a brilliant social life.

1869   *L'Éducation sentimentale* (definitive version) completed and published. Death of Louis Bouilhet.

1870   Works on yet another version of *La Tentation de Saint Antoine*.

1872   Flaubert's mother dies. Third version of *La Tentation* completed.

1874   *La Tentation* published. Begins work on *Bouvard et Pécuchet*.

1875–7 Writes *La Légende de Saint Julien l'Hospitalier*, *Un Cœur simple*, and *Hérodias* (*Trois contes*).

1877   *Trois contes* published. Returns to *Bouvard et Pécuchet*.

1877–80 Works on *Bouvard*, which will remain unfinished.

1880   8 May: dies.

1881   *Bouvard et Pécuchet* published.

TO

MARIE-ANTOINE-JULES SÉNARD*

Member of the Paris Bar
Ex-President of the National Assembly and
Former Minister of the Interior

Dear and Illustrious Friend,
allow me to inscribe your name on the first page of this
book, which I dedicate to you as having been chiefly
responsible for its publication. As a result of the
magnificent way in which you conducted my case, my
work has conferred upon me, its author, an authority
which I had no reason to anticipate. I should like you,
therefore, to accept this token of my gratitude.
However great it be, it can never adequately repay
either your eloquence or your devoted loyalty.

GUSTAVE FLAUBERT

Paris, 12 April 1857

PART ONE

CHAPTER I

WE were in the preparation room* when the head came in, followed by a new boy in ordinary day clothes, and by a school servant carrying a large desk. Those of us who were asleep woke up, and we all rose to our feet doing our best to give the impression that we had been interrupted in the midst of our labours.

The head made a sign to us to be seated: then, turning to the master on duty:

'Monsieur Roger,' he said in a low voice, 'I am putting this boy in your charge. He will start in the fifth. Later, should his work and general conduct warrant promotion, he will be moved into the senior class where, at his age, he ought to be.'

The new boy had withdrawn so completely into the corner behind the door as to be scarcely visible. He was a country lad, about fifteen years of age, and a good deal taller than any of the rest of us. He wore his hair cut in a straight fringe on his forehead like a village choirboy. He looked solemn and very shy. Though he was not particularly broad in the shoulders, his green cloth jacket with its black buttons seemed to irk him uncomfortably under the arms, and a pair of red wrists, accustomed to exposure, showed through the openings in his cuffs. His legs, encased in blue stockings, emerged from yellowish trousers braced very high. On his feet he wore heavy, badly-polished shoes, studded with nails.

We began to recite our lessons. He listened with all his ears. So intent was he on what was being said that it might have been a sermon. He was far too frightened either to cross his legs or to lean on his elbow. When the bell sounded at two o'clock, the master had to tell him to fall in with the rest of us.

It was our custom on entering the classroom to throw our caps on the ground so as to leave our hands free. We used to stand at the door and fling them under the bench in such a way that they would strike the wall and raise a great cloud of dust. We regarded this as being the 'thing to do'.

But either because he had not noticed what we did, or because he was too shy to follow suit, he was still holding his on his knee when prayers were over. It was a nondescript sort of object, combining a number of different features—part woollen comforter, part military head-dress, part pill-box, part fur bonnet, part cotton night-cap; one of those shoddy affairs which, like the face of an idiot, seems to express a certain secretive significance. Its general shape was that of an egg, and the upper part, stiffened with whale bone, rose from a base consisting of three bulging, circular, sausage-like protuberances. Above these was a pattern of alternating lozenges of rabbit-fur and velvet separated from one another by strips of some scarlet material. Higher still was a species of sack ending in a polygon of cardboard covered with a complicated design in braid, and finished off with a long, and excessively thin, cord from which hung a small truss of gold threads in place of a tassel.

It was new and had a bright, shiny peak.

'Stand up,' said the form-master.

He rose. His cap fell to the ground. The class began to laugh.

He bent down to pick it up. The boy next to him knocked it out of his hand with a jerk of the elbow. He picked it up again.

'I should be obliged if you would get rid of your—er—helmet——' said the form-master who had a pretty wit.

There was a roar of laughter which put the poor chap quite out of countenance. So confused was he that he did not know whether to keep the cap in his hand, to leave it lying on the ground, or to put it on his head. He resumed his seat and laid it on his lap.

'Stand up!' said the form-master again, 'and tell me your name.'

The new boy stammered out something wholly unintelligible.

'Again!'

Once more we heard the sound of garbled syllables drowned by the shouts of the class.

'Louder!' said the master, 'louder!' The new boy, as though making a desperate resolve, opened his enormous mouth, and, with the full force of his lungs, as though he were calling to someone at a distance, enunciated the single word— '*Charbovaril*'*.

At that pandemonium broke loose, rising to a confused crescendo of shrill voices (shrieks, yells, stamping of feet, and *Charbovaril*—*Charbovaril* repeated again and again) which gradually dispersed in single syllables. Finally, and with great difficulty, it was got under control, only to be taken up again by the occupants of another bench, as some burst of stifled laughter exploded on a sudden like a badly extinguished squib. To the accompaniment of a rain of impositions, order was eventually restored, and the form-master having at last succeeded in getting hold of the name, Charles Bovary, by dint of having it dictated, spelled out and read over to him, immediately told the poor wretch to take his place on the 'dunces' bench' which stood immediately below his own rostrum. The boy started to move, but hesitated before actually leaving his place.

'What are you looking for?' asked the form-master.

'My c——' replied the new boy timidly, with an anxious glance about him.

'Five hundred lines—the whole lot of you!' The words, uttered in a furious voice, quelled the rising storm like *Quos ego*.*

'I *will* have quiet!'—went on the outraged pedagogue, adding, as he mopped his forehead with a handkerchief which he took from under his cap, 'as for the new boy, he will copy out for me the verb *ridiculus sum* twenty times!'

Then in a kinder voice:

'Better go and retrieve that hat of yours: no one's stolen it.'

Calm settled down once more. Heads were bent over exercise-books, and for the next two hours the new boy behaved in exemplary fashion, though, from time to time, a pellet of paper, propelled by a pen-holder, hit his face with a moist thud. He merely wiped away the mess with his hand, not moving at all, and keeping his eyes on the ground.

In prep that evening he took a pair of protective cuffs from his desk, put his few odds and ends in order, and carefully ruled his paper. We noticed how conscientiously he did his work, what pains he was at to look up every word in the dictionary. Thanks, no doubt, to this evidence of good intentions, he managed not to be sent down to the class below: for, though he had a fairish acquaintance with the rules of grammar, his phrasing lacked elegance. He had been grounded in Latin by his local curé, because his parents, from reasons of economy, had delayed sending him to school as long as possible.

His father, Monsieur Charles Denis Bartholomew Bovary, formerly an assistant surgeon-major in the army, had become involved, about 1812, in some scandal connected with conscription cases, and been compelled to leave the service. As a result of this he had exploited his personal appearance, and had leaped at the chance of pocketing a dowry of sixty thousand francs which went with the daughter of a hosier who had become enamoured of his good looks. He was a handsome man, and a bit of a boaster, who strutted round with much jingling of spurs, sported a pair of whiskers which joined up with his moustache, always wore rings, and dressed in loud colours. Though he looked the devil of a fellow, he combined with his aspect of the warrior all the easy familiarity of a commercial traveller. Once married, he lived for two or three years on his wife's money, doing himself well in the matter of food, getting up late, smoking large porcelain pipes, going to the theatre of an evening before returning home, and becoming a familiar figure at various cafés. The father-in-law died, leaving little in the way of an estate. Indignant at being so treated, the ex-soldier tried his luck as a manufacturer, lost a bit of money at that, and then retired into the country with the intention of 'making the land pay'. But, since he knew no more about farming than he had done about cotton goods, rode his horses instead of sending them to the plough, drank his bottled cider instead of selling it, ate the best of his fowls, and greased his riding-boots with the fat of his pigs, he very soon realized that he had better abandon speculation altogether.

He found, in a village lying on the borderline between the district of Caux and Picardy, a dwelling, half farm, half country house, which was to let for two hundred francs a year. There, at the age of forty-five, morose, gnawed by regrets, full of resentment against heaven and envy of his fellow-men, he shut himself away. He was, he said, disgusted with the world, and determined to live in peace.

At one time his wife had been mad about him. Her love had expressed itself in an attitude of servility the only effect of which was to estrange him still more. Once gay, generous and fond, she became, as she grew older (like flat wine which turns to vinegar) a woman of difficult moods, shrill-voiced and nerve-ridden. In the early days of their marriage she had suffered much but complained little: had seen him run after all the village drabs, hang about all the places of ill-fame, and come home to her at night physically exhausted and stinking of liquor. At last her pride had rebelled, but she had said nothing, swallowing her anger and taking refuge in a silent stoicism which she maintained until the day of her death. She was forever occupied in various chores and matters of business. She made appointments with the solicitor and the local Justice, remembered when bills would fall due, and carried through all the arrangements to have them renewed. At home she ironed, sewed, did the washing, kept an eye on the workmen and saw that they were paid, while her lord and master bothered his head about nothing, spent his time drowsing ill-temperedly, and roused himself only for the purpose of saying hurtful things to her. All day long he sat in the corner of the hearth, smoking and spitting into the fire.

When her child was born it had to be put out to nurse, and when the little brat was eventually brought home he was thoroughly spoiled and treated like a young prince. His mother stuffed him with sweets, his father let him run about barefoot, and, wishing to pose as a philosopher, went so far as to say that he might go naked for all he cared, like the beasts of the field. In opposition to her maternal solicitude, he developed a theory that childhood should be a time of manly rigours. He did his best to rear his son on these lines, determined that he should be brought up in a school of Spartan austerity, and so grow strong in body. He made him sleep in a room without a fire, taught him to indulge in long draughts of rum, and trained him up to insult all religious processions. But the boy, who was of a mild temperament, responded ill to these attempts. His mother dragged him about with her wherever she went, cut out cardboard figures for him, told him stories, and indulged with him in endless monologues full of melancholy gaiety and baby-talk. Living, as she did, in unbroken loneliness, she lavished on the child her few shreds and shards of vanity. She dreamed of a great position for him, saw him in imagination a grown man, handsome and intelligent and settled in life as a civil-servant or a magistrate. She taught him to read and even to sing a few sentimental ballads to the accompaniment of an old piano which was one of her possessions. To all of which, Monsieur Bovary, caring little for the humaner arts, reacted by saying that it *wasn't worth the trouble*! How could they ever afford to send him to a government school, buy him a post or set him up in business? Besides, *all a man needed in order to get on in this world was plenty of cheek*. Madame Bovary bit her lip, and the boy ran wild about the village.

He followed the men at the plough and put the crows to flight with clods of earth. He ate the blackberries that grew in the hedgerows, kept watch over the turkeys, armed with a stick, helped in the hay-making, wandered about the woods, played at hopscotch in the church porch when it was raining, and, on the great feast-days, wheedled the sexton into letting him ring the bells, so that he might hang with his full weight on the end of the great rope and feel himself jerked off his feet as it bounced up and down.

He grew like a young oak tree. He acquired strong hands and a good colour.

When he was twelve, his mother made it her business to see that he should learn something. He was put in the charge of the curé. But the lessons were so short and so ill-planned, that he got little from them. They were hurried affairs, given at odd moments standing in the vestry, sandwiched between a christening and a funeral. Occasionally, after the angelus, the curé, when no duties called him from home, would send for his pupil. On these occasions they sat upstairs in his room while the midges and moths fluttered about the candle flame. It was hot: the boy dozed. Very soon, the good priest, his hands clasped on his stomach, grew drowsy and began to snore with his mouth hanging open. At other times, on his way home from administering the sacrament to a sick parishioner, and seeing Charles up to some mischief in the fields, he would call him over, lecture him for fifteen minutes or so, and take advantage of the occasion to make him conjugate a verb beneath a tree. Frequently the rain would interrupt these sessions, or some passing acquaintance. The curé, too, always expressed himself as satisfied with his charge, and went so far as to say that the *young man* had a remarkably good memory.

Charles could not go on like that. His mother was a woman of energy. His father, from a sense of shame, or, more probably, from sheer exhaustion, gave up the struggle. It was agreed that they should wait a year until after the urchin had made his first communion. Six months passed, and the next year Charles was finally sent to the College in Rouen,* whither his father accompanied him in person towards the end of October, at the time of the Saint-Romain Fair.

We should all of us now find it impossible to remember a thing about him. He was an even-tempered youth who joined in our games, did his work in prep, listened carefully in class, slept soundly in the dormitory and ate heartily in hall. He had been put in the charge of a wholesale ironmonger in the rue Ganterie, who asked him out on one Sunday in each month after the shop was closed, told him to take a walk down to the harbour and look at the ships, and delivered him back at school about seven, just before supper. Each Thursday evening the boy wrote a long letter to his mother in red ink, and this he sealed with three wafers. Having thus done his duty, he would revise his history notes, or read an old copy of *Anacharsis** which used to lie about in the classroom. When he went on our regular walks he always talked to the school servant, who was, like himself, from the country.

By dint of constant application he managed to maintain his place somewhere about the middle of the form-list. Once he even got a 'highly commended' in natural history. But at the end of his third year, his parents took him away, and sent him to study medicine,* convinced that he could get on sufficiently, without outside help, to be sure of a degree.

His mother took a room for him on the fourth floor of a house facing on to the Eau-de-Robec,* belonging to a dyer of her acquaintance. She made all necessary arrangements for his board, bought some furniture—a table and two chairs—sent him a cherry-wood bedstead from home, and provided him, in addition, with a small iron stove and enough wood to keep him warm. Having stayed with him for a week, she took her departure, after giving him a thousand lectures about being on his best behaviour now that he was to be left to his own devices.

The list of lectures which he read in the official time-table set his head in a whirl. They covered anatomy, pathology, physiology, pharmacy, chemistry, botany, clinical medicine and therapeutics, to say nothing of hygiene and materia medica—all words about the etymology of which he knew nothing, words which seemed to him like the portals of sanctuaries in which dwelt the shades of the august. He understood absolutely nothing. No matter how hard he listened, he made but heavy weather of the lectures. Nevertheless, he worked, equipped himself with bound notebooks, attended all the courses, and never played truant. He accomplished his little daily task in the manner of a mill horse, which goes round and round in blinkers, doing what he does without knowing the reason for it.

In order to save him expense, his mother sent him each week by the carrier a piece of baked veal, off which he made his luncheon every morning when he got back from the hospital, stamping his feet to keep himself warm. As soon as he had finished eating, he had to run off to a further lot of lessons, either in the lecture theatre or at the hospital, returning home, when they were over, along the endless streets. In the evening, after the scanty dinner provided by his landlord, he went up to his room, and once more settled down to work, his damp clothes steaming on his body as he sat in front of his glowing stove.

On fine summer nights, when the hot streets were deserted, and the servant-girls were playing at battledore and shuttlecock on the doorsteps, he would open his window and lean on his elbow, looking out. The river, which makes this part of Rouen seem like a miniature and squalid edition of Venice, flowed beneath, yellow, violet or blue, crossed by bridges and edged with wharves. He could see the workmen squatting on the banks, washing their arms in the current. Great skeins of cotton hung drying in the open air suspended from poles which projected from the windows of lofts. Opposite, above the roofs, was a wide stretch of cloudless sky, and the sun setting in a scarlet haze. How lovely (he thought) it must be now in the country, beneath the beeches! He would distend his nostrils hoping to catch a whiff of the good country smells, though these could never reach him at his perch. He grew thinner and more lanky, and his face took on a sort of mournful expression which made him look almost interesting.

Naturally, through sheer carelessness, the good resolutions he had made came gradually to lose their hold on him. A day came when he failed to turn up at the hospital, and next morning he missed a lecture. So sweet were the hours of idleness, that, little by little, he gave up all attempts to keep to his time-table. He formed the habit of frequenting bars, and developed a passion for dominoes. To sit of an evening cooped up in a grubby public room, for the sole purpose of stacking little oblongs of sheep's bone, marked with black dots, on a marble-topped table, seemed to him now to be a significant gesture of freedom, something which raised him in his own estimation. He grew to regard it as a ritual of initiation into the great world, as the key to forbidden pleasures. Each time he entered the place he turned the knob of the door with a thrill that had about it something almost sensual. As he stepped across the threshold a great weight of frustration was lifted from his spirit. He learned by heart snatches of song with which he entertained the women who were always welcome visitors there, came to have a passion for Béranger,* mastered the secret of making punch, and eventually had his first experience of love.

Thanks to these preparatory labours, he failed to pass his examination for the Public Health Service.* On the fatal evening his parents were waiting for him at home with all preparations made to celebrate his success. He set out on foot, halted at the outskirts of the village, sent a message asking his mother to come to him, and told her all. She found plenty of excuses for him, and put the blame for his failure on the unfairness of the examiners. Having thus, to some extent, drawn the sting from his smart, she undertook to arrange matters.

It was not until five years later that Monsieur Bovary learned the truth. By that time it had become ancient history, and he accepted his son's defeat the more readily since he found it impossible to admit that any child of his could be a fool.

Charles once more settled down to work, and studied uninterruptedly for his examination, taking the precaution of memorizing all the questions in advance. He passed reasonably high on the list. It was a proud day for his mother, and was marked with a grand dinner.

Then came the question of where he was to practise. The choice fell on Tostes.* There was only one old doctor in the place. For a long time Madame Bovary had been hoping that he would die, and almost before he had taken his departure, Charles was installed opposite as his successor.

But it was not enough for her to have brought up a son, had him taught medicine, and found in Tostes a happy hunting-ground for his abilities. He needed a wife. She found him one, the widow of a Dieppe bailiff, a woman of forty-five with a yearly income of twelve hundred francs. Ugly though she was, thin as a lath and with as many pimples as the spring has buds, she had had no lack of suitors from whom to choose. Before Madame Bovary the elder could achieve her object, she had to send the lot of them packing, and succeeded very cleverly in outwitting the intrigues of a pork-butcher who had Church influence behind him.

Charles had hoped that marriage would open up for him a brighter future. He had imagined that he would enjoy greater freedom than he had previously known, and might now do as he pleased both with himself and with his money. But his wife took control. She ordained what he should and should not say in public, made him fast on Fridays, dress as she thought fit, and dun those of his patients who were slow in settling their accounts. She opened his letters, spied on his movements, and listened through the wall whenever he had women in his consulting-room.

She had to have her chocolate brought to her every morning, and expected to be waited on hand and foot. She was for ever complaining of her nerves, of the state of her lungs, of her many and various ailments. The noise of people moving about made her feel ill, but no sooner was she left alone than she found her solitude unbearable. If anyone came to see her, it was, she felt sure, because they wanted to make certain that she was dying. When Charles came home of an evening, she would bring her long skinny arms from beneath the bedclothes, clasp them about his neck, make him sit on the edge of the bed, and then tell him of her woes. She accused him of neglect, of loving someone else, and always ended by asking for something to take for her health, and a little more love-making.

CHAPTER II

ONE night, about eleven o'clock, they were awakened by the sound of a horse stopping at their door. The maid-servant opened the attic window and spent some time in parley with a man in the street below. He had come for the doctor, and was the bearer of a letter. Nastasie shivered her way downstairs, turned the key and drew the bolts. The man left his horse where it was and entered the house in her wake. From the inside of his woollen cap with grey tassels he drew a letter wrapped in a scrap of linen, and presented it with scrupulous care to Charles, who propped himself on his elbow to read it. Nastasie stood by the bed, holding a light. Madame, from a sense of modesty, remained with her face to the wall, and presented only her back to the room.

The letter, which was fastened with a little blue wafer, begged Monsieur Bovary to go at once to Les Bertaux* farm to set a broken leg. Now, the distance from Tostes to Les Bertaux farm is a good six leagues by the road through Longueville and Saint-Victor. The night was extremely dark. Madame Bovary the younger feared lest some accident befall her husband. It was finally decided, therefore, that the groom should go on ahead, and that Charles should set out three hours later, when the moon was due to rise. A boy would be sent to show him the way to the farm, and to open the gates.

About four in the morning, Charles, well muffled in a cloak, started for Les Bertaux. Still only half aroused from the warmth of his slumbers, he surrendered himself to the easy amble of his mount. Whenever, at one of the holes fenced with thorn which had been dug along the highway, it stopped of its own accord, Charles woke with a jerk, hastily remembered the broken leg, and tried hard to rehearse all the fractures that he knew. The rain was no longer falling: day was breaking, and on the leafless branches of the apple-trees, the birds sat motionless, ruffling their tiny feathers in the cold dawn wind. The flat countryside stretched as far as eye could see, and the clumps of trees about the scattered farms showed as spaced splashes of an inky violet upon the vast grey surface which merged, on the far horizon, into the sky's funereal depths. From time to time Charles opened his eyes, but soon, his mind growing weary and sleep irresistibly return-ing, he would fall into a drowsy, half-conscious state where outward sensations grew confused with memories, and he saw, as it were, a double image of himself, student and married man, lying, as he had been but a while ago, in bed, and, at the same time, crossing an operating theatre as in the not so distant past. The warm stench of poultices assailed his nostrils, mixed with the fresh smell of dew. He could hear the rattle of iron curtain-rings above the ranged beds of the ward, and the sound of his wife sleeping. . . .

As he passed through Vassonville, he saw a small boy sitting on the grassy verge of the ditch.

'Are you the doctor?' asked the lad.

At Charles's answer, he took up his clogs and started running on in front, holding them in his hand.

As the medical officer continued on his way he gathered from the prattle of his guide that Monsieur Rouault was a farmer in easy circumstances, who had broken his leg the evening before as he was coming home from Twelfth Night celebrations at a neighbour's house. His wife had died two years before. No one lived with him but the 'young lady' who helped him to keep house.

The ruts became deeper. It could not be much further to Les Bertaux. The small boy vanished through a gap in the hedge, and reappeared to open the gate of the farmyard. The horse slipped on

the damp grass. Charles had to bend his head beneath low branches.
The kennel dogs barked, and dragged at their chains. At the
entrance to Les Bertaux his horse took fright and shied violently.

The farm had a prosperous appearance. Above the open half-
doors of the stables, great draught-animals could be seen placidly
taking their feed from brand-new mangers. A long manure heap
flanked the buildings and gave off a thin steam. Among the chickens
and the turkeys strutted five or six peacocks—exotic symbols of
luxury in the farmyards of that land of Caux—pecking for food. The
sheep-run was extensive, the barn tall, with walls that were smooth
as the back of a man's hand. Beneath the wagon-shed stood two large
carts and four ploughs complete with their whips, their yokes and all
their harness, the blue-dyed fleeces dirtied by the fine dust which
had drifted down from the lofts. The yard ran up hill. It was planted
with trees symmetrically spaced, and the cheerful gabble of a flock of
geese came from a corner near the pond.

A young woman, wearing a dress of blue merino adorned with
three flounces, welcomed Monsieur Bovary at the front door, and
showed him into the kitchen where a huge fire was blazing. Breakfast
for the farm-hands stood bubbling in little pots of different sizes.
Wet clothes hung drying within the great chimney-place. The
shovel, the tongs and the nozzle of the bellows, all of gigantic pro-
portions, shone like polished steel, and along the walls were ranged a
rich variety of kitchen utensils, which reflected the flicker of the
clear flames mingled with the first beams of the sun striking through
the window panes.

Charles went upstairs to see the invalid. He found him in bed,
sweating beneath the blankets, his cotton nightshirt flung to the
other end of the room. He was a small but thickset man of about fifty,
with a white skin, blue eyes, hair that was receding from his forehead, and rings in his ears. Beside him, on a chair, stood a big
decanter of brandy, from which he poured himself a drink now and
again to cheer his stomach. But the moment he set eyes on the
doctor, all sign of excitement vanished from his face, and, instead of
cursing and swearing as he had been doing for the last twelve hours,
he took to moaning feebly.

The fracture was a simple affair without any sort of complication.
Charles could never have dared to hope for anything easier. Recalling
the bedside manner of his masters, he comforted his patient with

cheerful talk—that favourite resource of the profession, which serves as the oil with which the surgeon prepares his instruments. A bundle of laths was brought from the wagon-shed to provide him with splints. He picked out one of them, cut it into lengths, and smoothed it with a scrap of broken glass, while the servant tore up sheets for bandages, and Mademoiselle Emma did her best to make pads. She took a long time, however, to find her needle-case, and her father grew impatient. She did not answer him, but pricked her fingers in the course of her work, and then proceeded to suck them.

Charles was surprised at the whiteness of her nails. They were bright and pointed, more highly polished than the ivories of Dieppe, and cut to an almond shape. Her hands, for all that, were not beautiful. Perhaps it was that they lacked pallor and had rather bony knuckles. In addition, they were too long, and had no softness of outline. But her eyes were lovely. Though they were brown, the lashes made them look black, and their gaze was candid and bold.

When the dressing had been completed, the doctor was invited by Monsieur Rouault to 'take a bite' before starting back.

Charles went downstairs to the principal room. Two plates with silver covers had been laid on a small table at the foot of a large, canopied bed with hangings of printed muslin showing a design of Turkish figures. A smell of orris-root and damp linen came from the tall oaken press which faced the window. Sacks of wheat stood in the corners of the room—an overflow from the nearby granary which was approached by three stone steps. A black chalk drawing of a head of Minerva, framed in gold, was the sole decoration. It hung from a nail in the middle of one of the walls, the green paint of which was scaling off through the action of the lime. Beneath the picture were the words 'To my dear Papa' in gothic lettering.

They talked first of the patient, then of the weather: of the extreme cold, and of the wolves which roamed the fields after nightfall. Mademoiselle did not find much to amuse her in the country, especially now, when most of the work of the farm fell on her unaided shoulders. The room was chilly and she shivered as she ate, thereby causing her rather full lips, which, in moments of silence, she was in the habit of biting, to fall slightly apart.

Her neck rose from a white, turned-down collar. Her hair was so smooth that the two black wings in which it was dressed seemed all of a piece. It was divided down the middle by a thin parting which followed the curve of her skull, and only the lobes of her ears were visible beneath it. It was gathered at the back into a large chignon, and showed a faintly perceptible wave over the temples—a feature of the human head which the country doctor now found himself observing for the first time in his life. There was a slight flush on her cheek bones. A pair of shell-rimmed glasses was stuck, masculine fashion, between the buttons of her bodice.

Charles went upstairs to say good-bye to her father, and, on coming back into the room on his way out, found her standing by the window, her forehead pressed against the pane, looking into the garden, where the bean-sticks had been blown down by the wind. She turned.

'Are you looking for something?' she asked.

'My riding-whip,' he said.

She began to rummage on the bed, behind the doors, under the chairs. It had fallen between the sacks and the wall. Mademoiselle Emma caught sight of it, and leaned forward across the sacks of wheat. Charles hurried forward politely, and, as he stretched his arm in a movement similar to her own, felt his chest brush against her back, bent beneath him. Blushing, she straightened herself, and looked at him over her shoulder as she held out his crop.

Instead of waiting for three days, as he had said he would before paying another visit to Les Bertaux, he came back the very next day, after which he turned up regularly twice a week, to say nothing of the unexpected visits which he paid now and again as though by accident.

All went well. The cure proceeded according to rule, and when, at the end of forty-six days, old Rouault began hobbling unaccompanied about the house, the opinion grew that Monsieur Bovary was a man of exceptional ability. Rouault said that he could not have been better looked after by the leading doctors of Yvetot,* or even of Rouen. Charles, for his part, did not so much as let himself wonder why it was that he found such pleasure in going to Les Bertaux. Had he done so, he would, no doubt, have attributed his zeal to the seriousness of the case, or, perhaps, to the profit which he hoped to derive from it. But was that the reason why his trips to the farm formed so delightful an exception to the humdrum routine of his life? On the days when they took place, he rose early, set off at a gallop, rode his horse hard, and then, before entering the house, dismounted in order to clean his boots on the grass, and to put on a pair of black gloves. He liked to visualize the manner of his arrival in the forecourt of the farm, feeling in imagination the pressure of the swinging gate against his shoulder, hearing the cock crowing from the wall, seeing the boys race down to meet him. He had grown to love the stables and the barn, old Rouault, who would give him a smacking hand-clasp and call him his 'preserver', and the sight of Mademoiselle Emma's tiny clogs standing on the scrubbed paving of the kitchen floor. Their high heels added something to her stature. As she walked in front of him, their wooden soles, rising briskly to meet the little ankle-boots she wore, gave out a clear, sharp sound.

She always saw him out, accompanying him to the top of the outside flight of steps. If his horse had not yet been brought round, she waited with him there. Good-byes had been said, and not a word passed between them. The wide spaces of the air were about them, bringing disorder to the wanton curls at the back of her neck, or blowing the apron strings in a flurry of streamers round her waist. One day in particular he remembered, a day of thaw, when the bark of the trees about the yard was all astream with moisture, and the snow was melting on the roofs of the outbuildings. She was standing on the threshold, and went in to fetch her parasol. She opened it, and the sun, striking through the fabric which was of the colour of a pigeon's breast, threw flickering lights upon the white skin of her face. She smiled within its shadow at the damp warmth of the day, and he could hear the drops of water falling one by one upon the tight-stretched silk.

At first, when Charles took to going to Les Bertaux, his wife never failed to ask after his patient, and had even reserved a fine blank page for Monsieur Rouault in the ledger which she kept by double-entry. But when she heard of the existence of his daughter, she set herself to find out more. She discovered that Mademoiselle Rouault had been brought up at an Ursuline convent* where, as the saying goes, she had received a 'good education', had learnt dancing, geography, drawing, embroidery, and to play the piano. It was the last straw!

'That', said she to herself, 'is why he looks so radiant when he sets off on his rounds. That's why he puts on a new waistcoat at the risk of getting it spoiled by the rain. He's after the girl!'

Instinctively, she hated her, and began to relieve her feelings by allusions which Charles completely failed to understand, and then by more direct comments which he carefully ignored for fear of raising storms. At last she resorted to point-blank charges which he did not know how to answer. Why, she asked, did he keep on going to Les Bertaux? Monsieur Rouault was as right as rain, and the account had not yet been settled. *She* knew well enough what the attraction was. *She* had heard all about the young woman who could talk and do fine needlework and display her wit! So that was what he wanted, was it, town-bred chits! Town-bred, indeed!—so would her tongue run on: old Rouault's daughter! Why, her grandfather was no better than a shepherd, and one of her cousins had nearly been taken to court for a bit of dirty work in some dispute or other! By what right did *she* put on airs and graces? Why should *she* show herself at church on Sundays got up like a countess in a silken gown? If it came to that, if it hadn't been for last year's colza crop, the beggarly old man would have been hard put to it to pay up his arrears of rent!

Charles grew so tired of these scenes that he gave up going to Les Bertaux. Héloïse had made him swear that he would discontinue his visits, making him take an oath upon the Mass. This particular incident had been preceded by a storm of sobs and kisses and a great outburst of passionate protestation. He obeyed, but the strength of his desires rose up to challenge so servile an attitude, and, by a sort of native hypocrisy, he persuaded himself that the very fact of being forbidden to see the girl gave him a sort of right to love her. Besides, his widow-wife was skinny, her teeth were long, and she wore, at all times of the year, a little black shawl with the point hanging down between her shoulder-blades. Her unattractive body was encased in scabbard-like dresses which were so short that they revealed her grey-stockinged ankles criss-crossed by the laces of her large and uncouth shoes.

From time to time his mother came to visit them, and always, at the end of a few days, her daughter-in-law seemed to have imparted to her something of her own sharpness. Like two knives, they took to scarifying him with comments and remarks. He oughtn't to eat so much. Why must he be for ever offering casual visitors a drink? It was sheer obstinacy in him not to wear flannel undervests!

It so happened that early in the spring, the solicitor at Ingouville* who administered the widow Dubuc's property, set sail on a favourable tide, taking all his client's money with him. Héloïse, it is true, was still left with her share in a ship valued at six thousand francs, and a house in the rue Saint-François. But out of the fortune which had been the subject of so much talk, the Bovary household had seen little more than a few odds and ends of furniture and some clothes. It was essential that they know precisely how they stood. The house in Dieppe turned out to be eaten up with mortgages. God alone knew how much had been deposited with the solicitor, and the share in the ship was found to amount to no more than three thousand francs. She had lied to them. So furious was old Monsieur Bovary that he broke a chair on the floor. He accused his wife of ruining their son by tying him up to an old broken-winded jade whose trappings were worth as little as her carcass! They travelled to Tostes. Explanations followed—and scenes. Héloïse flung herself weeping into her husband's arms, calling on him to protect her against his parents. Charles took her part, and the old people left in a fury.

But the blow had struck home. A week later, while she was hanging out some washing in the yard, Madame Bovary the younger began to spit blood, and the next day, while Charles was drawing the curtains with his back to her, she cried out 'Oh, God!' uttered a sigh and lost consciousness. She was dead! What a surprise!

When the funeral was over, Charles went home. He met no one on the ground floor. Upstairs, he saw her dress hanging at the foot of the alcove in their bedroom. Leaning against the bureau, he remained until evening in a state of painful reverie. After all, she *had* loved him.

CHAPTER III

ONE morning, old Rouault came over to pay Charles for the setting of his leg—seventy-five francs in two-franc pieces, and a turkey. He had heard about the doctor's trouble, and said what he could to comfort him.

'I know what it's like,' he said, giving him a hearty slap on the back: 'been through it myself! When I lost my late-lamented, I went out into the fields to be alone, threw myself down under a tree, and cried. I called on the good God and said all sorts of stupid things to him. I wanted to be like the moles I saw strung up on the branches with worms crawling in their bellies—in other words, dead as a door-nail. When I thought of all the other chaps lying snug in bed with their wives in their arms, I thumped the ground with my stick. I was pretty near out of my mind, and ate hardly anything. You wouldn't credit how the very idea of going to a café disgusted me! And then, quite gradually, as day followed day, as spring followed winter, and autumn caught up on summer, bit by bit and scrap by scrap, it all went, just passed, or, rather, burrowed deep down, because, you know, it'll always be there, a sort of weight on my chest! But we all come to it sooner or later. It's not for the likes of us to pine away and want to die just because others are dead. . . . You must get a hold on yourself, Monsieur Bovary—it'll pass. Come out and pay us a visit. My daughter thinks about you quite a lot, and says you've forgotten her. The spring'll be here quite soon now. We'll fix you a bit of rabbit shooting, just to take your mind off.'

Charles took his advice and returned to Les Bertaux. He found everything as it had been. He felt as though it was only yesterday that he had been there last, though actually it was five months. The pear-trees were already in bloom, and old Rouault, now up and about again, was in and out the whole time, so that the farm seemed to be more full of life than he remembered it.

Thinking it right and proper to be as polite as possible to the doctor in view of his unhappy circumstances, the farmer begged him not to take off his hat, spoke in a low voice as though to a sick man, and even pretended to fly into a temper because nothing had been done to prepare something a little lighter for him, *petits pots de crème*, or stewed pears. He told stories. Charles found himself laughing; but the memory of his wife suddenly returned and subdued him. Coffee was brought in, and he thought no more about her.

He thought about her less and less as the habit of living alone grew on him. The new delights of independence made solitude easier to bear. He could have his meals when he liked, come and go as he pleased without having to account for his movements to anybody, and, when he was really tired, spread himself at ease all over the bed. In these and other ways he indulged himself, made himself thoroughly comfortable, and took what consolations came his way. The death of his wife had done him no ill service in his profession. For a whole month he was regarded as 'the poor young man' who had been through 'such a terrible time'. His name began to be known far and wide, and his practice grew. He could go now to Les Bertaux without bothering his head about anyone. He was filled with a hope which he did not specify, with a sense of vague happiness. As he stood in front of the mirror brushing his whiskers, he decided that he was beginning to look more attractive.

One day, he turned up at the farm about three o'clock. Everybody was out in the fields. He went into the kitchen but at first did not notice Emma. The shutters were closed. Through the wooden slats the sunlight struck across the floor in long thin lines which broke into fragmentary brightness on the corners of the furniture, and flickered on the ceiling. On the table flies were crawling over the glasses which had been used at the meal just over, buzzing as they drowned in the cider lees. The daylight, shining down the chimney, laid a soft veneer upon the soot, and touched the burned-out embers with a hint of blue. Emma was sitting between the window and the hearth, sewing. She wore no kerchief, and small drops of sweat stood out upon her bare shoulders.

Following the fashion of the countryside, she asked him whether he would take something to drink. He refused, but she insisted, and finally, with a laugh, begged him to join her in a liqueur. From the cupboard she took a bottle of curaçao, reached down two small glasses, filled one to the brim, poured a few drops into the other, then, touching them, raised hers to her mouth. Since it was almost empty, she had to lean back in order to drink. With head tilted, lips pouting and neck extended, she laughed to find that she could taste nothing, while, with the tip of her tongue projecting between her exquisite teeth, she licked the bottom of the glass with little darting movements.

Then she sat down again and resumed her task of darning a white cotton stocking. She bent her head above it, saying nothing. Charles, too, was silent. A draught from under the door imparted a faint movement to the dust lying on the flags. He watched the tiny eddy, hearing only the blood pulsing within his own head and the cry of a distant hen which had just laid an egg in the yard. Now and again Emma cooled her cheeks with the palms of her hands, which she then chilled again upon the metal knob of the great andirons.

She complained of an occasional fit of giddiness since the hot weather had begun, and asked him whether sea-bathing might be a good thing. That started them both talking, she of her convent, he of his school. Words came easily to their lips. They went upstairs to her room, where she showed him her old music portfolios, the little books she had been given as prizes, and the wreaths of oak-leaves lying forgotten in the bottom of her wardrobe. She went on to speak of her mother, of the cemetery, and even pointed out the particular bed in the garden where, on the first Friday in every month, she gathered flowers to lay upon her grave. But the gardener they had knew nothing of his job and served them badly. She would have liked, she said, to live in town, if only for the winter months, though, perhaps because of the long days, the country was even more tedious in the summer. The tone of her voice changed with the subject of her talk, passing from clear to shrill, veiling itself in languor, modulating to a drawl which dropped almost to a whisper when she spoke about herself. At moments she was gay, and looked at him with innocent wide eyes, then suddenly her lids would droop, and her eyes founder in a tide of boredom, while her thoughts took aimless flight.

That night, on his way home, Charles pondered one by one the phrases she had used, trying to remember each in turn, seeking to supply the sense of what she had left unuttered, so as to reconstruct that period of her life when he had not known her. But he could never see her in imagination save as she had been at their first meeting, or as he had left her just a moment back. Then he began to wonder what would happen to her, whether she would marry, and who the man would be. Old Rouault, alas! was very rich, and she . . . so very lovely! But her face kept on rising before his eyes, and in his ears was the monotonous drone as of a top—'Suppose you married! Suppose you married!' That night he could not sleep. His throat was dry and he was plagued with thirst. He got up to take a drink of water from his jug and threw the window wide. The sky was covered with stars, and a warm breeze was blowing. Far away the dogs were barking. He turned his head to look towards her home.

Telling himself that, after all, he would be risking nothing, he made up his mind to put the question when next occasion offered. But each time the moment came, the fear of not finding the right words kept his lips tight shut.

Old Rouault would by no means have objected to having his daughter taken off his hands, for she was of little use to him in the house. Secretly, he made excuses for her, telling himself that she had too good a mind for farming—a calling on which the curse of Heaven must surely rest, since who had ever seen a farmer millionaire? Far from making a fortune, he was losing money every year.

True, he was a redoubtable bargainer on market-days, loving the tricks and haggling of the trade, but against that must be set his failure with the land and in the running of the farm which, more than most farmers, he detested. Only very grudgingly did he take his hands out of his pockets, nor was he sparing of money in anything that concerned his comfort, liking to feed well, to be warm, and to sleep soft. He loved hard cider, underdone joints, and coffee generously laced with brandy. He took his meals alone in the kitchen, by the fire, on a small table which was brought to him ready laid, as in a stage-play.

When, therefore, he noticed how flushed Charles looked whenever he was sitting with his daughter—a sure sign that one of these days he would ask her hand in marriage—he pondered the matter so as to be ready for the time when he should have to give an answer. He thought the fellow rather puny, and not at all the sort of son-in-law for whom he had hoped. But he was said to be a steady young man, careful of his money, and well educated. Almost certainly he would strike no hard bargain in the matter of a dowry. That was a great point, for old Rouault was faced with the necessity of selling twenty-two acres of his land. He owed money to the builder, money to the harness-maker, and the beam of the cider-press stood in need of repair.

'If he asks me,' he decided, 'I shall say yes.'

At Michaelmas, Charles went to stay at Les Bertaux for three days. The last of these passed, like those which had preceded it, in a series of postponements from one quarter of an hour to another. Old Rouault saw him off. They walked together down a deep lane. Now or never was the moment. Charles gave himself as far as the corner of the hedge, and at last, when it was behind them:

'There's something, sir,' he murmured, 'I want very much to say to you.'

They came to a halt and Charles fell silent.

'Well, come on, out with it! D'you think I don't know what's in the wind?' said old Rouault with a quiet chuckle.

'Père Rouault . . .' stammered Charles . . . 'Père Rouault . . .'

'Nothing'd please me better,' went on the farmer, 'and I've no doubt that girl of mine thinks much as I do, but she'd best be asked. Get along with you now, and I'll walk back to the house. If the answer is "yes"—you'd better not show up just yet—too many people about, besides, the excitement might be too much for her. Tell you what I'll do, so's you shan't have to eat your heart out—I'll open the window-shutter flat against the wall. You'll be able to see it from the back of the house if you lean over the hedge . . .'—and he moved off.

Charles tied his horse to a tree. Then he ran to the footpath and waited. Half an hour passed, after which he counted another nineteen minutes by his watch. Suddenly there was a noise of something striking the wall. The shutter had been thrown open: the catch was still vibrating.

Next morning he was at the farm about nine. Emma blushed as he entered, though she tried to laugh in order to keep herself in countenance. Old Rouault embraced his future son-in-law. All talk about money matters was postponed. After all, there would be plenty of time for that, because the wedding could not decently take place until the period of Charles's mourning was over, that is to say, not until the spring of the following year.

In this state of waiting the winter passed away. Mademoiselle Rouault was busy with her trousseau. Part of it was ordered from Rouen, and she spent much time making nightdresses and nightcaps with the help of fashion-plates which she borrowed. Charles's visits to the farm were taken up with discussion of plans for the ceremony. In which room, they wondered, should the wedding-breakfast be laid, how many courses should they have, and what should the main dishes be?

Emma, for her part, would have liked a marriage at midnight* by the light of torches, but her father thought such an idea nonsensical. At last, matters were settled, and the wedding-party took place. The guests numbered forty-three, and sixteen hours were spent in eating. Next day the whole business began over again, and was repeated, on a miniature scale, during the rest of the week.

CHAPTER IV

THE guests arrived early, and in a variety of vehicles—dog-carts, two-wheeled traps, old cabs minus their hoods, furniture vans with leather curtains. The young people from the nearer villages came standing packed together in wagons, holding on to the sides to keep themselves from falling, and jolted unmercifully by the trotting horses. There were visitors from as far as ten miles off, from Goderville and Normanville and Cany. All the relations on both sides had been invited. Broken friendships had been patched up for the occasion, and letters had been written to former acquaintances not seen for years.

The crack of a whip sounded from behind the hedge and was repeated. A few moments later the gate swung open and a trap drove in. It advanced at a spanking pace to the steps and there pulled up short. Its occupants spilled out on either side, rubbing their knees and stretching their arms. The ladies, crowned with bonnets, were dressed in the fashion of the city, with gold watch-chains, capes with long ends crossed beneath their girdles, or little neck-handkerchiefs fastened behind with a pin, and leaving the napes of their necks uncovered. The small boys, got up to resemble their fathers, seemed irked by their new suits (some were wearing boots for the first time in their lives). With them came gawky girls of fourteen or sixteen, speechless in white communion frocks lengthened for the occasion—cousins or elder sisters, presumably—pink-cheeked, in a condition of abject shyness, their hair plastered down with rose-pomade, and terrified of getting their gloves dirty. Since there were not enough grooms to unharness all the horses, the gentlemen rolled up their sleeves and did the work themselves. They wore, according to their differing social positions, dress-coats, frock-coats, short jackets, jackets with full skirts—good dress-coats, symbols of family importance, brought from the wardrobe only for occasions of high solemnity, full-fashioned frock-coats flapping in the wind, with cylindrical collars and pockets as large as small sacks, jackets of heavy cloth, worn, as a rule, with leather-peaked caps, very short-skirted jackets, with two buttons set close together like eyes, in the back, looking as though the side flaps had been hewed by the local carpenter from a solid block of wood. There were even a few (though they, most certainly, would be relegated to the bottom end of the table) who sported their extra-special smocks; smocks, that is to say, with collars turned down on to their shoulders, backs gathered into little pleats, and belted very low down with girdles sewn on to the material.

Shirts were bulging like so many breast-plates. Heads were freshly barbered, ears showed scarlet, cheeks were close-shaven. Some, who had risen before dawn and used their razors in a bad light, displayed great gashes beneath their noses, or scars as big as crown-pieces where they had scraped the skin from their chins. The wind during their drive had inflamed these sore spots, and the big, pale, fleshy faces were blotched with red.

The Mairie being no more than half a mile from the farm, the company proceeded there on foot, and returned in the same manner after the church ceremony. The procession, at first close-knit as a coloured scarf, undulating over the countryside and stretching along the path which wound through the fields of green corn, soon became extended, and broke up into little groups which stopped to talk. The fiddler went on ahead, his instrument gaily garlanded with ribbons. Next came the bride and groom, followed by their relations and a nondescript clutter of friends. The children brought up the rear, amusing themselves by plucking the ears of sprouting oats, or indulging in games among themselves, unseen by their elders. Emma's dress was too long and just touched the ground. Now and again she stopped to raise it, and daintily, with her gloved hands, to pick off the wild grasses and prickly thistles, while Charles, empty-handed, waited for her to finish. Old Rouault, a new silk hat on his head, and the cuffs of his dress-coat covering his knuckles to the very finger-tips, walked with Madame Bovary the elder on his arm. Old Monsieur Bovary, who to show his contempt of the company was wearing a frock-coat adorned with rows of military-looking buttons, was busy lavishing pot-house gallantries on a fair-haired country girl who curtsied, blushed, and knew not what to say. The other guests talked business or nudged one another in the ribs as a stimulating preliminary to the gaieties to come. It was possible, with a little straining of the ears, to hear the fiddler who all this while was scraping away across the open countryside. Whenever he noticed that he had left the company far behind, he stopped for breath, applied resin to his bow with much elaboration in order to get a fuller caterwauling from the strings, and then went on again, alternately raising and lowering the neck of his violin, the better to mark the time. The noise he made put the little birds to flight long before he had reached them.

The table had been laid under the wagon-shed. It was laden with four sirloins, six fricassées of chicken, a casserole of veal, three legs of mutton, and, as centrepiece, a handsome roast sucking-pig flanked with meat-balls cooked in sorrel. Decanters of brandy stood at each corner, and bottles of sweet cider were frothing round their corks. The glasses had all been filled to the brim with wine in advance. Great dishes of yellow cream, which quivered whenever the table was shaken, bore on their smooth surfaces the initials of the newly-married couple picked out in hundreds-and-thousands. A pastry-cook from Yvetot had been employed to provide the tarts and sweet-stuffs. Being new to the district, he had excelled himself, and appeared in person when the sweet stage was reached, bearing aloft an elaborate confection which drew cries of admiration. The base was formed of a cube of blue pasteboard representing a temple with a portico, colonnades and statuettes of white plaster, with, between them, little alcoves studded with stars of gold paper. Above this was a castle made of Savoy cake, surrounded by tiny battlements of angelica, almonds, dried raisins and oranges cut into quarters. Finally, at the very top, which depicted a green meadow complete with rocks, lakes composed of jam and little boats made out of nut-shells, was a small cupid balancing himself on a chocolate swing, the two uprights of which were topped with natural rosebuds by way of finials.

Eating went on until evening. When the guests were tired of sitting they wandered about in the yards or played at shove-ha'penny in the barn, after which they returned to the table. When the feast was nearing its end, some of them fell asleep and snored, though they woke up again when coffee appeared. Later still, they started to sing songs and perform feats of strength, lifting weights, doing gymnastics, trying to raise carts on their shoulders, making broad jests and kissing the ladies. When the time came to go home, it was only with great difficulty that the horses, gorged with oats to their nostrils, were forced between the shafts. They reared and stampeded: harness was broken, their masters laughed and cursed. And all night long, by the light of the moon, carts were seen dashing along country lanes at a gallop, trundling into ditches, bumping over piles of stones, jolting over the grass, with the women leaning out of the doors in an effort to get hold of the reins. Those who remained at Les Bertaux spent the night drinking in the kitchen. The children had fallen asleep under the benches.

The bride had begged her father to spare her the customary horseplay. One of the cousins, however, a fishmonger by trade (he had gone so far as to give them a pair of soles as a wedding-present), was just preparing to squirt water from his mouth through the key-hole, when old Rouault arrived in time to stop him, explaining that his son-in-law's dignity did not permit of such improprieties. The cousin was at last made to see the force of his argument, though only with considerable difficulty. To himself he said that old Rouault was puffed up with pride, and withdrew into a corner of the room where he found four or five other guests who, having, on more than one occasion, had the worst cuts off the joints, considered that they had been badly used, and were now whispering at the expense of their host, and muttering that they hoped he would come to a bad end.

Madame Bovary the elder had not opened her lips the entire day. She had been consulted neither about her daughter-in-law's dress, nor about the arrangements for the party. She withdrew at an early hour. Her husband, instead of following her, sent to Saint-Victor for cigars, and smoked until dawn, drinking kirsch-punch—a concoction unknown to the company, who consequently regarded him with more respect than they had done previously.

Charles was not gifted as a humourist, and had not shone during the festivities. He replied with no great brilliance to the various witticisms, puns, jokes with double meanings, compliments and broad examples of humour which the others regarded it as a duty to level at him from the soup onwards.

His appearance next morning, however, quite made up for this inadequacy. He seemed a different man. He was the one who gave the impression of having lost his virginity, whereas Emma gave no indication whatever that anything had happened to her. Even the wags were silenced and could only look at her when she drew near with an air of extreme puzzlement. But Charles made no attempt to hide his feelings. He kept on referring to 'my wife', and talked to her familiarly. He asked everyone he met what they thought of her, hunted for her up and down the house, and kept taking her out into the yard, where he could be seen in the distance, through the trees, walking with his arm round her waist, half bending towards her and ruffling her tucker with his head.

Two days after the ceremony, the newly-wedded pair left. Charles could not remain away from his patients any longer. Old Rouault lent them his trap, and went with them himself as far as Vassonville. There, he kissed his daughter for the last time, got down and started back for home. When he had gone a hundred paces or so, he stopped and sighed deeply at the sight of the trap vanishing into the distance, its wheels spinning in a cloud of dust. He was remembering his own wedding, the days of his youth, his wife's first pregnancy. He, too, had been very happy that day when he had taken her home from her father's house. She had ridden behind him on his horse along the snowy roads—for the time had been near Christmas, and the landscape was all white. She had clung to him with one arm, the other being occupied with her basket. The wind was busy with the long lace streamers of her Normandy head-dress, and now and again they blew across her mouth. When he turned his head he could see, there on his shoulder, close to his cheek, her little pink face smiling silently from beneath the golden ornament which she wore in her bonnet. From time to time she would slip her fingers under his coat to warm them against his chest. How long ago it all was! Their son would have been a man of thirty. He looked back along the road but could see nothing. He felt desolate and empty like a house from which the furniture has been taken. In his brain, fuddled with the fumes of last night's junketing, black thoughts jostled with sentimental memories. He felt tempted at one moment to take a turn in the churchyard. Fearing, however, lest that should make him still more melancholy, he went straight home.

Monsieur and Madame Charles arrived at Tostes about six o'clock. The neighbours crowded to their windows to catch a glimpse of the doctor's new wife.

The old servant appeared, curtsied, and apologized for not having dinner ready. She suggested that, while they were waiting, Madame should take a look over the house.

CHAPTER V

THE brick front stood flush with the street, or, with what might, more accurately, be called the high-road. A greatcoat, made to button high in the neck, was hanging behind the front-door, a horse's bridle, and a black leather cap. Standing on the floor in a corner were a pair of gaiters still covered with dried mud. To the right was the main room of the house, used both for eating and for sitting. Wallpaper of a canary-yellow, relieved along its upper edge by faded swags of flowers, trembled perpetually over its whole extent because the canvas on which it was hung had been imperfectly stretched. Curtains of white calico, edged with a red stripe, fell over the windows in overlapping folds. The diminutive mantelpiece was dominated by the splendours of an ornamental clock with a head of Hippocrates, flanked by candlesticks of plated silver crowned with oval glass shades. On the other side of the passage was Charles's consulting-room. It was small, about six foot square, and contained a table and four chairs, one of which was of the large, armed, desk variety. The many volumes of the *Dictionary of Medical Sciences*,* their pages uncut, but showing on their bindings signs that they had changed hands more than once, were almost the sole occupants of a six-shelved deal bookcase. So thin were the walls that the smell of cooking was distinctly noticeable, while anyone in the kitchen could be sure of hearing the patients next door, coughing and relating the details of their ailments. A few steps further down the passage, and opening directly on to the yard with its stables, was a large dilapidated room equipped as a bakehouse, but now used for storing wood, wine and all sorts of lumber. It was full of odds and ends of old iron, empty barrels, disused garden implements, and an assorted medley of other objects the precise nature of which it was impossible to determine. Everything was smothered in dust.

The garden was long and narrow, and stretched between daub and wattle walls on which apricot trees had been trained, to a thorn-hedge which separated it from the open fields. In the middle of it stood a slate sundial on a foundation of masonry. Four flower-beds of wilting rose-bushes were set symmetrically about the more utilitarian patch devoted to the serious purpose of vegetable growing. In a little grove of fir-trees, at the far end, was the plaster figure of a priest reading his breviary.

Emma went upstairs to the bedrooms. The first was unfurnished, but the second, which was to be hers and her husband's, contained a mahogany bedstead standing in an alcove hung with red draperies. A box, decorated with shells, stood on the chest of drawers, while, on a writing-table in the window was a jug in which had been placed a bunch of orange-blossom tied with ribbons of white satin. It was a wedding-bouquet—her predecessor's! She looked at it. Charles noticed the direction of her glance, removed the object and took it up into the attic, while Emma, seated in the armchair (her own belongings were being arranged about the room), thought of her own bouquet in its cardboard box, and wondered what they would do with it should she happen to die.

She spent the first few days planning changes in the house. She took the glass shades off the candles, had new wallpaper hung, the staircase repainted, and seats placed in the garden round the sundial. She went so far as to wonder whether it might not be possible to have a pond built with a fountain and a stock of fish.

After a while, her husband, knowing that she enjoyed driving, found a second-hand phaeton, which, when he had fitted it with new lamps and a dashboard of quilted leather, almost resembled a tilbury. He was happy, and without a care in the world. A meal taken alone with her, an evening walk together along the road, the feel of her hair beneath his hand, the sight of her straw-hat hanging from the hasp of a window—all these things, and many others, in which, till then, Charles had never suspected happiness to reside, went now to make up the continuity of his bliss. Lying in bed of a morning, with her head beside his on the pillow, he would watch the sunlight playing upon the golden down of her cheeks which were only half hidden by the scalloped flaps of her night-cap. Seen at such short range, her eyes looked larger than at other times, especially when she blinked her lids on waking. In shadow they seemed black, but in broad day, blue. It was as though they were composed of layer on layer, each of a different colour. Dense and solid in the depths, they grew lighter and lighter as his gaze traced its way upward to their enamelled surface. His own lost themselves in the profundities of hers. He could see himself imaged in miniature as far down as his shoulders, the handkerchief which he wore about his head, and the unbuttoned neck of his nightshirt, reflected with meticulous accuracy. Then he would get up, and she, going to the window, would watch him leave upon his rounds, leaning there on the sill between two pots of geraniums, wrapped in a dressing-gown which fell loosely about her. Charles, below in the street, would buckle on his spurs at the mounting-block, while, from her post above, she went on talking to him, tearing off scraps of flower and foliage with her teeth, and blowing them towards him. They fluttered and floated through the air, describing half circles like so many birds, clinging, before finally they reached the ground, to the ill-groomed mane of the old white mare standing motionless before the door. Then Charles would mount, blow her a kiss (to which she replied with a wave of the hand, before closing the window), and ride away.

Along the high-road, whose dusty ribbon stretched as far as the eye could see, he ambled on; through hollow lanes beneath low-hanging branches, and on narrow tracks where the growing corn reached almost to his knees, with the sun on his back and the breath of the morning in his nostrils, his heart filled with delight of the hours just past, his mind at rest, his body satisfied. And as he jogged along he ruminated his happiness, much as those who have dined well chew the savour of the truffles which their stomachs are busy digesting.*

Till then there had been few blessings in his life. He had spent his schooldays shut in between high walls, solitary in the midst of comrades who were richer than he was, or better at their work, who laughed at his accent and jeered at his clothes, whose mothers came to see them with muffs stuffed full of cakes. Later, when he was studying medicine he had never had enough money to treat to a dance some little working girl who might then have become his mistress. Later still, he had lived for fourteen months wedded to that widow whose feet, as they lay together in their bed, were as cold as icicles. But now, the lovely woman whom he adored was his for life. The world, for him, was all contained within the silky rondure of her skirts. He reproached himself for not loving her enough. He longed to see her again, and hurried home to climb the stairs with beating heart, to find Emma seated in their room, busy at her toilet. Tiptoeing across the floor, he kissed the back of her neck. She uttered a little cry. He was for ever touching her comb, her rings, her neckerchief. Sometimes he gave her great smacking kisses on the cheek, sometimes fluttered his lips along her naked arm from finger-tips to shoulder. And she would shake him off, half laughing, half annoyed, as she might have done some troublesome child.

In the days before her marriage she had fancied that she was in love. But the happiness love should have brought her did not come. She must, she thought, have been mistaken, and set herself to discover what it was that people in real life meant by such words as 'bliss', 'passion' and 'intoxication'—words, all of them, which she had thought so fine when she read them in books.

CHAPTER VI

SHE had read *Paul et Virginie*;* she had dreamed of the bamboo hut, of the negro, Domingo, of Faithful, the dog, but, above all, of the sweet friendship of a dear little brother who would have brought her red-rinded fruit plucked from trees higher than church-towers, or would have run to her barefooted on the sand with a gift of birds' nests.

When she was thirteen years old, her father had gone with her to the city, in order to place her in a convent. They had alighted at an inn of the Saint-Gervais quarter, where they had eaten off plates painted with scenes from the life of Mademoiselle de la Vallière.* The explanatory legends, broken here and there by the scratches left by many knives, were all designed to glorify religion, sentiment, and the splendours of the court.

Far from feeling bored during her first term at the convent, she delighted in the company of the good sisters who, for her entertainment, took her into the chapel, whence a long corridor led to the refectory. She showed but little interest in the games which were played in the hours of recreation, displayed an excellent understanding of her catechism, and was always the one who answered the visiting priest's most difficult questions.

Living continuously in the close atmosphere of classrooms, and in the company of pale-faced women who were never without their rosaries adorned with crosses of brass, she moved in a sort of mystic dream compounded of altar scents, the cool touch of holy water, and the glow of candles. Instead of following the mass, she spent her time in church looking at the pious pictures, framed in azure borders, which ornamented her service-book, and grew to love the sick lamb, the Sacred Heart pierced with sharp arrows, and the touching image of Jesus weighed down by his cross on the road to Calvary. She tried, by way of mortification, to go one whole day without eating, and sought some vow which she might set herself to perform.

When she went to confession, she invented trivial sins, hoping thereby to remain longer on her knees in the darkness, her face pressed to the grill beneath the murmured admonitions of the priest. The metaphors of affianced lover, husband, divine wooer and eternal marriage, which were for ever recurring in the sermons that she heard, moved her heart with an unexpected sweetness.

Each evening, before prayers, there was reading from some sacred book in the schoolroom. On weekdays this took the form of excerpts from the life of one of the saints, or from the Abbé Frayssinous's *Lectures*;* on Sundays, as a treat, of passages from the *Génie du christianisme*.* With what eagerness, at first, did she listen to those sonorous lamentations of romantic melancholy, which seemed to carry within them the echoes of nature and eternity. Had her youth been spent in the back-parlour of some city merchant's shop, her ears might have been opened to the lyric call of green fields, such as reaches us, as a rule, only through the medium of books. But she knew the country too well for that, was familiar with the bleating of flocks, the routine of the dairy and the plough. Accustomed to still-ness, she sought its opposite in tumultuous scenes. If she loved the sea, it was because of its storms. She never enjoyed the greenness of the grass save as a meagre accompaniment of ruins. Objects she valued merely for the profit, as it were, that she could draw from them, and rejected as useless everything that did not at once con-tribute to the consummation of her heart—for she was by tempera-ment sentimental rather than artistic, and engaged in the pursuit not of landscapes but of emotions.

There was at the convent a certain old maid who used to come for a week each month to repair the linen. Belonging, as she did, to an old family of gentlefolk ruined by the Revolution, she enjoyed the special favour of the archbishop, took her meals at the sisters' table in the refectory, and always engaged in a few minutes' chat with them afterwards, before returning to her work. Quite often the boarders would play truant from the schoolroom to pay her a visit. She knew by heart the love songs of the previous century, and these she would sing in a low voice as she plied her needle. She told stories, brought news of the outside world, executed small commissions in the town, and secretly lent to the older girls one or other of the novels that she carried in the pockets of her apron, and that she herself devoured in the intervals of labour. They were concerned only with affairs of the heart, with lovers and their lasses, with persecuted damsels for ever swooning in solitary pavilions, with outriders meeting a violent death on every journey, and horses foundering on every page, with dark forests and agonies of sentiment, with vows, sobs, tears and kisses, with moonlit gondolas, with groves and nightingales, with cavaliers who were always brave as lions, gentle as lambs, and virtuous as real men never are, always elegantly dressed and given to weeping with the copious fluency of stone fountains. For six months, when she was fifteen, she soiled her hands with this dusty nonsense of old libraries. A little later, in the pages of Walter Scott, she grew enamoured of historic scenes, and dreamed of old oak chests, guard-rooms and medieval minstrels. She would have loved to spend her days in some ancient manor-house like the damsels in long-waisted gowns who dawdled away their time beneath Gothic traceries, chin in hand, their elbows resting on stone sills, watching white-plumed horsemen come galloping from afar on sable chargers. At that period of her life she cultivated a passion for Mary Stuart, and indulged in an enthusiastic veneration of all illustrious and ill-starred ladies. Jeanne d'Arc and Héloise, Agnès Sorel,* La Ferronnière the beautiful,* and Clémence Isaure,* shone for her like comets from the dark immensities of history, whence also emerged, but more thickly shadowed and entirely unrelated one with another, Saint Louis and his oak,* the dying Bayard,* certain violent crimes of Louis XI,* a few scrappy incidents from the Massacre of Saint-Bartholomew,* the white plume of Henry IV,* and always the memory of the painted plates extolling Louis XIV.*

The ballads which she sang at her music lessons were concerned with nothing but little angels with golden wings, Madonnas and lagoons and gondoliers—mild compositions which, through the childish simplicity of their style and the defects of their musical expression, gave her glimpses of the seductive fantasy world of sentimental realities. Some of her companions brought back to the convent copies of the 'keepsakes'* which they had been given at the New Year. These had to be hidden: it was quite a complicated business. The girls read them in the dormitory. Handling their beautiful satin bindings with the utmost care, Emma feasted her dazzled eyes on the names of the unknown authors appended to each piece, and, more often than not, made glorious with the title of Count or Viscount. She actually trembled as she blew beneath the tissue paper to raise it from the engravings which it covered. It would rise, half-folded, and fall back softly against the opposite page. The image revealed would be that of some young man in a short cloak, pressing in his arms a white-robed maiden with a purse at her girdle; or portraits of nameless English ladies with fair, curled hair, looking out from under round straw hats, with large and limpid eyes. They were shown reclining in carriages, gliding through a parklike landscape, with greyhounds leaping in front of the equipage with its two diminutive postillions clad in white breeches. Others there were, day-dreaming on sofas with an opened letter, looking at the moon through a half-open window draped with a black curtain. Innocence was indicated in the form of young girls, who with tears upon their cheeks pouted at doves through the bars of gothic cages or, head to one side, smiled as they plucked the petals from a daisy with tapering fingers that curved backwards like medieval shoes. Sultans, too, played their part, taking their ease in the arms of dancing-girls in green-trellised arbours, giaours and Turkish scimitars and little Grecian caps, and pallid country scenes (these above all) of dithyrambic lands often miraculously endowed with a simultaneous flora of palms and pine trees, with tigers on the right hand, lions on the left and Tartar minarets on the horizon. In the foreground would be Roman ruins, and, beyond, a line of camels—the whole enclosed in a frame of nice clean virgin forest, with a great perpendicular beam of sunlight shimmering upon the water, where, white scratches on a steel-grey ground, swans, elegantly dispersed, were swimming.

The shaded wall-lamp above her head would shine upon these visions of the world.* One by one they passed before her in the silence of the dormitory, nor was the illusion broken save by the sound of some distant and belated cab driving along the boulevards.

For the first few days after her mother's death she wept bitterly, and had a mourning picture made from the dead woman's hair. She wrote home a long letter filled with melancholy reflections on human life, and begged that, when it was her turn to die, she should be buried with her mother in the selfsame grave. Her father thought she must be ill and came to see her. She got much secret satisfaction from the thought that, in one triumphant moment, she had achieved that exquisite ideal of wan decline from which the mediocre heart is ever excluded. She let herself be carried on the slow current of a Lamartinian melancholy,* lulled by the sound of harps upon the lake, and songs of dying swans, listening to the fall of autumn leaves, consoled by the vision of pure virgins mounting to heaven, and, in their ears, the voice of the Eternal echoing among the valleys. Soon she grew bored, but would not admit her boredom, continuing, first from force of habit then from vanity, only to find herself, at last, cured of her gloom, with no more sadness in her heart than there were wrinkles on her brow.

The good sisters, who had been so sure of her vocation, noticed with much astonishment that Mademoiselle Rouault seemed to be slipping from their grasp. So prodigal had they been, in fact, of sacred offices, of prayers and retreats and sermons, so constantly had preached the veneration due to saints and martyrs, so often had instilled the principles of modesty and salvation, that she had reacted like a horse ridden on too tight a rein. She stopped short, and the bit slipped from between her teeth. Her spirit, positive and assertive for all its wild enthusiasms, that had loved the church for its flowers, music for the words of ballads, and literature for its sentimental thrills, revolted when faced by the mysteries of the faith. She felt the irk of a discipline which was at odds with her temperament. When her father removed her from the school, no one was sorry to see her go. The Superior even discovered that, during her last weeks there, she had shown a lack of respect towards the community.

At first, after reaching home, she took pleasure in ordering the servants about, but soon grew out of love with country scenes, and began to regret her convent. By the time Charles first came to Les Bertaux she saw herself as stripped of all illusions, with nothing more to learn and nothing more to feel.

But the anxieties of her new duties, or, perhaps, the stimulus of a man's mere presence in the house, had been sufficient at that time to convince her that she was finally within grasp of that marvellous passion which hitherto had hovered, like a great red-winged bird, in the skies of poetry. But now she could not believe that this uneventful existence was the happiness she had dreamed of.

CHAPTER VII

SHE used to reflect at times that these ought none the less to be the best days of her life, the honeymoon, as they called it. To taste its sweetness, she should doubtless have travelled to those lands with sounding names where newly-wedded bliss is spent in exquisite languor.* Seated in a post-chaise behind curtains of blue silk, she should have climbed, at walking pace, precipitous mountain roads, listening to the postillion's song echoing from the rocks to the accompaniment of goats' bells and the muted sound of falling water. She should have breathed at sunset, on the shores of sea-bays in the south, the scent of lemon trees, and at night, alone with her husband on a villa terrace, have stood hand in hand, watching the stars and planning for the future. It seemed to her that happiness must flourish better in some special places than elsewhere, as some plants grow best in certain kinds of soil. Why was it not her fate to lean upon the balcony of a Swiss chalet* or hide her melancholy in some Highland cottage, with a husband dressed in a black, long-skirted velvet coat, soft leather boots, a pointed hat, and ruffles at his wrist?

Maybe she would have liked to speak of all these things to some companion. But how is it possible to find words for an inexpressible melancholy which changes like the changing clouds, and eddies like the wind? She had no language for such confidences, no opportunity, and not sufficient courage.

Had Charles but shown the will to listen, had he but suspected the movement of her thoughts, or seen but once into her mind, her heart would, she felt, suddenly have released all its wealth of feeling, as apples fall in profusion from a shaken tree. But as their lives took on a greater intimacy, so did detachment grow within her mind and loose the bonds which bound them.

Charles's talk was flat as a city pavement trodden by all men's thoughts dressed in the clothes of every day. They could not rouse emotion in her, nor laughter, nor excuse for dreams. He had never, he told her, felt any temptation, when he lived in Rouen, to see the Paris actors in the local theatre. He could not swim or fence or shoot with the pistol, and once, when, in a tale, she came upon a term of horsemanship, he could not tell her what it meant. But a man, surely, should be all-knowing, should excel in multiple activities, be capable of initiating his wife into the violence of passion, the refinements of life, and all the mysteries of existence? Charles, however, taught her nothing, knew nothing, desired nothing. He thought her happy, and she resented his assured tranquillity, his ponderous peace of mind, the very happiness she brought him.

Sometimes she sketched, and Charles found much delight in standing at her side, watching her bend above her drawing-board, half closing her eyes the better to judge the effect of her work, or rolling little pellets of bread* between finger and thumb. The quicker her hands moved when she played the piano, the greater his surprise. She struck the notes with a sure touch, and could run down the keyboard from treble to bass without a moment's pause. Thus shaken from its slumbers, the old instrument with its jangling strings could be heard at the other end of the village when the window was open, and often the bailiff's clerk, on his way down the street, hatless, wearing list slippers, and holding a sheet of paper in his hand, would pause to listen.

But there was another side to Emma. She knew how to run her house. She sent out the accounts for her husband's professional services, expressing herself in well-turned phrases which had nothing about them of the ordinary language of commerce. When, on a Sunday, they occasionally invited a neighbour in to dine, she always managed to provide some elegant dish, served greengages arranged in pyramids on vine leaves, had the pots of preserves turned out on plates, and even talked of buying finger-bowls for dessert. Because of all this the consideration shown to Bovary increased.

Charles came to value himself the more highly for possessing such a wife. Proudly he would point out to his guests two little pencil sketches of hers in the parlour, which he had had framed in large mounts and hung against the wallpaper on green cords. The parishioners going home from church could always see him standing at his door wearing handsome carpet-slippers.

He came back of an evening very late, usually about ten, but sometimes not till midnight. As soon as he got in he asked for something to eat and, since the servant had gone to bed, it was Emma who served him. He took off his frock-coat, the better to dine at his ease. He regularly detailed to her all the people he had met, the villages he had visited, the prescriptions he had written, and, in a mood of comfortable self-satisfaction, ate what was left over of the midday stew, peeled the rind from his cheese, munched an apple, emptied the decanter, and then went to bed where he lay snoring on his back.

Because he had long been in the habit of wearing a cotton nightcap, his silk handkerchief often slipped awry, so that his hair, next morning, hung untidily over his face, whitened by the feathers from his pillow, the strings of which had a way of coming unfastened during the night. He always wore heavy boots which showed two deep folds running from instep to ankle. The rest of the upper was straight and taut as though encasing a wooden boot-tree. He said that they were *good enough for the country*.

His mother encouraged him in these habits of economy, for she came to see him, as she always had done, whenever there had been some particularly violent upheaval in her own house. All the same, she seemed to have a prejudice against her daughter-in-law. She found her *too grand for them*. Wood, sugar, candles were consumed as prodigally (so she maintained) as in some *great house*, and the amount of coal used in the kitchen would have sufficed to cook a meal for twenty-five persons! She arranged Emma's linen for her in the presses, and taught her to keep a careful eye on the butcher when he brought the meat. The young woman submitted to this instruction; Madame Bovary the elder was not sparing in her application of it. All day long the house echoed to 'daughter', 'mother', spoken with a little tightening of the lips, each of the two women dealing out little verbal courtesies in a voice trembling with anger.

The old lady had always felt, in the days of Madame Dubuc, that she was still her son's favourite, but now, Charles's love for Emma seemed to her like an act of treachery to her affection, a trespassing on ground which was hers by right. She looked on at her son's happiness in a mood of melancholy silence, as an impoverished householder might stare through the window at strangers feasting in his former home. She was for ever indulging in fond memories, thereby reminding him of her pains and sacrifices on his behalf, comparing them favourably with Emma's more easy-going ways, and drawing the conclusion that it was unreasonable on his part to adore her so exclusively.

Charles did not know how to answer these outbursts. He respected his mother but was deeply in love with his wife. He held the former's judgement to be impeccable, yet found the latter beyond reproach. When old Madame Bovary had left, he would try, with great timidity, and in her very words, to repeat one or two of her less offensive observations. On these occasions, Emma, proving in a few curt words that he was wrong, would send him back to his patients.

But in accordance with the theories she believed in, she tried to induce feelings of love in herself. On moonlit nights, in the garden, she recited all she could remember of the passionate lyrics she had read, and sang to him, with many sighs, a number of melancholy strains. The only result was that she felt herself to be as calm as before, and that Charles seemed neither more in love nor more deeply stirred.

When she had thus struck flint upon her heart without getting the smallest spark, she persuaded herself without much difficulty, being by nature incapable either of understanding what she did not feel, or of believing anything not expressed in conventional forms, that Charles's passion was not of the excessive kind. His emotional manifestations had, by now, fallen into a regular pattern. He made love to her at certain fixed times. It was a habit like any other, a sort of sweet course to look forward to after the monotony of dinner.

A gamekeeper whom he had cured of an inflammation of the lungs gave Emma a little Italian greyhound. She took it out with her on her walks—for she did occasionally venture abroad to escape her everlasting solitude, and have something on which to rest her eyes other than the eternal garden and the dusty road beyond.

It was her custom to go as far as the beechwood of Banneville, to a point where an abandoned pavilion formed an angle with the wall towards the open country. There, in the ha-ha, long reeds grew sharp-spiked among the grass.

She always began these visits by glancing round to see whether anything had changed since last she had been there. She found the same foxgloves, the same wallflowers, in the same spots, the clumps of nettles growing round great stones, the lichen creeping up the three long windows whose closed shutters gave out a smell of rotting wood, and over the iron bars. Her thoughts, aimless at first, played as chance directed, like the dog who scampered round in circles, yelping at butterflies, hunting shrew-mice, and snapping at the poppies along the edges of the sprouting corn. But little by little they would grow to a point, and, sitting on the turf, stabbing at it with the point of her parasol, she would say to herself, over and over again:

'Oh why, in heaven's name, did I ever get married!'

She kept wondering whether, if things had turned out differently, she might not have met a different man. She tried to imagine what all those things which had never happened might have been like, the life she might have lived so alien to the one she knew, the husband who had never come her way. Surely all men were not like Charles? He might, that dream-lover, have been handsome, witty, distinguished, attractive, just such a one as the girls she had known at school had doubtless married. What were they doing now, those childhood friends? Living a city life, probably, surrounded by the bustle of streets, the chatter of theatres, the bright lights of ballrooms;

familiars of an existence in which the heart dilates, the senses open and expand. But her own life was as cold as an attic with a north light. Boredom silently wove its spider's web across the corners of her heart. She remembered prize-days of old when she had gone up to the platform to get her little wreaths. With her hair in plaits, her white frock with the cloth boots showing beneath it, she had made a sweet picture. As she went back to her place, the gentlemen in the audience had had a way of leaning forward, to pay her compliments. The courtyard in front of the school used to be full of carriages on those occasions. Farewells were called to her across their fastened doors, and the music-master, passing with his violin-case, had raised his hat. How far away it all seemed! how very far away!

She called Djali, held him between her knees, and stroked his long, sleek head.

'You've nothing to worry about,' she told him: 'come, give your mistress a kiss.'

The slim creature indulged in a leisurely yawn, and she, struck by its air of melancholy, would wax sentimental. Seeing an analogy between herself and him, she would speak her thoughts out loud, as though to some afflicted friend in need of comfort. Sometimes there were squalls of wind, gusts that blew suddenly from the sea, sweeping the Caux countryside with instantaneous fury, and carrying a salty tang for many miles inland. It blew with whistling sound through the reeds at ground level: the leaves of the beeches rustled in a sharp spasm of agitation, while the tree-tops continued to sway to the sound of their old deep murmuring. She drew her shawl closer about her shoulders and got up.

In the avenue, a green light, muted by the foliage, lit the smooth moss which creaked softly beneath her feet. The sun went down. The sky between the branches was red, and the long straight lines of trees, all exactly alike, looked like a brown colonnade seen in relief upon a golden ground. She was seized with panic, and, calling Djali, hurried back to Tostes by the main road. When she reached home, she fell into an easy chair, and stayed there all the evening, saying nothing.

But towards the end of September, an extraordinary event occurred in her life. She was invited to La Vaubyessard, to the house of the Marquis d'Andervilliers.

The Marquis, who had been a Secretary of State under the

Restoration, was now eager to re-enter politics, and was embarking on a long-range campaign with the object of ensuring his election to the Chamber of Deputies. In winter he distributed large quantities of firewood, and, as a member of the local council, showed much vigour in putting forward constant demands for new roads in this constituency. During the hot weather he had had an abscess in his mouth which Charles had lanced and quite miraculously relieved. The steward who had been sent to Tostes to pay the doctor reported, when he got back that evening, that he had seen some magnificent cherries in his garden. Now, it so happened that the cherry-trees at La Vaubyessard were far from healthy. The Marquis, therefore, asked Bovary to let him have a few slips for grafting, made a point of going to thank him in person, caught sight of Emma, and decided that she had a pretty figure and manners far superior to those of a mere country-girl. So deeply was he impressed that an invitation was duly sent. This did not, in the opinion of his family, overstep the bounds of decent condescension, and need not be viewed as constituting a social indiscretion.

At three o'clock one Wednesday, therefore, Monsieur and Madame Bovary got into their phaeton, and set off for La Vaubyessard with a large trunk strapped behind, and a hat-box in front. In addition to these, Charles had a cardboard box wedged between his legs.

They arrived at nightfall just as the lamps in the park were being lighted to show the carriages the way.

CHAPTER VIII

THE château was a modern building in the Italian style,* with two projecting wings and a flight of three steps. It lay spread out at the far end of a great expanse of greensward on which a few cows were grazing among the well-spaced clumps of large trees. Small groups of shrubs, rhododendrons, syringa and white-flowering hawthorn, showed rounded and uneven tufts of green along the winding course of the gravelled drive. There was a river with a bridge, and it was possible to discern through the misty air the thatched roofs of various buildings scattered about the park which was flanked by the gentle slopes of two thickly wooded hills. Behind the house, in a grove of trees, stood the coach-houses and stables set in two parallel lines, all that remained of the old château now demolished.

Charles's phaeton drew up before the central steps. Servants appeared. The Marquis came forward, and, offering his arm to the doctor's lady, led her into the hall.

It was very high and paved with marble flags. Footsteps and voices echoed as in a church. Opposite the entrance rose a staircase, and to the left, a gallery, looking on to the garden, led to the billiard-room, whence came the click of ivory balls. As she passed through it on her way to the drawing-room, Emma saw a number of men round the table, all with solemn faces and chins balanced on high cravats. They wore decorations, and smiled silently as they plied their cues. Large gold frames hung on the dark-panelled walls, each bearing, on its lower edge, a name in black lettering. 'Jean-Antoine d'Andervilliers d'Yverbonville', she read, 'Count of La Vaubyessard and Baron of La Fresnaye, killed at the Battle of Coutras, 20th October, 1587', and, on another, 'Jean-Antoine-Henry-Guy d'Andervilliers de la Vaubyessard, Admiral of France and Knight of the Order of St Michael, wounded at the Battle of Hougue-Saint-Vaast, 29th May, 1692, died at La Vaubyessard, 23rd January, 1693'.* The succeeding names were hard to see, because the lamps, so shaded as to throw their light on to the green cloth of the billiard-table, left the rest of the room in shadow. All that illuminated the canvases was a brown glow which, here and there, picked out the sharp ridges of the cracked varnish. A few details of the great black squares in their gold frames were accentuated, here a pale forehead, there two eyes gazing into the room, wigs rippling over the powder-flecked shoulders of scarlet coats, the clasp of a garter showing above a rounded calf.

The Marquis opened the door of the drawing-room. A lady rose (no less a lady than the Marquise) and came forward to greet Emma. She made her sit next to her on a little sofa, and began to chat in the most amiable manner, as though they had been old friends. She was a woman of about forty, with handsome shoulders, a high-bridged nose and a drawl. She was wearing over her brown hair a simple lace shawl which fell on her back in a point. A fair young woman was sitting by her in a straight-backed chair, and several gentlemen, with flowers in the buttonholes of their evening coats, were clustered round the fireplace, talking to the ladies.

Dinner was served at seven o'clock. The men, who were in a

majority, sat at the first table, in the hall, the ladies at the second, in the dining-room, with the Marquis and his wife.

As soon as Emma entered the room, she felt herself enveloped in a gust of warm air which smelled of flowers, fine linen, roast meat and truffles. The flames of the candles in the sconces rose long and straight above bell-shaped casings of silver. The cut-crystal lustres, misted over with a dull sheen of moisture, gave back a dull glow. There were bunches of flowers all down the long table, and, on the wide-bordered plates, the napkins, in the form of bishops' mitres, held small oval rolls in the yawning gap between their folds. The red claws of lobsters hung over the china rims of dishes. Luscious fruit, set in open baskets, stood piled on beds of moss. The quails were served with all their plumage. A cloud of steam rose to the ceiling. The butler, in silk stockings, knee-breeches, a white cravat and a lace frill, looking as solemn as a judge, handed the courses, ready carved, between the shoulders of the guests, and, with a deft movement of his spoon, picked out for each the portion she had indicated as her choice. From the great porcelain brass-fitted stove, the statue of a woman, draped to the chin, gazed at the crowded room in frozen immobility.

Madame Bovary noticed that several of the ladies had not put their gloves in their glasses.*

At the far end of the table, alone among all these women, an old man crouched over his well-filled plate, a napkin tied round his neck like a child, and gravy slobbering over his lips. His eyes were bloodshot, and he wore his hair in a little queue bound with black ribbon. This was the Marquis's father-in-law, the old Duc de Lavardière, once an intimate of the Comte d'Artois in the days when the Marquis de Conflans had given hunting parties at Le Vaudreuil. He had, so the story went, been sandwiched between Monsieur de Coigny and Monsieur Lauzun,* as one of Marie-Antoinette's lovers. His life had been notoriously self-indulgent, full of duels, bets and abductions. He had run through his fortune and terrified his family. A servant stationed behind his chair shouted in his ear the names of the dishes at which the old man pointed to an accompaniment of noisy spluttering. Emma's eyes kept turning of their own accord in his direction. She gazed at his pendulous lips as though he were something august, something out of the general run of nature. He had lived at Court and lain in a queen's bed!

Iced champagne was served. She shivered all over her body as she felt the cold liquid in her mouth. Never before had she seen pomegranates or tasted pineapple. Even the sifted sugar seemed whiter and finer than elsewhere.

When dinner was over, the ladies retired to their rooms to prepare for the ball.

Emma dressed with the meticulous care of an actress on a first night. She arranged her hair as the hairdresser had advised, and put on the filmy dress which lay spread out upon the bed. Charles's trousers were too tight round the waist.

'These straps will get in my way when I dance,' he said.

'Dance?' exclaimed Emma.

'Why not?'

'You must be mad! They'll all laugh at you! You'd much better spend the evening sitting down. Besides,' she added, 'that would be more becoming in a doctor.'

He said nothing, but paced up and down the room until she should be ready.

He could see her from behind reflected in the mirror between its flanking candles. Her black eyes looked blacker. Her hair, slightly puffed over her ears, glittered with a bluish sheen. The rose in her chignon quivered on its flexible stem. At the tip of each leaf there was an artificial drop of water. Her dress was of pale saffron yellow, relieved by three tight bunches of roses complete with their leaves.

He made as though to kiss her on the shoulder.

'Don't!' she said, 'you'll crumple my dress!'

The playing of a violin and the notes of a horn reached their ears. She went down the stairs only just keeping herself from running.

The quadrilles had begun. More guests were arriving. People were pushing their way here and there. She took up a position on a settee close to the door.

When the quadrille was over, the floor was left free for the gentlemen who were standing about talking and for the liveried footmen laden with great salvers. Along the line of seated ladies painted fans were fluttering, smiling lips half hid themselves behind bouquets of flowers, and little gold-stoppered bottles twinkled in half-opened hands the nails of which showed clearly marked beneath the tight white kid of gloves so closely fitting that they made a mark about their owners' wrists. Lace trimmings, diamond brooches, bracelets adorned with hanging lockets, trembled on bodices, darted points of fire from bosoms and jingled on bare arms. Hair, dressed well forward on the forehead and twisted in the nape, was crowned with clusters and fronds of forget-me-nots, jasmine, pomegranate, wheat-ears and cornflowers. The mothers of these many partners sat tranquil on their chairs, with red turbans* on their heads and an expression of discontent on their faces.

Emma's heart gave a faint flutter as she stood in the line of dancers, her partner's fingers lightly laid upon her arm, waiting for the first stroke of the fiddler's bow to give the signal for starting. But very soon her emotion vanished. Moving to the rhythm of the orchestra, she swam forward with a gentle undulation of the neck. A smile showed upon her lips at certain tender passages on the violin, when, now and again, it played alone and the other instruments were hushed. The sound of gold coins chinking on the baize surfaces of card-tables was clearly audible. Then, with a crash of brass, the music would once more strike up loudly. Feet took up the measure, skirts swelled, swishing as they touched one another, hands were given and withdrawn, eyes, downcast a moment before, were raised again in silent colloquy.

Several men—fifteen or so—of all ages ranging from twenty-five to forty, scattered among the dancers, or standing in the doorways, talking, were distinguished from the general crowd by a sort of family likeness which linked them in spite of differences in age, face or dress. Their evening-coats, better cut than those of their fellow-guests, seemed to be made of a more elastic cloth; their hair, which they wore in clustered curls over their temples, and lustrous with pomade, of a silkier texture. They had the colouring which comes of wealth, that pallor which is enhanced by the white sheen of china, the iridescence of watered satin, the polish of fine furniture, and is maintained by a diet of exquisite food never indulged in to excess. Their necks moved freely above low cravats, their long whiskers fell over turned-down collars, and they wiped their lips with embroidered handkerchiefs marked with large monograms and diffusing a sweet perfume. Those on the threshold of middle age looked young, while the more youthful of their company had an air of maturity. Their indifferent glances told of passions dulled by daily satisfaction, and through their polished manners showed that

peculiar aggressiveness which comes of easy conquests, the handling
of thoroughbred horses and the society of loose women.

Close to Emma a man in a blue coat was talking of Italy to a young
woman with a pale face and a pearl necklace. Together they extolled
the size of the pillars of St Peter's, Tivoli, Vesuvius, Castellamare
and the Cascine, the roses of Genoa, the Coliseum seen by moonlight. With her other ear she listened to a conversation which was
full of words she did not understand. There was a group surrounding a very young man who, the week before, had beaten *Miss Arabella*
and *Romulus* and had won two thousand louis by leaping a ditch in
England.* Someone complained that his racers were getting fat:
someone else that a printer's fault had distorted the name of his
horse.

The air of the ballroom grew heavy. The lights shone dim. There
was a general movement towards the billiard-room. A servant got up
on a chair and broke two panes. At the sound of the shattered glass,
Madame Bovary turned her head and saw in the garden the faces of
peasants pressed against the windows. Suddenly she remembered
Les Bertaux, and saw in imagination the muddy pond, her father in
his smock beneath the apple-trees, and herself as she once had been,
skimming with her fingers the great bowls of milk in the dairy. But in
the rich glow of the present her own past life, till then so clear,
vanished entirely, and she began to wonder whether indeed it had
ever been hers at all. Here was she: beyond, outside the radius of the
ball, everything lay in a vague, obliterating shadow. She ate an ice
flavoured with maraschino which she held in her left hand in a silver-
gilt cockle-shell. With the spoon between her teeth she half closed
her eyes.

A lady nearby let fall her fan. A dancer was passing.

'I wonder, sir,' said the lady, 'whether you would be so very kind as
to pick up my fan which has fallen behind this sofa.'

The gentleman bowed, and, as he stretched his arm, Emma saw
the young woman's hand drop something white and three-cornered
into his hat. The gentleman recovered the fan and held it out
politely. The lady thanked him with a movement of the head, and fell
to inhaling the perfume of her flowers.

After supper, at which many wines of Spain and of the Rhine were
served, soup *à la bisque** and *au lait d'amandes*, Trafalgar puddings,*
and many varieties of cold meat set about with jellies which trembled

in their dishes, the carriages, one by one, began to drive away. If one lifted the corner of the muslin curtains the light of their lamps could be seen slipping away into the darkness. The sofas began to empty. A few gamblers still stayed on. The musicians were sucking their finger-tips to cool them. Charles stood leaning against a door-jamb, half asleep.

At three o'clock in the morning, the cotillion* began. Emma had never learned how to waltz. Everyone in the room was waltzing, even Mademoiselle d'Andervilliers and the Marquise. No one was left except the guests who were staying in the house, about twelve persons in all.

In spite of her ignorance of the steps, one of the waltzers, whom the others called familiarly 'Vicomte', and whose very low-cut waistcoat seemed as though moulded on his torso, twice asked her to dance, saying that he would guide her, and that she would manage very well.

They began slowly, then started to move more swiftly. They turned and twisted, and everything about them turned and twisted too, the lamps, the furniture, the panelled walls, the floor—like objects on a pivoted disk. As they passed close to the doors, the lower edge of Emma's dress blew against her partner's trousers: their legs became intertwined. He lowered his glance and looked at her. She raised her eyes to his. A languorous dizziness came over her. She stopped. They started again, and, quickening his pace, the Vicomte swung her away to the far end of the gallery, where, quite out of breath, she all but fell and rested her hand for a moment on his breast. Then, still twirling, but more soberly, he led her back to her place. She stumbled against the wall and put her hand over her eyes.

When she opened them again, a lady was sitting on a stool in the middle of the floor with three dancers on their knees before her. She chose the Vicomte, and the music struck up once more. Everybody looked at them. Up and down the room they went, she, keeping her body motionless and her chin lowered, he, in the same posture as before, with back straight, elbows rounded and lips protruded. She certainly knew how to waltz! They continued a long time, out-dancing all the others.

The company stayed a while longer, talking: then, after bidding one another good-night, or, rather, good-morning, the guests went to their rooms.

Charles clung to the balusters on his way upstairs. His knees felt as weak as water. He had spent five long hours standing by the card-tables, watching people playing whist, a game of which he was entirely ignorant. As he took off his boots, he heaved a deep sigh of relief.

Emma flung a shawl over her shoulders, opened the window and leaned out.

The night was very dark. A few drops of rain were falling. She breathed in the damp air and felt its coolness on her eyes. The music of the ball still echoed in her ears, and she forced herself to stay awake in order to prolong the illusion of that luxurious life which she must leave, so soon, behind her.

The first light of dawn began to show in the sky. She stared long at the windows of the château, trying to guess which were the rooms of all those whom she had seen in the course of the evening. She would dearly have loved to know the manner of their lives, to enter them, and make them her own. But she was shivering with cold. She undressed and snuggled between the sheets against the sleeping Charles.

There were a lot of people at breakfast. The meal lasted for ten minutes. No strong drink was served, which surprised the doctor. When it was over, Mademoiselle d'Andervilliers collected some scraps of rolls in a basket to take to the swans on the lake, and the guests visited the greenhouses where exotic plants with hairy skins rose in pyramids beneath hanging urns which, like nests filled to overflowing with snakes, drooped long, green, twisted tentacles. The orangery at the far end led by a covered way to the back premises. The Marquis, to amuse the young woman, took her to see the stables. Above the basket-shaped mangers were china plaques on which the names of the horses were written in black letters. The animals stamped in their stalls when anyone passing made a clucking sound with his tongue. The boards of the saddle-room shone like a drawing-room floor. Carriage harness was hung in the middle on two revolving pillars, and bits, whips, stirrups and curb-chains were ranged in rows along the wall.

Charles asked a servant to have his phaeton got ready. It was led round to the steps, the luggage was stowed, and the Bovarys, after making their compliments to the Marquis and his lady, started off for Tostes.

Emma watched the turning wheels, but said nothing. Charles, sitting well forward, drove with his arms spread wide, and the little cob ambled along between the shafts which were too big for him. The slack reins bounced up and down on his crupper, and soon grew moist with his lather. The corded box behind bumped rhythmically against the body of the vehicle.

They were on the rising ground near Thibourville when suddenly a group of horsemen passed them, coming from the opposite direction. They were laughing and smoking cigars. Emma thought that she recognized the Vicomte. She turned her head but could see in the distance only the movement of heads rising and falling to unequal motion of trot and gallop.

A quarter of a league further on they had to stop to tie up a broken trace with string. But Charles, giving one last look to the harness, saw something lying on the ground between the horse's legs. He picked it up. It was a cigar-case, edged with green silk and bearing a coat of arms in the middle, like a carriage door.

'There are actually two cigars in it,' he said. 'I'll smoke them tonight after dinner.'

'Do you mean to say you smoke?' she asked.

'Sometimes, when I get the chance.'

He put his find in his pocket, and whipped up the cob.

When they reached home dinner was not yet ready. Madame flew into a temper, Nastasie answered insolently.

'Leave the room!' said Emma. 'This is more than I can stand. Take your notice!'

They had onion soup with a piece of veal cooked in sorrel. Charles, sitting opposite Emma, rubbed his hands with a cheerful look.

'It's nice to be back!' he said.

They could hear Nastasie crying. He was rather fond of the poor creature. In the old days she had kept him company during the many empty evenings he had spent as a widower. She had been his first patient, and he had known her longer than he had known anyone in the district.

'Did you mean that about sending her away?' he said at length.

'Yes, why do you ask?' she answered.

They sat in the kitchen for warmth while their bedroom was being got ready. Charles began to smoke. He did so with his lips pushed forward, constantly spitting, and drawing himself back at every puff.

'You'll make yourself sick!' she said scornfully.

He laid his cigar aside and ran to the pump for a drink of cold water. Emma snatched up the cigar-case and flung it violently into the cupboard.

The next day seemed inordinately long. She took a walk in the tiny garden, pacing up and down the same paths again and again, stopping to look at the flower-beds, the trellised fruit-trees, the plaster statue of the priest. She felt struck by a sort of wonderment at the sight of all these once familiar objects. How far away the ball already seemed! What was it that so completely severed this evening from the morning of the day before yesterday? Her journey to La Vaubyessard had opened a yawning fissure in her life, a fissure that was like one of those great crevasses which a storm will sometimes make on a mountain-side in the course of one short night. She resigned herself, however, to the inevitable, and reverently locked away in the chest of drawers the lovely dress which she had worn and the satin slippers with their soles still stained with the yellow beeswax of the dance-floor. Her heart was like them: the touch of wealth had stamped it with a mark which would never be effaced.

To remember the ball became for Emma a daily occupation. With the return of every Wednesday she said to herself on waking, 'A week ago—a fortnight—three weeks—I was *there!*' Little by little, the faces she had seen became confused in her memory. She forgot the tune to which they had danced the quadrille. The liveries of the servants, and the furniture of the rooms, lost their former precision. Details faded but regret remained.

CHAPTER IX

OFTEN, when Charles had gone out, she would open the cupboard and take, from amid the folded linen where she had put it, the green silk cigar-case.

She looked at it, opened it, even sniffed the mingled smell of tobacco and verbena which hung about its lining. Whose was it?— the Vicomte's. Perhaps it was a present from his mistress, embroidered on a frame of rosewood, some delicate little piece of furniture, hidden from all eyes but her own.

Doubtless the work had taken hours of application, doubtless, soft curls had bent above it, and in a mood of sweet day-dreaming, stitch had been added to stitch. The meshes of the canvas had caught the very spirit of love, each prick of the needle had fixed a memory or a hope. Those little twined and knotted threads of silk held passion's record. A morning had come when the Vicomte took it away with him. What chatter it must have heard as it lay on many mantel-pieces above great canopied hearths, between vases of flowers and Pompadour* clocks. And now, here was she in Tostes; he, probably, in Paris. What sort of place was this Paris of the sounding name? She spoke it half aloud from mere pleasure in the word. It echoed in her ears like a cathedral chime, it flamed before her eyes, so that she almost saw it written on the labels of her toilet bottles. At night, when the fishmongers passed in their wagons beneath her window, singing the *Marjolaine*,* she would lie awake listening to the noise of iron-shod wheels dying quickly into the distance, thinking to herself: 'Tomorrow they will be there.' She followed them in imagination, up hill and down, through villages and along the starlit roads. Always at some indeterminate distance, was a confused amorphous place, and there her dream died.

She bought a map of Paris and with her finger-tip traced walks about the capital. She sauntered along the boulevards, stopping at each corner, exploring the long lines of streets between the white squares which stood for houses. At length her eyes grew tired, and she would close them, seeing in the darkness of her drooping lids the flames of gas-lamps flickering in the wind, and the steps of carriages let down with a rattle before the porticoes of theatres.

She surrendered to the magic of *Corbeille*, a magazine devoted to women's interests, and of the *Sylphe des Salons*.* She devoured the accounts of first-nights, race-meetings and balls, not missing a single word. She took an interest in the début of a singer or the opening of a shop. She knew the latest fashions, the names of the best dress-makers, the days on which the fashionable world drove in the Bois or went to the opera. She pored over the description of furniture in the works of Eugène Sue.* She read Balzac* and George Sand,* seeking in their pages satisfaction by proxy for all her longings. Even at meals she sat with a book before her, turning the pages while Charles ate his food and chatted. Always, as she read, the memory of the Vicomte kept her company. She established a connexion between

him and the characters of her favourite fiction. But the circle of
which he was the centre gradually expanded, and the glow which
was like a nimbus about his face spread outwards, shedding a light on
dreams in which he played no part. Paris, vaster than the ocean,
shimmered for her in a rosy vapour. Its swarming, noisy life ceased
to be a mere generalized tumult, and was seen as an agglomeration of
parts, each with its own colour and form. But of these, it was two or
three only which held the forefront of her stage, blocking out everything else and imaging within their own small compass the whole
panorama of humanity. First was the world of high diplomacy,
whose denizens trod on polished floors in rooms panelled with mir-
rors and filled with oval tables covered with velvet, gold-fringed,
cloths. The women wore trains and had faces of mystery. Aching
hearts beat behind their smiling lips. Next in importance came the
circle which revolved about the great ducal houses, peopled by won-
drous creatures, late-rising and pale-faced. The women, poor, sweet
angels, wore dresses trimmed with English lace, the men, keen
brained for all their fatuous looks, spent their days in the hunting
field, riding horses until they dropped, dawdled away the summer
months in Baden, and, round about the age of forty, wedded heir-
esses. At midnight, in the private rooms of restaurants, the gay
crowd, diversified by an admixture of actresses and men of letters,
supped to the sound of laughter in candle-lit intimacy. Spendthrift
as kings, they were, full of idealistic ambitions and outlandish fantasies. The world they lived in was high above that of the common
herd, somewhere in tempestuous regions suspended between earth
and heaven. The rest of the universe was no more than a place of
shadows, ill-defined, anonymous, barely existing. From all that was
close and familiar she turned her thoughts. Her own daily scene—a
tedious countryside, a half-witted, middle-class society, an unceasing
round of mediocrity—she saw as an exception to some more glorious
rule, as something in which, by mere ill-chance, she had been caught
and held. Beyond it, stretching as far as eye could see, was a world of
joy and passion. In the heat of her desire she confounded heart's
happiness with the sensual pleasures of luxury, true refinement of
sentiment with elegance of manners. Did not love, like Oriental
blooms, need carefully tended earth to grow in, and a special climate? Moonlit sighs and lingering embraces, tear-stained hands at
parting, burning desires and languorous tenderness—such things

could have place only on the balconies of noble mansions where leisure marks the passing of the days, in boudoirs with silken blinds, deep-piled carpets, flower-filled bowls and beds raised high in stepped recesses: could go only with the sparkle of jewels, the shoulder-knots of liveried footmen.

The ostler from the post-house, who came each morning to tend her mare, stumped along the passage in his heavy clogs. His smock was full of holes, his feet unstockinged—a wretched substitute for grooms in well-cut breeches! When his work was done he left, and came no more that day. For Charles, when he got back, would look after his horse himself, taking off the saddle, removing the harness, while the servant-girl would bring a load of hay and toss it, as best she could, into the manger.

In place of Nastasie (who did, indeed, leave Tostes in floods of tears), Emma had taken into her service a girl of fourteen, an orphan with a gentle face. She was forbidden to wear cotton caps, instructed to use the third person only when addressing her mistress, and taught always to carry a salver when bringing in a glass of water. Emma planned to make of this child her own personal maid, who would darn and starch her linen and help her to dress. The new girl, not wishing to be sent away, obeyed without a murmur, and, since her mistress was in the habit of leaving the key in the sideboard, made off each evening with a little store of sugar which she ate in solitude after she had gone to bed and said her prayers. Sometimes, of an afternoon, Félicité (for that was her name) would go across the road for a chat with the postillions, while her mistress was upstairs in her room.

Emma would wear a loose dressing-gown which revealed between its crossed lapels a pleated under-skirt adorned with three gold buttons. Her girdle was a cord with large tassels, and on her feet she had wine-red slippers with big bunches of ribbon at the instep. She had bought a letter-case, a supply of paper, a penholder and envelopes, though there was no one to whom she could write. She dusted the shelves, looked at herself in the mirror, took up a book, and then, falling into a day-dream as she read, let it fall upon her knees. She would have liked to travel, or to have gone back to her convent. She wished she could die, and she wished she could live in Paris.

Charles rode through the country lanes in rain and snow. He ate omelettes at farm-house tables, thrust his arm into damp beds, had his face splashed when he let blood, listened to death-rattles, examined chamber-pots, and rolled up a deal of dirty linen. But always when he got home at night he found a roaring fire, the table laid for dinner, an easy chair and a charming, beautifully dressed wife smelling so fresh that he never, for the life of him, knew whence the sweet scent came, and thought her body must impart it to her clothes.

She charmed him by a thousand little refinements, sometimes a new way of fashioning paper shades for the candles, sometimes a new trimming to her dress, sometimes an outlandish name for a very simple dish which, though the servant had spoiled it, he ate with relish to the bitter end. She had seen women in Rouen wearing bunches of trinkets on their watch-chains, so she bought some for herself. She longed to have big blue glass vases on her mantelpiece and—this was rather later—an ivory work-box with a silver-gilt thimble. The less Charles understood these elegancies the more was he enthralled by them. They added something to the pleasures of his senses as well as to the comfort of his home. They were like gold-dust scattered over the narrow footpath of his life.

He enjoyed good health and looked well. His reputation was by now completely established. The country people liked him because he was not proud. He petted their children and never drank at the inn. Moreover, his morals were of a kind to inspire confidence. He was particularly successful with colds and affections of the lungs. Fearful of killing his patients, he rarely prescribed anything more drastic than soothing draughts, occasional emetics, a foot-bath or an application of leeches. Not that he was frightened of surgical operations. He bled people as freely as he did horses, and when it came to taking out teeth, he had *the devil of a wrench*!

As time went on, he became a subscriber to *La Ruche Médicale*, a new magazine of which he had been sent a prospectus. This he did *to keep himself up to date*. He would dip into it after dinner, but the warmth of the room combined with the process of digestion usually sent him to sleep after about five minutes, and he would sit there with his head on his arms and his tousled hair spread out like a mane under the lamp. Emma would look at him and shrug.

Why had she not as husband one of those taciturn enthusiasts who, after a lifetime spent in burning the midnight oil, carry into the rheumatic retirement of sixty a cross to pin upon their ill-cut evening coats? The name of Bovary was hers, and she would have liked to know it illustrious, to have seen it displayed in book shops, quoted in newspapers, known throughout the length and breadth of France. But Charles was entirely without ambition. A doctor from Yvetot with whom he had recently been in consultation had humiliated him before his patient and the assembled relatives. When, on his return that evening, he had related the occurrence, she had railed against his colleague. Charles, touched by the outburst, had kissed her on the forehead with a tear in his eye. But she, ashamed, exasperated, had felt like boxing his ears. She had had to go into the passage, open the window and breathe in the cool night air in order to get control of her feelings.

'What a poor, craven creature!' she had muttered to herself, biting her lips.

As he grew older he irritated her in more ways than one. He began to contract coarse habits. When he sat at his wine he would cut up the corks of the empty bottles. After meals, he sucked his teeth. He made a gurgling noise whenever he ate soup, and, as he grew fatter, his eyes, which were small in any case, looked as though they were being pushed upwards and outwards towards his temples by the increasing puffiness of his cheeks.

Sometimes she would tuck the edge of his red knitted jersey out of sight beneath his waistcoat, straighten his cravat and throw away the faded gloves which he was quite gaily proposing to put on. It was not for him—as he thought—that she did these things, but for herself. Her action was dictated by her egotism, was the expression of a nervous irritability. Sometimes, too, she talked to him of things that she had read, passages from novels or from plays, or would repeat some anecdote of *high society* which she had seen in the gossip column of her paper. For at least, he was better than nobody, was always there, ready to listen and agree. Many were the secrets which she told her dog! She would have told them to the logs in the fireplace or the pendulum of the clock.

But deep in her heart she was waiting for something to happen. Like sailors in distress, she gazed around with despairing eyes upon the loneliness of her life, seeking a white sail on the immensities of the misty horizon. She did not know what chance, what wind would bring it to her, to what shore it would carry her, whether it would turn out to be an open boat or a three-decker laden to the gunwale with pain or happiness. But each morning when she woke she was agog for what the day might bring forth. She listened to the sounds of the world, jumped from her bed, and never ceased to be surprised that nothing happened. Then, when night came on again, sadder than ever, she longed for the morrow.

Spring returned. With the first of the hot weather, when the blossom showed upon the pear-trees, she had spasms of breathlessness.

At the beginning of July she began to count on her fingers how many weeks must elapse before it was October, thinking that the Marquis d'Andervilliers might give another ball at La Vaubyessard. But September slipped away without bringing either a letter or a visit.

After the vexation of this disappointment her heart grew once more empty, and the old procession of identical days began again.

So they would go on, day after day, innumerable, indistinguishable, and bringing nothing! Other lives, no matter how flat they might be, held at least the possibility of happenings. A single adventure sometimes brought changes of fortune which held an infinity of possibilities and new scenes. But nothing ever happened to her! God had willed it so! The future stretched ahead like a dark corridor with a locked door at the end.

She gave up her music. What was the point of playing? Who was there to hear? Since she would never sit in a concert hall in a short-sleeved dress of black velvet, letting her fingers ripple over the ivory keys of an Erard grand, and hearing murmurs of ecstatic appreciation blow round her like a breeze, what was the point of subjecting herself to all the boredom of practising? She left her sketch-books and her embroidery untouched upon the cupboard shelves. What was the use? what was the use? Sewing got on her nerves.

'I have read everything,' she said to herself, and could find nothing better to do than heat the tongs red-hot and watch the falling rain.

How sad she felt on Sundays when the bell rang for vespers! In a mood of listening lassitude she heard the cracked notes sound. A solitary cat moving slowly along a roof arched its back in the pale sunlight. The wind raised little eddies of dust on the high-road. Sometimes, from far off, a dog howled, and at regular intervals the bell gave forth its monotonous note which sounded only to be lost above the empty fields.

But on those days at least something happened—the congregation came out of church, the women in waxed clogs, the peasants in new smocks, the small children skipping and hopping in front. Soon all had dispersed homewards, and then, till darkness fell, there was nothing to be seen but a group of men—always the same men—playing at shove-ha'penny in front of the main door of the inn.

The winter was cold. The window-panes each morning were thick with frost, and the light, striking palely through them, as through unpolished glass, often showed no change the whole day through. The lamp had to be lit by four in the afternoon. On fine days she went into the garden. The frost had trimmed the cabbage leaves with silver lace, and stretched long shining threads between them. No birds sang, and all life seemed asleep. The trellised fruit-trees on the wall were swathed in straw, and the vine lay like an ailing serpent beneath the coping. If she went close she could see the wood-lice creeping with their many legs. In the little grove of pines close to the hedge, the priest, in his three-cornered hat, reading his breviary, had lost his right foot, and the plaster scaled by the frost had left white blotches on his face.

Going back into the house, she would shut the door of her room, poke the fire, and, relaxing in the warmth, feel the dead weight of boredom heavier still. She would have enjoyed going downstairs and chatting with the maid, but did not quite like to.

Every day, at the same time, the schoolmaster, wearing a black silk skull-cap, flung wide his shutters, and the village constable passed by, his sabre slung over his smock. Evening and morning the horses from the post-house went by, three by three, to be watered at the pond. Now and again the door of one of the taverns set its little bell a-tinkling, and, when the wind blew, she could hear the miniature copper basins which served as a sign before the barber's shop, creaking on the two rods which held them suspended. It boasted, this shop, by way of decoration, an old fashion-plate stuck on one of the panes, and the wax bust of a lady with yellow hair. The barber, too, bewailed frustration in his calling and a future that would never be his. Dreaming of a shop in some great city, Rouen, maybe, on the water-front or close by the theatre, he spent the day pacing up and down between the Mairie and the church, gloomily awaiting customers. Whenever Madame Bovary looked up she saw him there, like a sentry on his beat, with a little cap stuck over one ear, and his flannel jacket.

Sometimes, in the afternoon, a man's face would show outside the parlour window, a tanned face with black whiskers and a beaming smile which displayed a row of white, shining teeth. The notes of a waltz would be heard, and, in a tiny box, on the hurdy-gurdy's top, made in the semblance of a drawing-room, she could see dancers no bigger than her finger, ladies in red turbans, Tyrolean peasants in short coats, monkeys in black evening suits, gentlemen in knee-breeches, turning, turning, among diminutive chairs and sofas and pier-tables, all reflected in scraps of glass joined at their corners by strips of gilded paper. The man would turn his handle, looking to right, to left and at the windows. Now and again, aiming a long jet of brown saliva at the mounting-stone, he would lift the instrument with his knee to ease the drag of the brace across his shoulder. The music, now mournful and hesitant, now quickening to a joyful rhythm, would issue from the box, wheezing through a pink silk curtain held by a decorative brass claw. The tunes it played had once been part of the repertoire of theatre orchestras, had been sung in drawing-rooms, danced to by couples beneath the glow of crystal chandeliers. They were echoes from the great world. Endless sarabands began to weave within her head, her thoughts leaping to the notes, like dancing-girls on a flowered carpet, swimming from dream to dream, from sadness to sadness. When the man had received her offering in his cap he would cover up his organ with a piece of blue cloth, hoist it on to his back, and move off with heavy tread. She watched him go.

But it was at meal-times, in particular, that she felt as though she were at the end of her tether, at meal-times in the little parlour on the ground-floor, with its smoky stove, its creaking door, its sweating walls and its damp flags. All the bitterness of existence lay heaped on her plate. With the steamy vapour of the meat stale gusts of dreariness rose from the depths of her heart. Charles took a long time over his food. She sat nibbling nuts or, with her elbow on the table and her head on her hand, amusing herself by tracing lines with her knife on the waxed surface of the cloth. She no longer took any interest in the running of her house, and her mother-in-law, who spent part of Lent at Tostes, was much surprised by the changes which she saw there. Once so neat and careful of her person, Emma now would spend the whole day in a loose wrap, with grey stockings on her legs. There were candles instead of lamps. Being so poor, she said, they must economize, adding that she was perfectly content and happy; that she liked Tostes. With such phrases, and with others more unexpected still, she stopped the older woman's mouth. No longer did she seem disposed to take advice. Once, when her mother-in-law was rash enough to say that employers ought to keep a watchful eye on the religious observances of their servants, she answered with so angry a glance, with so chilly a smile, that the good woman never touched on the subject again.

Emma became difficult and capricious. She would order special dishes for herself, and then not touch them: one day would drink nothing but plain milk, and, on the next, cups of tea by the dozen. Often she refused obstinately to leave the house, and then, saying that she was stifling, throw the windows wide and put on the flimsiest of dresses. When she had been particularly harsh with the servant, she would load her with presents, and tell her to go off and amuse herself at some neighbour's house. Similarly, she would throw all her loose change to a beggar, though not naturally of a kindly temperament, nor easily sensitive to another's feelings, as is often the case with the children of country folk whose hearts always show a resemblance to their fathers' horny hands.

Towards the end of February, old Rouault, wishing to mark the anniversary of his cure, came in person to Tostes with the gift of a superb turkey, and stayed three days. Since Charles was busy with his patients, it was Emma who kept him company. He smoked in his bedroom, spat on the fire-irons, talked farming and livestock, poultry and local politics, to such purpose that she shut the door on his departing back with a feeling of satisfaction which surprised even herself. No longer, in any case, did she trouble to conceal her scorn of things and persons, and at times went out of her way to make outrageous statements, condemning what was usually approved, approving what was perverse or immoral—all of which made her husband open wide eyes.

Would this wretched state of affairs go on for ever?—would she never escape? She was as good as, if not better than, all the women whose lives were happy! She had met duchesses at La Vaubyessard who had heavier figures than her own and coarser manners. She kicked against the pricks of God's injustice; would lean her head against the wall and weep, envious of those who knew tumultuous days and nights of dance and domino and all the desperate joys which come with arrogant pleasures—but not to her!

She grew pale and began to suffer from palpitations of the heart. Charles prescribed valerian and camphor baths. But no matter what he tried, it seemed only to increase her irritability.

On some days she prattled with a sort of feverish gaiety. But these exalted moods would be suddenly succeeded by periods of languor when she sat motionless and silent. She could be brought out of these fits only by having her arms rubbed with eau de cologne.

Since she was for ever complaining of Tostes, he imagined that some local influence must lie at the root of her ill-health. Such a hold did this idea take on his mind that he seriously considered setting up in practice somewhere else.

She took to drinking vinegar in order to grow slim, contracted a dry cough and completely lost her appetite.

To leave Tostes meant a sad wrench for Charles. He had been there for four years, and his practice was by now solidly established. But if he must, he must. He took her to Rouen to see his former master. She was suffering, said the latter, from a nervous ailment and needed change of air.

After making a prolonged search, Charles was told about a large market-town called Yonville-l'Abbaye,* in the parish of Neufchâtel. The doctor there, a Polish refugee,* had decamped only the week before. He wrote to the local chemist to find out the size of the population, how far off the nearest medical practitioner lived, how much a year his predecessor had made, etc., etc. The replies to all these questions being satisfactory, he decided that he would move there when spring came, unless Emma's health improved in the meantime.

One day when she was rearranging a drawer in anticipation of their departure, she pricked her finger on something. It was the wire which bound her wedding bouquet. The orange-blossom was yellow with dust, and the satin ribbon with its silver fringe was frayed at the edges. She threw it on the fire, where it flared up quicker than dry straw. Soon it was no more than a glowing twig on the cinders, slowly falling to ash. She watched it burn. The little pasteboard berries crackled, the wire thread twisted, the tinsel melted. The paper leaves shrivelled, hung like black butterflies upon the fire-back, and, in a few moments, flew up the chimney.

When they left Tostes in the month of March, Madame Bovary was pregnant.

PART TWO

CHAPTER I

YONVILLE-L'ABBAYE* (so called from a former Capuchin Abbey of which not even the ruins now exist) is a market-town lying about eight leagues from Rouen, between the Abbeville and the Beauvais roads, in a valley watered by the Rieule, a small tributary of the Andelle. Before joining the larger stream it serves to turn three mills, where ponds hold a number of trout which provide amusement on Sundays for the local youth who fish for them with rod and line.

The traveller leaves the main road at La Boissière, and continues straight on to the top of the hill of Leux, whence he gets his first view of the valley. The river in its winding course cuts it into two parts, each of which has a distinctive appearance. To the left is pasture, to the right arable. The grasslands extend beneath a range of low hills, ultimately joining up with the western section of the Bray grazing district. But eastwards, the level bottoms begin to rise gently and to expand their acreage in a great expanse of golden corn which stretches as far as eye can reach. The stream skirts the border of the pastures, and looks like a white line separating the colour of the meadows from that of the plough, so that the landscape resembles a spread cloak having a velvet collar trimmed with silver braid.

Walking on towards the horizon, one finds, at length, the oaks of the Argueil forest and the steep escarpment of the Saint-Jean uplands streaked by long red gashes. These are the marks left by the rain. The brick-red colouring, graven in thin lines upon the greyish background of the hillside, comes from the numerous iron-impregnated streams which flow through the surrounding country.

This is the meeting-place of Normandy, Picardy and the Île-de-France, a bastard land where the accents of the people and the contours of the ground are characterless. The worst cheeses of the whole Neufchâtel district are made here, and farming is an expensive business, because much manure is needed to enrich a friable soil mostly composed of sand and pebbles.

Until 1835 there was no practicable route into Yonville, but about that time a local highway was built to join the Abbeville and Amiens roads. It is used occasionally by travellers from Rouen into Flanders. Despite its new outlets, however, Yonville has remained stationary. Its inhabitants, instead of making an effort to improve their farming methods, have clung obstinately to the raising of cattle, though at a loss, and the sleepy town, standing with its back to the plain, has shown a natural tendency to extend towards the river. It lies spread out along the bank like a cowherd taking his siesta by the waterside.

A metalled causeway, planted with aspens, leads from the bridge at the bottom of the hill in a straight line to the first of the outlying houses. These are surrounded by hedges and stand with yards about them which boast a multiplicity of scattered buildings, wine-presses, wagon-sheds and distilleries, all sheltering beneath bosky trees with ladders, poles and hay-forks leaning against their branches. The thatched roofs, looking for all the world like fur caps pulled down over the wearers' eyes, overhang, to about a third of their depth, the windows, the coarse, whorled panes of which have knots in the middle after the manner of bottle-ends. Here and there a few weakly pear-shoots are trained over the plaster walls with their diagonal timber beams, and the doors on the ground-floor level have little swinging gates intended to keep out the chickens which cluster round the threshold pecking at crumbs of rye-bread soaked in cider. Closer to the town, the yards become narrower, the houses more closely packed. There are no more hedges. A bundle of bracken swinging from a broom-stick beneath a window marks the black-smith's forge, and next it is the wheelwright's shop with two or three new wagons standing outside and encroaching on the roadway. A little further on, standing behind a wrought-iron screen, is a white house facing on to a patch of lawn containing a small figure of Cupid with his fingers to his lips. Two metal urns are set one at each end of the low flight of steps. Heraldic shields shine on the door-panels. This is the home of the local lawyer. It is the handsomest house for miles around.*

The church is on the other side of the street, twenty yards further on, at the point where it debouches into the market-place. The little churchyard, surrounded by a waist-high wall, is so crammed with graves that the older tomb-stones, laid flat on the ground, make an unbroken expanse of paving on which the unchecked grass has set a pattern of neat green squares. The church was entirely rebuilt during the last years of Charles X. The wooden frame of the roof is beginning to decay in its upper part, and shows a few black worm-holes in its blue colour-wash. Above the porch, where the organ pipes should be, is a gallery for the men, approached by a winding stair which echoes to the sound of their clogs.

The daylight, striking through the plain glass of the windows, shines obliquely on rows of benches placed at right angles to the wall on which is nailed an occasional piece of straw matting with, beneath it, in large letters, the words—'Mr So-and-so's Pew'. The confessional stands at the point where the building narrows, and is balanced, on the other side of the aisle, by a statue of the Virgin dressed in a satin robe and crowned with a muslin veil sewn with silver stars. Her cheeks are touched with red like a Sandwich-Islands totem. At the far end, a copy of the *Holy Family* (presented by the Minister of the Interior) dominates the high altar and closes the view.

The market-hall—in other words, a tiled roof supported by about twenty wooden posts—fills one half of the main square of Yonville. At the corner, next to the chemist's shop, is the town hall, a building constructed *in accordance with the plans of an architect from Paris.* It is in the form of a Greek temple. On the ground level are three Ionic columns with, above them, a semi-circular gallery. The tympanum is filled by a Gallic cock which is shown with one foot resting on the charter,* while in the other it holds the scales of justice.

The chief focus of interest, however, is the chemist's shop belonging to Monsieur Homais. It faces the Golden Lion inn. The time to see it is after dark when the lamps are lit and the red and green jars which adorn the window cast their coloured radiance on the pavement. For then, as though behind a screen of Bengal lights, the shadow of the chemist can be observed leaning above his desk. The whole front of his house is placarded with inscriptions, in Italian, round and copperplate script—EAUX DE VICHY, DE SELTZ ET DE BARÈGES , ROBS DÉPURATIFS, MÉDECINE RASPAIL, RACAHOUT DES ARABES, PASTILLES DARCET, PÂTE REGNAULT, BANDAGES, BAINS, CHOCOLATS DE SANTÉ,* etc. The sign, which covers the whole width of the façade, bears the words HOMAIS—CHEMIST. At the back of the shop, behind the great scales which are riveted to the counter, the single word LABORATORY is visible above a glass door, in the middle of which, in gold on a black ground, the name HOMAIS is repeated.

Apart from this, there is nothing to be seen in Yonville. The street (the only one) is about a gunshot in length and lined with a few shops. It ends abruptly where the road makes a turn. Leaving it on one's right, and continuing to the bottom of the Saint-Jean hill, one comes, almost at once, to the cemetery.

When it had to be enlarged at the time of the cholera epidemic,* a section of wall was pulled down and a few adjoining acres were purchased. But this new section is almost entirely unused. The graves, now as in the past, are crowded about the gate. The curator, who is also sexton and grave-digger (thus deriving a double benefit from the corpses of the parish) has turned the empty patch to account by growing potatoes on it. Each year, however, the available space has grown less, and when a particularly heavy bout of sickness attacks the town, he is in doubt whether to rejoice at the number of deaths or to bemoan the increase in the quantity of graves.

'You live by death, Lestiboudois!' said the curé to him one day.

This gloomy comment made him think, and for a while he stopped his gardening activities. But recently he has resumed his cultivation of tubers, and goes so far as to maintain, without turning a hair, that they grow of their own accord.

Since the events which I am about to relate, nothing has changed in Yonville. The tin tricolour* still twists and turns on the church steeple; the two calico streamers still flutter in the wind over the fancy-goods shop; the pickled foetuses in the chemist's window still look like bundles of white tinder, and decay a little more each year in their jars of viscous alcohol. Above the front-door of the inn the old golden lion, discoloured by the rain, still exhibits his poodle's curls to the eyes of travellers.

The evening on which the Bovarys were due to arrive at Yonville, the widow Lefrançois, who at that time kept the inn, was so fearfully busy that she sweated over her pots and pans. Tomorrow was market-day, and meat had to be carved, chickens drawn, tea and coffee made, in readiness for the occasion. She had, in addition, the meals of her 'regulars' to prepare, as well as a dinner for the doctor, his wife and their servant. Peals of laughter came from the billiard-room, and the three millers in the small parlour were calling for brandy. The wood fire roared, the coal crackled, and on the long kitchen table, among the raw joints of mutton, huge piles of plates clattered in response to the shaking of the block on which spinach was being chopped. From the yard came the frightened clucking of fowls striving to avoid the serving-maid who was doing her best to round them up for slaughter.

A man in green leather slippers, with a slightly pock-marked face, wearing a velvet cap with a gold tassel, was warming his back at the fire. His face expressed nothing but self-satisfaction, and he seemed to take life as calmly as the goldfinch hanging in a wicker cage above his head. This was the chemist.

'Artémise!' cried the mistress of the establishment, 'get the wood cut, fill the jugs and hurry up with the brandy! I wish I knew what sweet to give the company you're going to get! Heavens! What a row the removal men are making in the billiard-room! And they've left their van right under the archway, too! The Swallow might smash into it. Shout to Polyte to shift it. Would you believe it, Monsieur Homais, they've played something like fifteen games and drunk eight pots of cider since the morning! . . . They're going to ruin my cloth . . .'—she went on, looking at them in the far room, her skimmer in her hand.

'It might be no bad thing,' replied Monsieur Homais: 'for then you'd have to buy another!'

'What, another billiard-table!' exclaimed the widow.

'Well, this one's quite worn out, Madame Lefrançois. If I've said it once, I've said it a hundred times, you're doing yourself a lot of harm, a *lot* of harm. Besides, enthusiasts for the game nowadays like narrow pockets and heavy cues. No one's interested in *marbles* any more! Those days are dead and gone. We must move with the times. . . . Look at Tellier, now. . . .'

The landlady flushed with annoyance. The chemist continued:

'His billiard-table is a good deal handsomer than yours. It's no use denying it, and if anybody had the idea of getting up a patriotic tournament, for Poland,* say, or the victims of the Lyons floods.* . . .'

'I'm not afraid of rubbish like him!' broke in the landlady with a shrug of her enormous shoulders. . . . 'Come on, Monsieur Homais, as long as the Golden Lion's here, we'll have customers . . . we've been feathering our nest, we have, but as for the Café Français, one of these fine mornings you'll see it with the shutters up, and a nice big notice of sale pasted on the front! . . . A new billiard-table, indeed!'—she went on to herself—'when the old one's so handy for laying out the washing. Why, in the shooting season, I've bedded no less than six casuals on it. . . . Where can that slowcoach of a Hivert have got to?'

'Are you waiting until he comes before dishing up the gentlemen's dinner?' inquired the chemist.

'Waiting?—but what about Monsieur Binet, then? In he'll come on the stroke of six—there's not his equal for punctuality in the world. And always has to have the same place kept for him in the small parlour. Rather die, he would, than take his dinner anywhere else. And fussy! So particular about his cider! Very different from that Mr Léon. Seven o'clock it is, sometimes, or half-past, before *he* turns up, and never so much as looks at what's set before him. A good young man if ever there was—never raises his voice, and . . .'

'Which only goes to show that there is a world of difference between a man who's had a good education and an ex-soldier tax-collector!'

At that very moment six o'clock struck and Binet came in.

He was dressed in a blue frockcoat which hung stiff and straight about his bony form. On his head was a leather cap with ear-flaps tied together on the top. The peak was turned up and revealed a forehead from which the hair had receded as a result of his having had to wear a military helmet in early life. He had on a black cloth waistcoat and a cravat of horsehair. His trousers were of some grey material, and his boots, which, no matter what the weather, he always kept well polished, showed two parallel bulges caused by the prominence of his big toes. Not a hair encroached on the white collar which followed the line of his jaw, and, like the edge of a flower-bed, framed a long, sallow face with small eyes and an aquiline nose. He was good at all card games, an excellent shot, and wrote a beautiful hand. He had a lathe at home on which he turned napkin-rings as a hobby; he filled the house with them, combining the jealous pride of an artist with bourgeois self-absorption.

He made straight for the small parlour, but, before he could take his place, the three millers had to be dislodged. While his plate was being laid, he sat near the stove, saying nothing. When all was ready, he closed the door and removed his cap, as he always did.

'*He* won't wear out his tongue with courtesy!' remarked the chemist as soon as he was left alone with the landlady.

'Never says anything,' she replied. 'There were these two linen salesmen here last week—jolly young chaps—told such stories one night I laughed till I cried—and he sat there like a stuffed trout, never said a word.'

'No imagination, that's what it is,' said the chemist: 'no small-talk, none of the qualities which go to make the social being!'

'Still, they say he's no fool,' protested the landlady.

'No fool? No fool, eh?' rejoined Monsieur Homais. 'Not in his own line, maybe'—he added more calmly.

'That a business-man,' he went on, 'with a wide connexion, a lawyer, a doctor, a chemist, should be so absorbed in his work as to become odd or even boorish, is but natural. History is full of them. But that is because the minds of such folk are constantly working. Take my own case, for instance: many's the time I've hunted all over my desk for a pen with which to write a label, only to find that I'd stuck it behind my ear!'*

But by this time Madame Lefrançois had gone to the door to see whether the Swallow had put in an appearance. She gave a start. A man dressed in black had suddenly entered the kitchen. The fading daylight showed him to have a red face and an athletic body.

'What can I do for your reverence?' asked the lady of the inn, reaching for one of the brass candlesticks which stood in a row on the mantelpiece ready for lighting. 'Would it be a drop of something, now?—a little cassis or a glass of wine?'

The gentleman of the cloth refused her offer politely. He had come, he said, to fetch the umbrella which he had left a day or two earlier at the convent of Ernemont. After asking Madame Lefrançois to have it sent down to the presbytery in the course of the evening, he took his departure in the direction of the church where the angelus was being rung.

As soon as the sound of his footsteps had died away in the square, the chemist began to inveigh against his behaviour. His refusal to take anything seemed to him to be a sign of the most revolting hypocrisy. All priests, he said, tippled in secret, and were trying to reintroduce the tithe system. The landlady rushed to do battle in defence of the parish priest.

'He could lay four of you across his knee any day, if it comes to that! Last year, when he was helping my men to get in the straw, he carried six trusses at a time. Strong as a horse, he is!'

'Good for him!' said the chemist. 'Just the sort of strapping fellow to take young girls in confession! If I was the government I'd have all priests bled regularly once a month. Yes, Madame Lefrançois, a good, generous blood-letting once a month, in the interest of public well-being and sound morality!'

'For shame! that's plain wickedness, that is! You've no respect for religion!'

'I have plenty of respect for religion,' replied the chemist: 'for my own religion, that is, and a good deal more than they have with their tricks and their mummery! I worship God! I believe in the Supreme Being,* in a Creator—of what nature I do not inquire—who has put us into this world to fulfil our duties as citizens and fathers. But I don't feel called upon to go kissing silver dishes in church, or to pay good money in order to fatten a lot of play-actors who live a great deal better than we do. A man can worship God just as well in the woods and fields, or by merely contemplating the wide vault of heaven, like the ancients. *My* God is the God of Socrates, of Franklin, of Voltaire and of Béranger!* I stand for the creed of the *Vicaire savoyard** and the immortal principles of '89.* I have no use for any god who walks in his garden with his stick in his hand, entertains his friends in the bellies of whales, dies with a loud cry, and rises again after three days—all of them things which are not only absurd in themselves, but altogether contrary to the laws of the physical universe—which proves, by the way, that priests have always wallowed in slothful ignorance, and are for ever trying to drag down their flocks with them!'

He stopped and looked about him for an audience. Carried away by his own eloquence, he had imagined himself, for a moment, to be attending a full session of the municipal council.

But the mistress of the house was no longer listening to him. She was straining her ears to catch the distant rumble of wheels. The sound of a carriage became audible, and the rattle of loose chains bumping on the roadway. In a few moments the Swallow drew up in front of the door. It was a huge, yellow, chest-like object mounted on two large wheels which, since they rose as high as the tilt, prevented the passengers from seeing anything of the road, and spattered their shoulders with mud. The small panes of its narrow windows shook in their frames when the conveyance was closed, and exhibited, here and there, splashes of fresh dirt on an undercoating of old dust which no rain storm ever succeeded in wholly washing away. It was drawn by three horses, one of which acted as leader. Whenever it went down hill, the bottom bumped against the road.

A few citizens of Yonville began to collect in the square, all talking at once, asking for news and explanations and demanding anticipated packages. Hivert was thoroughly muddled, not knowing whom to answer first. It was he who carried out local commissions in town, making the round of the shops, and bringing back rolls of leather for the cobbler, old iron for the smith, a barrel of herrings for his mistress, hats from the milliner, hair-pieces from the barber. All the way along the road on the homeward journey, he delivered these various parcels, throwing them over farmyard walls, standing on his seat and shouting at the top of his lungs, while the horses continued on their way unattended.

An accident had delayed him. Madame Bovary's greyhound had dashed away across the fields. They had wasted a quarter of an hour whistling for him. Hivert had even gone back half a mile, thinking at each moment that he saw him. Finally, however, they had had to go on. Emma had cried and worked herself into a temper. She told Charles that he was to blame for this misfortune. Monsieur Lheureux, the draper, who was with them in the carriage, had tried to console her by telling stories of lost dogs who had recognized their masters many years later. He had heard of one, he said, who had travelled all the way from Constantinople to Paris, while another had covered fifty leagues in a straight line and swum four rivers. His own father had had a poodle which, after an absence of four years, had suddenly jumped up on him in the street one evening as he was going out to dine.

CHAPTER II

EMMA got out first, followed by Félicité, Monsieur Lheureux and a nurse. It was necessary to wake Charles who had fallen fast asleep in his corner when darkness fell.

Homais introduced himself. He offered his respects to Madame, his compliments to Monsieur, and said that he was delighted to think that he had been able to do them some small service. He added that, in the absence of his wife, he had taken upon himself the duty of receiving them.

No sooner had Madame Bovary entered the kitchen than she went straight to the fire. She took hold of her skirt at the knee with two fingers, lifted it just sufficiently to reveal her ankles, and extended her black-shod foot to the blaze, across the joint which was turning on the spit. The flames irradiated her whole figure, the fierce glow penetrating the stuff of her dress, the pores of her smooth white skin, and even the lids of her eyes which she kept constantly blinking. A flood of red rippled across her as the wind blew through the half-open door.

A young man with fair hair was gazing at her in silence from the other side of the fireplace.

Since he was vastly bored at Yonville, where he worked in the office of Maître Guillaumin, the lawyer, Léon Dupuis (for he it was, the second of the Golden Lion's 'regulars') often postponed the hour of his dinner, hoping that some traveller might turn up at the inn with whom he might spend the evening chatting. Having nothing to occupy him when his day's work was done, he was under the necessity of arriving punctually, and of enduring Monsieur Binet's intimate company through the whole meal, from soup to cheese. It was with a feeling of delight, therefore, that he had acceded to the landlady's suggestion to take his dinner with the new arrivals.

The party moved into the large parlour where, in order to impress, Madame Lefrançois had had the four places laid.

Homais asked permission to keep his skull-cap on his head for fear of catching cold.

'I expect, Madame,' he said, turning to his neighbour, 'that you must be feeling weary. Our Swallow jolts its occupants most abominably.'

'That is true,' replied Emma, 'but I always find something to amuse me in the hurly-burly of travel. I love change.'

'It is inexpressibly tedious,' sighed the lawyer's clerk, 'to be tied down always to the same spot.'

'If you were like me,' said Charles, 'perpetually condemned to spend whole days in the saddle. . . .'

'But', went on Léon, addressing himself to Madame Bovary, 'nothing, I should say, could well be more pleasant. One so seldom gets the opportunity.'

'Besides,' put in the chemist, 'a doctor's rounds are easy enough in this part of the world. The state of our roads makes it possible to employ a trap, and, generally speaking, the fees are good, seeing that most of our farmers are in easy circumstances. Medically, the work is not hard. Apart from such normal ailments as enteritis, bronchitis, biliousness, etc., and an occasional fever at harvest time, there is very little serious illness hereabouts, nothing which calls for special attention, unless it be the scrofula, which is caused, undoubtedly, by the deplorably unhygienic conditions in which our farm-labourers live. You will find, however, that you will have a good deal of prejudice to overcome, an obstinate belief in traditional methods against which your science will have to wage daily warfare, Most of the folk round here would rather have recourse to prayers, relics and the parish priest, than take the more natural course of going to the doctor or the chemist. Not that you could call our climate, to any serious extent, deleterious—we even run to a few nonagenarians. The thermometer (I give the data from personal observation) drops in winter to four degrees, and, in the hot season, touches twenty-five degrees centigrade—never going higher than thirty, that is to say, expressed differently, twenty-four Réaumur, or fifty-four Fahrenheit* (which is the English measure). That, believe me, is the extreme limit. We are sheltered from the north winds by the forests of Argueil, and from the west by the hill of Saint-Jean. But the resultant heat—caused by the moist vapour which rises from the river and the presence of so many cattle in the meadows—for animals, as you know, give off considerable quantities of ammonia—a mixture, that is, of azote, hydrogen and oxygen (not nitrogen and hydrogen only)—sucks up the goodness of the soil, commingling and uniting these various emanations into a single bundle—if I may so express myself—and combining with such electricity as is distributed by the atmosphere, and might in the long run, as in tropical countries, produce unhealthy miasmas—the resultant heat, as I was saying, is tempered precisely in that quarter from which it comes—or would come, namely, from the south—by the south-east winds, which, after being cooled in their passage across the Seine, reach us—at times with great suddenness—like breezes from Russia!'

'Are there any nice walks in the neighbourhood?' inquired Madame Bovary of the young man.

'Not many,' he replied: 'though there is one place, known as the Pasture, on top of the hill, at the forest edge, where I sometimes go on Sundays. I lie there with a book, watching the sunset.'

'There is nothing lovelier than a sunset,' she said, 'especially at the sea-side.'

'I adore the sea,' said Monsieur Léon.

'Don't you think', remarked Madame Bovary, 'that the spirit spreads its wings more freely over the limitless expanse of ocean? Don't you find that the mere sight of that wide horizon elevates the soul, and brings to the mind thoughts of the infinite and the ideal?'

'The same is true of mountains,' said Léon. 'One of my cousins made a trip to Switzerland last year, and he says that we can't imagine what poetry there is to be found in its lakes, what charm in its waterfalls, what a sense of grandeur in its glaciers. Pine trees of an unbelievable size span the torrents, huts cling to the sides of precipices, while, thousands of feet below, the eye catches glimpses of whole valleys through rifts in the cloud. Such sights must fill the heart with enthusiasm, must make one want to pray, must move the soul to ecstasy! I am no longer surprised when I hear tell of a famous musician, who, in order to stimulate his imagination, was in the habit of playing the piano in full view of the sublime expanses of Nature.'

'Do you play?' she asked.

'No, but I am very fond of music,' he replied.

'Don't listen to him, Madame Bovary!' Homais broke in, leaning forward across his plate: 'that's just his modesty! What about the other day, my boy, when you were singing the *Guardian Angel** so beautifully, up in your room? I could hear you from my laboratory. You delivered it like a professional!'

It was true that Léon lived in the chemist's house where he occupied a small room on the second floor, looking out on to the square. At this compliment from his landlord, he blushed. The latter, however, had again turned to the doctor, and was giving him an account of the principal citizens of Yonville, telling stories about each one and supplying information. No one really knew how rich the lawyer was, and the Tuvache family was always giving itself airs.

Emma went on:

'What is your favourite music?'

'German—because it sets one dreaming.'

'Have you heard the Italian singers?'

'Not yet, but I shall pay them a visit next year when I am in Paris, finishing my studies.'

'I was just telling your husband that, thanks to poor Yanoda being so foolish and clearing out in such a hurry, you will find yourselves the proud possessors of one of the most comfortable houses in Yonville. What makes it particularly convenient for a doctor is that it has a door on to the lane, which enables him to go out without being seen. Besides, it is beautifully fitted up—wash-house, kitchen with scullery, family parlour, fruit-loft, etc. He was a gay old dog and thoroughly improvident! He had an arbour specially built at the end of the garden, by the river, so that he could have somewhere to drink his beer in summer-time. If you like gardening, Ma'am, you'll be able. . . .'

'My wife takes little interest in such things'—said Charles: 'she prefers to spend her time in her room, reading, though she has been advised to take exercise.'

'Just like me'—remarked Léon. 'What pleasanter way of passing the hours can there be than to sit by the fire of an evening with a book, when the lamp shines bright and the wind is battering at the windows?'

'Oh, I do so agree!' she said, gazing at him with wide-open black eyes.

'One thinks of nothing,' he went on, 'and time passes. Without leaving one's chair, one travels in imagination through many lands. One becomes one with what one is reading. One revels in its details and conforms to the pattern of its adventures. One becomes identified with the characters of the story, so that one seems to feel with their hearts and to wear their clothes.'

'How true!' she said: 'How true!'

'Has it ever happened to you', he continued, 'to come across in a book some vague idea which you have already had, to find yourself confronted by some misty image from afar which seems to embody your most exquisite feelings?'

'I know precisely what you mean,' she answered.

'That is why', he said, 'I love poetry above all things. Verse, for me, is far more tender than prose, and can more easily bring tears to my eyes.'

'But, in the long run,' said Emma, 'it exhausts one. What I love now is the kind of story which one can read at a single sitting, which can give one a thrill of terror. I hate *low* heroes and lukewarm sentiments of the sort one finds in real life.'

'Works that fail to touch the heart', observed the lawyer's clerk, 'miss, it seems to me, the true end and object of Art. Life is so full of disillusionment that it is lovely to be able to dwell in imagination on noble characters, pure affections and the delineation of delight. Living here, cut off from the world, I find in reading my sole means of distraction. There are so few resources in Yonville!'

'No doubt it is much like Tostes,' said Emma, 'but I made a point of always having a library subscription.'*

'In my own house, Ma'am,' interrupted the chemist who had caught these last words, 'I have a library comprising the best authors, and should feel honoured if you would make use of it. Voltaire, Rousseau, Delille, Walter Scott,* you will find them all, as well as the *Écho des feuilletons*, etc. I also take in regularly a number of periodicals, including the *Fanal de Rouen*,* which appears daily. I am in the happy position of acting as its agent in several of the local towns— Buchy, Forges, Neufchâtel, Yonville and its environs.'

The meal had taken two and a half hours, because the servant, Artémise, dawdling along in her old list slippers, insisted on bringing in each plate separately, was in a constant state of forgetting something, never listened to what was said to her, and kept on leaving the door of the billiard-room ajar so that the latch rattled.

So absorbed had Léon been in his conversation, that, without noticing what he was doing, he had put his foot on the cross-bar of Madame Bovary's chair. She was wearing a little cravat of blue silk which supported a stiff ruff of frilled cambric, and each time she raised or lowered her head, her chin sank into, or emerged from, the stuff with a movement of exquisite grace. Seated there side by side while Charles and the chemist continued their conversation, the two of them had drifted into one of those vague interchanges of talk where each casual phrase seems to lead unerringly back to the fixed centre of a mutual sympathy. Paris theatres, the titles of novels, new dances and high society (of which neither of them knew anything), Tostes where she had lived, Yonville, the present scene of their meeting—all these things and places they passed in review, chatting of everything that came into their heads, until dinner was over.

When coffee had been brought in, Félicité departed to prepare the bedroom in the new house, and very soon the diners began to disperse. Madame Lefrançois was dozing by the fire, and the ostler was waiting with a stable-lantern to conduct Monsieur and Madame Bovary homewards. Odds and ends of straw were sticking to his red hair, and he limped with his left leg. He took the curé's umbrella in his free hand, and they started off.

The town was fast asleep. The pillars of the market hall threw deep shadows. The ground looked silvered as on a summer's night.

But since the doctor's house was only about fifty yards from the inn, the moment soon came to say good night, and the company separated.

As soon as she entered the hall, Emma felt the chill of damp plaster like a wet cloth upon her shoulders. The walls had been freshly whitewashed, and the wooden treads of the staircase creaked. In the rooms on the first floor a pallid light came through the uncurtained windows. She could see the tops of trees, and, beyond them, the meadows half drowned in mist which wreathed like smoke in the moonlight along the course of the river. In the middle of the room stood a disorderly pile of assorted objects, drawers, bottles, curtain-rods, gilt bedposts. Mattresses lay sprawled over chairs, basins littered the floor. The two men who had moved the furniture had left things just anyhow.

This was the fourth occasion on which she had gone to bed in a strange place. The first had been as a new girl at the convent, the second, when she moved to Tostes, the third at La Vaubyessard. This was the fourth. Each had, as it were, marked the beginning of a new phase in her life. She could never believe that things were going to be the same in one place as they had been in another: and, since her experiences had, so far, been unfortunate, she felt convinced that the future would be an improvement on the past.

CHAPTER III

WHEN she got up next morning, she saw the lawyer's clerk standing in the square. She was wearing a dressing-gown. He looked up and bowed. She gave him a quick nod and closed the window.

Léon spent the whole day waiting for six o'clock to come, but when he entered the inn he found only Monsieur Binet in the dining-room.

The previous evening's meal had been a considerable event for him. It was the first time in his life that he had passed two whole hours in conversation with a *lady*. How came it that he had been able to talk to her so eloquently of things about which he could never, previously, have discoursed so well? He was by nature timid, and normally maintained an attitude of reserve which was part modesty, part dissimulation. The general opinion in Yonville was that he had 'very nice' manners. He lent an obedient ear to the discussions of his elders, and appeared to hold no extreme political views—qualities which were, indeed, remarkable in a young man. Nor was he without talents. He painted in watercolour, could read the key of G, and liked to immerse himself in literature after dinner whenever he was not playing cards. Monsieur Homais respected him for his learning, and his wife liked him because he was kind and would often take her children into the garden. They were grubby urchins, thoroughly ill brought up. They had something of their mother's listlessness, and were normally looked after by the servant and by Justin, the young apprentice, a distant cousin of Monsieur Homais, who had been taken into the house out of charity, and combined a certain amount of domestic work with his duties in the shop.

The apothecary proved himself to be the best of neighbours. He advised Madame Bovary on the subject of tradesmen, arranged for his own cider merchant to call on her, personally tasted the liquor he provided, and superintended the proper placing of the cask in the cellar. He told her how she could get her butter cheap, and made a deal on her behalf with Lestiboudois, who, in addition to his ecclesiastical and mortuary functions, lent a hand with all the best gardens in Yonville, working by the hour or by the year, as might be preferred.

It was not sheer altruism that prompted the chemist to this show of obsequious cordiality. What he did he did with a purpose.

He had infringed article 1 of the Law of 19th Ventôse of the Year XI,* which forbids anyone to practise medicine unless he holds a doctor's diploma. Information had been laid against him—he had never quite known by whom—as a result of which he had been summoned to Rouen to wait on the King's Procurator in Chambers. The magistrate had received him standing, fully robed, his ermine on his shoulder and his official cap on his head. The heavy tread of a gendarme could be heard in the corridor, and there was a distant sound of keys being turned in massive locks. So loud was the singing in the chemist's ears that he thought he was about to have a stroke. He conjured up a vision of dungeons, of his family in tears, of his shop put up for sale and of all his precious bottles scattered. He found it necessary to go into a café for a glass of rum and seltzer in order to raise his spirits.

The memory of this reprimand had grown gradually fainter, and he had continued, as formerly, to give harmless consultations in his back room. But the Mayor had a grudge against him, his colleagues were jealous, and he feared the worst. His object in lavishing polite attentions on Monsieur Bovary was to place him under an obligation. He hoped that a sense of gratitude would keep the doctor from talking should he notice anything. Every morning, Homais brought him the daily paper, and quite often, of an afternoon, would go round to the house of the 'medical officer' for a little conversation.

Charles was in a gloomy mood. Patients were slow in turning up. He would sit for long hours saying nothing, dozing in his consulting-room, or watching his wife at her sewing. In order to occupy himself he did odd jobs about the house, and even tried to brighten up the loft with some paint left behind by the workmen. But he was preoccupied with money worries. He had spent so much on repairs at Tostes, on his wife's clothes and on the move, that he had got through the whole of her dowry—more than three thousand crowns—in two years. Many of their possessions had been damaged or lost between Tostes and Yonville, including the plaster statue of the priest, which had been jerked out of the wagon by a more than usually deep pot-hole, and been broken into a thousand pieces* on the metalled surface of the street at Quincampoix.

For the moment, however, a pleasanter anxiety filled his mind— Emma's pregnancy. As her time approached, so did his tender concern for her increase. He felt that a new bond of the flesh held her to him, that their union had become more complex, their feeling for one another more constant. When he saw her at a little distance moving heavily about the house, and watched the slow swaying of her uncorseted figure as she walked: when, in moments of quiet intimacy, he gazed on her at his ease and noticed how tired she looked as she lay slumped in her chair, his joy knew no bounds. He would get up, go over to her, give her a kiss, put his hand under her chin, call her 'little mother', try to make her dance, and, half crying, half laughing, say all the loving nonsense that came into his head. The thought that he had begotten a child delighted him. Nothing was lacking now. He knew all that there was to be known about human existence, and he sat down to the feast, leaning comfortably on his elbows with a feeling of quiet happiness in his heart.

Emma's first sensation had been one of surprise. This was succeeded by an eagerness to be brought to bed and so know what it was like to be a mother. But since she could not afford to have all that she would have liked to have—a cradle shaped like a boat with pink silk curtains, and embroidered caps for the baby—she abandoned, in an access of bitterness, all idea of a layette, and ordered an outfit from a working-woman in the village, without choosing or discussing anything. Consequently, she found no pleasure in those preparations which, as a rule, whet a mother's appetite, and it may be that, from the very beginning, her affection for the child was, to some extent, diminished on that account. Since, however, Charles did nothing but talk about the brat at every meal, she soon began to give more constant thought to it.

She longed for a son. He would be strong and dark, and she would call him George. This idea that she might have a male child was a sort of anticipatory compensation for all the frustrations of her past life. A man, at least, is free. He can take his way at will through all the countries of the world and all the passions of the heart; he can surmount all obstacles and sink his teeth deep into the pleasures of life, no matter how fantastic or far-fetched. But a woman is for ever hedged about. By nature both flexible and sluggish, she has to struggle against the weakness of the flesh and the fact that, by law, she is dependent upon others. Her will, like the veil fastened to her hat by a string, eddies in every wind. Always she feels the pull of some desire, the restraining pressure of some social restriction.

She was brought to bed about six o'clock one Sunday morning, just as the sun was rising.

'It's a girl!' said Charles.

She turned her head and lost consciousness.

Almost at once Madame Homais ran in to give her a kiss, followed by old Madame Lefrançois of the Golden Lion. The chemist, as befitted a man of his cautious temperament, merely offered her his professional congratulations through the half-open door. He was anxious to see the child, and, when he did so, gave it as his opinion that it was well formed.

She spent much of her convalescence thinking what name she should give her daughter. First of all she ran over in her mind all

those with an Italian termination—Clara, Louisa, Amanda, Atala.*
She had rather a weakness for Galsuinde, and, still more, for Yseult
or Léocadie.* Charles wanted the child to be named after his mother,
but Emma was against this. They went through the calendar of
saints' names from end to end. They consulted various strangers.
'Monsieur Léon,' said the chemist, 'with whom I was discussing the
matter a few days ago, expressed some surprise that you had not
settled on Madeleine which is very fashionable just now.'

But Madame Bovary the elder objected strongly, on the ground
that it was the name of a fallen woman. Monsieur Homais had a
personal preference for names which recalled great men, illustrious
events or liberal ideas—and had always adopted that principle in the
case of his own four children. Napoleon stood for glory, Franklin for
liberty. Irma,* maybe, was a concession to the romantic spirit, but
Athalie* was an act of homage to the most immortal of all the master-
pieces of the French stage. For his preoccupation with philosophy in
no way lessened his admiration for the arts, nor did the thinker, in
his case, oust the man of feeling. He could discriminate, and give due
weight to imagination as well as to fanaticism. While, for instance,
taking grave exception to the ideas expressed in this particular tragedy, he yielded to no man in his admiration of its style. He exe-
crated its 'message' but reverenced the details of its composition.
The characters moved him to fury, but their speeches roused his
enthusiasm. When he read the great passages he was transported
with delight: but the thought that the clergy could use them as fine
window-dressing material filled him with gloom. This confusion of
feeling was, for him, a matter of acute embarrassment, and he would
have liked, while setting the laurel-wreath with his own two hands
on Racine's brow, to have argued with him for a quarter of an hour at
least. Finally, Emma remembered having heard the Marquise at La
Vaubyessard address one of the young women guests as Berthe.
Berthe, therefore, it should be, and, since old Rouault was unable to
be present at the christening, Monsieur Homais was asked to stand
in as godfather. His presents all came from the shop—six boxes of
lozenges, a whole bottle of invalid food, three packets of marshmal-
lows, and, to crown all, six sticks of sugar-candy which he had found
in a cupboard. On the evening of the day on which the ceremony was
performed, there was a grand dinner-party. The curé was invited,
and feelings ran high. Over the liqueurs, Monsieur Homais recited

Le Dieu des bonnes gens,* Monsieur Léon sang a barcarolle,* and old Madame Bovary a ballad dating from the days of the Empire. Finally, Charles's father insisted on the child being brought down, and baptized it all over again by pouring a glass of champagne over its head. This mockery of the first of all the sacraments roused the Abbé Bournisien to indignation. Old Bovary countered him by quoting from *La Guerre des dieux*.* The curé wanted to leave but the ladies begged him not to. Homais intervened, and the gentleman of the cloth was prevailed upon to resume his seat. This he did, and sat peacefully sipping from his saucer the cup of coffee which he had only half drunk.

Monsieur Bovary the elder stayed on at Yonville for a month, dazzling the inhabitants by his display of a superb police cap trimmed with silver braid, which he put on whenever he went out into the square to smoke his pipe. Being accustomed to drink large quantities of brandy, he constantly sent the servant across to the Golden Lion to buy a bottle, which he had entered to his son's account. He used up all his daughter-in-law's stock of eau-de-cologne on his pocket-handkerchiefs.

She found his company far from unpleasant. He had seen much of the world, and loved to talk about Berlin, Vienna and Strasbourg, as he had known them in the days when he was serving as an officer in the army. He told her of the mistresses he had had and of the splendid dinners he had eaten. Besides, he was attentive, and at times, on the stairs or in the garden, would put his arm round her waist and cry:

'Better look out, Charles, my boy!'

His wife, however, began to grow alarmed for her son's happiness. She feared that if this sort of behaviour went on too long, the old man might have a bad influence on the young woman. So she pressed on with her preparations for their departure. It may be that her anxieties were even more serious. Monsieur Bovary was not the sort of man to respect anyone or anything.

One day, Emma was seized with a sudden desire to see her small daughter,* who had been put out to nurse with the carpenter's wife. Without bothering to look at the calendar to see whether the six weeks of the Virgin* had expired, she set out for the Rollets' cottage which was situated at the far end of the village, at the bottom of the hill, between the main road and the meadows. It was noon. The shutters of all the houses were tight closed. The slate roofs were glittering in the harsh glare of the cloudless sky so blindingly that the sharp edges of the gable-ends seemed to give off a shower of sparks. A sultry wind was blowing. Walking made her feel weak. The stones of the footpath hurt her feet. She began to wonder whether she had not better return home or go into one of the houses on her way and sit down for a while.

At this moment, Monsieur Léon emerged from a nearby doorway with a bundle of papers under his arm. He came forward to greet her, and stood there in the shade of the grey canvas awning which projected over the window of Lheureux's shop.

Madame Bovary said that she was on her way to see her child, but that she was beginning to feel tired.

'If . . .' began Léon, but was too shy to continue.

'Are you busy?' she asked, and, on the lawyer's clerk assuring her that he was not, begged him to keep her company. By evening, the incident was known all over Yonville, and Madame Tuvache, the Mayor's wife, declared in her servant's hearing, that *Madame Bovary was compromising herself.*

To reach the nurse's cottage they had to turn left at the end of the street and take a little path which led in the direction of the cemetery. It ran between small houses and the walls of yards, and was bordered by privets. They were in flower, as were the veronica, the dog-roses, the nettles and the young brambles projecting from the bushes. Through a hole in a hedge they could see pigs on a dung-hill in one of the tumbledown buildings, and a few tethered cows rubbing their horns against a tree-trunk. Side by side they walked in a mood of quiet happiness, she leaning on his arm, he shortening his pace to keep step with hers. In front of them a swarm of flies danced in the sunlight and buzzed in the warm air.

They recognized the cottage by an old nut-tree in the shadow of which it stood. It was low-built and roofed with brown tiles. On the wall, beneath the window of the loft, hung a string of onions. Some faggots were leaning against the thorn-hedge round a patch of lettuces, a few lavender bushes and some sweet-peas trained on sticks. Dirty water was seeping over the grass, and all around lay odds and ends of nondescript garments—a pair of woollen stockings, a red calico nightdress. A coarse linen sheet was festooned along the hedge. At the sound of the gate, the nurse appeared with a child in her arms which she was suckling. With her other hand she was leading a wretched undersized little creature, its face a mass of spots. This was the baby son of a Rouen hosier whose parents were too busy to look after it, and had left it in the country.

'Come in,' she said: 'yours is asleep over there.'

A single room comprised the whole of the ground-floor. A large uncurtained bed stood against the far wall, while a kneading-trough filled the side by the window, one of the panes of which had been mended with a circular patch of blue paper. In the corner behind the door, beneath the draining-board of the sink, was a row of boots with shining nails, and, close by, a bottle full of oil with a feather stuck in its neck. A copy of *Mathieu Laensberg** had been left on the dusty mantelpiece amid a litter of gun-flints, candle-ends and scraps of tinder. The room's latest superfluous acquisition was a picture of Fame blowing a trumpet, cut, doubtless, from some advertisement for scent, fastened to the wall by six shoemaker's nails.

Emma's child was sleeping on the ground in a wicker cradle. She took it up, wrapped in its blanket, and started to dandle it, singing the while in a low voice.

Léon moved about the room. It seemed strange to him to see this fine lady in her nankeen gown against a background of such poverty. Madame Bovary blushed, and he turned away, fancying that his eyes might have betrayed him into some impertinence. The child had just been sick over the collar of her dress, and she put it back into its cradle. The nurse hurried forward to wipe up the mess, declaring that it would not show.

'Always doing that, she is! I spend all my time washing out her things. I'd be obliged, I'm sure, if you'd tell Camus the grocer to let me have a bit of soap now and again. Make it easier for you, too, it would, for I shouldn't have to be bothering you all the time.'

'Certainly, I'll see to it'—replied Emma: 'Good day to you.'

She went out, wiping her feet on the threshold.

The woman accompanied her into the yard, talking all the while about how hard it was on her to have to be continually getting up in the night.

'That worn out I am, I sometimes fall asleep in my chair. A pound or so of ground coffee wouldn't come amiss, for me to have in the morning with a drop of milk. Last me a month, it would.'

Emma had to endure her thanks before she could get away. She had gone a few yards along the path when a sound of clogs made her turn her head. It was the nurse.

'Yes, what is it?'

The country-woman drew her aside behind an elm and started to talk about her husband, who, with his job and the six francs a year which the captain . . .

'Come to the point,' said Emma.

'Well, it's like this,' said the nurse, sighing heavily between each word. 'It might make him feel sad seeing me drinking coffee all by myself . . . you know what men are. . . .'

'If that's all, I'll see that you get sufficient. You are becoming wearisome.'

'The fact is, m'dear, he gets the most horrible cramps in his chest, on account of his wounds—says that even a drink of cider makes him go all weak.'

'Do please hurry up.'

'Well, then'—dropping a curtsy—'if it's not asking too much'—another curtsy—'I was just wondering whether you *might* spare us'—a pleading look came into her eyes—'just a drop of brandy now and again, so's I could rub your little lamb's feet for her—sensitive as the skin on your tongue, they are!'

At last she got rid of the woman, and once again took Monsieur Léon's arm. For some distance she walked quickly, then dropped to a slower pace. She was staring straight ahead, and her eyes encountered the young man's shoulders. He was wearing a frock-coat with a black velvet collar over which his auburn hair fell in straight, well-combed locks. She noticed that he wore his nails considerably longer than was usual in Yonville. Keeping them in order was one of his main preoccupations, and for this purpose he kept a special pen-knife in his desk.

They walked home along the bank of the river. In the hot season the fall of the water left more of the bank than usual uncovered, so that the lower courses of the garden walls were revealed. Shallow flights of steps led down from them to the stream which flowed silent, swift and cold-looking beneath. Tall thin grasses leaned above it, responding to the drag of the current, and lay on its clear surface like hair forlorn and green. Here and there, on the tip of a reed or the leaf of a water-lily some delicate-footed insect crawled or lay basking. The rays of the sun struck through the little blue bubbles made by the ripples as they broke. The trunks of the old pollarded willows showed a grey reflection. All around and beyond stretched the meadows, seemingly empty. It was the farmers' dinner-time, and nothing reached the ears of the young woman and her companion but the sound of their footsteps on the path, the words they spoke, the rustle of Emma's dress on the grass. The garden walls with their coping of broken bottles were as hot to the touch as conservatory windows. Wallflowers were growing between the bricks. The edge of Madame Bovary's sunshade scraped the withered blossoms as she walked, starting a small cascade of yellowish dust, and, now and again, a twig of loose-trailing clematis or honeysuckle dragged along the stretched silk or caught in its fringe.

They spoke about a company of Spanish dancers who were about to appear at the Rouen theatre.

'Are you going to see them?' she asked.

'If I can,' he replied.

Had they nothing else to say to one another? If their lips were silent their eyes were eloquent of more important matters. Even while they sought to speak of ordinary things, each was conscious of a languorous sweetness, of, as it were, an unbroken murmur from the secret places of the heart, which rose above the sound of uttered words. Caught by the wonder of this new delight, they did not think to tell one another of their feelings, nor yet to seek their cause. Happiness which is still to come sends, like some tropic isle to the voyager approaching over spreading tracks of sea, a foretaste of the bliss that is its birthright, a perfumed breeze which makes him swoon with heady vapours, so that no thought of what may lie below the yet unreached horizon troubles his mind.

At one point in their walk the earth had been trodden soft by cattle's hooves, and they had to step across the mire on great mossed stones set at intervals. More than once she paused, looking to see where next to place her foot. Uncertainly balanced on a stone which rocked beneath her weight, with elbows spread, body curved and the light of indecision in her eyes, she stood there laughing, fearful of falling into a puddle.

When they reached her garden, she opened the little gate, ran up the steps and disappeared.

Léon went back to his office. His employer was out. He glanced at the files, then cut himself a pen, took his hat, and left the house.

He walked to the Pasture high on the hill of Argueil, by the forest edge, and, lying down beneath the pines, looked through clasped fingers at the sky.

'How bored I am!' he said to himself: 'how bored!'

He was much to be pitied, he thought, for having to live in this village with Homais for friend and old Guillaumin for master. The latter, who was entirely absorbed in the details of business, with his gold-rimmed spectacles, his red side-whiskers and white cravat, was a stranger to intellectual refinement, though his assumption of the English phlegm had impressed the young man when first he came to work for him. As for the chemist's wife, she was the best wife in all Normandy, gentle as a sheep, devoted to her children, her parents and her cousins, shedding tears over the misfortunes of others, easy-going in her home and a sworn enemy of corsets. But she moved so heavily and talked so tediously, was so vulgar in her appearance, so limited in her conversation, that it had never occurred to him— though she was no more than thirty and he twenty, though they slept in adjoining rooms, though he talked to her every day of his life— that anyone could possibly think of her as a woman, or indeed, that she was a woman at all except in dress.

Who else was there? Binet, a few shopkeepers, two or three publicans, the curé, and, finally, Monsieur Tuvache, the Mayor, with his two prosperous, churlish and stupid sons who farmed their own land, gave family parties, went to church regularly, and were quite intolerable.

But against the background of all these faces, Emma's stood out alone, remote. For, between her and him, there stood, he felt, a great and sundering gulf.

At first he had called upon her often in the chemist's company. But Charles had not seemed particularly glad to see him, and he was at a loss how to behave, caught, as be was, between a fear of seeming indiscreet, and the longing for an intimacy which he regarded as being almost impossible.

CHAPTER IV

WHEN the cold weather began, Emma abandoned her bedroom and installed herself in the parlour, a long room with a low-pitched ceiling and a piece of branched coral spreadeagled in front of the mirror. Seated in an armchair close to the window, she watched the inhabitants of the village walking along the pavement.

Twice each day, Léon made the journey from his office to the Golden Lion. Emma could hear him coming while he was still some distance off, and used to lean forward, listening. The young man slid past the curtains, always dressed in the same clothes, and never once turned his head. But when the light had faded, and she sat with her chin in her left hand and her half-finished embroidery lying unnoticed on her lap, she often gave a start at the sudden appearance of his gliding shadow. On such occasions she would get up and order dinner to be laid.

Monsieur Homais had a way of turning up during the meal. With his skull-cap in his hand, he entered quietly on tip-toe so as not to disturb anyone, and always with the same phrase on his lips: 'Good evening, everybody!' Then, after taking his usual chair set between husband and wife, he would ask the doctor for news of his patients, while the latter sounded him on his chances of ever getting paid. Next, they discussed the news in the morning's paper. By that hour, Homais had it nearly by heart, and could repeat it word for word together with the editorial comments and a catalogue of all the accidents recorded as having happened to people both in France and abroad. That subject exhausted, he at once began to launch out into a series of observations on the dishes which he saw before him. Sometimes, half rising from his chair, he would point out the most delicate morsels to Madame, or, turning to the maid, give her advice how best to deal with stews, or speak about the health-giving properties of various sauces. He talked, in a manner calculated to dazzle all who heard him, of osmazome,* natural juices and gelatine. He had more recipes in his head than there were jars in his shop. He excelled in the concoction of preserves, of vinegar and sweet cordials, and was fully versed in the newest improvements in fuel-saving ranges, as well as in the best methods of maturing cheeses and treating sickly vine-plants.

At eight o'clock Justin fetched him to lock up the shop. Monsieur Homais would give him a roguish glance, especially if Félicité happened to be in the room, having noticed that his nephew had a particular weakness for the doctor's house.

'That young fellow of mine is beginning to get ideas,' he said: 'devil take me if I don't believe he's fallen in love with your maid!'

But a far graver fault, and one for which he was always lecturing him, was a habit he had contracted of continually listening to conversations with which he had no concern. On Sundays, for instance, it was almost impossible to get him out of the drawing-room, whither he had been summoned by Madame Homais to take charge of the children who had fallen asleep in the armchairs, thereby disarranging the ill-fitting loose-covers.

Not many people came to these evening receptions given by the chemist, for his spiteful tongue and political opinions had estranged him from several highly respectable members of the community in turn. The lawyer's clerk, however, never failed to put in an appearance. As soon as he heard the bell he would run forward to greet Madame Bovary, relieve her of her shawl, and put away beneath the desk in the shop the large list slippers which she wore over her shoes when it was snowing.

The gaieties began with a few rounds of trente-et-un, after which Monsieur Homais would play at écarté with Emma. Léon would station himself behind her and give advice. With his hands resting on the back of her chair, he would fix his gaze on the teeth of the comb which she wore thrust deep into her chignon. At each movement she made in playing her hand, her dress would ride up on the right side. From her high-piled hair a rich umber reflection fell upon her back, modulating off into paler and paler densities until it was lost altogether in the shadow. The lower part of her dress hung in ample folds on either side of the chair, and spread on the floor about her feet. When Léon, from time to time, felt the fabric beneath his boot-sole, he started back as though he had trodden on a living body.

When cards were finished, the apothecary and the doctor played a game of dominoes, and Emma, changing her place, would lean with her elbows on the table, looking at *l'Illustration*. She had brought her fashion-magazine with her. Léon sat beside her. Together they looked at the plates, waiting for one another before turning the pages. Often she asked him to read her some poetry, and he would declaim the lines in a drawling voice which he was careful to let die away in the love passages. But the noise of the dominoes worried him. Monsieur Homais was good at the game, and used to beat Charles by a full double six. Having finished their three hundred up, they would both stretch themselves at length in front of the fire and very soon be fast asleep. The fire fell into ash, the tea-pot was empty;

Léon went on reading and Emma listened, mechanically twirling the shade of the lamp on the surface of which the figures of pierrots driving carriages and tight-rope walkers with their poles were painted. With a gesture towards his sleeping audience, Léon would stop reading, and then they would talk together in low voices, what they had to say seeming the sweeter for not being overheard.

In this way a sort of bond grew up between them, a continual exchange of books and ballads. Monsieur Bovary, who was not easily moved to jealousy, showed no surprise at this development.

He received, on his birthday, a head for use in the study of phrenology, marked with figures as far down as the thorax, and coloured blue. This was a little attention from the lawyer's clerk, nor was it the only one, for he went so far as to undertake commissions for the doctor in Rouen. A recent novel having started a fashion for cactus plants, Léon bought one for Madame, and sat with it on his lap in the Swallow, pricking his fingers on its sharp leaves.

She had a little shelf constructed with a rail, suitable for holding flower-pots, and set it in her window. Léon, too, had a hanging garden, and each saw the other at work watering the plants.

But among all the windows of the village, there was another which was still more frequently occupied. For every Sunday, from morning till night, and on every afternoon when there was a good light, Monsieur Binet could be seen in his attic bending over his lathe, the monotonous whine of which could be heard as far as the Golden Lion.

One evening, Léon, on returning home, found a mat of velvet and wool, with a design of leaves on a pale ground. He called Madame Homais, Monsieur Homais, Justin and the children and the cook. He mentioned the incident to his employer. Everyone wanted to see the mat. Why, it was asked, should the doctor's wife show such generosity to the lawyer's clerk? It was really very odd, and a firm conviction arose that she must be his *bonne amie*.

There was some excuse for this conclusion, so voluble was he in praise of her charm and her intelligence. Things went so far that, on one occasion, Binet rudely interrupted him by saying:

'A lot I care—she doesn't take any notice of *me*!'

The young man went through torments in an attempt to discover some way in which he might declare the state of his feelings. Fearful of displeasing her, yet ashamed of being so spiritless, he wept from discouragement and desire. At last he decided to do something definite, and wrote a number of letters. These, however, he destroyed, endlessly postponing the moment of action to some future date. Often he started out from the house with the full intention of putting everything to the test, but his heart failed him as soon as he was in Emma's presence, and when Charles, coming into the room, suggested that he accompany him on his rounds in the phaeton, he at once accepted, took his leave of Madame, and departed. After all, was not her husband, to some extent, a part of her?

As to Emma, she made no attempt to ask herself whether she were in love with him. Love, she believed, should come with the suddenness of thunder and lightning, should burst like a storm upon her life, sweeping her away, scattering her resolutions like leaves before a wind, driving her whole heart to the abyss. She did not know that when the gutters are stopped up, the rain forms in puddles in front of the house. She would have remained secure in her ignorance had she not suddenly discovered a crack in the wall.

CHAPTER V

It was on a Sunday in February, an afternoon of snow.

They had all of them, Monsieur and Madame Bovary, Homais and Monsieur Léon, gone to see a flax mill* which was being built about half a league from Yonville, in the valley. The apothecary had taken Napoleon and Athalie with him for the sake of the exercise, and Justin accompanied them, carrying a load of umbrellas.

Nothing could well have been less curious than this curiosity. In the middle of a large patch of waste land, amid a litter of rusty cogwheels, piles of sand and a wealth of pebbles, stood a long, rectangular building, the walls of which were pierced by several small windows. It was not yet finished, and they could see the sky through the joists of the roof. Attached to a beam in the gable-end was a bundle of straw and wheat-ears tied together with tricolour ribbons* flapping in the breeze.

Homais held forth. He explained to the 'company' the future importance of the establishment, calculated the strength of the floors and the thickness of the walls with many expressions of regret that he did not, like Monsieur Binet, possess a rod marked off in metres.*

Emma had taken his arm and was leaning lightly on his shoulder, looking at the dazzling whiteness of the sun's disk as seen through the mist. Charles was there. His cap was pulled down low on his forehead, and his thick lips were twitching—which increased his general look of stupidity. Even his back, the calm expanse of his back, got on her nerves. All the flat nonentity of his character seemed to be displayed upon the surface of his coat. While she was gazing at him and savouring her irritation with a sort of depraved gusto, Léon took a step forward. The cold wind which had driven the blood from his face, had given to it a listless look which she found more than usually appealing. The collar of his shirt was a little loose, and she could see the skin of his neck behind his cravat. The tip of one ear was visible beneath a lock of hair, and his large blue eyes, turned upward to the sky, seemed to her more limpid and more beautiful than the colour of the heavens reflected in some mountain tarn.

'You little wretch!' exclaimed the apothecary in sudden wrath.

He darted at his son who had just jumped into a heap of lime in order to whiten his shoes. Under the volley of reproaches aimed at him, Napoleon began to howl, while Justin set about wiping his shoes with a wisp of straw. But he needed a knife, and Charles offered him his own.

'So he carries a knife about with him in his pocket—like a farm-labourer,' she said to herself.

It began to freeze, and they returned to Yonville.

That evening Madame Bovary did not visit her neighbours, and when Charles had started out and she was left alone, she realized again the contrast between the two men, this time with all the sharpness of an immediate sensation, and with that lengthening of perspective which memory imparts to objects. Lying in bed and looking at the bright fire, she conjured up a picture of Léon standing as he had done that afternoon, one hand leaning on his cane, the other holding Athalie who was peacefully sucking a piece of ice. She thought him charming and could not get him out of her mind. She remembered him in other attitudes on other days: she remembered things he had said, the sound of his voice, every detail of his person. Forming her lips, as though for a kiss, she said again:

'Quite, quite, charming'—and then—'I'm sure he's in love. . . . With whom? . . . if not me?'

All the proofs were suddenly vivid before her eyes. Her heart gave a bound. The flame in the hearth made a cheerful flickering on the ceiling. She turned on her back and spread her arms wide.

Then began that complaint which is as old as the world:

'If only Fate had been kind! . . . Why didn't things turn out so? . . . What prevented it?'

When Charles came in at midnight, she gave the impression that she had just woken up. He made some little noise while he was undressing, and she complained of a headache, after which she asked him with a casual air what the evening had been like.

'Monsieur Léon went upstairs very early . . .' he said.

She could not repress a smile, and fell asleep again, filled with the sense of a new enchantment.

On the evening of the next day, Monsieur Lheureux, the dealer in fancy goods, paid her a visit. He was an exceptionally clever salesman.

Gascon by birth, but Norman by adoption, he combined the talkativeness of the southerner with the canniness of the native of Caux. His fat, soft, beardless face looked as though it had been stained with liquorice juice, and his white hair enhanced the glitter in his small black eyes. No one knew his past history. Some said that he had travelled the roads as a pedlar, others that he had been a banker at Routot. The only certain thing about him was that he could do in his head sums so intricate that even old Binet was frightened of him. Smooth to the point of obsequiousness, his body was always bent in the attitude of one who bows in salutation or conveys a request.

After leaving his hat with its crape band at the door, he laid a green cardboard box on the table, and began to complain to Madame, politely enough, that so far he had failed to gain her custom. A poor shop like his was not calculated to appeal to a lady of *fashion*. He dwelt on the word. But she had only to express her wishes, and he would undertake to get her anything she wanted, silks or linens, stockings or fancy goods, for he went to town four times a month regularly. He had dealings with all the best houses. She could ask about him at the Trois Frères, at the Barbe d'Or or at the Grand Sauvage—there wasn't much *they* didn't know about him As he had happened to be passing he thought he would just drop in and show her a few odds and ends which he happened to have with him, thanks to an unusually good stroke of luck. From the box he took a dozen embroidered collars.

Madame Bovary examined them.

'There's nothing I need,' she said.

With great dexterity, Monsieur Lheureux proceeded to exhibit three Algerian scarves, several packets of English needles, a pair of straw slippers, and, to crown all, four eggcups carved from coconut shells in filigree by convicts. Then, spreading his hands on the table, leaning forward, and stretching his neck, he watched, open-mouthed, while Emma looked through his merchandise, unable to make up her mind. Every now and again, as though to remove a speck of dust, he gave a flick with his fingernail to the silk of the scarves which were displayed at full length. When he did this they quivered with a faint rustling sound, and the gold spangles woven into their tissue gleamed in the green evening light like stars.

'How much are they?'

'The merest trifle!' he replied: 'hardly worth mentioning! I don't mind a bit waiting for my money. Pay whenever you find it convenient. You're not dealing with a pack of Jews, you know!'

She turned the matter over in her mind for a few moments, and then declined Monsieur Lheureux's offer with thanks. He did not seem to be in the least put out, but said:

'Oh well, some other time, perhaps. I'm sure we shall get on together. I always do get on with the ladies—except my own!'

Emma smiled.

'What I mean is, it's not the money I'm worrying about,' he went on in a friendly tone, after firing off this little joke. . . . 'I'd *give* you some of *that* if you happened to want any. . . .'

She made a movement of surprise.

'And without having to go far to find it, either,' he added quickly, lowering his voice: 'make no mistake about it!'

Then he changed the subject, asking for news of old Tellier, the proprietor of the Café Français, whom Charles was attending.

'What exactly's wrong with him? . . . He coughs loud enough to shake the house. . . . I'm afraid a nice made-to-measure suit of planking will be more in his line than a flannel nightshirt . . . and that before we're very much older. Sowed too many wild oats when he was a young man, that's the trouble. No self-control, ma'am. Inside all burned out with brandy. Still, can't say I like seeing an old acquaintance kick the bucket. . . .'

While strapping up his box, he chatted on about the doctor's patients.

'Suppose it's the weather's the cause of all this illness we're having,' he said, looking gloomily at the window. 'Don't feel too chipper myself—must come along one of these days and have a talk to your good man about this pain in the back. Well, good night, Madame Bovary—yours to command at any time —your very humble servant.'

He closed the door softly behind him.

'How sensible I was,' she reflected, her mind still on the scarves.

She heard footsteps on the staircase: it was Léon. A pile of dusters waiting to be hemstitched was lying on the chest-of-drawers. She took up the first one that came to her hand. When he entered the room she gave the impression of being very busy.

Conversation dragged. Madame Bovary kept on breaking off every few moments in what she was saying, and he, for his part, seemed to be very much embarrassed. He sat on a low chair by the fire, turning her ivory needle-case over and over in his fingers. She stitched away, pausing every now and again to arrange a little gather in the material, on which she was working, with her nail. She said nothing, and he, too, was mute, as much enchanted by her silence as he would have been by her words.

'Poor boy!' she was thinking.

'What have I done to annoy her?' he was wondering.

At last, however, he did come out with the news that he had got to go to Rouen in the course of the next few days on business connected with his legal work.

'Your subscription to the music library has run out: would you like me to renew it?'

'No,' she replied.

'Why not?'

Pursing her lips, she slowly drew out a long needleful of grey thread.

This work of hers got on his nerves. It seemed to roughen the tips of her fingers. A verbal gallantry occurred to him, but he dared not risk it.

'Are you giving up your music, then?' he asked.

'What?'—she spoke quickly—'my music?—Heavens, yes! Haven't

I got a house to look after, a husband to keep tidy, and a thousand domestic duties, which have got to come before music?'

She looked at the clock. Charles was late. She assumed an expression of anxiety. More than once she said:

'He's such a good man, you know.'

The lawyer's clerk was fond of Monsieur Bovary, but this tenderness of hers on his account gave him an unpleasant shock. Nevertheless, he continued to sing his praises. Everybody thought well of him, he said, including the chemist.

'So upright!' continued Emma.

'Indeed, yes!' said the young man. Then he began to speak of Madame Homais whose untidiness was usually a subject for laughter between them.

'But what *does* it matter?' said Emma, interrupting him. 'A good mother never minds what she looks like.'

Then she relapsed into her former silence.

It was the same on the following days. Her talk, her behaviour, everything, was different. People began to notice that she was taking her housekeeping seriously, that she was once more becoming a regular attendant at church, that she rode her servant with a tighter rein.

She fetched Berthe home from her nurse. Félicité would bring her down when there were visitors, and Madame Bovary would undress her to display her limbs. She adored children, she said: they were her consolation, her delight, her mania. She hugged her daughter to an accompaniment of lyrical transports which, to ears other than those of the good people of Yonville, would have brought echoes of Sachette in *Notre-Dame de Paris*.*

When Charles came home he would find his slippers warming by the fire. The linings of his waistcoats were never torn now, his shirts never without buttons, and he even had the pleasure of seeing his cotton nightcaps all neatly ranged in equal piles on the shelf of the wardrobe. She never sulked, as once she had done, when he suggested a turn in the garden. He had only to make a proposal for her to agree at once, though she might find it impossible to guess what it was that prompted the wishes to which she gave such unmurmuring obedience. When Léon watched him sitting, after dinner, by the fire, his hands clasped over his stomach, his feet on the fender, his face reddened by the process of digestion, his eyes moist with happiness, while the child crawled over the carpet, and his young, slim-waisted wife leaned over the back of the chair to kiss him:

'What madness'—he said to himself—'to think that I could ever win her!'

So virtuous, so inaccessible, did she seem to him, that he abandoned all hopes, however vague.

But his renunciation set her in a very extraordinary light. Her body was entirely beyond his reach. He grew to think of her, therefore, as something disincarnate. The image of her which he cherished in his heart was of someone untrammelled by the flesh, and ever winging upwards like a radiant goddess. The emotion that he felt was entirely detached from mundane affairs—the sort of emotion a man cultivates for its very rarity, the loss of which would outweigh in misery what its possession might give of joy.

Emma grew thinner, her cheeks lost their colour, her face became longer. With her black hair, her straight nose, her birdlike movements and her new moods of silence, it was as though she were passing through life with scarce an earthly contact, as though her forehead bore the signature of some predestined blessedness. So sad she was, so calm, so sweet yet so reserved, that when he was by her he felt as though an icy charm were laid upon his heart, felt as he might have done in church, shivering with cold, yet conscious of the sweet smell of flowers mingled with the chill of marble. Others besides himself succumbed to her fascination.

Said the chemist: 'She is a woman of great gifts: a woman who would not be out of place in a sub-prefecture.'

The tradesmen's wives admired her abilities as a prudent housewife. Her husband's patients appreciated her good manners; the poor, her charity.

But her heart was filled with frenzy, hatred, and consuming desires. The long straight folds of her dress concealed a spirit in turmoil. But no word of this inner torment ever reached her modest lips. She was in love with Léon and cherished solitude the better to revel in her thoughts of him. The sight of him troubled the delicious self-indulgence of her brooding. The sound of his step thrilled her nerves. But as soon as he was present in the flesh, these feelings vanished, leaving behind nothing but a sense of limitless astonishment with a flicker of sadness in its wake.

Léon did not know that when he left her door with despair in his heart, she would get up from her chair as he turned from her, that she might watch him through the window walk away along the street. She worried about his movements, scrutinized his looks, and made all sorts of excuses to visit his room. She envied the chemist's wife the happy fate which permitted her to sleep under the same roof, and her thoughts were for ever winging to the house, like the pigeons of the Golden Lion who wetted their pink feet and white wings in its gutters. But the more she realized her love, the more deliberately did she tread it down that no sign of it might be visible to others and that its hold on her might be diminished. She would have liked Léon to know of its existence, and built fantasies of chance and accident which might make recognition easy. What held her back, no doubt, was laziness and fear of consequences quite as much as modesty. She thought she had repulsed him over-long, that the time for encouragement was past, that all was lost. Then pride, and the pleasure of being able to say to herself—'I am a virtuous wife', of watching herself in the glass striking attitudes of resignation, consoled her to some extent for the sacrifice she thought she was making.

But then the hunger of her senses, her greed for money, and the melancholy bred of passion, would all swirl together in a spasm of pain, and, instead of thinking no more about him, she let imagination dwell on him, finding stimulus in sorrow and seeking to indulge it. A badly served meal, a door left ajar, rasped her nerves. She sighed over the velvets that she had not got, the happiness she might have had: over dreams that were too vast and a house that was too small.

What exasperated her was the fact that Charles seemed to have no idea of the torments through which she was passing. His fixed conviction that he could make her happy she regarded as a stupid insult, and his sense of security where she was concerned, as ingratitude. On whose account, then, had she been so 'sensible'? Was it not Charles who stood between her and any hope of happiness?—who was the cause of all her wretchedness, the sharp point of the buckle, as it were, in that belt of complexities which bound her in on all sides?

It was on him, therefore, that she visited the many manifestations of hatred which sprang from her troubles. Any attempt to lessen them merely increased them. For this useless anguish was but something added to her other motives for despair and merely served to widen the gulf between them. She was over-kind in judging herself, and, consequently, the more prone to rebellion. The drabness of her home life prompted fantastic dreams of luxury, uxorious tenderness a longing for the pleasures of adultery. She would have been glad if Charles had beaten her, for that at least would have given her a reasonable excuse for loathing him and seeking out ways to be revenged. She was amazed, at times, by the appalling thoughts which came into her mind. Yet she must go on smiling all the time, all the time must hear herself saying over and over again that she was happy, must somehow contrive the appearance of happiness and make him believe in its reality.

There were moments, all the same, when such hypocrisy disgusted her. She was tempted to run away with Léon to some distant spot where life might begin again. But no sooner did her mind play with the idea than she was conscious of an abyss within her soul full of strange threats and darkness.

'And, anyhow, he no longer loves me'—she thought. 'What is going to happen? What help can I expect? What consolation, what relief from pain?'

She would sit, bruised and broken, all energy drained from her, with streaming eyes, uttering low sobs.

'Why not talk to Monsieur?' said the maid when she had entered the room during one of these crises.

'It's nothing but my nerves,' replied Emma. 'You mustn't breathe a word of it to him. It would only make him wretched.'

'It was just the same with Guérin's girl,' went on Félicité, 'the fisherman's daughter I knew in Dieppe, before I came to you. She was so sad, so terribly sad, that seeing her standing on the front step, you'd have thought she was a shroud stretched out in front of the door. Her trouble, I heard, was a sort of a fog she had in her head. The doctors couldn't do anything, nor the curé either. When she was taken really bad, she used to go walking all alone down by the sea, and the customs officer when he was making his rounds often found her lying flat on her stomach on the shingle, crying her eyes out. But they say it all passed away when she got married.'

'But in my case', said Emma, 'it didn't start until after I was married.'

CHAPTER VI

ONE evening when she was sitting by the open window watching Lestiboudois, the sexton, trimming the box-hedge, she suddenly heard the sound of the angelus bell.

It was at the beginning of April, when the primroses are in bloom. A warm wind was blowing over the dug flower-beds, and the gardens, like women, seemed to be furbishing their finery for the gaieties of summer. Through the lattice of the arbour, and all around beyond it, she could see the river meandering slow and carefree through the meadow grasses. The mist of evening was drifting between the leaf-less poplars, blurring their outline with a violet haze, paler and more transparent than a fine gauze hung upon their branches. Cattle were moving in the distance, but her ear could catch neither the noise of their hooves nor the sound of their lowing. The bell, continuously ringing, struck upon the air with its note of peaceful lamentation.

The repeated tolling took the young woman's mind back to the memories of childhood and of her school. She remembered the branched candlesticks which used to stand upon the altar, overtop-ping the flower-filled vases and the tabernacle with its little columns. She would have liked, as then, to be an unnoticed unit in the long line of white veils in which, here and there, the stiff coiffs of the good sisters kneeling at their desks showed as accents of black. At mass, on Sundays, whenever she raised her head, she could see the sweet face of the Virgin in a blue cloud of eddying incense. At such moments she had been conscious of deep emotion, had felt alone and immaterial, like a piece of down from a bird's breast at the mercy of a raging wind. It was, therefore, almost without knowing what she was doing, that she set out towards the church, ready to enter into any act of devotion provided only that her feelings might be wholly absorbed, and the outer world forgotten.

As she crossed the square, she met Lestiboudois on his way home. For, in order that too great a hole might not be made in his day, he would leave the job in hand, perform his church duties, and then go straight back to what he was doing. The result was that the angelus was rung at such times as he found convenient. It didn't, he felt, really matter, because if it sounded a little earlier than it should, it would serve to remind the children of the hour of catechism.

Some of them had turned up already, and were playing at marbles on the flagstones of the churchyard. Others, astride upon the wall, were swinging their legs and kicking down the giant nettles which grew on the patch of ground between it and the most recent graves. It was the only piece of greenery to be seen. Everying else in the neighbourhood was stone and always covered with a fine dust, no matter how much sweeping the sexton did. The boys and girls of the village in their canvas shoes used it as a playground, as though it had been deliberately designed for that purpose, and their high-pitched voices could be heard above the booming of the bell, which rose and fell with the movement of the great rope which hung from the belfry, dragging on the ground beneath. Swallows were darting hither and thither with little cries, cutting the air with the sharp edge of their flight, hurrying back to their yellow nests beneath the tile-hung coping. At the far end of the church, a lamp was burning, or, rather, the wick of a nightlight in a hanging glass receptacle. Seen from afar, its glow looked like a patch of white, flickering on the surface of the oil. A long ray of sunlight struck down the full length of the nave, accentuating the darkness of the side-aisles and the corners.

'Where is the curé?' asked Madame Bovary of a small boy who was amusing himself by rattling the kissing-gate which was loose on its hinges.

'He's just coming,' was the reply. And, indeed, at that very moment, the door of the presbytery squeaked, and the Abbé Bournisien appeared.

The children fled headlong into the church.

'The young ruffians!' murmured the priest: 'always the same. . . .'

He picked up a tattered catechism over which he had just stumbled.

'No respect for anything,' he said. He caught sight of Madame Bovary.

'Do please forgive me,' he remarked: 'I didn't recognize you.'

He stuffed the catechism into his pocket and came to a halt, still twiddling the heavy vestry key between his fingers.

The light of the setting sun, shining full in his face, drained the colour from his woollen soutane which was shiny at the elbows and frayed at the bottom. Stains of grease and snuff followed the row of little buttons on his broad chest, increasing in number the farther they got from his neckband and the thick red folds of his chin which was marked with little yellow blotches half hidden by a growth of grey, wiry stubble. He had just finished his dinner, and was breathing stertorously.

'I trust you are in good health?' he remarked.

'No, indeed,' replied Emma, 'I am far from well.'

'Same with me,' said he: 'The first warm days are terribly taxing, don't you find? But there, we are born to suffering, as St Paul says. But what is Monsieur Bovary's opinion?'

'Oh he!' she murmured with a disdainful toss of the head.

'What!' said the good man with an air of surprise: 'surely he has prescribed something for you?'

'It is not', remarked Emma, 'earthly remedies that I need.'

The curé, all this while, was shooting occasional glances towards the church, where the small boys, now on their knees, were nudging one another and falling about like packs of cards.

'I wanted to know . . .' she went on.

'Just you wait, Riboudet!' cried the priest. 'I'll give you such a box on the ears if you don't look out!' Then turning to Emma:

'He's the son of Boudet the carpenter. His parents are comfortably off and let him do as he pleases. He could learn fast enough if he wanted to, for he's an intelligent lad. Sometimes, for fun, I call him Riboudet (after the hill between here and Maromme). *Mon* Riboudet, I say. Ha! ha! *Mont*-Riboudet—you see the joke? I told it to Monsignor the other day, and you should have heard him laugh— yes, he was actually so pleased as to laugh. . . . And how is Monsieur Bovary?'

She seemed not to have heard the question. He went on:

'As busy as ever, I don't doubt. I shouldn't think there's anyone in the parish who has as much to do as he and I—the one doctors their bodies'—he finished up with a chuckle—'the other their souls!'

There was an imploring look in the eyes which she turned upon him.

'Yes . . .' she said, 'it is in your power to relieve all wretchedness.'

'You mustn't say that, Madame Bovary! Only this morning I was sent for to Le Bas-Diauville, to look at a cow which was suffering from wind—they thought it had been bewitched, and not just one cow only, but the whole herd—how on earth it happened I don't know . . . but just a moment, if you'll forgive me . . . Longuemarre and Boudet! . . . Saints above! . . . stop it! d'you hear me!'—and off he rushed into the church.

The boys were crowding round the great reading-desk, clambering over the precentor's stall, opening the missal. Others were tiptoeing into the confessional. Suddenly the curé was on top of them, cuffing them right and left, taking them by the scruff of the neck and depositing them on their knees in the choir as violently as though he meant to root them in the pavement.

'I must say,' he began again, when he had rejoined Emma and started to spread a large bandana handkerchief, one corner of which he held in his teeth, 'farmers have a good deal to complain of, too.'

'So have other people,' she rejoined.

'I should be the last to deny it . . . workmen in the large cities, for instance.'

'They're not the ones . . .'

'Believe it or not, I have known cases of poor mothers of families, thoroughly good souls, all of them, real saints, actually going without bread.'. . .'

'But how about women,' retorted Emma (and the corners of her mouth twitched nervously as she spoke), 'how about women who have bread but no . . .'

'Fuel in winter, you were going to say?' broke in the priest.

'But that matters so little . . .'

'What do you mean, it matters so little? In my opinion anyone who's well warmed and well fed . . .'

'Oh, my God! My God!' she moaned.

'Are you feeling unwell?' he asked, stepping forward with a worried expression: 'perhaps it's indigestion? You should go home, Madame Bovary, and drink a little tea. You'll find it very strengthening, or a glass of cold water with some sugar . . .'

'What for?'

She looked like someone who has just awakened from a dream.

'Well, you passed your hand over your forehead: I thought that perhaps you felt giddy.'

Then, recollecting himself: 'But there was something you wanted to ask me? What was it? I have forgotten.'

'I? . . . Oh, nothing. . . .'

She had been gazing about her, but now brought her eyes back till they slowly came to rest on the old man in the soutane. They stood there, the two of them, looking at one another, but saying nothing.

'In that case, Madame Bovary'—he said at length, 'I will ask to be excused. Duty first, you know. I must get these young rascals off my hands. First communion is coming uncomfortably close, and I very much fear that we may he caught napping. As soon as Ascension is past, I am going to insist on an extra hour every Wednesday! Poor little things! One can never start too soon setting their feet in the way of the Lord—as, indeed, he enjoined on us by the mouth of his divine son . . . Good day, Madame, and please remember me to your husband.'

He went into the church, pausing at the door to make his genuflexion.

Emma watched him disappear between the double row of benches, treading heavily, his head leaning a little to one side, his arms spread and his hands half open.

Then she turned on her heel with a single, sharp movement, like a statue swivelling on a pivot, and went home. But still behind her she could hear the curé's deep voice, and the shrill tones of the children.

'Are you a Christian?'

'Yes, I am a Christian.'

'What is a Christian?'

'A Christian is one who, being baptized . . . being baptized . . . bapt . . .'

She held to the banisters on her way upstairs, and, as soon as she was in her room, collapsed into an armchair.

The pale white light from the windows grew dimmer with a sort of quiet and regular pulsation. The various pieces of furniture, each in its accustomed place, seemed to take on a tenser immobility, losing themselves in the encroaching dusk as in a misty ocean. The fire was out, the clock ticked on. She was struck with a vague wonder that outward things could be so calm when all her being was in turmoil. Between the window and the work-table, baby Berthe, in her little knitted boots, moved uncertainly, trying to reach her mother and cling to her apron-strings.

'Leave me alone!' exclaimed Emma, pushing her away.

But a moment later the little girl was back again, this time pressing against her knees, and staring up at her with large blue eyes, while a dribble of clear saliva ran down her chin on to her silk bib.

'Leave me alone!'—the young woman said again in a sudden access of irritability.

The expression of her face frightened the child and she started to cry.

'Oh, do get *away!*' cried her mother, elbowing her aside.

Berthe stumbled and fell against a brass fitting at the foot of the chest-of-drawers. She cut her cheek and it bled. Madame Bovary pounced on her, picked her up, broke the bell-pull, called for the servant at the top of her voice, and was just beginning to heap bitter reproaches on herself, when Charles appeared. It was dinner-time, and he had only that moment come in.

'Look, dear'—said Emma calmly: 'she had a fall while she was playing, and hurt herself.'

Charles reassured her. The injury was not serious. He went off to look for some diachylon.*

Madame Bovary did not go down to the parlour. She wanted to be left alone to tend the child. As she watched her sleeping, the last of her anxiety vanished, and she began to think that she had been both foolish and too good-natured to worry, as she had been doing, over so trivial an incident. That it had been no more than trivial was obvious, for Berthe's sobbing had stopped, and her breathing barely stirred the cotton coverlet. Two big tears still hung at the corners of her eyelids, which were not so completely closed as to hide from view the pale-coloured pupils which seemed to be withdrawn behind the lashes. The strip of sticking-plaster on her cheek had the effect of stretching the skin and drawing it slightly sideways.

'Curious',—thought Emma—'how ugly that child is.'

When, at seven o'clock, Charles returned from the chemist's shop (whither he had gone after dinner to take back what remained of the diachylon) he found his wife standing by the cradle.

'I told you it was nothing,' he said, kissing her on the forehead. 'Don't worry, darling. You'll only make yourself ill.'

He had spent a long time with the apothecary. He had given no sign of having been badly shaken, but Monsieur Homais had thought it as well to cheer him up and put new heart into him. After discussing the matter in hand, they had gone on to talk about the many dangers to which the young are exposed, and of the careless-ness of servants. Madame Homais had strong views on the subject, for she still carried on her breast the marks made by some hot embers which a former cook had let fall on her pinafore when she was a child. Consequently these excellent parents took every kind of precaution. They had never permitted the presence of sharp knives in their house, and had seen to it that the wooden floors were always left unpolished. There had been iron gratings on the windows, and strong bars in front of the fires. The Homais children, for all their independence, were never allowed to go out without someone to watch their movements. At the slightest sign of a cold their father swathed them in mufflers, and even when they were well past their fourth birthdays they were mercilessly compelled to wear quilted caps. This latter precaution was due to a mania of Madame Homais, and her husband was secretly worried about it, fearing the possible effect of such tight headwear on the organs of the intellect. He would so far forget himself as to say to her:

'Do you want to turn them into little Caribs or Botocudos?'*

Charles more than once attempted to interrupt the flow of conversation.

'I should like to have a word with you,' he whispered to the lawyer's clerk. The latter had at once led the way upstairs.

'Does he suspect anything?' Léon wondered, and lost himself in a welter of conjectures.

When they reached his room, Charles closed the door and asked him, when next he was in Rouen, to find out how much a good daguerrotype would cost. He wanted to give his wife a portrait of himself in his black dress-coat, as a sentimental surprise. It would, he felt, be a delicate attention on his part. But, before he did anything, he wanted to know *what it would let him in for.* Since Monsieur Léon went regularly to town almost every week, the commission would not put him to any inconvenience.

What was the object of these visits? Monsieur Homais suspected some youthful adventure, an intrigue of sorts. But he was wrong. Léon had no love-affair on hand. He was more melancholy than ever, as Madame Lefrançois deduced from the quantity of food which he left untasted on his plate. Avid for details, she began to question the tax-collector. Binet replied haughtily that he was not a professional police-spy. Not but what his young friend seemed to him to be behaving in a very odd manner, for Léon would constantly throw himself back in his chair, fling out his arms, and complain vaguely about life.

'The trouble with you is that you don't know how to relax.'

'And what's the best way of doing that?'

'If I were you, I should invest in a lathe.'

'But I don't know how to work a lathe.'

'I hadn't thought of that,' said the other, stroking his chin with a mingled air of contempt and satisfaction.

Léon was sick of loving to no purpose. He began to experience that sense of despondency which comes of doing the same things over and over again, day in, day out, aimlessly and without hope. He was so bored by Yonville and its inhabitants that the sight of certain people and certain houses irritated him almost beyond bearing. Excellent man though the chemist was, Léon was beginning to find him well-nigh intolerable. Yet, the prospect of looking for a new situation, attractive though it was, frightened him. Apprehension, however, quickly turned to impatience, and in his ears there sounded the distant fanfare of Paris with its masked balls and the laughter of its women. Sooner or later he would have to complete his law-training there, so why not go now?* What was there to prevent him? He began to indulge in secret anticipations, planning in advance what he would do with his time in the capital. He dreamed of the little flat he would furnish, of how he would live the life of an artist. He would learn the guitar, would invest in a dressing-gown, a Basque beret, a pair of blue velvet slippers! He was already delighting in the vision of two fencing-foils suspended over his mantelpiece with a skull beneath them and the guitar above.

The chief difficulty would be to get his mother's consent, though no plan could well seem more sensible. Even his employer wanted him to work for a while with someone else, and so get a chance of developing his gifts. By way of compromise he started to look for an opening as assistant-clerk with a Rouen lawyer. But in this he failed, and at last wrote his mother a long and detailed letter, in which he gave his reasons for wanting to settle down in Paris at once. She gave her consent to the scheme.

He was in no hurry. Each day, for one whole month, Hivert transported on his behalf from Yonville to Rouen and from Rouen to Yonville a quantity of packing-cases, trunks and parcels. After renewing his wardrobe, having his three armchairs freshly stuffed, and buying a supply of silk scarves: after, in fact, equipping himself as thoroughly as though he were about to start on a world tour, Léon still put off his departure from week to week, until at last he received a second letter from his mother in which she urged him to make the move if he were really anxious to sit his examination before the holidays.

When the moment for leave-taking arrived, Madame Homais wept, Justin sobbed, and Homais, as befitted a strong man, concealed his emotion. He offered to carry the young man's overcoat as far as the lawyer's gate, the latter having promised to drive Léon in to Rouen. There was just time to say good-bye to Madame Bovary.

At the top of the stairs he paused, so breathless did he feel. As he entered the room, Madame Bovary got up quickly.

'It's me again,' said Léon.

'I knew it!'

She bit her lips, and a wave of colour flooded her face till it showed all pink from the roots of her hair to the edge of her collar. She stood there, leaning against the wall.

'Is your husband not in?' he went on.

'No, he's out.'

She repeated the words: 'He's out.'

A silence fell between them. They looked at one another, and their thoughts, caught in a single wave of anguish, clung together like two bodies shaken with passion.

'I should like to give Berthe a kiss'—said Léon.

Emma went a little way down the stairs and called Félicité

Léon glanced hurriedly round at the walls, the book-cases, the mantelpiece, as though to make them part of himself, as though he wanted to take them with him.

But she came back, and, in a moment or two, the maid appeared with Berthe who was dragging a windmill upside down on the end of a string.

Léon kissed her several times on the neck. 'Good-bye, you poor little mite: good-bye, darling!'

He handed her back to her mother.

'Take her away,' said she. They were left alone.

Madame Bovary turned her back on him and pressed her face to the window. Léon had his hat in his hand, and kept on tapping it softly against his leg.

'It's going to rain,' said Emma.

'I've got an overcoat,' said Léon.

'Ah!'

She averted her gaze, her head drooping. The light shone on the upper part of her face, illuminating it as far down as the line of her brows. She looked like a bust carved in marble. She was staring into the distance, but what she saw, or what she was thinking in the secrecy of her mind, it was impossible to tell.

'I suppose we'd better say good-bye,' he murmured.

She looked up with a sharp movement of the head.

'Yes . . . good-bye . . . and now go, please.'

They advanced a few paces towards one another. He held out his hand: she hesitated.

'English fashion, then,'* she said, surrendering her own and forcing a laugh.

Léon felt it between his fingers, and the very substance of his being seemed to melt into the moist palm.

Then he loosened his grip, their eyes met once again, and he vanished.

Beneath the roof of the market-hall he stopped, and, from the shelter of a pillar, took one last look at the white house with its four green shutters. He thought he saw a shadow at the window of her room, but the curtain fell loose from its hook as of its own accord, and the long, slanting folds dropped slowly into place, spreading out in a single movement, and then hanging as motionless as though they had been a plaster wall. He started to run.

He could see his employer's carriage in the distance, standing in the road with a man in an apron beside it, holding the horse. Homais and Maître Guillaumin were chatting. They were waiting for him.

'Let me give you a hug,' said the apothecary with tears in his eyes. 'Here is your overcoat, dear friend. Don't catch cold—look after yourself—be careful!'

'Jump up,' said the lawyer.

Homais leaned across the dashboard and, in a voice shaken by sobs, let fall these two sad words:

'Bon voyage!'

'Good evening to you,' said Maître Guillaumin: 'Let her go!'

They drove off, and Homais turned away

Madame Bovary had opened the window which gave on to the garden, and stood watching the clouds.

They were piling up in the west, towards Rouen, in dense black masses, from behind which great bars of light shot like the golden arrows on a panoply of arms. The empty sky all around had the whiteness of china. A gust of wind bent the tops of the poplars, and, all at once, the rain came, pattering on the green leaves. Then the sun reappeared, the hens began to cackle, the sparrows fluttered their wings in the wet bushes, and the pools of water drained away over the sandy soil, carrying with them the pink blossoms of an acacia.

'He must be far away by now,' she thought.

Monsieur Homais, as was his custom, dropped in at six o'clock while Emma and her husband were at dinner.

'Well, well,' he said, sitting down, 'so we've got our young friend off.'

'So it seems,' replied the doctor: then, turning about in his chair: 'What's the news with you?' he asked.

'Nothing much, except that my wife was a bit upset this afternoon. You know what women are, the least little thing puts them out—mine especially. One can't blame them—their nervous systems are so much less stable than ours.'

'Poor Léon!' said Charles. 'I wonder how he'll get on in Paris. . . . Do you think he'll manage to shake down?'

Madame Bovary sighed.

'Not a doubt of it!' replied the chemist, making a clucking sound with his tongue. 'Nice little parties in restaurants, masked balls, champagne—he'll have a fine time, you mark my words.'

'But I don't think he's likely to go wild,' protested Bovary.

'Nor do I'—Monsieur Homais hastened to assure him, 'though he must do as others do if he's not to be taken for a Jesuit.* You've no idea what those young rascals of the Quartier Latin get up to, they and their actress friends. Besides, students are made very welcome in Paris. If they have any social gifts at all they get asked to the best houses. Some of the great ladies of the Faubourg Saint-Germain even fall in love with them, which gives many of them the chance of making a good marriage.'

'All the same,' said the doctor, 'I'm not altogether happy in my mind about him. . . . Paris, you know. . . .'

'And you're quite right'—broke in the apothecary: 'there's another side to the medal, and a man can never be too careful. He may, for instance, be walking in one of the public gardens. Up comes a stranger, well-dressed, and perhaps even sporting a decoration, the kind of fellow one might take for a diplomat. He worms his way into his confidence, offers him a pinch of snuff, say, perhaps even picks up his hat for him. The intimacy grows. The stranger takes him to a café, invites him down to his place in the country, introduces him to all sorts of people over a glass of wine, and in nine cases out of ten all he's after is to steal his new acquaintance's purse or to get him into bad company.'

'True enough,' replied Charles. 'But I was thinking rather of illness—typhoid fever, for instance, to which students from the provinces are particularly prone.'

Emma gave a start.

'Because of the change of diet'—the chemist took him up—'and the violent disturbances to which the newcomer's whole system is exposed. Then there's the Paris water—we mustn't forget that, and all the feeding out in restaurants. Highly seasoned dishes end by heating the blood. When all's said and done, they're no patch on a good stew. Personally, I always say that you can't beat good middle-class cooking—the healthiest in the world! When I was studying to be a chemist in Rouen, I used to take my meals in a boarding-house, along with the professors.'

He talked on, expounding general opinions and discussing his personal preferences, until Justin came to fetch him to make an egg-flip for which some customer was asking.

'No rest for the wicked!' Homais exclaimed: 'always on the go . . . can't get away even for a few minutes. Always sweating blood and water like a cart-horse! Never out of harness!'

Then, just as he was leaving the room: 'By the by, have you heard the news?'

'What news?'

'Only', said the chemist, raising his eyebrows and assuming a more serious expression, 'that the Agricultural Show for Seine-Inférieure looks like being held this year at Yonville l'Abbaye. Anyhow, that's the rumour. There was something in the paper about it this morning. It would be a most important event for the district. But we'll talk about that later. I really must be off—many thanks: Justin has the lantern.'

CHAPTER VII

THE morrow was for Emma funereal. A black mist seemed to lie over everything, drifting aimlessly across the surface of objects, while misery swept through her heart, moaning softly like the winter wind in a deserted castle. She was in the mood which afflicts one when one dreams of things that have gone, never to return. She felt in her bones the sort of lassitude which deadens the heart when something has come to an end. She felt the pain that strikes at one when an accustomed rhythm has been broken or when some prolonged vibration ceases.

She fell a prey to the same sort of dull melancholy and numb despair as she had known on returning from La Vaubyessard with the music of the dance still echoing in her ears. The Léon whom she saw now in imagination was taller, handsomer, more charming, less clearly defined. Though they were separated, he had not left her. He was still there, and his ghost seemed to haunt the house. She could not take her eyes from the carpet which he had trod, from the empty chairs in which he had sat. Still the river flowed, rippling slowly beneath the muddy bank. How often they had walked beside it, hearing the murmur of its waters, watching the mossy stones. How brightly the sun had shone! What lovely afternoons they had spent alone together in the shade of the trees at the bottom of the garden, he, reading aloud, bareheaded, reclining against a bundle of dried faggots, while the cool wind from the meadows fluttered the pages of his book and the nasturtiums growing on the arbour. . . . And now he was gone, the one delight of her life, her only possible hope of happiness! Why had she not snatched at the chance while she had had it within her reach? Why had she not clung to him with both hands, knelt to him, so that he should not flee? She cursed herself for not having loved Léon. She hungered for his lips. She was seized with a desire to run after him, to throw herself into his arms, to say to him: 'Here I am! I am yours!' But she foresaw the difficulties of such an enterprise, and her desires, increased by regret, became the more imperative.

Henceforth the memory of Léon lay at the centre of her feeling of boredom. It sparkled more brightly than a traveller's fire lit and left on the snows of the Russian steppe. She ran towards it, huddled over it, stirred the dying embers with the utmost care, hunting round for such scraps of fuel as would keep it alive—half-forgotten memories as well as events just past, what she felt and what she imagined only, cravings for luxury now melting into nothingness, plans for some future happiness which cracked like dead branches in the wind, her barren virtue, her vanished hopes, the dreary duties of domestic life—all these she gathered, taking what came to her hand in an effort to keep the fire of misery from being extinguished.

But the flames died down, perhaps because the supply of fuel ran low, perhaps because they were smothered with excess of it. Gradually absence did its work of quenching love, and habit deadened longing. The furnace glare which once had flushed to scarlet the pale sky of her life dimmed in the thickening darkness, and died away by slow degrees. As the intensity of her feelings became numb, mere dislike of her husband figured in her mind as a craving for her lover, and she mistook the burning touch of hatred for tenderness rekindled. But as the tempest raged on, and passion burnt itself to ashes, no help came, nor did the sun shine: all around was deepest night. She lived on like a lost soul racked by an icy cold.

The worst days of the old time at Tostes began again. But now she thought herself much more miserable, for a sharp pain was added which she knew would never end.

One who, like herself, had set upon her back the weight of so much sacrifice, might well indulge her fancies. She bought a gothic prie-dieu, and spent fourteen francs in a single month on lemons with which to clean her nails. She wrote to Rouen ordering a dress of blue cashmere, and bought herself one of Lheureux's loveliest scarves. She tied it round her waist over her dressing-gown, and, thus garbed, would spend whole hours behind closed shutters, lying full length on the sofa with a book in her hand.

She was forever changing the way she did her hair, sometimes wearing it Chinese fashion, in soft swathes and plaited tresses, sometimes, manlike, with pendent curls and a parting at the side. She made up her mind to learn Italian, and, with that end in view, bought dictionaries, a grammar and a supply of paper. She embarked on a course of serious reading in history and philosophy. Sometimes at night, Charles would wake with a start, thinking that he had been called to a case of sickness.

'I'm coming,' he would mutter, but it was only the sound of Emma striking a match to light the lamp again. But her reading went the way of her embroidery which lay half finished in her wardrobe. She would begin some book, lay it aside, and embark upon another.

She had fits in which she might easily have been led into the most extravagant actions. On one occasion she wagered her husband that she would drink off half a glass of brandy at a single draught, and, when Charles was mad enough to dare her, swallowed the brandy to the last drop.

Despite her 'fancy airs' (as the Yonville housewives called them) she did not give the impression that she was happy. She had, as a rule, that tightness of the lips which one sees on the faces of old maids or of ambitious folk who have been disappointed of their goal. Her complexion was uniformly pale, white as a sheet. The skin of her nose looked as though it were stretched downwards, and there was an unfocused stare in her eyes. Finding three grey hairs on her temples, she said that she was growing old.

She often had attacks of giddiness, and one day spat a little blood. Charles was all solicitude and could not conceal the fact that he was anxious.

'What *does* it matter?' she said.

He retired to his consulting-room and sat there in his armchair beneath the phrenological bust, his elbows on the table, weeping.

It was then that he wrote to his mother, begging her to come. They had many long discussions about Emma.

What conclusions could they reach? What could be done, since she refused any form of treatment?

'What your wife needs', said his mother, 'is a spell of hard manual labour! If she had to earn her bread, as many women have, she wouldn't have time for all these fancy ailments! The trouble is that she has nothing to do and stuffs her head with a whole lot of nonsense!'

'But she does find things to do,' said Charles.

'Finds things to do?—what, may I ask? Reading novels—a lot of wicked books full of quotations from Voltaire which hold the priests up to ridicule. You mark my words, this won't be the last of it! People without religion always come to a bad end!'

It was decided that Emma must be prevented from reading novels.* Such a plan would not be easy to put into operation, and the old lady took it upon herself. When next she was in Rouen, she would go to see the proprietor of the lending-library, and would tell him that Emma was giving up her subscription. If, after that, the man went on providing poison for her mind, couldn't they call in the police?

There was a coldness between daughter and mother-in-law when they said good-bye. During all the three weeks they had spent together, they had not exchanged above four words except for the usual inquiries and compliments when they met at meals or parted for the night.

Old Madame Bovary left on a Wednesday—which was market-day at Yonville.

From early morning the square was filled with a line of carts standing up-ended, with their shafts in the air all the way along the row of houses which stood between the church and the inn. On the opposite side was a range of canvas booths devoted to the sale of cotton-goods, blankets, woollen stockings, halters for horses and bunches of blue ribbons fluttering in the wind. On the ground stood piles of pots and pans flanked by pyramids of eggs and hampers of cheeses from which protruded a quantity of sticky straw. Near some agricultural machinery, a number of fowls were clucking, thrusting their necks through the bars of their cages. The crowd, gathered in one spot, and showing no sign of movement, looked, now and again, like damaging the chemist's window. His shop, on Wednesdays, was never empty. People elbowed their way into it, not so much with the idea of buying anything as to consult its owner, so great was old Homais's reputation in the surrounding villages. His air of hearty reassurance had fascinated the country folk. They thought him a greater doctor than all real doctors put together.

Emma was leaning on her elbow at her window (as she frequently did, for windows in country towns are a substitute for theatres and public walks), amusing herself by watching the rustic mob) when she noticed a gentleman dressed in a frocked coat of green velvet. He was wearing yellow gloves in spite of the heavy gaiters on his legs, and was coming towards the doctor's house, followed by a country fellow with head bent and a thoughtful look on his face.

'Could I, I wonder, see your master?' he said to Justin who was chatting to Félicité on the doorstep.

It was obvious that he took him for a servant.

'Tell him that Monsieur Rodolphe Boulanger of La Huchette* would like a word with him.'

It was not from any idea of vaunting his status as a landed propri-etor that he had added the territorial appellation to his name, but in order to identify himself. La Huchette was an estate not far from Yonville, the manor of which he had recently purchased together with two farms which he worked himself, though without bothering overmuch about them. He was a bachelor who was generally credited with having not less than *fifteen thousand livres a year*.

Charles came into the room. Monsieur Boulanger introduced his man who wanted to be bled because of *a tingling sensation all over his body*.

'It will clean me out,' was his reply to every argument.

Bovary busied himself with bandages and basin, asking Justin to help him. Then, turning to the village lad, who had already gone as pale as a sheet:

'No need to be frightened, my good man,' he said.

'I'm n–not f–frightened—go ahead,' said the other.

He held out his great arm with an air of swagger. At the prick of the lancet the blood spurted out and splashed the looking-glass.

'Hold the bowl nearer!' exclaimed Charles.

'See that!' said the young peasant. 'Like a fountain. Got red blood, ain't I? Good sign, ain't it?'

'Sometimes', replied the doctor, 'a man feels nothing at first, but later on, syncope may set in, especially with great strapping fellows like you.'

At these words, the countryman dropped the little box with which he had been fiddling, and jerked his shoulders so violently that the chair made a cracking sound. His hat fell off.

'I thought something of this kind would happen,' said Bovary pressing his finger on the vein.

The bowl began to tremble in Justin's hands, his knees shook and he turned pale.

'My dear!' called Charles, 'come down here a moment!'

Emma was with them in a few seconds.

'Vinegar!' she ordered: 'Oh, heavens! two of them at once!'

So upset was Charles that he had great difficulty in applying the compress.

'It's nothing,' said Monsieur Boulanger in a level voice, lifting Justin in his arms.

He sat him on the table in such a way that his back was supported against the wall.

Madame Bovary busied herself with unfastening his cravat. The strings of his shirt had got tangled in a knot, and for some minutes her fingers moved lightly about the young man's neck. Then she poured some vinegar on her cambric handkerchief and proceeded to dab his temples, blowing on them gently the while.

The carter recovered consciousness, but Justin's syncope lasted longer, and his pupils quite vanished into the surrounding white of his eyes, so that they looked like blue flowers floating in milk.

'We must hide that from him,' said Charles.

Madame Bovary took the bowl, intending to put it under the table. As she leaned down to do so, her dress (it was a light summer dress of a yellow colour, long in the waist, with four flounces and a very full skirt)—spread round her on the floor. And since, thus bending, she trembled slightly with the effort of stretching her arm, the ballooning of the material collapsed here and there in response to her movements. She went to fetch a jug of water, and was just melting some pieces of sugar, when the chemist arrived. In the general confusion, the maid had gone to look for him. As soon as he saw that his apprentice's eyes were open, he paused for breath. He looked down at him, moving round his recumbent form.

'Fool!'—he said: 'that's about the long and short of it, f-o-o-l! just because of a little blood-letting—a great hulking chap like you who thinks nothing of shinning up trees after nuts as nimbly as any squirrel! Come on, say something! Pretty proud of yourself—eh? A fine chemist *you'll* make, I must say! Why, you might be called on to give evidence in the courts in some serious case, just so's to clear the magistrate's mind for him. You'd have to have your head screwed on right then, *and* follow complicated arguments, if you wanted to show you were a proper man and not a little idiot!'

Justin said nothing, and the apothecary continued:

'Who *asked* you to come? You're always making a perfect nuisance of yourself to Monsieur and Madame, especially on Wednesdays when I particularly need you. At this very moment there are twenty persons over at the shop. I let everything slide because of the interest I take in you. Up with you now—and be off! wait for me and keep an eye on the bottles!'

When Justin had readjusted his clothes and taken himself off, the talk turned to the subject of fainting. Madame Bovary had never had that particular experience.

'Very extraordinary, I must say, for a lady!' remarked Monsieur Boulanger: 'not but what men are often more sensitive in that way. I was present at a duel once at which one of the seconds fainted clean away merely at the sound of the pistols being loaded.'

'The sight of other people's blood', said the apothecary, 'has no effect whatever on me. But just to think of my own flowing is enough to bowl me over, if I dwell on the idea for too long.'

Meanwhile, Monsieur Boulanger had packed his servant off, telling him not to worry now that his whim had been gratified.

'It has done one good thing,' he added: 'it has given me the pleasure of making your acquaintance.'

He looked hard at Emma while he said this. Then he laid three francs on the edge of the table, bowed nonchalantly, and departed.

In a very short while he was across the river (on his way back to La Huchette), and Emma could see him walking through the meadows beneath the poplars, slackening his pace now and again, like one deep in thought.

That doctor's wife is charming, he was thinking: really charming: good teeth, black eyes, neat ankles, and carries her- self like a Parisienne! Where the devil does she come from? and how on earth did that oaf manage to pick her up?

Monsieur Rodolphe Boulanger was thirty-four, a man with a coarse nature and a shrewd brain. There had been many women in his life, and he knew the sex pretty thoroughly. He had found this particular specimen of it remarkably pretty, and therefore he let his mind dwell on her and on her husband.

I should say he's as stupid as they make 'em, and it's pretty obvious that she's sick of him. His nails are dirty and he goes about with a three days' growth of beard on his chin. While he's off jogging on his rounds, she stays at home darning his socks. I bet she's bored!— wants to live in a town and go dancing the polka every night. Poor little woman—gasping for love like a carp on the kitchen table for water! If I paid her a few compliments, she'd be at my feet—I'm dam' sure of that! And a very charming, sweet little morsel she'd be. . . . But how to get rid of her afterwards 'd be a bit of a problem.

He could see in advance the difficulties which would beset his pursuit of this new pleasure, and his thoughts, by way of contrast, turned to his mistress, a Rouen actress whom he was keeping. The idea of her, the memory of her, brought with it a sense of satiety, and——

Madame Bovary, he reflected, is a great deal prettier, and quite unspoiled. Virginie is beginning to put on fat, and she's so fussy about her pleasures. Besides, she's got a perfect mania for shrimps!

There was no one about in the meadows, and Rodolphe could hear nothing but the swish of his feet in the grass and the scraping of the distant crickets in the oats. He conjured up a picture of Emma dressed as he had seen her in the parlour, and he began mentally to undress her.

'I'll have her yet!' he exclaimed, and crushed a clod of earth with a blow of his stick.

At once, he started to consider the tactical possibilities of the situation.

Where can I manage to meet her—and how? She's always got that kid hanging to her apron-strings, to say nothing of the servant, the husband and the neighbours—all sorts of tiresome obstacles. Bah! It's too much like work!

But he could not get his mind off the subject: she's got eyes that go through you like a drill: and that wonderful pallor of hers—I adore pale women!

By the time he had reached the top of the hill at Argueil, he had made up his mind.

It's only a question of finding an opportunity. I'll call on them once or twice, send them some game and a few chickens. If need be, I'll have myself bled. We'll strike up a friendship: I'll invite them to my place. By Jove—the agricultural show'll be coming off shortly, she'll be there and I shall see her. That's where I'll make a beginning, and I'll go straight to the point—it's always the best way!

CHAPTER VIII

THE day of the famous show* arrived. From early in the morning of the great occasion the inhabitants stood about on their doorsteps discussing the preparations. The front of the town hall had been festooned with ivy. A tent had been set up in one of the meadows for the banquet, and in the middle of the square, opposite the church, a sort of rocket apparatus had been placed in position which was to be discharged when the Prefect arrived, and when the names of the prizewinners were announced. The National Guard from Buchy (there was no detachment at Yonville) had come over to add body to the fire brigade which was parading under the captaincy of Binet. He wore an even higher collar than usual, and so tightly had he been buttoned into his tunic that the whole upper part of his body was stiff and motionless. The vital principle seemed to have descended into his legs which, when he marked time, rose rhythmically in a single movement. Since there existed a rivalry between the colonel and the collector of taxes, each manœuvred his men apart, in order to display his own particular talents. Red epaulettes and black facings marched and counter-marched, turn and turn about, endlessly. When the drill seemed to be finished, it would begin all over again. Never had there been such a display of pomp and circumstance! Many of the citizens had washed their houses on the previous evening. Tricolour flags hung from the half-opened windows. All the taverns were full, and, the day being fine, the starched bonnets, gold crosses and coloured neckerchiefs shone whiter than snow, glittered in the bright sun, and, with their spots of bright colour here and there, relieved the dull monotony of frock-coats and blue smocks. The farmers' wives from the outlying districts, as they got off their horses, undid the huge pins which kept their dresses rolled up round their waists for fear of splashes, while their husbands spread pocket-handkerchiefs over their hats as a protection, holding one corner between their teeth.

The crowd surged into the main street from both ends of the village. They came from the lanes, the alleys and the houses. From time to time the bang of a knocker could be heard as a door was slammed behind the tradesmen's wives who had come out to see the merrymaking with thread gloves on their hands. Especially admired were two lofty erections, covered with fairy lamps, which flanked the platform on which the authorities were to sit. In addition to these, there had been placed against the four columns of the town hall four differently shaped posts, each bearing a smallish standard of green material enriched with inscriptions in gold lettering. One carried the words—'To Commerce', another, 'To Agriculture', a third, 'To Industry', and a fourth, 'To the Fine Arts'.

But the jubilation which brightened every face seemed to have cast a gloom over Madame Lefrançois, the landlady of the inn. Standing on the steps of her kitchen, she muttered under her breath:

'What tomfoolery!—the idiots, with that great canvas marquee! Do they really think the Prefect will feel comfortable dining under a tent like a strolling player? They say that all this fuss is good for the place! Why should I go to all the expense and trouble of bringing a cook-boy over from Neufchâtel just for a lot of cowherds and tramps . . .'

The apothecary walked past. He was wearing a black dress-coat, nankeen trousers, shoes of beaver, and—wonder of wonders!—a hat—a low-crowned hat!

'Your servant!' he said: 'please excuse me, I am in a hurry!'

The fat widow asked him where he was off to.

'I expect it must seem strange to you—eh?' he replied: 'I, who as a rule, am more strictly confined to my laboratory than the rat in the cheese* . . .'

'What cheese?' asked the landlady.

'Oh, no matter, no matter—I merely wished to give expression to the truth that in general I live the life of a recluse in my shop. But today, in view of the special circumstances, I must. . . .'

'So you're off yonder?' said she, with an expression of contempt.

'Certainly I am,' replied the apothecary, in a tone of considerable astonishment. 'Am I not one of the executive committee?'

Old Madame Lefrançois stared hard at him for a few seconds, and then said with a smile:

'That's quite another matter. But what have you got to do with farming? D'you know anything about it?'

'Of course I know something about it since I am a pharmacist by trade, that is to say, a chemist! And chemistry, Madame Lefrançois, having as its object the knowledge of the reciprocal and molecular action of all natural bodies, it follows that farming falls within its domain. The composition of manure, the fermentation of liquids, the analysis of gases and the influence of miasmas—what is all that, think you, if not chemistry pure and simple?'

The landlady said nothing, and Homais continued:

'Do you think that before a man can concern himself with the agronomic sciences, he must himself have walked behind the plough or fattened chickens? What is really important is that he should know the composition of those substances with which he will have to work; of geological strata, of the effects of atmospheric conditions, of the qualities of soils, minerals and liquids, of the density of different bodies, their powers of capillary attraction or repulsion—and a whole lot else. He must, too, have a thorough grounding in the science of health, so that he may with knowledge oversee and criticize the erection of buildings, the dietary of animals, the feeding of his domestic staff! Furthermore, Madame Lefrançois, he must know something of botany, for he should be able to distinguish various plants—sorting, if you understand me, those that are salutary from those that are harmful, those that produce nothing from those that have a high nutritive value. He will have to decide whether to root them out from one part of his land, or to re-sow them elsewhere, whether to encourage some and destroy others. It is, in short, his duty to keep himself up-to-date in the matter of scientific developments by the reading of public pamphlets and papers, to be ever on the watch for possible improvements . . .'

The eyes of the landlady never left the door of the Café Français, and the pharmacist went on:

'Would to God that our agriculturists were chemists, or that, at least, they paid more attention to the counsels of science! I myself recently wrote an admirable *brochure*, a memorandum running to seventy-two pages, entitled—*Cider: Its Manufacture and Effects; Together with Original Comments on the Subject*, which I sent to the Agronomical Society of Rouen.* As a result, I had the honour of being enrolled a member of that body, Agricultural Section, Pomological Sub-Section. Had my work been given to the public . . .'

Here he stopped, perceiving that Madame Lefrançois was wholly preoccupied.

'Just look at 'em!' she exclaimed: 'I can't understand it—a low eating-house like that!'

With a mighty shrug which stretched her bosom's knitted covering, she pointed with both hands at the ale-house kept by her rival, from which now came the sound of singing.

'Well, anyways, it won't be for long—a week at the most!'

Homais started back in amazement. She came down the three steps and whispered in his ear:

'Didn't you know? The bailiffs will be in this week. Lheureux's selling him up. Been dunning him till the man's all but out of his mind.'

'What a terrible catastrophe!' exclaimed the apothecary, who was always well supplied with phrases suited to every possible occasion.

The good woman embarked on the story which had reached her by way of Théodore, Maître Guillaumin's servant. Great though her detestation of Tellier was, she did not spare Lheureux, who, she said, was a cringing, crawling, nasty creature.

'Ah look!' she said, 'There he is in the market-hall, bowing to Madame Bovary, who's got a green hat. And arm-in-arm with Monsieur Boulanger, too!'

'Madame Bovary!' said Homais. 'I must go and offer my respects. Maybe she would like to have a seat in the enclosure, under the porch.'

Without listening to Madame Lefrançois who called him back that she might continue her story at greater length, the pharmacist hastened away, smiling and very upright, distributing bows right and left, and taking up a great deal of room, with his coat-tails flying behind him in the breeze.

Rodolphe, seeing him while he was still some distance away, had quickened his pace. But Madame Bovary was soon out of breath, and he slowed down again. With a smile on his lips, but in a rough and boorish tone, he said:

'I wanted to avoid that great lump of a fellow: you know, the chemist.'

She nudged him with her elbow.

'And what, I wonder, does that mean?' he said to himself.

They walked on, he looking at her out of the corner of his eye.

Her profile was so calm that it was impossible to guess anything from it. It stood out in the bright sunlight, against the oval of her bonnet with its pale-coloured ribbons which looked like the leaves of a water-plant. Her eyes gazed straight ahead from beneath their long curled lashes. They were wide open, but seemed to lose something of their effect by reason of the blood which throbbed gently below the delicate skin of her flushed cheeks. A faint pink showed on her nose, between the nostrils. Her head was slightly leaned to one side, and the pearly tips of her white teeth were visible through her parted lips.

'Is she laughing at me?' he wondered.

But Emma's movement had been intended as no more than a warning, for Monsieur Lheureux was close at hand, and was addressing a few words to them now and again, as though he would have liked to begin a conversation.

'What a lovely day! Everyone's out of doors! The wind is in the east!'

Neither she nor Rodolphe made the slightest effort to reply, but at their least movement he drew near, murmuring – 'I *beg* your pardon?' and lifting his hand to his hat.

In front of the blacksmith's forge, Rodolphe, instead of keeping straight on to the toll-house, turned off sharply into a footpath, pulling Madame Bovary after him.

'Good day, Monsieur Lheureux!' he said. 'I expect we shall be meeting again soon.'

'You got rid of *him* all right!' she said with a laugh.

'Why should I have to put up with other people?' he replied: 'and today of all days, when I have the happiness of being with you. . . .'

Emma blushed. He left the phrase unfinished, and went on, instead, to speak of the lovely weather and of the pleasure of walking on grass. A few daisies were showing.

'Pretty little things,' he said: 'Easter flowers we call them. There are enough here for all the love-lorn girls of the neighbourhood to tell their fortunes by.'

A moment later, he added:

'What would you say if I picked a few?'

'Are *you* love-lorn?' she said with a little cough.

'Maybe I am, maybe I'm not,' answered Rodolphe.

The meadow began to fill, and they found themselves being jostled by mothers of families with their large umbrellas, their baskets and their babies. They had frequently to stand aside while long files of country-women, servants in blue stockings and flat-heeled shoes and silver rings, smelling of milk, passed close to them. They walked holding one another by the hand, and, in this way, stretched the whole length of the field, from the line of aspens to the banqueting tent. But the moment of judging had now arrived, and the farmers, one after the other, were filing on to a sort of race-course which was divided off from the rest of the ground by a long rope carried on stakes. The cattle were already in position, their muzzles turned towards the rope, their rumps of all shapes and sizes roughly aligned. The pigs, drowsy from too much food, were routing about in the earth: the calves were mooing: the cows, their legs doubled beneath them, were lying on their bellies, slowly chewing the cud, blinking their heavy lids under attack from the flies which were buzzing all around them. Carters, with rolled-up sleeves, were busy holding by the halter a number of rearing stallions which were neighing with distended nostrils in the direction of the mares. The latter stood peaceably by, stretching their necks with their long hanging manes, the foals clinging to their shadow or, now and again, trotting up to suck. Down the whole line of these packed and undulating bodies could be seen white manes rising in the wind like waves, the sharp jerk of horns, the heads of running men. Herded apart, about a hundred yards away and well outside the ring, was a huge black bull, muzzled, and with an iron ring in his nose, motionless as though he had been cast in bronze. A small, ragged urchin had hold of him by a rope.

Several gentlemen were moving ponderously between the two rows, examining each animal, and talking to one another in low voices. One of them, who seemed to be of more importance than the others, made notes in a small book as he walked. This was the President of the jury, Monsieur Derozerays, from Panville. No sooner did he see Rodolphe than he hurried forward and said with a friendly smile:

'Not deserting us, are you, Monsieur Boulanger?'

Rodolphe protested that he was just coming. The moment the President had turned his back, however,

'Hanged if I go!' he said: 'I'd very much rather have your company than his.'

Though he never ceased poking fun at the whole show, Rodolphe made full use of his blue ticket, showing it to the gendarmes on duty, and thereby managing to move more freely. Now and then he even stopped in front of one or other of the exhibits, in spite of Madame Bovary's lack of interest. This he noticed, and immediately began to joke at the expense of the Yonville ladies and the way they were dressed, hastening to apologize for the carelessness of his own get-up. It exhibited that mingling of the ordinary everyday with the elegant which the vulgar herd always interprets as evidence of an eccentric life, the influence of uncontrolled emotions, a subjection to the imperative demands of art, and, invariably, of a certain contempt for the social conventions. All this it finds either definitely or actively exasperating. His cambric shirt, for instance, with its pleated wristbands, was permitted to blow in a fine disorder through the opening of his waistcoat of grey drill, and his wide-striped trousers reached only to the ankle and displayed nankeen boots with uppers of varnished leather. These were so highly polished that they reflected the grass. He trod the horse-dung nonchalantly as he walked with one hand in the pocket of his jacket and his straw hat tilted to one side.

'You know how it is,' he said, 'when one lives in the country . . .'

'. . . Everything seems just a waste of time'—Emma finished the sentence for him.

'Precisely! Not one of these good folk would know a well-cut coat if he saw one.'

They went on to speak of the mediocrity of life as lived in the provinces, of how stifling it was, of how it destroyed every illusion.

'In me it produces a state of profound gloom,' said Rodolphe.

'You gloomy!'—Emma voiced her astonishment—'I should have called you extremely cheerful!'

'On the surface, perhaps. But that is because I can assume a mask of mockery in my dealings with other people. But many's the time, when I see a churchyard by moonlight, that I wonder whether I shouldn't he better off sleeping with those who lie there. . . .'

'But your friends?' she said, 'what about them?'

'My friends?—what friends? I am not sure that I have any—any, that is, who really concern themselves about me.'

These words were accompanied by a sort of hissing intake of breath.

They were obliged to draw apart by the approach from behind of a man who was carrying a great pile of chairs. So overloaded was he, that only the toes of his clogs and the extremities of his outstretched arms were visible. It was Lestiboudois, the grave-digger, who was distributing the seats from the church among the crowd. Fully awake, as always, to his own interests, he had found this means of making something for himself out of the show, and so successful had the scheme proved to be, that he was at his wits' end to know whom to serve first. The village folk, exhausted by the heat, were busy quarrelling over these straw-bottomed chairs which smelled of incense. They leaned against their heavy backs, stained with the droppings of candle-grease, with a kind of reverence.

Once again, Madame Bovary took Rodolphe's arm. He went on speaking as though to himself:

'I have been cheated of so much, and am so utterly alone! If only I had something to live for, if only I had found someone. . . . Ah, *then* I would have put forth all the energy of which I am capable, would have surmounted all obstacles, broken through all difficulties!'

'Still, I don't really feel that you are to be pitied,' said Emma.

'Do you honestly mean that?'

'Because, when all is said and done'—she went on—'you are free.' She hesitated before adding—'and rich.'

'Please don't laugh at me!' he replied.

She swore that the thought had never entered her head.

At that moment the report of a gun rang out, and there was a general rush towards the village. But it turned out to be a false alarm. The Prefect had not arrived, and the members of the jury found themselves in something of a quandary, not knowing whether they ought to open the proceedings or continue to wait.

At length, a large hired landau appeared at the far end of the square, drawn by two skinny horses which a driver in a white hat was belabouring with might and main. Binet had barely time to shout 'Fall in!' and the colonel to follow suit. The men made a dash for their piled muskets, some, in their hurry, even forgetting to fasten their collars. But the official equipage, seemingly anticipating the confusion, had slowed down. The two jades ceased to strain at their coupling chain and fell into an easy amble, arriving in front of the porch of the town hall at a jog trot, just as the National Guard and the fire brigade took up position to a roll of drums, and began to mark time.

'Steady there!' shouted Binet.

'Halt!' yelled the colonel: 'dress by the left!' After a 'Present!' the clatter of which sounded like a copper kettle bumping downstairs, arms were ordered.

A gentleman with a pale face and a benign expression was seen to alight from the carriage. He had a bald forehead, a shock of hair at the back of his skull, and was wearing a short coat trimmed with silver braid. He screwed up his prominent eyes under their heavy lids, the better to scan the attendant multitude, at the same time raising his pointed nose and stretching his sunken lips into a smile. He recognized the Mayor by his sash and explained that the Prefect had been unable to come.* He was himself, he said, one of the counsellors of the prefecture, and hastily added a few apologies.

Tuvache replied in one or two well-chosen words, and the newcomer expressed himself as being overwhelmed. They stood face to face, their foreheads almost touching, surrounded by the members of the jury, the officials of the municipal council, the local big-wigs, the National Guard and the crowd. The Counsellor, pressing his little black three-cornered hat to his bosom, reiterated his greetings, while Tuvache, bent double like a bow, smiled, stammered, tried to find the right thing to say, declared his loyalty to the throne, and voiced the honour which was being done to Yonville.

Hippolyte, the ostler from the inn, took the two horses by the bridle and limping along on his club-foot, led them away through the yard gates of the Golden Lion, where a number of peasants had gathered to have a good look at the carriage. The drum rolled, the gun roared, and the distinguished gentlemen, climbing up on to the platform in single file, proceeded to take their places in the chairs upholstered in red Utrecht velvet which had been lent for the occasion by Madame Tuvache.

They all looked exactly alike. Their pale, flabby faces, slightly touched by the sun, had the colour of sweet cider, and their bushy whiskers emerged from stiff collars held in position by white cravats tied in large bows. They all wore double-breasted velvet waistcoats and watches with oval cornelian seals on long ribbons. They all sat with their hands resting on their thighs, their legs deliberately spread, the smooth cloth of their trousers shining more brilliantly than the leather of their heavy boots.

The leaders of local female society were ranged behind them between the columns of the portico, while the common people were massed facing the platform, standing or seated on chairs.

'*I* think', said Monsieur Lheureux (addressing the chemist who was pushing past him on his way to his seat), 'that they ought to have had two Venetian masts with some rich but severe drapery. They would have added novelty to the decorations and would have made a brave show.'

'I agree,' replied Homais: 'but what can you expect with the Mayor superintending everything? Poor old Tuvache hasn't much taste, you know—completely devoid of what you might call the genius of art.'

Rodolphe, with Madame Bovary in tow, had gone up to the council chamber on the first floor of the town hall. There was no one in it, and he declared that it made an admirable grandstand from which they could watch the proceedings in comfort. He took three stools from under the table which was presided over by a bust of the monarch, and moved them over to one of the windows. They sat down side by side.

There was some commotion on the platform, much whispering and parleying. At last, the Counsellor rose. Word had gone round that his name was Lieuvain, and it was passed from mouth to mouth in the crowd. When he had shuffled his notes, and held them close to his eyes for easier reading, he began.

'Gentlemen: I should like to say before passing to the serious business of the day, and in doing so, I feel sure that I am voicing your own sentiment—I should like to say that we all, I know, would wish to offer a tribute of respect and gratitude to the Administration of which we form a part, to the government, and, gentlemen, to that Monarch, that Sovereign, that dearly beloved King, to whom nothing that touches the public well-being or private prosperity of his people is ever a matter of indifference; to that sure pilot who guides the car of state amidst the ceaseless perils of a stormy sea, knowing well that peace is no less glorious than war, nor the pursuit of industry, commerce, agriculture and the fine arts. . . .'

'I think I must move my seat back a bit,' said Rodolphe.

'Why?' asked Emma.

But at this moment the voice of the Counsellor rose in a remarkable manner as he warmed to his declamatory effort:

'The times are past, gentlemen, when civil discord stained our public places red, when the owner of wide acres, the man of business, and even, yes, gentlemen, even the humble artisan, as he sank at night into his peaceful slumbers, trembled lest he be awakened by the din of incendiary tocsins, times when the most subversive theories dared brazenly to sap the very foundations. . . .'

'Because', went on Rodolphe, 'I might be seen from down there, and that would mean that for the next fortnight I should have to explain myself to all and sundry. My reputation being what it is. . . .'

'You are too hard on yourself,' said Emma.

'Not at all, my reputation is quite appalling—I swear it is . . .'

'But, gentlemen'—continued the Counsellor—'if I banish such dark pictures from my memory, and glance round me for a moment at our beautiful country as it now is, what do I see? I see commerce and arts everywhere flourishing. I see new systems of communication which have come into being like so many fresh arteries in the body politic, establishing new contacts. Our great centres of manufacture have resumed their ancient activity: religion, more firmly grounded than ever before, smiles in all our hearts: the ports are full of shipping: confidence has been born anew, and France, at long last, breathes again. . . .'

'As a matter of fact,' went on Rodolphe, 'in what people say of me, they may not, from a worldly point of view, be altogether wrong.'

'How do you mean?' queried Emma.

'You must surely know that there are on this earth men who are never at peace. For them the see-saw between dream and action never ceases. The purest passions, the most extravagant forms of indulgence are a daily necessity. They must be for ever plunging into a turmoil of fantasies and follies.'

She looked at him as she might have looked at some traveller who has journeyed through strange lands.

'But to us poor women', she said, 'even that distraction is forbidden.'

'A sad distraction, since happiness is never found by such means.'

'But is happiness ever to be found at all?' she asked.

'Yes,' he replied; 'sooner or later it is.'

'And that', the Counsellor was saying, 'is what you have understood. You agriculturists and tillers of the soil, you peaceful pioneers in the great task of civilization, you men of progress and sound morality—you, let me repeat—have understood that the storms of politics are more to be feared than the disturbances of Nature. . . .'

'Yes, sooner or later'—continued Rodolphe, 'it *is* to be found, sometimes quite suddenly when all has seemed despair. The horizon opens up, and it is as though a voice cried: "There!" Someone comes, someone to whom one feels the need to unburden all one's troubles, someone to whom one wants to give everything, to whom one would willingly sacrifice life itself. There's no need for words—people just find one another—they have glimpsed each other in dreams' (and here he looked hard at her). 'The treasure so long sought is within one's reach. It shines and sparkles. But still one doubts, still one dare not hope. One is dazzled like a man coming from a place of shadows into the light of day.'

As he said this he added pantomime to speech. He passed his hand

over his face like one who is overcome with dizziness. Then he let it
drop to Emma's. Hers she withdrew.

But the Counsellor was still busy with his reading:

'. . . And why, gentlemen, should that cause you any surprise? Such an
emotion could be felt only by those so blinded, so deeply plunged (and
this I say without fear or favour)—so deeply plunged in the prejudices
of another age as even now to wholly have misunderstood the minds
and feelings of our country folk. Where is a truer patriotism to be found
than in our fields and pastures, a more complete devotion to the public
weal—in one word—a keener intelligence? Nor, gentlemen, do I mean
by that word the merely superficial cleverness which is but the adorn-
ment of lazy minds. I mean, rather, the deep, the balanced intelligence
which is concerned, above all else, to pursue useful ends and so
contribute to the prosperity of each, to the betterment of our common
life and to the maintenance of the body politic—that intelligence, in
short, which is born of a respect for law and of an habitual devotion to
duty. . . .'

'Just listen to him!' said Rodolphe: 'always this talk of duty! I'm
sick to death of the very word! We're always having it dinned into
our ears by a bunch of old fogeys in flannel waistcoats, a gaggle of
pious humbugs with rosaries in their hands and foot-warmers under
their boots! Duty! duty! The only duty *I* recognize is the duty to feel
sublime emotions, to love and to cherish what is beautiful—*not* the
duty which would have us accept the conventions of society and the
ignominies of acquiescence! . . .'

'Still . . .' objected Madame Bovary . . . 'still . . .'

'No, no! Not a word against the passions! Are they not the one
thing of beauty in this world?—The one and only source of heroism
and enthusiasm, of poetry, music and the arts?—of all, in short, that
makes life worth living?'

'But', said Emma, 'we must, to some extent, respect the opinions
of our neighbours and conform to their morals. . . .'

'But there are two moralities,' he answered: 'one is petty and
conventional; it is the invention of men and changes endlessly, stirring up as much empty fuss and clamour as the imbeciles you can see
down there. But the other lives in that eternity which is all around
and all above us, like the fields and the woods and the blue sky
spreading its radiance on our earth.'

Monsieur Lieuvain had just wiped his mouth with his pocket-handkerchief. He continued:

'. . . It would he a strange thing, gentlemen, if *I* were to ask *you* of what use is agriculture? How are our needs provided, our substance assured if not by the man who has devoted his life to agriculture? It is he, gentlemen, who, scattering seed along the fruitful furrows of our fields with hard and horny hand, raises the corn, which then is bruised, beaten and reduced to powder by many ingenious mechanisms: and this powder, under the name of flour, is then transported to our cities and delivered there to the baker who fashions it into nourishing food for rich and poor alike. Is it not he, too, who fattens the abundant herds that cover our grazing lands, that they may afford us clothing? How should we clothe ourselves, how find food, were it not for the agriculturist? Nor, gentlemen, need we go so far afield to find examples of my meaning. Who among us has not oftentimes reflected on the important part played by that humble creature who is the pride and ornament of our farmyards, providing soft pillows for our beds, succulent flesh for our tables, and eggs? I should never have done were I to enumerate in detail the many products which the well-farmed soil, like a generous mother, showers upon its children. Here it is the vine, there the cider apple: in one place the colza crop, in another the cheese and the flax which, in recent years, has been more abundantly grown, and to which I would more particularly draw your attention. . . .'

But he had no need to do anything of the sort, for all around him mouths were gaping as though to drink his words. Tuvache, beside him, was listening with wide-open eyes: Monsieur Derozerays blinked his lids from time to time, while, further off, the chemist, with his son Napoleon between his knees, was cupping his ear with his hand in an effort not to lose a syllable. The other members of the jury were nodding approving chins within the folds of their waistcoats. The firemen, drawn up beneath the platform, stood leaning on their bayonets, and Binet, quite motionless, and with his elbow projecting at an angle, was keeping his sword-point upwards. No doubt he could hear, but he most certainly could not see because the vizor of his helmet was crammed down on his nose. His lieutenant, the younger son of the great Tuvache, was still more extravagantly topped, for he had equipped himself with a headgear so enormous that it rocked to and fro upon his crown, with one end of a cotton neckerchief emerging from beneath it. His smile was that of an amiable child, and upon his small, pale face, beaded with sweat, was an expression which betokened enjoyment, exhaustion and sleepiness.

The whole square was chock-a-block with people up to the very house-fronts. There were spectators leaning on the sill of every window and standing on the step of every door. Justin, stationed in front of the chemist's shop, seemed as though turned to stone, so fixedly was he staring at the scene. In spite of the silence, Monsieur Lieuvain's voice was lost upon the air. It reached his audience only in broken snatches, and even these were drowned, at moments, by the creaking and scratching of chairs among the crowd. Suddenly, from behind the listeners, would come the prolonged mooing of cows or the bleat of lambs calling to one another from the corners of the streets. The cowmen and the shepherds had brought their charges right into the town, and from time to time they voiced their feelings, the while, with their tongues, they pulled at the twigs which dangled above their noses.

Rodolphe had drawn very close to Emma, and now, speaking quickly and in a low voice, he said:

'Does not this world-conspiracy revolt you? Is there one single sentiment it does not condemn? The noblest instincts, the purest sympathies, are persecuted and befouled. If two poor souls at length encounter, all is so ordered that they shall not join their fates. Yet, they will try to do so, beating their wings and crying one to another. Not that it matters, for, sooner or later, whether in six months or in ten years, they will meet again and love, since fate has planned it so, and they are made for each other.'

He sat with his arms crossed upon his knees, his face raised to Emma's. Across the narrow space that separated them, he gazed fixedly upon her. She could see in his eyes little golden streaks which spread a brightness all about the coal-black pupils; could even smell the scented pomade which gave such lustre to his hair. She was overcome by a sudden weakness, remembering the Viscount who had made her waltz with him at La Vaubyessard, whose beard had exhaled the same odour of lemon and vanilla as this head beside her. Instinctively she half closed her eyes the better to savour its sweetness. But as she straightened herself on her chair, she caught a glimpse, far away in the distance, of the old Swallow diligence slowly coming down the hill of Leux, trailing behind it a long plume of dust. It was in that yellow vehicle that Léon had so often come back to her, and along that same road that he had gone for ever from her sight. She imagined for a moment that she could see him at the window opposite. Then the vision grew confused: clouds passed, and it seemed to her that once again she was turning in the waltz beneath the crystal lustres, the Viscount's arms about her—that Léon was close at hand, would come now at any moment. . . . Yet it was Rodolphe's head of which she was aware at her side. The sweetness of this feeling mingled with her old desires which, like grains of sand before a blustering wind, eddied in the faint gusts of perfume that seemed to spread about her soul. Several times she expanded her nostrils that she might sniff the freshness of the ivy twined about the capitals. She drew off her gloves and wiped her hands. Then, with her handkerchief, she fanned her face, while, through the throbbing of her temples, she could hear the murmurs of the crowd and the voice of the Counsellor chanting his periods.

He was saying:

'Continue in your ways and persevere! Heed not the promptings of routine, nor yet the over-hasty urgings of a rash empiricism! Set yourselves, above all, to the task of bettering the soil and improving your manures, to the developing of still finer equine, bovine and porcine breeds! May this show be for you as a peaceful arena where the conqueror may stretch the hand of friendship to his vanquished foe in the hope of nobler triumphs yet to come! And you, venerable servitors, humble domestic helps, whose toilful labours no government till now has duly recompensed, take the reward of all your silent virtues, and be assured that henceforth the state is watchful of your interests and ranged as your protector: that it will see your just claims honoured, and, so far as in it lies, will lighten the burden of your arduous sacrifices!'

At this point, Monsieur Lieuvain resumed his seat. Monsieur Derozerays then rose and embarked upon another speech. It was not, perhaps, so florid as the Counsellor's, but it held his auditors' attention by something more positive in its style, for it was inspired by greater knowledge and expressed more clearly-defined views. It was less concerned to praise the acts of government, and gave greater consideration to questions of religion and of agriculture. It brought out the connexion between the two, and showed how, at all periods, they had worked together in the development of civilization.

Rodolphe spoke to Madame Bovary of dreams and omens and magnetic attraction.

Surveying the eras when human societies were in their infancy, the orator drew a picture of those rough old days when men, deep buried in their forests, had lived off acorns. Later, he went on, they had shed the skins of beasts and clad themselves in woven stuffs, had learned to plough the fields and cultivate the vine. Had that, he asked, been altogether an advantage? Had it not brought to mankind more troubles than benefits? That was the problem which Monsieur Derozerays set before himself.

From magnetic attraction Rodolphe had progressed to affinities, and, while the President cited Cincinnatus* and his plough, Diocletian* and his cabbages, and the emperors of China* inaugurating the year by the planting of seed, the young man explained to the young woman that these irresistible attractions could be traced back to states of former existence.

'How did it come about', he said, 'that you and I should meet? What chance willed it? The truth is that, like two rivers flowing to a common meeting-point, the propensities of our natures thrust us, across the intervening space, towards one another.'

He seized her hand. She did not withdraw it.

'We must work together for good farming,' cried the President.

'Recently, for instance, when I came to your house. . . .'

'. . . To Monsieur Bizet of Quincampoix. . . .'

'Did I know that we should be together in this place?'

'. . . Seventy francs?'

'A hundred times I even strove to break from you, but ever followed, ever stayed. . . .'

'. . . Manures. . . .'

'As I should so dearly love to stay this evening, tomorrow, all the days of my life!'

'. . . To Monsieur Caron of Argueil, a gold medal. . . .'

'For never have I found a charm so powerful in the companionship of anybody. . . .'

'. . . To Monsieur Bain of Givry-Saint-Martin . . .'

'This memory of you will be with me always. . . .'

'. . . For a merino ram . . .'

'But you will forget me: I shall be for you as a shadow that has passed. . . .'

'. . . To Monsieur Belot of Notre-Dame . . .'

'But no! Tell me I shall count for something in your thoughts and in your life!'

'Pig class—a prize of sixty francs, divided between Monsieur Lehérissé and Monsieur Cullembourg . . .'

Rodolphe pressed the hand which lay in his, warm and quivering like a captive dove struggling to escape. But whether because she was really striving to free it, or because she was responding to his pressure, she made a little movement of the fingers. He exclaimed:

'Oh thank you!—You do not repulse me, then! How good you are! You understand that I am wholly yours! Let me but see you, gaze upon your face!'

A little breeze from the windows puckered the tablecloth. In the square beneath, the great headdresses of the countrywomen flapped like the wings of white butterflies.

'. . . For the best use of oilseed cake'—went on the President, and hurried through his catalogue:

'Flemish manure—flax-growing—drainage—long-term leases— domestic service . . .'

Rodolphe had stopped speaking. They sat there looking at one another. An overmastering desire set their dry lips quivering. Softly, without self-consciousness, their fingers intertwined.

'. . . Catherine-Nicaise-Élisabeth Leroux,* of Sassetot-la-Guerrière, for fifty-four years of unbroken service on the same farm, a silver medal—value, twenty-five francs!'

'Where is Catherine Leroux?' said the Counsellor.

She did not come forward, and voices could be heard whispering:

'Go on!'

'No.'

'Over there, to the left!'

'Don't be frightened!'

'How silly she is!'

'For the last time, is Catherine Leroux present?' cried Tuvache.

'Yes . . . there she is.'

'Then let her come forward.'

A little old woman, with a frightened expression on her face, was seen advancing across the platform. She looked all shrunken in her shabby clothes. On her feet were large wooden clogs and round her waist an expansive blue apron. Her thin face, framed in a cap without a border, was more wrinkled than a shrivelled apple, and a pair of long hands with bony knuckles dangled from the sleeves of her red bodice. They were so engrained, so roughened and coarsened, with barn-dust, soap-suds and the grease of sheep's wool, that they looked dirty, though they had been washed in clean water. From having worked so long they remained half bent, the humble witnesses of many years of suffering and toil. An almost nunlike rigidity gave dignity to her face. No hint of sadness or of softness showed in the faded stillness of her gaze. From long intimacy with the beasts of the field she had caught an air of mute placidity. This was the first time that she had ever found herself in so numerous a company. Secretly terrified by the bunting and the drums, by the gentlemen in black coats and by the Counsellor's cross of the Legion of Honour, she stood there motionless, not knowing whether to move forward or take to her heels, nor why the crowd was urging her on and the judges were smiling. In such guise did half a century of servitude stand rooted before that group of sleek, self-satisfied notables.

'Approach, venerable Catherine-Nicaise-Élisabeth Leroux!'— said the Counsellor, who had taken a list of the prize-winners from the hand of the President.

Glancing, turn and turn about, at the sheet of paper and at the ancient crone, he said again in fatherly tones:

'Come nearer—nearer!'

'Are you deaf?' said Tuvache, bouncing from his chair.

Going close to her, he shouted in her ear:

'Fifty-four years of faithful service!—a silver medal!—Twenty-five francs!—It's all for you!'

When, at last, the medal was in her hand, she stood there staring at it. A beatific smile slowly spread across her face, and she could be heard murmuring as she moved away:

'I'll give it to our priest, so he'll say masses for me.'

'What bigotry!' exclaimed the chemist, leaning across to the lawyer.

The business of the day was over. The crowd began to disperse. Now that the speeches had been read, each of those present resumed his social rank. Daily habits once more reasserted themselves. The masters spoke sharply to their servants, who, in their turn, be-laboured the dumb animals. These, apathetic in their hour of triumph, ambled back to their byres with wreaths of green between their horns.

Meanwhile, the National Guard had climbed to the first floor of the town hall with brioches spitted on their bayonets, accompanied by the battalion drummer carrying a basket full of bottles. Madame Bovary took Rodolphe's arm. He led her home, and they separated on her doorstep. Then he went for a lonely saunter in the meadow until such time as the banquet should be ready.

The meal was long, noisy and badly served. So tightly packed were the guests that it was only with difficulty that they could move their arms at all, and the narrow planks which served for benches well-nigh broke beneath their weight. They ate enormous quantities of food, each determined to get his full share. Sweat poured down the assembled faces, and a whitish steam, like morning mist above a brook in autumn, floated over the table between the hanging lamps. Rodolphe, leaning back against the canvas of the tent, was so engrossed by thoughts of Emma, that he heard nothing. Behind him, servants were piling dirty plates upon the grass. His neighbours spoke to him but he made no answer. His glass was filled and silence took its stand within his thoughts, though the noise around grew louder. He brooded on what she had said and on the shape of her mouth. Her face glimmered on the polished surface of the shakos as in a magic mirror. The walls seemed draped in the folds of her dress, and before his inward gaze there spread an infinite vista of long days of love.

He saw her again that evening during the firework display. But she was with her husband, Madame Homais and the chemist, who was worrying a good deal about stray rockets. He was continually breaking from the company in order to give Binet pieces of advice.

The fireworks, consigned to Tuvache, had, from excess of caution, been stored in his cellar, with the result that the damp powder was only with great difficulty ignited at all, and the chief set-piece, representing a dragon biting its own tail, failed completely. Every now and again some wretched roman candle went off to an accompaniment of shouts from the gaping crowd mingled with shrieks from the women when some amorous swain squeezed a waist in the darkness. Emma said nothing, but rested her head quietly on Charles's shoulder, raising her face now and then to follow the bright track of a rocket in the blackness of the night. Rodolphe watched her by the light of fairy-lamps. One by one these went out. The stars were kindled. A few drops of rain fell. She tied her scarf over her bare head.

At this moment the Counsellor's carriage emerged from the inn yard. The coachman was drunk and had fallen into a doze. The huge bulk of his body could be seen above the hood, sitting between the lamps, swaying to and fro to the pitching of the springs.

'Drunkenness', said the chemist, 'ought to be severely punished. I should like to see the names of all who had made beasts of themselves on alcoholic beverages inscribed daily at the entrance to the town hall on a notice-board provided expressly for the purpose. Not only would it be a warning, but would supply a public record of the greatest statistical value, which, should occasion arise—but, forgive me. . . .'

He ran across once more to say something to the captain.

The latter was going home, back to his lathe.

'It mightn't be a bad thing', remarked Homais, 'if you sent one of your men, or went yourself.'

'Leave me alone!' replied the tax-collector, 'there's no danger.'

'It's all right,' said the chemist, as he rejoined his friends. 'Monsieur Binet assures me that all necessary measures have been taken. No sparks have fallen and the pumps are fully charged. We can go to our beds with minds at rest.'

'Bed is just what I need'—exclaimed Madame Homais who was yawning prodigiously. 'It doesn't matter what happens now, we have had a lovely day for the show.'

In a low voice, and with a tender glance, Rodolphe repeated:

'Lovely, indeed!'

Two mornings later a long article on the agricultural show appeared in the *Fanal de Rouen*. Homais had dashed it off the very next day.

'Why all these swags and flowers and garlands? Whither surges the crowd like the waves of a stormy sea beneath a tropical sun which pours its heat upon our fields and furrows?'

He went on to speak of conditions among the rural population. The government, no doubt, was doing much, but not enough.

'Deal courageously with the problem!' he adjured it: 'many indispensable reforms are needed: provide them!'

Then, touching on the arrival of the Counsellor, he was careful to refer to 'the martial air of our fine militiamen', to 'our sprightly village maidens'—not omitting the bald-headed ancients—'those patriarchs, not a few of whom, the remnants of our deathless legions, felt their old hearts beat again to the manly rolling of the drums.' He mentioned himself as having occupied a prominent place among the judges, and recalled, in a note, that Monsieur Homais, pharmacist, had sent a memorandum on cider to the Agricultural Society. In his description of the prize-giving, he waxed lyrical over the delight of the successful entrants. 'Fathers embraced their sons, brothers brothers, husbands wives. Not a few of them exhibited with pride their simple medals, and, doubtless, on returning to those homes where the good wife was awaiting them, hung these trophies with tears upon the modest walls of humble cots.

'At six o'clock a banquet was served in Monsieur Liégeard's paddock, to which were invited the most prominent of those who had taken part in the festivities. A number of toasts were drunk. Monsieur Lieuvain proposed the health of the King, Monsieur Tuvache that of the Prefect. Monsieur Derozerays raised his glass to Agriculture, Monsieur Homais his to Industry and the Fine Arts, those inseparable sisters! Monsieur Leplichey called on the company to drink to Progress! After dark, the night was made brilliant by a display of fireworks. The scene took on the appearance of a kaleidoscope, of an opera, and, for a moment, our little town might have thought itself transported to the heart of some dream of the *Arabian Nights*.

'It should be put on record that no untoward incident occurred to mar this happy family party.' He added:

'It was noticed that only the clergy were absent. Those who dwell in sacristies understand progress, no doubt, rather differently than we do. No one, dear followers of Loyola,* will question your right to do so.'

CHAPTER IX

SIX weeks passed. Rodolphe had not come back. Then, one evening, he appeared.

It would be a mistake to return too soon, he had said to himself.

At the end of the week he had gone away for the shooting. When that was over, he had thought at first that he had delayed too long, but then had come this reflection:

If she loved me from the first, having to wait to see me again must have made her love me even more! On with the good work!'

To what extent his reasoning had been sound he realized when he saw Emma turn pale as he entered the room.

She was alone. Dusk was falling. The short muslin curtains over the window intensified the twilight, and the gilt mouldings of the barometer, touched by a gleam of sun, drew sparks of fire from the mirror which hung between the branches of the coral ornament.

Rodolphe remained standing, and at first Emma scarcely replied at all to his opening compliments.

'I have been busy,' he said, 'and far from well.'

'It wasn't anything serious, was it?' she exclaimed.

Rodolphe sat down beside her on a stool.

'No . . . the truth is, I had made up my mind not to see you again.'

'Why?'

'Can't you guess?'

He looked at her again, but with such smouldering passion that she blushed and hung her head. He went on:

'Emma . . .'

'Sir!' said she, slightly increasing the distance between them.

'Ah!' he replied in melancholy tones, 'you see now how right I was in my decision that I had better not return, since you refuse me the use of that name which has filled my every thought, and slipped just now unbidden from my lips! Madame Bovary! . . . that is the name by which all may call you . . . yet, it is not your name but another's!'

He repeated: 'Another's!'

He buried his face in his hands.

'You are never out of my mind! . . . The memory of you drives me to despair! . . . Ah, forgive me! . . . I will go . . . Farewell! . . . I will journey far . . . so far that no mention of my name will ever reach your ears . . . and yet . . . today . . . some power, I know not what, impelled me hither! There is no fighting against heaven, no resistance possible when the angels smile! One cannot but be drawn onwards by what is beautiful, charming, adorable!'

It was the first time Emma had ever heard such words, and her pride, like one who lets himself relax in a vapour bath, stretched itself languidly, and without resistance, in the warmth of his protestations.

'But', he continued, 'if I did not come, if I could cheat myself with no hope of seeing you, I could at least fill my eyes with the sight of all

that lay about you. Every night I used to get up—yes, every night—
and come here. I would stand gazing at your house, its roof brilliant
beneath the moon, the trees in the garden swaying before your windows where a little lamp, a tiny point of brightness, shone in the
darkness from behind the panes. You never knew that there, so close
and yet so far, a poor wretch . . .'

She turned towards him with a sob.

'How good you are!' she said.

'No, I love you: that is all. You do not doubt it, surely. Say that you
do not! Speak but one word!'

Imperceptibly, Rodolphe let himself slip from the stool to the
floor. But the sound of clogs reached his ears from the kitchen, and
he noticed that the parlour door was ajar.

'What sweet charity it would be in you,' he went on, rising to his
feet, 'to satisfy a foolish whim of mine.'

It was, that whim, to see over the house. He wanted to know it
wholly, nor did Madame Bovary think the request unreasonable.
They were both of them preparing to leave the room when Charles
came in.

'How-d'you-do, Doctor,' said Rodolphe. The man of medicine,
flattered by this unexpected appellation, was all obsequiousness. The
other took advantage of this opportunity to regain something of his
composure.

'Your wife', he said, 'was talking to me about her health. . . .'

Charles interrupted him. His mind, as it happened, was far from
easy on that subject. Emma was again suffering from attacks of
breathlessness. Rodolphe inquired whether riding might not be
beneficial.

'Excellent! nothing could be better! . . . What a good idea. . . . You
ought to follow it up, my dear.'

She objected that she had no horse, and Rodolphe immediately
offered one of his. She refused, and he did not insist. Then, to give
some colour to his visit, he explained that his carter—the one who
had been bled—was still suffering at times from giddiness.

'I'll have a look at him,' said Bovary.

'You mustn't dream of putting yourself out! I'll send him over: we'll
come over together. That will be much more convenient for you.'

'All right, then—and many thanks.' As soon as husband and wife
were alone—

'Why wouldn't you accept Monsieur Boulanger's offer? It was so extremely kind of him to make it.'

She pouted, sought a thousand excuses, and at last declared that it *might look strange*.

'A lot I care about that!' said Charles, pirouetting on his heel. 'Your health is the only thing that matters. You did wrong to refuse!'

'And how am I to go riding without a habit?'

'You'd better get one made,' he replied. The habit decided the matter.

When it was ready, Charles wrote to Monsieur Boulanger that his wife was at his disposition, and that he was counting on his kindness.

At noon next day, Rodolphe turned up at Charles's door with two riding-horses. One had pink rosettes at its ears, and a lady's doe-skin saddle on its back.

Rodolphe was wearing a pair of high boots made of some soft leather. He had acted on the assumption that Emma had probably never seen anything of the sort before. She was, indeed, delighted with his appearance when she saw him on the stairs wearing a full-skirted coat of velvet and white stockinette breeches. She was quite ready, and was waiting for him.

Justin slipped out of the shop to see her, and even the apothecary stopped work to do honour to the occasion. He was profuse in his advice to Monsieur Boulanger.

'Accidents can happen so quickly! Do, please, be careful! Your steeds, maybe, are mettlesome!'

She heard a sound above her head. It was Félicité tapping on the window to amuse little Berthe. The child blew a kiss, and her mother raised the handle of her crop in acknowledgment.

'A pleasant ride!' said Monsieur Homais. 'Be careful, now! What-ever you do, be careful!'

He waved his newspaper as he watched them move off.

Emma's horse broke into a gallop as soon as it felt soft earth. Rodolphe kept close beside her. Now and then they exchanged a few words. With her head slightly bent, her bridle-hand held high, and her right arm extended, she surrendered to the rhythmical move-ment of her horse as though she were being rocked in a cradle.

At the bottom of the hill, Rodolphe let his mount have its head, and they leaped forward together. When they reached the top, the horses suddenly stopped, and her long blue veil again hung drooping.

It was early October, and a mist lay over the countryside. As far as the eye could reach, long scarves of vapour clung to the outline of the hills, rising here and there, and vanishing in the upper air. Now and again, when the haze parted, the roofs of Yonville could be seen glittering in a stray beam of sunlight, the little gardens running down to the river, the yards, the walls and steeple of the church. Emma half closed her eyes in an effort to make out her own house, and never had the wretched village in which she lived seemed so small. From the high ground on which they were halted, the whole valley showed as an immense pale lake, gauzy and insubstantial. Its occasional clumps of trees stood out from the background like black rocks, and the line of tall poplars which over-topped the mist had the appearance of a sea-shore blown by the wind.

Beside them, on the grass between the pines, a muted radiance spread in the warm air. The earth, reddish in colour like snuff, deadened the noise of their horses' hooves scattering pine-cones as they moved.

Rodolphe and Emma skirted the wood. Occasionally she turned away her head to avoid his glance, and when she did this, she could see nothing but the ordered rows of tree-trunks—a dwindling vista which turned her slightly dizzy. The horses breathed noisily: the saddle-leathers creaked.

Just as they were entering the forest, the sun came out.

'God is on our side!' said Rodolphe.

'Do you think so?' she replied.

'Come on!'

He made a clicking noise with his tongue, and the two horses broke into a trot.

The high bracken beside the path kept getting entangled in Emma's stirrups. Rodolphe, without slowing down, leaned across whenever this happened, and pulled it loose. At other times, when there were branches to be pushed aside, he edged close to her, and she could feel his knee against her leg. The sky turned blue. There were great rides full of flowering heather, and carpets of violets showed among the litter of dead leaves, grey, tawny and gold according to the trees from which they had fallen. Several times they heard a tiny flutter of wings in the undergrowth, or the hoarse, soft cry of rooks, as they flew off among the oaks. They dismounted, and Rodolphe tethered the horses. She walked ahead of him on the mossy turf between the ruts. But her long skirt got in her way, though she was holding up the train, and Rodolphe, following behind, kept his eyes fixed on the strip of thin white stocking which showed between the black stuff of her habit and her black boots. It held for him something of the quality of her bare flesh. She stopped.

'I am tired!' she said.

'Come on, make an effort!' he replied: 'Keep your courage up!'

A hundred yards further on she stopped again, and, through the meshes of her veil which hung down to her waist obliquely from her man's hat, he could see her face in a sort of blue transparency, as though she were swimming beneath a summer sea.

'Where are we going?'

To this question he made no reply. She was panting slightly. Rodolphe looked about him, gnawing his moustache.

They reached a rather larger clearing where young trees had recently been felled, and sat down on a fallen trunk. He began to speak of his love. He was careful at first not to frighten her by too many compliments. He was calm, serious, melancholy.

Emma listened to him with bowed head, stirring with her toe the wood-shavings that lay upon the ground.

But, when he said:

'Are not our destinies henceforth united?'

'No!' she replied. 'You know quite well that's impossible.'

She got up and made ready to go. He seized her by the wrist. She stood quite still, then, after looking at him for a space with a moist and loving eye, said quickly:

'Let's not speak of it any more. . . . Where are the horses? We ought to be getting back.'

He made a movement expressive of anger and vexation. She repeated her question:

'Where are the horses?—where are the horses?'

Then, with a strange smile on his lips, a fixed look in his eyes, and his teeth fast clenched, he came towards her, his arms spread wide. She recoiled, trembling, and stammered:

'You're frightening me!—you're hurting me!—let us go!'

'If we must, we must, I suppose,' he said, and a change came over his face. He was once again considerate, fond and shy. He gave her his arm. They turned back. He said:

'What was the matter with you? Why did you behave like that?—I don't understand. You had an entirely wrong idea of my intentions. I keep you in my heart like a Madonna on a pedestal, high above this base world, in a place apart, strong and inviolable. But you are necessary to my life! I need your eyes, your voice, your thoughts! I would have you be a dearly loved friend, a sister, an angel!'

He put his arm round her waist. Very gently she tried to free herself. He supported her thus as they walked.

They could hear the sound made by the horses as they cropped the leaves.

'Oh stay just a little longer!' said Rodolphe: 'let us not go! Stay with me here, I beg!'

He drew her further onwards, skirting a little pool where the duckweed made a carpet of green upon the water's surface. Dead water-lilies lay motionless among the reeds. At the sound of their footsteps frogs leaped hurriedly out of their way.

'It's wrong, it's wrong,' she kept saying. 'I'm mad to listen to you!'

'Why? . . . Emma . . . Emma . . .'

'Oh, Rodolphe! . . .' She spoke his name slowly, and leaned upon his shoulder.

The cloth of her habit caught upon the velvet of his coat. She threw back her head, and her white throat fluttered in a sigh. She melted, and then, with tears streaming down her cheeks, with a shudder, hiding her face, she gave herself to him.

Evening was closing in. The sun struck level through the branches, dazzling her eyes. Here and there among the leaves and on the ground, little patches of light flickered, as though humming-birds in flight had shed their feathers. All around was silence. A sweet influence seemed to come from the trees. She could feel her heart begin to beat again, and the blood surging through her veins like a river of milk. Far off, beyond the wood, and on the further hills, she heard a long and wordless cry, a voice that seemed to hang in the air. Silently she listened. It mingled like music with the dying vibrations of her strained nerves. Rodolphe, a cigar between his teeth, was busy with his knife, mending a break in one of the bridles.

They took the same road back to Yonville. They could see in the mud the marks of their two horses, side by side; they passed the same bushes, the same boulders scattered in the grass. Nothing in the outward scene had changed. But for her something so important had happened, that it was as though the very hills had moved.

From time to time Rodolphe leaned across, took her hand and kissed it.

How charming she looked on horseback!—upright and slim-waisted, her knee crooked about the pommel, her colour heightened by the air, in the red evening glow.

As they entered Yonville her horse grew skittish, and pranced upon the stone setts of the street. Eyes watched her from the windows.

At dinner her husband remarked on how well she was looking, but when he began to ask about her ride, she pretended not to hear, but sat with her elbows on the table beside her plate, between the two lit candles.

'Emma!' he said.

'What?'

'I was calling on Monsieur Alexandre this afternoon. He's got a mare—a bit old to be sure, but a nice-looking animal, though a trifle broken-winded. I am pretty certain I could get her for a hundred crowns. . . .'

A moment later, he added:

'Thinking you'd like her, I made an offer . . . in fact, I bought her. . . . Did I do right?'

She nodded assent.

A quarter of an hour passed.

At last: 'Are you going out this evening?' she asked.

'Yes—why?'

'Oh nothing, dear, nothing.'

As soon as she had got rid of Charles, she went upstairs and shut herself into her room. At first she experienced a sort of giddiness, seeing with reminiscent eyes the trees, the roads, the ditches, and Rodolphe: feeling again his arms about her waist, while the leaves quivered and the wind moaned through the reeds.

But when she looked at her face in the glass she was surprised by what she saw. Never had her eyes looked so large, so black, so fathomless. Some subtle influence, diffused about her person, had transfigured her.

She kept on saying to herself: 'I have a lover—a lover!' thrilled by the idea, as if she had experienced a sort of second puberty. So, after all, she was to know the happiness of love! of those fevered moments of delight which she had despaired of finding. She stood on the threshold of a magic land where passion, ecstasy, delirium would reign supreme. A blue immensity was round her: the high peaks of sentiment glittered for her in imagination. Mere ordinary existence seemed a thing far off and tiny, glimpsed far below in the shadows cast by those high immensities.

Then she called to mind the heroines of the books that she had read; the lyrical legion of those adulterous ladies sang in her memory as sisters, enthralling her with the charm of their voices. She became, in her own person, a living part, as it were, of that imaginary world. She was realizing the long dream of her youth, seeing herself as one of those great lovers whom she had so much envied. But that was not her only feeling. In what had happened she saw vengeance gratified. She had had more than her share of suffering! Now, at last, she had triumphed, and love, so long repressed, leapt like a living fountain in her heart, bubbling upward in ecstatic freedom. She revelled in it without remorse, without disquiet, without anxiety.

The whole of the next day passed in a sweet delight such as she had never known before. They exchanged vows. She told him of her sorrows . . . Rodolphe silenced her with kisses, and she, looking at him through half-closed eyes, begged him to call her once more by her name, to say again he loved her.

All this happened, as on the previous afternoon, in the forest, under a lean-to used by clog-makers. Its walls were of straw, and it had a roof so low that they had to stoop. They sat close together on a bed of dry leaves.

From that day forward, they wrote to one another regularly every evening. Emma took her letters to the end of the garden and hid them in a crack of the terrace, close to the river. Rodolphe fetched them, and left his own in the same hiding-place. Always she found them too short.

One morning, when Charles had gone out before it was light, the whim took her to see Rodolphe without a moment's delay. It was possible to reach La Huchette quickly, spend an hour there, and be back in Yonville before its inhabitants were awake. The very thought of such an expedition set her panting with desire, and she was soon half-way across the meadows, walking fast, and not once looking back.

Day was beginning to break. From far off Emma recognized her lover's house by the two fan-tailed vanes which stood out black in the half-light.

Beyond the farmyard stood a solid mass which could only be the château. She entered it as though the walls at her approach had opened of themselves. A great staircase rose in a single flight to the upper corridor. She turned the handle of a door, and at once, on the far side of the room, saw the figure of a man asleep. It was Rodolphe. She uttered a cry.

'You!' he said: and again, 'you!—how on earth did you get here? . . . Your dress is all wet!'

'I love you!' she replied: and threw her arms about his neck.

This first bold stroke having succeeded, Emma got into the way, whenever Charles left the house early, of dressing quickly and creeping stealthily down the terrace steps to the water-side.

Sometimes she would find that the plank which served as a bridge for cattle had been removed, and on those occasions she had to pick her way along by the garden walls which fronted the river. The bank was slippery, and she clung for support to the clumps of withered wallflower growing between the stones. Further on she turned off into the ploughed fields, sinking deep in the soggy soil, stumbling, and getting her thin boots covered with mud. The handkerchief which she wore tied about her head fluttered in the wind as she crossed the meadows. Terrified, as she was, of cattle, she would break into a run, arriving quite out of breath, with pink cheeks, and exhaling a fresh sweetness of vigorous young life, of green, growing things, and the open air. At this early hour Rodolphe was still asleep. It was as though a morning of spring came with her into his room. The yellow curtains which hung to the full length of the windows, gave muted passage to a golden but oppressive light. She would grope her way across the floor, blinking her eyes, while the drops of dew on the thick waves of her hair made, as it were, a topaze aureole about her face. He would draw her to him with a laugh and press her to his heart.

The first moment past, she would begin to investigate his room, opening the drawers, combing her hair with his combs, and looking at herself in his shaving-mirror. Often she would take the big pipe which lay on the bed-table* beside a jug of water, among a litter of lemons and bits of sugar, and put the mouth-piece between her teeth.

It took them a good quarter of an hour to say good-bye. Emma would weep. It was her dearest wish never to leave him. Something stronger than herself led her relentlessly to seek his presence.

One day, when she had made such an unheralded appearance in his room, he welcomed her with an air of frowning discontent.

'What is the matter?' she asked. 'Are you ill?—Tell me, what is troubling you?'

Finally, taking a serious tone, he told her that her visits were becoming reckless, and that she was compromising herself.

CHAPTER X

LITTLE by little she began to catch the infection of his nervousness. The first onset of love had gone to her head like wine. So largely did it bulk in her field of vision, that she could see nothing else. But now, she could no longer live without it and began to be obsessed with fears lest something of it be lost, or its smooth course disturbed. On her way home from these visits she glanced anxiously about her, scanning each figure that crossed her path, each cottage window which might hide prying eyes. Her ear grew quick to catch the sound of steps, of voices and of plough-teams at work in the fields. Now and then she came to a standstill, pale of face, and trembling like the poplar leaves above her head.

One morning, as she was thus returning, she suddenly thought that she saw the long barrel of a gun pointed directly at her. It was sticking out at an angle from behind a small cask half buried in the grass at the edge of a ditch. She was almost ready to faint with terror, but continued to move forward, and a man emerged from the cask like a jack-in-the-box. He was wearing gaiters reaching to his knees, and a cap was pulled well down over his eyes. His teeth were chattering and his nose was red. It was Captain Binet on the look out for wild duck.

'You ought to have called out before you got so near!' he exclaimed. 'You must always give warning of your approach when you see a gun!'

In these words did the collector of taxes seek to disguise the fright he had had, for a prefectoral decree had forbidden the shooting of duck except from boats. Consequently, Monsieur Binet, in spite of his respect for the law, was actually guilty of a contravention, and kept on thinking that he heard the approaching steps of a game-keeper. But this cause for nervousness gave an edge to his pleasure. Alone in his cask, he had been savouring the delights of the chase and applauding his own cunning.

The sight of Emma seemed to take a great weight off his mind, and he at once began a conversation with her.

'It's far from warm! There's a decided nip in the air!'

She said nothing, and he went on: 'Isn't it very early for you to be about?'

'Yes,' she said, stumbling a little over her words. 'I've just been to see my child's nurse.'

'Quite so, quite so . . . I've been here since the crack of dawn, but the weather's so dirty that unless a bird plops down bang at the end of . . .'

She broke in on his speech with a 'Good day, Monsieur Binet,' and turned on her heel.

'Your obedient servant, ma'am,' he said dryly, and went back into his cask.

Emma repented of having parted so unceremoniously from the collector. No doubt he would draw the most unfavourable inferences from the event. That story of hers about the nurse was the worst thing she could have thought of as an explanation, since everybody in Yonville knew perfectly well that the Bovary child had been back now with its parents for a whole year. Besides, no one lived on that side of the town. The path she had taken led only to La Huchette. Binet must have guessed, therefore, whence she had come, and would certainly not keep silent, but would turn their meeting into matter for gossip. She spent the whole day till dusk tormenting herself in an endeavour to find a plausible lie, and ever before her eyes she had the picture of that old fool with his game-bag.

Charles, noticing after dinner that evening how worried she looked, suggested a visit to the chemist, thinking it might prove a means of distraction.

Who should be the first person she set eyes on in the shop but the collector! He was standing by the counter, with the light from the red jar full upon him. He was saying:

'Half-an-ounce of vitriol, please.'

'Justin!' shouted the apothecary, 'bring me the sulphuric acid!'

Then, to Emma, who was about to go upstairs to Madame Homais's room:

'It's not worth giving yourself the trouble. She's just coming down. Warm yourself by the stove while you're waiting. . . . Pray excuse me . . . Good day, Doctor'—for the chemist always found a special pleasure in using the word *doctor*, as though by addressing the other thus, he gained a sort of reflected glory—'better bring the chairs from the small parlour'—he said to the boy—'You know perfectly well that the armchairs in the drawing-room are never to be disturbed! . . .'

In his anxiety to put his own easy-chair back in its proper place, Homais was just about to hurry away from the counter when Binet asked him for half-an-ounce of sugar-acid.

'Sugar-acid,' said the chemist contemptuously, 'don't know it, never heard of the stuff. Perhaps you mean oxalic acid—that's what you want, isn't it, oxalic?'

Binet explained that he wanted something to make a copper solvent for scouring some of his shooting equipment which had got rusty.

Emma began to tremble.

Said the chemist:

'Indeed, this weather is far from propitious: an excess of humidity in the air.'

'All the same,' remarked the collector with a sly expression, 'there are *some* people who don't seem to mind it!'

She appeared to be on the point of choking.

'There's something else I want too, give me . . .'

'Will he never go away!' she thought.

'. . . half an ounce of colophony and some turpentine, four ounces of yellow wax and an ounce and a half of animal black, please, to clean my polished leather straps.'

The apothecary was just beginning to cut the wax when Madame Homais appeared with Irma in her arms, Napoleon beside her, and Athalie behind. She went across to the window and sat down on the velvet-covered bench which stood beneath it. The boy squatted on a footstool, while his elder sister prowled round the box containing jujube paste* which was close by her dear papa. The latter went on with his work of filling containers, corking bottles, sticking on labels and making up packages. No one spoke, and the only thing to be heard was the occasional tinkle of weights in the scales, and a few muttered words addressed by the chemist to his apprentice.

'And how may *your* young lady be doing?' asked Madame Homais suddenly.

'Silence!' exclaimed her husband, who was entering figures on his scribbling block.

'Why didn't you bring her?' went on the lady in a lower voice.

'Ssh!' Emma replied, pointing to the apothecary.

But Binet, intent on examining his bill, had probably heard nothing of all this. At last he went out, and Emma heaved a deep sigh of relief.

'How heavily you're breathing!' said Madame Homais.

'It's on account of the heat,' she replied.

As a result of this incident, they discussed next day how best to arrange their meetings. Emma suggested bribing his servant with a present, but it seemed wiser to find some discreet house in Yonville. Rodolphe promised to look out for one.

All through that winter, he came after dark, three or four times a week, to the garden. Emma had been careful to remove the key from the wicket gate, and Charles had come to the conclusion that it was lost.

To warn her of his presence, Rodolphe would throw a handful of gravel against the shutters. Emma, as soon as she heard the sound, would jump to her feet, but quite often had to wait, because Charles had a mania for sitting by the fire endlessly chattering.

She could scarce contain her impatience. If she could have made him jump out of the window by merely looking at him, she would have done so. Finally, she began to make herself ready for the night. This done, she would take up a book and go on reading quite quietly as though she were enjoying it mightily. But Charles, who was already in bed, would call to her to come.

'Come to bed, Emma,' he would say: 'It's late.'

'I'm coming.'

But finding that the glare of the candles got into his eyes, he would turn his face to the wall and at once fall asleep. Then she would creep from the room, holding her breath, trembling with eagerness, wearing her nightdress and with a smile upon her lips.

Rodolphe had a large cloak. In this he wrapped her, putting his arm about her waist, and leading her in silence to the bottom of the garden. Their chosen spot was under the arbour, the same bench of rotting wood where once, on summer nights, Léon had gazed so languishingly upon her. Nowadays, she scarcely gave him a thought.

The stars shone through the leafless branches of the jasmine bush. They could hear at their backs the rippling of the river, and, now and again, the rattle of dry reeds on the bank. Great masses of shadow, here and there, swelled about them in the darkness, and sometimes, swept by a single shuddering movement, seemed to rise and hang above their heads like huge blurred waves advancing to overwhelm them. The cold of the night air made them cling closer together. Their sighs seemed louder, their eyes, which only with difficulty each could see, looked larger, and the silence between them was broken now and then by muted whispers which struck on their hearts with a crystal clearness and spread with a myriad echoes through the darkness.

When it rained they took refuge in the consulting-room which stood between the out-house and the stable. She would light one of the kitchen candles which she had hidden behind the books. Rodolphe would make himself as comfortable as though he had been at home. The sight of the bookshelves, the desk and the general arrangement of the room, provoked him to a show of mirth, and he could not refrain from making a number of jokes at Charles's expense which Emma found distinctly embarrassing. She would have liked him to be more serious, even, at times, more dramatic, as, for instance, on one occasion when she thought she heard the sound of approaching footsteps on the garden path.

'Somebody's coming!' she said.

He blew out the light.

'Have you got a pistol?'

'Whatever for?'

'Why . . . to defend yourself!' said Emma.

'Against your poor unfortunate husband?' Rodolphe finished the phrase with a movement which seemed to signify—I could crush him like a fly with a flick of the finger!

She was amazed by his courage, though frequently rather scandalized by a sort of indelicacy and naïve coarseness in his attitude.

He gave a good deal of thought to this mention of the pistol. If she had meant it seriously, how ridiculous it was, he decided, rather hateful, even, for he had no reason whatever to dislike the excellent

Charles, being himself in no way 'devoured by jealousy'—as it is generally styled. In this matter of her husband, Emma had sworn a solemn oath which he, in his turn, had regarded as being rather lacking in taste.

Besides, she was becoming extremely sentimental. She had insisted on an exchange of miniatures, and they had both cut off great handfuls of hair. She was now asking him to give her a ring—a real wedding-ring—as the symbol of their eternal union. Frequently she spoke to him of the bells at eventide, or of the *voice of Nature*, and would talk of her mother and of his, whom he had lost twenty years before. That, however, did not prevent Emma from consoling him in the kind of baby-language which might have been suitable in the case of a lost child. She even went so far as to say, gazing at the moon:

'I am sure that far away, up there, they are smiling down on our love!'

But how pretty she was! So few of the women he had possessed had been so frank and ingenuous! This love without wantonness was something quite new in his experience. It took him out of the habit of his easy conquests, and flattered at once his pride and his sensuality. Though his solid middle-class good-sense despised Emma's exalted emotionalism, he could not, in his heart of hearts, but find it charming, seeing that he was its object. Sure of her devotion, he no longer took pains to please her, and insensibly, his manner towards her changed.

No longer, as in the old days, did he say those sweet and tender things that once had drawn tears from her eyes, nor indulge now in the violent caresses which formerly had made her mad. The great love in which she swam as in an element, seemed to be growing less dense beneath her, like the water of a river contracting in its bed. She saw the mud, but would not believe her eyes and redoubled her tenderness. He took less and less trouble to conceal his indifference.

She did not know whether she regretted having yielded to him, or whether, on the contrary, she did not love him the more devotedly. The sense of humiliation which swept over her when she thought how weak she had been, turned to a bitter rancour which physical delights merely palliated. It was not so much attachment as a sort of state of permanent seduction which bound them to one another. He subjugated her, and she was almost frightened of him.

The surface of their lives, however, seemed as unruffled as ever now that Rodolphe had succeeded in conducting their adulterous relations in his own way, and when, at the end of six months, spring came round again, they were like an old married couple calmly tending a domestic flame. This was the time of the year at which old Rouault always sent a turkey in memory of his mended leg. A letter was regularly enclosed with the gift. Emma cut the string which fastened it to the basket, and read the following lines:

My dear children:

I trust that this finds you in good health, and that the bird will prove to be even better than the others, because it seems to me rather more tender as well as larger. Next time, for a change, I shall send you a cock, unless you still prefer the *peckers*, and please don't forget to send me back the hamper, and the last two also. I have had a misfortune with the cart-shed. The roof blew off one windy night and got hung up in the trees. And the harvest hasn't been any too good either. So I don't know when I shall be getting over to see you. Now that I am all by myself it is terribly difficult for me to leave the house, my poor Emma!

At this point there was a gap between the lines, as though the old fellow had dropped his pen while he indulged in a spell of day-dreaming.

I am pretty well except for a cold which I caught the other day at Yvetot Fair where I went to hire a shepherd having turned the old one off because he was too fanciful in the matter of food. One really is to be pitied having to deal with such rascals, besides he was very dishonest too. I was told by a pedlar who had a tooth pulled this winter when he was in your part of the world that Bovary is working as hard as ever. Which didn't surprise me and he showed me his tooth. We had some coffee together. I asked him if he had seen you. He said no but he had noticed two horses in the stable so I conclude that business is good. So much the better my dear children and may the good God send you all possible happiness. I am very sorry not to have made the acquaintance of my dearly beloved granddaughter Berthe Bovary yet. I have planted a wild plum for her in the garden underneath your window and I won't have anyone touch it except perhaps later on to make jam which I shall keep in the store-cupboard for her when she pays me a visit. Good-bye my dear children. I send you a kiss daughter and you too son-in-law and one on both cheeks for the little girl.

I am very sincerely
your loving father
Théodore Rouault

She sat for some minutes holding the coarse paper between her fingers. So densely interlaced were the spelling mistakes that to follow the chatter of kind thoughts embedded in it was, for her, like trying to find a hen half buried in a thorn-hedge. The writer had obviously dried the ink with ashes from the fire, because a little grey dust slid from the pages on to her dress. She could almost see her father bending towards the hearth and reaching for the tongs. What a long time it was since she had sat by him on the settle in the chimney-corner burning the end of a stick in the crackling fire of driftwood! . . . She remembered the summer evenings bright with sunlight, the whinnying of the colts as they sheered off at a gallop when anyone approached. . . . A beehive stood beneath the window, and sometimes the bees, circling in the sun, would strike against the panes like little bouncing balls of gold. How happy she had been in those far-off days!—how free!—how full of hope!—what illusions she had treasured!—and now they had gone for good! She had squandered these things in the waywardness of her heart, at every successive stage of her life— maidenhood, marriage, love—losing them one after the other as she grew older, like a traveller who leaves fragments of his wealth at every inn along his road.

But on whom could she pin the responsibility for her unhappiness? Where was the extraordinary catastrophe which had turned her life upside down? She raised her head and looked about her, as though seeking the cause of all her suffering.

A ray of April sunshine touched the cups and saucers on the dresser. The fire was burning. Beneath her slippered feet she could feel the soft surface of the carpet. The day was clear, the weather warm, and she could hear her child chortling with laughter.

As a matter of fact, the little girl was tumbling in the drying hay. She was lying flat on her stomach at the top of a rick, while her nurse kept her from falling by clutching her petticoat. Lestiboudois was close by, raking, and each time he came within reach, she leaned over the edge, beating the air with both arms.

'Bring her to me!' cried her mother running to take her. 'How I love you, my poor little mite!—how I love you!'

Then, noticing that the tips of the child's ears were dirty, she rang the bell for hot water, and set about cleaning her, changing her linen, her shoes and stockings, and asking her endless questions about her health, just as though she had that moment returned from a long journey. Finally, with one last kiss and a little shedding of tears, she handed her over again to the servant who had been standing there quite dumbfounded by so excessive a display of affection.

That evening, Rodolphe found her more serious than usual.

It'll pass—he said to himself: It's just one of her moods.

He failed to keep three successive appointments with her. When, at last, he did come, she received him coldly, almost disdainfully.

'You're wasting your time, my pet. . . .' He pretended not to notice her melancholy sighs, nor yet the handkerchief which she took out.

It was then that Emma repented.

She even began to ask herself why she detested Charles, and whether it might not be better for her were she able to love him. But so little nourishment did these revivals of sentiment get from him, that her desire for self-sacrifice had no outlet.

And then, at just the right moment, the apothecary provided her with the opportunity for which she was looking.

CHAPTER XI

HE had recently read high praise of a new method for the treatment of club-foot, and, being an enthusiast for progress, now conceived the patriotic idea of setting Yonville abreast of the times by giving it for its very own a surgical operation designed to cure this deformity.

'After all'—he said to Emma—'what do you risk? Look at the thing sensibly'—and he began to mark off on his fingers the many different advantages of such an experiment—almost certain success, relief from pain for the patient and a much improved appearance, immediate fame for the operator. 'Why should not your husband extend a helping hand to Hippolyte over at the Golden Lion? Incidentally, the lad would talk about his marvellous recovery to every traveller using the inn, and . . .'—here Homais dropped his voice and glanced cautiously about him—'. . . is there any reason why I shouldn't send a brief account of the incident to the papers? . . . a printed article is read by a lot of people . . . they talk . . . and in that way a snowball gets started. Who knows what the effect might not be!'

Why, if it came to that, shouldn't Bovary succeed? Emma had no reason for thinking that he lacked ability: and, if he did succeed, what a source of satisfaction it would be to her to know that she had persuaded him to adopt a course of action which might add to his reputation and provide a substantial increase to his income? She longed with all her heart for something more solid to lean upon than love.

Charles, attacked on one side by the apothecary and on the other by his wife, allowed his better judgement to be influenced. He sent to Rouen for Dr Duval's book,* and, every evening, sat with his head in his hands, studying its contents. While he read all about the equine, varine and valgine forms,* that is to say—talipes equinus, talipes varus and talipes valgus (or, to put the matter more simply, the different ways in which the foot can deviate from the normal— downwards, inwards or outwards) together with the cognate subjects of *strephypopody* and *strephanopody* (in plain words, depressant twisting or upward straightening), Monsieur Homais was using all his powers of persuasion in an effort to induce the young man at the inn to submit to the operation.

'You'll feel scarcely anything. At the worst you'll experience a mere momentary discomfort, a prick, as when you are being lightly bled—not nearly so bad as having a corn cut.' Hippolyte rolled unintelligent eyes in an agony of indecision.

'Not', continued the chemist, 'that it is any of my business. My feeling for you alone prompts me to speak as I do—my feeling for you and my love of mankind in general. I should be delighted, my dear fellow, to see you freed of your hideous malformation, and of that maladjustment in the lumbar region which, no matter how brave a face you may put upon it, must, of necessity, cause you considerable physical discomfort while in the exercise of your calling.'

Homais went on to point out how brisk, how agile, he would feel once the operation had been performed. He went further, and hinted that he would be a great deal more attractive to the ladies—at which suggestion the lad grinned sheepishly. The chemist then shifted his ground and proceeded to attack his vanity.

'Heavens above! Call yourself a man! Suppose you'd had to enlist, suppose you'd had to fight—what then, my boy?'

—with which words he took himself off, saying that he could not understand such obstinacy, such blindness, such a refusal to profit from the marvels of science.

At length the wretched youth consented. It was as though there were a conspiracy against him. Binet, who never meddled in other people's business, Madame Lefrançois, Artémise, the neighbours, even the Mayor, Monsieur Tuvache—everyone, in fact, took a hand in lecturing him, till he felt thoroughly ashamed. But what really decided him was the thought that the operation *would cost him nothing*. Bovary went so far as to promise that he would provide the necessary apparatus at his own expense. This act of generosity was Emma's idea, and Charles consented, saying to himself in his fondness, that his wife was an angel.

Acting under the chemist's directions, he got the local carpenter, with the assistance of a locksmith, to construct a kind of box weighing about eight pounds, in the fabrication of which neither iron nor wood, sheet-metal, screws nor nuts, were spared. Three times the work had to be scrapped and begun again from the beginning, but at last it was completed.

But before he could decide which of Hippolyte's tendons to cut, it was first necessary to determine the exact nature of his malformation. The foot, in his case, was in an almost completely straight line with the leg, though this did not prevent it from being turned inwards, so that it could be classified as an example of the equine variation with a slight tendency to the varus, or, alternatively, as a slight case of varus with strong equine symptoms. But in spite of the equine appendage which was, in fact, as large as a horse's hoof, with rough skin, brittle tendons, coarse big toe, and black nails which might well have been the rivets on a horse-shoe, the poor taliped ran about from morning to night as nimbly as a stag. He was to be seen continually in the square, jumping round the carts, always moving with his inadequate limb well forward. Indeed, it seemed actually to be stronger than its companion. By dint of being used, it had, as it were, developed the moral qualities of patience and energy, and the harder the work demanded of it, the better pleased it seemed to be.

Since the deformity was of an equine nature, it would be necessary to cut the Achilles' tendon, though it might be advisable, later, to deal also with the anterior tibial muscle in order to get rid of the varus—for the doctor did not dare undertake the two operations at one and the same time. As it was, he was trembling with anxiety lest he might injure some vital region about which he knew nothing.

Not Ambroise Paré practising the direct ligature of an artery for the first time since Celsus had done the same thing fifteen centuries earlier; not Dupuytren opening an abscess through a thick layer of brain; not Gensoul* attempting the first operation for the removal of the upper maxillary, can have experienced such a beating of the heart, so tense a concentration of the mental faculties, as Monsieur Bovary when he approached Hippolyte, tenotome* in hand. He had beside him, as in a hospital, a table on which were a pile of lint, waxed threads and a great number of bandages—every bandage, in fact, contained in the apothecary's shop. It was Monsieur Homais who had been busy from early dawn organizing all these preparations, which he did as much with the object of dazzling the multitude as of satisfying himself with the illusion of efficiency.

Charles made an incision in the skin. There was a dry, cracking sound. The tendon was cut, the operation finished. Hippolyte could not get over his surprise. He covered Bovary's hands with kisses.

'Now, you mustn't get excited!' said the apothecary. 'You can express your gratitude to your benefactor later.'

He went down to announce the result to six inquisitive loungers who were waiting in the yard, imagining that they would see Hippolyte walk out of the house without limping. Then Charles, having adjusted the mechanical aid to the patient's leg, went home.

Emma was on the doorstep, anxiously awaiting his return. She flung her arms round his neck. They sat down to dinner. Charles ate a large meal, and even expressed a desire for a cup of coffee with his dessert, a form of self-indulgence which he permitted himself only on Sundays, when they had guests.

The evening passed pleasantly in talk and shared dreams of the future. They spoke together of the fortune they would make, of the improvements they would introduce into their home. He saw his fame spreading far and wide, his prosperity growing, his wife for ever devoted to him. She, too, was happy at this opportunity of finding refreshment for her spirit in a new emotion, a healthier, a better emotion than she had so far known; of being able to feel some degree of tenderness for the poor fellow who was so dotingly fond of her. The thought of Rodolphe did, for a moment, pass through her mind, but her eyes found their way back to Charles's face, and she even noticed, with some surprise, that his teeth were not at all bad.

They were in bed when Monsieur Homais, braving the indignation of the cook, rushed into their room with a freshly written sheet of paper in his hand. It was the announcement which he meant to send to the *Fanal de Rouen*. He had brought it for them to read.

'*You* read it,' said Bovary.

Homais began:

'In spite of the prejudices which still cover a large part of the face of Europe like a net, light has begun to break through to our countryside. Last Tuesday, our little town of Yonville was the scene of a surgical experiment which was, at the same time, an act of the highest philanthropy. Monsieur Bovary, one of our most distinguished practitioners. . . .'

'Oh, but that's really going *too* far!' said Charles, who was almost speechless from emotion. . . .

'Nonsense. . . .'

'operated on a case of club-foot. . .'

'I have avoided using technical terms, because you know what newspapers are. Not everybody might understand. The masses must . . .'

'True,' said Bovary: 'please go on.'

'Well then, to resume'—said the chemist.

'. . . Monsieur Bovary, one of our most distinguished practitioners, operated on a case of club-foot, the patient being Hippolyte Tautain, who for the past twenty-five years has filled the office of ostler at the Golden Lion hotel on the place d'Armes, kept by Madame Lefrançois. The novelty of the attempt, and the interest aroused, had drawn so large a crowd of townspeople, that the entry to the house was positively blocked. The operation was performed as though by magic, and the few drops of blood visible on the surface of the patient's skin seemed to have appeared only in order to bear witness to the fact that the rebellious tendon had finally yielded to the surgeon's art. Strangely enough, the youth (and this assertion comes from an eye-witness) felt no pain. His condition at the moment of writing leaves nothing to be desired. Everything contributes to the belief that his period of convalescence will be short. It is by no means improbable that when the next local occasion of merry-making comes round, we shall see our good Hippolyte playing his part in the bacchic revels with a host of happy companions, proving by his high spirits and nimbleness of limb, the completeness of his cure. All honour to our generous men of learning! All honour to those indefatigable spirits who consecrate their nights to the betterment, to the relief, of their fellow men. Thrice honour where honour is due! Should we not cry aloud that the blind shall see, the deaf hear and the lame walk? All that fanaticism once promised to a chosen few, science has now brought within the reach of all mankind. We mean to keep our readers regularly informed of the successive phases of this remarkable cure.'

But all this did not alter the fact that, five days later, old Madame Lefrançois turned up in a terrible state, crying:

'Help! He's dying! I don't know what to do!'

Charles hurried to the Golden Lion, and the chemist, seeing him rush bare-headed across the square, left his shop to take care of itself, and was quickly on the scene. Breathless, flushed and anxious, he hastened up the stairs, asking everyone he passed:

'Has anything untoward occurred relative to our interesting taliped?'

The poor taliped in question was twisting and turning in the most appalling convulsions. So violent were his movements that the mechanical contraption in which his leg was encased struck against the wall with such vigour that it seemed likely to bring it tumbling about his ears.

With many precautions to avoid disturbing the position of the limb, the doctor removed the box. A hideous spectacle was revealed. The shape of the foot was completely obliterated by swelling, and the skin was drawn so tight that it seemed on the point of bursting. The whole surface of the member was covered by an ecchymosis* occasioned by the wonderful apparatus.

Hippolyte had been complaining for some time that it hurt him, but nobody had paid any attention to his protestations. It was impossible now to maintain that he had been altogether wrong, and the leg was left for a while unconfined. But scarcely had the swelling to some extent abated, than the two *savants* judged it advisable to re-adjust the mechanism, this time screwing it down more tightly than ever in order to expedite the process of the cure. Three days later Hippolyte could no longer endure the torture, and once again they removed the constriction. They gazed in amazement at the result of their efforts. A livid tumescence had spread from the foot to the leg, marked here and there with angry gatherings from which a black liquid was exuding. The case was taking an ugly turn. Hippolyte began to show signs of exhaustion, and Madame Lefrançois installed him in the small parlour next to the kitchen in order that he might at least have something to distract his mind. But the tax-collector, who came in every day for his dinner, complained bitterly of having so unpleasant a neighbour, and the patient was moved into the billiard-room.

He lay there beneath the coarse blankets, pale, unshaven, hollow-eyed. Occasionally he turned his sweat-soaked face on the dirty pillow which was crawling with flies. Madame Bovary paid him a visit, bringing linen for compresses, speaking words of consolation, and urging him to keep his spirits up. Not that he suffered from any lack of company, especially on market-days, when the room was filled with hobbledehoys knocking the balls about, fencing with the cues, smoking, drinking, singing and shouting.

'How goes it?' they would ask, slapping him on the back. 'Can't say you look up to much. But it's your own fault: you ought to have . . .'—done this, that or the other.

They told him stories of people who had been cured by quite other methods than those he had adopted and, just to comfort him, they would add:

'Fact is, you cosset yourself too much. Get up for a change instead of lolling in bed like a king! But king or no king, you don't exactly smell good, you old ruffian!'

The trouble was that the gangrene was moving higher and higher. The sight of it made even Bovary feel sick. He came every hour, every few minutes. Hippolyte gazed at him with eyes of terror, and stammered through his sobs—

'When will I get well? Oh save me! It's so bad, it's so bad. . . .'

Whenever the doctor took his departure he told his victim to be very careful about what he ate.

'Don't listen to him, my lad,' said Madame Lefrançois. 'They've made enough of a martyr of you as it is. You'll waste your strength. Come on now, swallow!'—and she would offer him bowls of rich soup, slices of mutton, hunks of bacon, and occasional glasses of brandy which he was too weak to raise to his lips.

The Abbé Bournisien, hearing that he was worse, insisted on being admitted to the sick-room. He began by sympathizing with the lad's sufferings, though he declared at the same time that he ought to rejoice in them, since it was God's will that he should be in his present state. He must seize the opportunity of making his peace with heaven. 'For', said the ecclesiastic, 'you must admit that you have somewhat neglected your religious duties. You were rarely, if ever, to be seen at the Divine Office. How many years is it since you last approached the Holy Table? I fully realize that your work and the hurly-burly of your daily life have left you little time in which to give thought to your eternal salvation, but now is the chance for you to examine your conscience. There is no reason to despair. I have seen many great sinners call on his mercy when they were about to be summoned to the Judgement Seat (though such, of course, is not your case) and they assuredly died in a state of spiritual comfort. It is to be hoped that you, no less than they, will be to us a salutary example. Why should you not, for instance, just as a matter of pre-caution, say each morning and evening one *Ave Maria* and one *Paternoster*? Do that—do it for me, as a kindness to me. After all, it will cost you nothing . . . will you promise?'

The poor devil promised. The curé came again in the course of the next few days. He chatted with Madame Lefrançois, and told a number of anecdotes salted with jokes and puns which Hippolyte was quite incapable of understanding. Then, snatching at any opportunity that occurred, he would turn the talk into religious channels, assuming for the occasion an expression of suitable solemnity.

His zeal apparently succeeded, for, in no long time, the taliped evinced a desire to go on a pilgrimage to Bon-Secours,* should he be cured. Monsieur Bournisien raised no objection to this scheme. Two precautions were better than one, he said, and the sufferer would be *risking nothing*.

The apothecary waxed indignant over what he called these *priestly manœuvres*, asserting that they were imperilling Hippolyte's con-valescence. More than once he said to Madame Lefrançois:

'Leave him alone! Leave him alone; you are weakening his stamina with all this mystery-mongering!'

But the good woman would not listen to him. It was, she main-tained, *entirely his fault* that all this had happened. Out of sheer perversity, she hung a stoup of holy water, adorned with a twig of boxwood,* above the bed.

Nevertheless, religion no more than surgery seemed capable of effecting a cure and there appeared to be no way of keeping the putrefaction from spreading upwards towards the stomach. However often the medicines were changed and the compresses renewed, the muscles grew slacker with each day that passed, and Charles finally replied with an affirmative nod when Madame Lefrançois suggested that she should, as a counsel of despair, be allowed to send for Monsieur Canivet of Neufchâtel, who was renowned far and wide for his skill.

This colleague, a qualified practitioner of about fifty, completely self-assured and in the enjoyment of a good practice, could not restrain himself from uttering a contemptuous laugh when he found the leg to be gangrened as far as the knee. Having declared that there was nothing for it but amputation, he took himself off to the chemist's house, there to inveigh against the fools who had reduced the wretched man to such a condition. Taking hold of Monsieur Homais by the button of his coat, and shaking him, he shouted in the full publicity of the shop:

'These damned Paris inventions! You see now what the theorizing of these metropolitan pundits leads to! It's all on a par with strabism chloroform and lithotropy,*—a farrago of monstrous nonsense which the government ought to forbid! All they care about is being clever! They stuff remedies down your throat without bothering about the consequences. We poor country dolts are not endowed with their brilliance. We hold no high-sounding degrees, and we don't dress ourselves up to the nines like a pack of coxcombs. *We* merely concern ourselves with the practice of medicine and the healing of the sick. It would never occur to us to operate on people who are perfectly sound in wind and limb! Straighten club-feet, indeed! D'you really think that club-feet *can* be straightened? It's about as sensible to believe that as that a hunchback can have his spine put to rights!'

Talk of this kind caused Homais acute suffering. But he dissimulated his embarrassment behind a courtier's smile, since it was in his interest to keep on the right side of Monsieur Canivet, whose prescriptions sometimes penetrated as far as Yonville. He made, therefore, no attempt to defend Bovary, and even refrained from uttering any observation touching the doctor's methods. False to his principles, he sacrificed personal dignity to the more important considerations of his trade.

A major amputation by Dr Canivet was a considerable event in the life of the village. When the great day came, the inhabitants were all early astir, and the main street, crowded though it was, had a somewhat lugubrious air, as though an execution were about to be carried out. There was much discussion of Hippolyte's case at the grocer's. The shops did no business, and Madame Tuvache, the Mayor's wife, never once stirred from her window, so eager was she to see the surgeon arrive. He came at last, driving his own trap. But because the right-hand spring had lost some of its resilience as the result of long submission to his obesity, the vehicle leaned slightly to one side, revealing on the seat beside him a huge box covered in sheepskin dyed red. Its three brass locks glittered with authority.

As soon as he had driven tempestuously into the inn yard, he shouted for somebody to come and take his horse out, after which he paid a visit to the stable to make sure that it was given a proper feed of oats. For whenever he made his rounds, he gave first attention to the welfare of his mare and the housing of his trap. This habit of his had led people to say that Monsieur Canivet was a 'card', and his refusal ever to be shaken out of his calm increased the estimation in which he was held. The universe might have crashed about him, and its inhabitants perished to the last man, he would not have abated one jot or tittle of his 'little ways'. Homais appeared.

'Remember, I'm counting on you!' said the surgeon. 'Is everything ready? Well, then, let's get started.'

But the apothecary confessed with a blush that he was too sensitive to witness so terrible an operation.

'When one is only a spectator,' he said, 'well, you know how it is. One's imagination gets all worked up. My nervous system is so highly strung. . . .'

'Fiddlesticks!'—broke in Canivet. 'I should have said, from the look of you, that blood-pressure was more likely to be *your* trouble—which doesn't surprise me in the least, seeing that you chemist fellows are for ever mugged up in your kitchen. That sort of life is bound to have a bad effect on the health. Look at me! Up every morning at four, shave in cold water (I never feel the cold), and not a flannel waistcoat to my name. Never catch cold—nothing wrong with my chest. I live any old how, eating what comes my way like a philosopher. That's why I'm not a delicate plant like you! Why, I'd as soon carve up a Christian as a fowl . . . Habit, I suppose you'll say, just habit. . . .'

Without so much as a glance at Hippolyte who was lying in bed sweating with terror, the two of them began a discussion in the course of which the apothecary compared the cool-headedness of the surgeon to that of a general. This analogy pleased Canivet, who waxed eloquent on the demands which his art made on a man. He regarded it, he said, as a sacred trust, no matter how much it might be degraded by local medicos. Then, turning to the sick man, he examined the bandages supplied by Homais—the same set had served at the operation for club-foot—and asked for somebody to hold the limb for him. Lestiboudois was sent for, and Monsieur Canivet, first rolling up his sleeves, went into the billiard-room, while the apothecary stayed with Artémise and the landlady, both of them looking whiter than their aprons and busily listening at the door.

Meanwhile, Bovary did not dare stir from his house. He remained downstairs in the parlour sitting by the fireless grate, his chin sunk on his chest, his hands clasped, his eyes set in a fixed stare. What a disaster, he thought: what a disappointment!—and after he had taken every imaginable precaution. Ill luck had dogged him. Nor could he take comfort from the thought that it did not matter. If Hippolyte died, *he* would be looked on as his murderer. What sort of an explanation could he give when questions were asked, on his rounds, about the incident? Could it be that he had made some mistake? He examined his conscience, but was aware of none. Even the most famous surgeons, if it came to that, sometimes made mistakes. That was what people would never believe. He would be a laughing-stock, a butt. The story would spread far and wide, to Forges, to Neufchâtel, even to Rouen! Members of the profession might even attack him in print. A regular rough and tumble of words would ensue. He would have to reply in the columns of the newspapers. Hippolyte might go so far as to take him to court. He saw himself dishonoured, ruined, lost! His imagination, assailed on all sides by hypothetical situations, bobbed about like an empty cask carried out to sea and left to the mercies of the waves.

Emma, on the opposite side of the fireplace, looked at him. She had no share in his particular humiliation, but that did not alter the fact that she was saddled with a special one of her own. What a fool she had been ever to imagine that a man like her husband could amount to anything!—as though she hadn't told herself twenty times in the past that he was the drabbest of mediocrities.

Charles began to walk up and down the room. His boots squeaked.

'Oh do sit down,' she said: 'you're getting on my nerves!'

He went back to his chair.

What had come over her that for the second time, she (as a rule so intelligent) should have made a mistake like that? Under the influence of what deplorable mania had she allowed her life to be swallowed up in a perpetual series of sacrifices? She remembered her instinctive longing for luxury, the spiritual privations of which she had been the victim, the many sordid aspects of her marriage and her home, the dreams that had fallen like wounded swallows in the mud, all the things she had desired, all the chances she had refused, all the things she might have had—and for what?

The silence which brooded over the village was rent by a blood-curdling scream. Bovary went so pale that she thought he was about to faint. A little nervous frown showed between Emma's eyes, but her thoughts continued to move in their previous direction. Everything she had done had been for *his* sake, for the sake of this creature, this man, who understood nothing, felt nothing! There he sat, quite calmly, quite blissfully unaware that the ridicule attaching to his name would henceforth sully hers no less. She had done her best to love him. She had bitterly repented in tears the fact that she had given herself to another.

'Maybe, after all, it *was* a valgus?' Bovary suddenly exclaimed from the depths of his private meditations.

The unexpected shock of the phrase, falling on her thoughts like a lead ball into a silver dish, made Emma start. She looked up, puzzled to think what he could mean, and in silence they gazed at one another, each half surprised to find the other there, so sundered had they been by secret thoughts. Charles fixed upon her the unsteady eyes of a drunkard, while, motionless in his chair, he listened to the final cries of the man whose leg was being amputated. They reached his ears in a series of long-drawn-out modulations, interspersed with thin, gasping screams, like the distant howling of some animal that was being killed. Emma bit her pale lips, twisting between her fingers a small piece of the coral which she had broken from the mantel ornament. She fixed on him her burning eyes, two fiery arrows ready to leap from the bow. Everything about him irritated her now—his face, his clothes, the things he did not say, his whole person, the mere fact that he was alive at all. She repented of her former virtue as she might have repented of a crime, and the little that now remained of it was crumbling beneath the furious blows dealt it by her pride. She took a positive delight in all the perverse ironies of adultery triumphant. The memory of her lover came back to haunt her with its heady charm. She gave herself heart and soul to it, and let her thoughts dwell upon it with a new zest. Charles seemed to be as completely cut off from all contact with her life, as eternally absent from the concern of her heart, as impossible and as wholly obliterated, as though he were really at the point of death and she saw him there before her in the last hopeless struggle of dissolving mortality.

There was a sound of footsteps on the pavement. Charles looked up. Through the slats of the lowered blinds, he could see Dr Canivet standing in full sunlight by the market-hall, mopping his brow with a silk handkerchief. Behind him was Homais carrying a large red box. The two men moved off towards the shop.

In a sudden impulse of tenderness and discouragement, he turned towards his wife, and said:

'Kiss me, dear.'

'Oh, leave me alone!' she answered, her face crimson with anger.

'What is the matter with you?' he said, amazed by her outburst, and again, 'what is the matter with you? Don't be so distressed. Cheer up, you know I love you . . . come, dear. . . .'

'Stop it!' she cried, and the expression of her face was terrible.

Running from the room, she slammed the door so violently that the barometer jumped from its nail on the wall and crashed to the ground.

Charles collapsed into his armchair, utterly shaken, wondering what could be wrong with her, imagining some nervous ailment, weeping, and conscious of some vague presence in the room beside him, a presence that was at once deadly and incomprehensible.

When Rodolphe turned up in the garden that evening, he found his mistress waiting for him on the bottom step of the terrace. They fell into one another's arms, and all the ill-feeling that had been between them melted like snow in the heat of their embrace.

CHAPTER XII

THEIR love-making began all over again. Emma would frequently sit down in the middle of the day, write him a letter and beckon through the window to Justin. Then the boy would take off his apron before setting off at full speed for La Huchette. A little later Rodolphe would appear. She only wanted to tell him how bored she was, how wholeheartedly she loathed her husband and the life she was called upon to endure.

'But what can I do about it?' he exclaimed one day in an access of irritation.

'You could do a great deal, if you only would. . . .'

She was sitting on the ground between his knees, her hair loose, a far-away look in her eyes.

'*What* could I do?' he asked.

She sighed.

'We could go away and live together . . . somewhere. . . .'

'You must be mad!' he answered with a laugh: 'how could we possibly do that?'

She returned to the subject. He pretended not to understand and edged the conversation into other channels. He could not see why she should make such a fuss about anything so simple as love. But there was a motive, a reason in what she did. She needed something over and above her attachment, something that should give it strength and purpose.

The tenderness of her feeling for him grew stronger as the days passed. It increased in proportion as the thought of her husband became more and more repellent. Surrender to the one bred hatred of the other. Never had Charles been so distasteful to her; never before had she found his fingers so spatulate, his mind so stodgy, his manners so common, as when she sat with him after one of her meetings with Rodolphe. All the time that she was playing the part of virtuous wife her mind was on fire with memories of the familiar head with its black hair falling in curls over a sun-tanned brow, of the figure at once so strong and so elegant, of the man who combined intellectual experience with such fervent desire. It was for him that she filed her nails with an artist's care. She could never put enough cold cream on her skin or patchouli on her handkerchief. She loaded herself with bracelets, rings and necklaces. Whenever he was due to come, she filled her two big blue vases with roses, giving as much thought to the arrangement of her room and to the attiring of her person as might some courtesan in readiness for the coming of a prince. The servant was kept for ever bleaching her linen, and all day long Félicité was confined to the kitchen where young Justin, who often kept her company, sat watching her at work.

With his elbow resting on the long board at which she did her ironing, he feasted his eyes on the feminine finery spread all about him—dimity petticoats, neck-handkerchiefs, collarettes, drawers with running strings, enormous round the hips and tapering at the bottom.

'What's that for?' he would ask, passing his hand over a crinoline, or touching a hook, an eye.

And Félicité would laughingly reply:

'Mean to tell me you've never seen one of *them* before? Your mistress, Madame Homais, must have lots like that!'

'Oh, yes, of course, *she* has.'

Then, in a thoughtful voice, he would ask:

'But she's not a lady—like Madame?'

But seeing him wandering about her kitchen gave Félicité the fidgets. She was six years his senior, and Théodore, old Maître Guillaumin's man, was beginning to pay court to her.

'Oh, get along, do, and leave me in peace!' she would say, moving her jar of starch. 'Go and pound some almonds. Always running round after the women. Time enough for that, you little wretch, when you start growing hair on your chin!'

'Don't be cross. I'll go and clean her boots for you.'

Then he would take down Emma's boots from their place on the shelf above the fire, all dirtied with the mud of her stolen meetings. It covered his hands with a fine powder which he watched as it rose slowly in the air caught in a beam of sunlight.

'How frightened you are of hurting them!' the cook would say. She herself treated them with far less consideration, because her mistress was in the habit of passing them on to her as soon as the fabric showed signs of wear.

Emma had several pairs in her cupboard, and, consequently, took no pains to preserve them. Charles never dared to comment on her extravagance.

Because of his timidity in this respect he was induced to spend three hundred francs on a wooden leg which she saw fit to present to Hippolyte. It was a complicated piece of mechanism with a cork-lined recess for the stump, and joints actuated by springs. It was concealed by a black trouser and ended in a polished boot. But Hippolyte, not wishing to subject so handsome a limb to the wear and tear of every day, begged her to get him another one which should be more convenient. Needless to say, it was the doctor who again defrayed the cost of this fresh acquisition.

Thus equipped, the ostler gradually resumed his duties. He could be seen, as of old, moving about the village. But whenever Charles heard the brisk tap-tap of his wooden leg on the pavement, he hurriedly walked a different way.

It was Monsieur Lheureux, the draper, who had undertaken the commission, and the business gave him an opportunity of paying Emma frequent visits. He told her of his new consignments from Paris, described the many novelties in feminine finery which he could supply, was ever anxious to please, and never asked for money.

Finding it thus easy to satisfy her every whim, Emma fell an easy victim to his cajolery. When she was seized with a sudden desire to give Rodolphe a very fine riding crop which she had seen in a Rouen umbrella shop, Lheureux laid it on her table the very next week.

But the day following he brought her a bill for two hundred and seventy francs odd. Emma did not know what to do. The drawers of the desk were all empty. They owed Lestiboudois for a fortnight's work, two quarters' wages to the servant, and a number of other items. Bovary was impatiently awaiting a remittance from Monsieur Derozerays, who was in the habit of settling his doctor's bill once a year, round about St Peter's day.

She managed at first to keep Lheureux waiting, but finally he lost patience. He himself was being pressed for money; his available capital was all tied up, and if he did not get some of what she owed him, he would be compelled to take back the goods with which he had supplied her.

'Take them, then!' said Emma.

'I was only joking,' he answered. 'The crop's the thing I'm really worrying about. I should hate to have to ask your husband for it.'

'Oh, but you mustn't do that!' she said.

Ah, I touched you on a raw spot, there, my fine lady—he thought, and, secure in the discovery he had made, took his departure, saying, in his usual sibilant whisper:

'Well, well . . . we'll see. . . .'

She was thinking how she could possibly get herself out of this embarrassing situation, when the cook came in and put a little roll of blue paper on the mantelpiece. It had been sent, she said, by Monsieur Derozerays. Emma pounced on it. It contained fifteen napoleons,* the amount of the fees still owing. She heard Charles coming upstairs, dropped the coins into her drawer and turned the key.

Three days later Lheureux paid her another visit.

'I have a proposal to make,' he said. 'If, instead of settling your account, you will take . . .'

'Here's your money'—she replied, putting fifteen napoleons into his hand.

The draper was struck dumb. He concealed his disappointment, however, under a flood of apologies and offers of service, all of which Emma refused. She stood there for a few minutes turning over in the pocket of her apron the two five-franc pieces which he had given her in change. She was determined to economize so as to be in a position to pay Charles back later.

'What's the use of worrying,' she thought: 'he'll forget all about it.'

Rodolphe had received from her, in addition to the crop with an enamelled handle, a seal with the device *Amor nel cor*,* a scarf to wear in cold weather, and a cigar-case just like the one belonging to the Vicomte which Charles had once, long ago, picked up on the road and Emma had treasured ever since. He felt humiliated by these gifts, and had refused more than once to accept them. But she had insisted and at last he had given way, though with the mental reservation that she was becoming tyrannical and importunate. Besides, she was getting the strangest ideas.

'You must think of me when midnight strikes,' she said, and, if he confessed that he had not done so, she overwhelmed him with reproaches which always ended with the same question:

'Do you love me?'

'Of course I love you.'

'A great deal?'

'Yes, a great deal.'

'And you've never loved anyone else?'

'Did you think I was a virgin?' he exclaimed with a laugh.

At that Emma started to cry, and he forced himself to console her, salting his protestations with little jokes.

'It's only because I love you so,' she said. 'Do you realize that I can't live without you? Sometimes, when I am seized by a craving to see you, I feel myself torn by all the violent rancours of love. Where is he? I wonder: perhaps he's talking to some other woman: perhaps she's smiling at him, perhaps he's going up to her. . . . That isn't true, is it? There's no one you like better than me, is there? I know there are heaps of women prettier than me, but none of them know how to love you better than I do, do they? I am your slave and your concubine! You are my king, my idol! You are good, you are handsome, you are intelligent and you are strong!'

He had heard these things so often, that by now they had lost all spice of originality. She was just like all the other mistresses he had had. As the charm of novelty slipped from her like a dress, Rodolphe saw nothing but the naked horror of an eternal monotony of passion, always with the same face, always speaking the same words. This practised seducer could see no difference in the sentiments concealed beneath a similarity of surface. Because wanton, mercenary lips had murmured similar protestations in his ear, he had no great belief in the sincerity of this, his latest conquest. Strip away the exaggerations of language, he thought, and there's nothing left but the same old mediocre emotions. As though the fulness of the heart does not sometimes overflow into the emptiest of metaphors. After all, no one can ever give the exact measure of his needs, of his thoughts or his sorrows. Human language is like a cracked kettle on which we beat out tunes for bears to dance to, when all the time we are longing to move the stars to pity.

But with that conscious superiority which belongs to a man who, in any involvement, holds back something of himself, Rodolphe perceived that there were further pleasures to be extracted from this affair. He decided that all modesty was pointless, and treated her with brutal frankness. He made her his creature, pliant and corrupt. Hers was a doting kind of attachment, full of admiration for him and sensual delights for herself, a state of beatitude in which her soul was gradually lulled to sleep, sinking ever deeper into intoxication and drowning there, shrivelled like the Duke of Clarence in his butt of malmsey. Her very appearance had changed as a result of this long habit of love. Her looks had become bolder, her talk freer. She would so far forget propriety as to go walking with Monsieur Rodolphe with a cigarette between her lips, as though deliberately to flout public opinion. A time came when those who, hitherto, had doubted saw her descend from the Swallow wearing a close-fitting waistcoat cut like a man's, and could doubt no longer. Madame Bovary the elder—who after an appalling scene with her husband had taken refuge with her son—was not the least shocked of the good ladies of the place. Other things, too, she found which displeased her. In the first place, Charles had not taken her advice about forbidding his wife to read novels. Besides, she disliked the general atmosphere of the house, and allowed herself to make a number of critical observations. There were angry scenes—one in particular which had to do with Félicité.

The old lady, walking down the passage one evening, had caught the girl in the company of a man, a man of about forty with a brown beard.* At the sound of her approach he had quickly slipped out of the kitchen. Emma laughed when she heard of the incident, but her mother-in-law had flown into a rage, declaring that if all standards of decent behaviour were not to go by the board, employers had better keep an eye on their servants.

'What sort of people do you move among?' said Emma, with so impertinent a look that Madame Bovary asked her whether she cared nothing about the kind of talk *she* was giving rise to.

'Leave the room!' exclaimed the young woman, springing to her feet.

'Emma! . . . Mamma!'—cried Charles in an effort to keep the peace.

But they were too far gone in exasperation. Emma kept stamping her foot and saying:

'What manners! A peasant would behave better!'

He ran to his mother who was quite beside herself.

'An insolent, flighty creature!' she fumed: 'and maybe something worse!'

She insisted that unless she received an apology she would leave the house there and then. Charles went back to his wife and implored her to give way. He even went on his knees to her. At last:

'All right,' she answered, 'I'll go and beg her pardon.'

She was as good as her word, holding out her hand to her mother-in-law with the dignity of a marquise, and saying:

'Please accept my apologies, madame.'

Then, going upstairs to her room, she flung herself face downwards on her bed, where she lay crying like a child, her head buried in the pillows.

It had been agreed between her and Rodolphe that, should anything out of the ordinary happen, she should fasten a little piece of white paper to her shutter, so that, if he happened to be in Yonville, he might hurry round into the lane at the back of the house. Emma made the signal and waited for three-quarters of an hour, at the end of which time she suddenly saw Rodolphe at the corner of the market-hall. She was tempted to open the window and call to him, but he had already disappeared, and she drew back in despair. In a little while, however, she thought she heard somebody walking on the footpath. It must be he. She ran downstairs, and across the yard. There he was, outside the gate. She threw herself into his arms.

'For heaven's sake be careful!' he said.

'If you only knew what I have been through!' She began to tell him all that had happened, hurriedly, inconsequently, exaggerating some facts and inventing others, and interspersing the narrative with so many asides that he quite failed to follow her.

'Cheer up, my sweet: dry your eyes. You really must be patient.'

'I have been patient for four years, and utterly, utterly miserable! . . . A love like ours should be declared openly in the face of heaven. They are torturing me! I can't stand any more! Save me!'

She clasped him to her. Her eyes, brimming with tears, shone like flames seen through water. Her breast rose and fell with her rapid breathing. Never had he found her so adorable. So completely was he carried away by his passion that he lost his head.

'What are we to do?' he asked. 'What do you want us to do?'

'Take me away!' cried Emma 'Please, please take me away!'

Her mouth fastened on his as though she would tear from his lips the unexpected consent which he breathed out in a kiss.

'But . . .' he said.

'What?'

'How about the child? . . .'

She thought for a few minutes and then replied.

'We'll take her with us. It can't be helped, we must . . .'

What a woman! he reflected, as she left him and he saw her move away.

She slipped into the garden, where somebody was calling her name.

In the course of the next few days, old Madame Bovary was amazed at the change which seemed to have come over her daughter-in-law. Emma was, indeed, far more docile than usual, and carried her deferential manner to the extreme of asking the older woman to give her a recipe for pickling gherkins.

Was this new attitude adopted only that she might the more successfully pull the wool over both their eyes, or did she really, in a mood of voluptuous stoicism, want to feel more deeply the bitterness of all that she was about to abandon? Not that she really heeded them. On the contrary, she was living as one lost in the anticipation of happiness. With Rodolphe it formed, this happiness to come, a never-ending subject of conversation. She would lean against his shoulder and murmur:

'Do you dream, as I do, of our being together in the mail-coach? Is it really going to happen? I feel that when the horses start it will be just as though we had gone up in a balloon bound for the stars. I am counting the days . . . are you?'

Never had she looked so lovely as at this time. She had that indefinable beauty which comes with happiness, with enthusiasm, with success, though in reality it betokens nothing but the harmonious adaptation of temperament to circumstance. Her longings, her troubles, the memory of the pleasures she had experienced and the illusions of her heart which time could not wither, acted upon her as do manure, rain, wind and sunlight on growing flowers. They worked a slow development in her so that she expanded into the full splendour of her nature. Her eyelids seemed moulded expressly for long, amorous gazing in which the pupils became submerged, while warm sighs distended her finely-chiselled nostrils and lifted the corners of her full lips which were shadowed, when the light fell full upon them, by a faint dark line of down. It was as though some artist, skilled in perversity, had disposed upon her nape the twisted coils of her hair. When the violence of her adulterous transports loosened them, they lay there in heavy and unstudied disarray. Her voice, nowadays, had taken on a softer timbre, and there was a softness, too, about her figure. A subtle, penetrating effluence seemed to come from the very folds of the clothes she wore and the curve of her foot. Charles found her as delicious and as irresistible as in the first days of their marriage.

When he came home at midnight, he dared not wake her. The nightlight in its porcelain bowl spread quivering circles of radiance on the ceiling, and the drawn curtains of the little cot bulged in the darkness beside the bed like a little white tent. He gazed at the two sleepers. He thought he could hear the child's gentle breathing. Soon, now, she would be growing up. Every season of every year would bring new evidence of progress. Already he could see her, in imagination, returning from school in the late afternoon, a small, laughing urchin, with ink-stains all over her smock and a basket on her arm. The next stage would be boarding-school, and that would mean a heavy drain on him. It would have to be managed somehow—but how? He turned the problem over in his mind. It occurred to him that he might rent a small farm near enough for him to keep an eye on it in the course of his professional rounds. He would lay aside any profits it might show, open a savings-bank account with them and, later on, invest the money in some kind of security. Besides, his practice was bound to grow. He counted on that happening, because he meant Berthe to have a good education, to be talented, to learn the piano. How pretty she would be at fifteen, just like her mother, and wearing big straw hats like hers in the summer. People would take them, at a distance, for two sisters. He could see her sitting with them in the evenings, when the lamp was lit, doing her work. She would embroider slippers for him, help with the household chores, fill his home with her sweetness and gaiety. Last stage of all, she would get married. He thought about that, too. They would find some decent, solid young man for her, and she would live happily ever after.

Emma was not asleep, but only pretending. While he dropped off beside her, she lay awake, her head full of quite other dreams.

For a whole week she had been journeying behind four galloping horses to a new country from which they would never return. On, on they went, sitting with linked arms, saying nothing. Sometimes, from high on a mountain-side they caught a sudden glimpse of some splendid city, all domes and bridges; harbours filled with shipping among groves of lemon, cathedrals of white marble with storks nesting on their pointed spires. The carriage moved slowly because of the great flagstones, and all around were huge banks of flowers and women in scarlet bodices selling them. The air was filled with the sound of bells, the neighing of mules, the low thrumming of guitars and the plash of fountains, the thin spray from which kept ever fresh the mountains of fruit displayed at the bases of pale statues smiling beneath the arching jets of water. As darkness fell, they arrived in some fishing village where brown nets were drying in the breeze before a row of cottages along the summit of a cliff. There they would settle down, living in a low house with a flat roof beneath the shade of palms, overlooking the sea, at the head of a gulf. They would float over the water in a gondola, they would recline in swinging hammocks. Life would be as free and easy as the silk clothes they would wear, as warm and star-spangled as the nights on which they gazed. Yet, in this vast canvas which she painted of their future, no special incident held the eye. One superb day resembled another with no more difference between them than between the waves of that sea which spread to the horizon, still and blue and sundrenched.

But at this moment in her reverie the child began to cough, or Bovary gave a louder snore than usual, and she lay there wakeful till the dawn showed pale behind the windows, and young Justin started to take down the shutters of the chemist's shop in the square.

She had asked Monsieur Lheureux to come to see her. She said:

'I shall need a cloak, a full, lined cloak with a long cape.'

'Are you going on a journey, then?' he asked.

'No, but ... Oh, no matter ... I rely on you, and I want it quickly.'

He bowed.

'I shall want a trunk, too,' she continued. 'Not too heavy a one, and of a convenient size.'

'I know precisely what you mean—something about three foot by one and a half—that's the most popular size just now.'

'And a hand-bag.'

There's something behind all this, or I'm a Dutchman! thought Lheureux.

'And you may as well take this,' said Madame Bovary, drawing her watch from her girdle: 'it will cover the cost of what I have ordered.'

But the man exclaimed that she had got an entirely wrong idea of him. They had known one another far too long for him to have any doubts of her. Really, she must not behave so childishly! But she insisted on his taking at least the chain, and he had put it in his pocket, and was already on his way out, when she called him back.

'Please leave everything for me at your shop. About the cloak'— she seemed to be turning something over in her mind—'it would be better if you did not bring that here either. Just tell me the name of the tailor, and say that I will send for it.'

Their departure was fixed for the following month. She would leave Yonville as though on a shopping expedition to Rouen. Rodolphe would have reserved their seats, seen to the passports, and even written to Paris to make sure that they should have the coach to themselves as far as Marseilles, where they would buy a carriage, and continue their journey, without stopping, as far as Genoa.* She, for her part, would see that her luggage was sent to Lheureux so that it could be loaded direct on to the Swallow. In that way, no one would have the least suspicion of what she was about to do. No mention was made of the child. Rodolphe was careful not to speak of her. Emma, quite possibly, was not thinking about her.

He wanted another two weeks in which to complete his arrangements, but, at the end of the first of them, asked for a further fortnight, saying that he had not been well. He went away for a while. August passed, and finally, after all these delays, he fixed Monday, the 4th September,* as the definite date for their departure.

Saturday came, and Sunday. Tomorrow they would be off.

Rodolphe turned up that evening earlier than usual.

'Is everything ready?' she asked.

'Yes.'

They took a turn round one of the flower-beds, and sat down on the wall near the terrace.

'You are sad,' said Emma.

'No I'm not: why should I be?'

All the same, there was a curious expression in his eyes, a sort of a tender look.

'Is it because you are going away?' she asked: 'because you are leaving all the things you love, saying good-bye to your old familiar ways? Oh, I do understand . . . I have nothing to care for in the whole world: you are my whole world. And I will be yours—your family, your country, I will look after you and love you.'

'How charming you are!' he said, taking her in his arms.

'Really?' she murmured with a laugh of pleasure. 'Do you love me? Swear you do!'

'Do I love you! I'm mad about you, my darling!'

The round crimson moon was coming up on the horizon beyond the meadows. It rose rapidly between the poplar branches, which obscured it here and there like a ragged black curtain. Then it emerged, brilliantly white, lighting up the empty sky; moving more slowly now, it let fall on the river a great splash of brightness which broke into an infinity of stars. The silver gleam appeared to turn and twist upon itself as though it had been a headless snake covered with shining scales. At other moments it resembled some monstrous candelabra scattering from each long arm a rain of melted diamonds. The mild night spread all round them. Vast expanses of shadow lay among the branches. Emma, with eyes half closed, drew in the breeze with her sighs. They spoke no word, so sunk were they in dreams. The tenderness of their first days of love had returned bank-high and silent, like the river which flowed so gently on that it brought to their senses the smell of syringa, and filled their memories with shadows deeper and more melancholy than those cast by the motionless willows on the bank. At times some night-prowling animal, hedgehog or weasel, ran hunting through the undergrowth, bringing to their ears a light rustle of leaves; and now and again they could hear the sound made by some ripe peach falling from the espaliered tree.

'How beautiful the night is,' said Rodolphe.

'We shall know others like it,' answered Emma, and then, as though speaking to herself, 'what wonder it will be to travel! . . . But why is my heart so heavy? Is it fear of the unknown . . . the breaking of old ties? . . . or is it . . . no, it is nothing but an excess of happiness! What a poor weak creature I am, am I not? . . . You must forgive me.'

'There is still time!' he exclaimed: 'think well of what you are about to do. You may repent it later.'

'Never!' she said impulsively, and then, snuggling closer to him— 'What sadness could there be in store for me? There is no desert, no precipice, no ocean I would not cross with you beside me. Our life together will be like an eternal embrace that each day grows more close and more complete. There will be nothing to trouble our happiness, no anxieties, no obstacles. We shall be alone, all in all to one another, for ever. . . . Say something . . . answer me!'

At regular intervals he interjected a 'Yes . . . yes! . . .' Her hands were playing with his hair, and she said repeatedly, in a childish voice, while great tears ran down her cheeks:

'Rodolphe! . . . Rodolphe! . . . my dear, darling Rodolphe!'

Midnight struck.

He got up to go, and, as though this movement of his had been the signal for their flight, Emma suddenly became gay and cheerful.

'Have you got the passports?'

'Yes.'

'You've forgotten nothing?'

'Nothing.'

'You're sure?'

'Certain.'

'And you will be waiting for me at the Hôtel de Provence at noon?'

He nodded.

'Till tomorrow, then!' said Emma with a final kiss.

She watched him walk away.

She did not turn back, but ran after him. Leaning out over the water, between the bushes, she cried:

'Till tomorrow!'

He was already on the other bank, walking quickly across the meadows. After a few minutes he stopped, and, seeing the white patch of her dress vanishing into the darkness like a ghost, felt his heart beating so violently that he had to lean against a tree to keep himself from falling.

'What a fool I am!' he said with a violent oath. . . . 'Oh well, she was a charming mistress while it lasted!'

As he spoke, Emma's beauty, and all the pleasure that their love had brought him, became once more vivid in his mind. At first he grew tender, then was seized with a revulsion of feeling against her.

'Damn it all!' he exclaimed with a gesture, 'why should I make myself an exile, and take on her brat as well?'

This he said to strengthen his determination.

'It's not only the encumbrance, but the expense too. . . . No, a thousand times no! . . . That would have been too idiotic!'

CHAPTER XIII

As soon as he got home, Rodolphe sat down hurriedly at his desk which stood beneath a shooting trophy in the form of a stag's head which was fastened to the wall. But with the pen already between his fingers, he could find nothing to say, and sat there, leaning on his elbows, thinking. Emma seemed to have vanished into the distant past. It was as though the resolution he had taken had suddenly opened a vast gulf between them.

To bring the thought of her more vividly before him, he started to rummage in the cupboard which stood at the head of his bed. He was looking for an old Rheims biscuit-tin in which he was in the habit of keeping the letters he had received from his many women. A smell of damp dust and withered rose-leaves came from it. The first thing he found was a pocket-handkerchief speckled with small pale stains. It was hers. She had used it on one of their walks when her nose had bled. He could remember nothing else about it. Beside it, its corners all dinted and battered, was the miniature she had given him. He thought the dress she was wearing pretentious, and the sidelong glance of her eyes rather common. But by dint of gazing on the picture and evoking the memory of its living model, he found that Emma's features were gradually losing their distinctness. It was as though the living face and its painted replica had so rubbed against one another that each had lost the clear edges of its definition. Finally, he set himself to read some of her letters. They were full of details about their journey: short, practical and urgent, like business memoranda. He was seized by a desire to read the longer ones which she had written at an earlier period. To find them at the bottom of the tin, he had to disturb the rest of its contents. Mechanically he started to turn up a mass of papers and small objects, coming at random on bouquets, a garter, a black domino, pins and locks of hair—dark hair, fair hair. Some of it, tangled in the fastenings of the box, had broken when he opened it.

Thus aimlessly wandering among the memories of his past, he began to examine the writing and the style of many different letters, letters as various in their contents as in their spelling. Here they all were, tender or jocose, facetious or melancholy. Some of the writers demanded love, some money. At times he would come on a word which brought to mind faces, gestures, the sound of a voice. Of some of the writers he could remember nothing at all.

All these women, crowding together in his thoughts, got in one another's way. They seemed to shrink in size, to assume an identity when reduced to the same level of love. He took a handful of the letters, just as they came, and amused himself for a while by tumbling them in a cascade from his right hand to his left. At length, bored by this game, and beginning to feel sleepy, he put the box back in the cupboard, saying to himself as he did so:

Just a lot of nonsense

The phrase did, in fact, sum up what he felt, for the succession of his pleasures, like boys in a school playground, had so trodden his heart under foot that now not a single shoot of green could show above ground, and what passed over it, more scatterbrained than children, did not, as they might have done, leave even a name scrabbled on the wall.

Well, he said to himself, I'd better get the thing done with. He began to write.

'Be brave, Emma, be brave. I don't want to be the cause of your life's unhappiness. . . .'

And that really is true, he thought. What I am doing is done in her interest. I am being honest with her.

'Have you ever seriously thought about this decision of yours? My poor angel, do you realize the abyss into which I was dragging you? The answer to both these questions is "No"—isn't it? You have been rushing ahead in a mood of mad confidence, believing that happiness lay round the corner. . . . What thoughtless, miserable creatures we are. . . .'

He paused, seeking some good excuse.

Suppose I told her I had lost all my money? Useless, it wouldn't have the slightest effect on her. Sooner or later I should have to start explaining things all over again. Women of her sort never listen to reason!

He thought for a moment or two, then continued.

'I shall never forget you, of that you may be sure. I shall always feel devotedly attached to you. But inevitably—(such is the fate of all human emotions)—our love would have grown less. We should have become exhausted by our own ardours, and I might have known the appalling misery of witnessing your remorse, and of sharing in it too, since who but I would have caused it? Merely to think of your present pain tortures me. Forget me, Emma! What evil fate threw us together? Why are you so beautiful? Am I to blame? No!—as God is my witness, no!—the fault was Fate's alone.'

Fate is always a telling word—he said to himself.

'If only you had been one of those many women whose hearts are trivial, I might, out of sheer selfishness, have embarked on an experiment which would have been without the slightest danger to you. But your exalted sentiments, which are at once your charm and your instrument of martyrdom, utterly prevented you—adorable creature that you are—from seeing how false a position we should have been forced into. But I share your guilt there, for I had given it no serious consideration either. I lay beneath the manchineel tree* of an ideal happiness, and did not foresee the consequences. . . .'

Perhaps she will think I am giving her up because I am afraid of the expense. . . . Oh well, that can't be helped . . . I've got to finish with her somehow!

'It is a cruel world, Emma. Wherever we went it would have pursued us. You would have been the victim of indiscreet questions, of calumny, of scorn, perhaps even, of insult. . . . You exposed to insult! . . . I have ever wished to set you on a pedestal . . . I carry the thought of you now as a talisman, and it will be with me through all my wanderings. For I am punishing myself for the evil I have done you by a self-imposed sentence of exile. I am going whither I know not. I am mad! Farewell! Be ever good, and do not forget the wretched man who has lost you. Teach your child my name, that she may remember me in her prayers.'

The wicks of the two candles flickered. Rodolphe got up to close the window. When he sat down again—

That, I think, is all, he said to himself. Ah, just one thing more, in case she tries to get on my tracks.

'I shall be far away by the time you read these melancholy lines, for I wish to fly as quickly as I can, lest I be tempted to see you again. I must not be weak. Some day I shall come back, and who knows but that in the future we may talk together calmly of our former love? . . . Adieu!'

He wrote the word a second time, separated—*A Dieu*—a touch which appealed to him as being in excellent taste.

How am I to sign myself? he wondered. Yours devotedly?—no . . .
Your friend? . . . yes, that'll do.

'Your friend.'

He read the letter through and found it thoroughly satisfactory.

Poor little woman, he thought tenderly: she will think me harder
than a rock. A few tear-stains wouldn't have done any harm, but I
can't cry . . . not that I can be blamed for that. Then, pouring out a
glass of water, he dipped his finger in it, and let a large drop fall upon
the paper. It made a pale blot on the ink.

Looking round for something with which to close the letter, his
eyes caught the seal with its motto *Amor nel cor*.

'Not perhaps altogether suitable. . . . Oh, hell, what does it
matter!'

After which, he smoked three pipes and went to bed.

Next morning, as soon as he was up (about two o'clock, for he had
slept late) Rodolphe gave instructions for a basket of apricots to be
packed. Into this he tucked the letter, concealing it beneath a layer of
vine leaves, and told his groom, Girard, to deliver it with the utmost
care to Madame Bovary. This had been his usual method of corres-
ponding with her, the basket being filled, according to the season,
with fruit or game.

'Should she ask for news of me,' he said, 'you must reply that I
have gone on a journey. The basket must be delivered personally to
her. . . . Now, off with you, and be careful.'

Girard put on his new smock, tied his handkerchief over the
apricots, and, walking with long, heavy strides in his nailed clogs, set
off tranquilly for Yonville.

When he arrived at Madame Bovary's house, she was in the
kitchen with Félicité, spreading out a bundle of linen on the table.

'A present from my master,' said the groom.

She was seized with sudden apprehension. While feeling in her
pocket for some money, she looked at the country fellow with a wild
expression in her eye. He, for his part, gazed at her in astonishment,
quite failing to understand why anyone should be so moved by so
trivial a gift.

At last he left the room. Félicité stayed where she was. Emma
could stand the strain no longer, but ran into the parlour as though to
arrange the apricots, turned the basket upside down, tore the leaves
apart, found the letter, opened it, and then, as though a terrible fire

were raging at her heels, fled in an access of terror to her room.

Charles met her. She saw him. He said something to her. She did not hear but continued on her way upstairs, panting, distraught, like a drunken woman, still clutching the horrible sheet of paper which crackled in her fingers like metallic foil. On the second floor she stopped in front of the door leading to the attic. It was shut.

She tried to calm her nerves. She remembered the letter. She *must* read it to the end, but dared not. And where? Somebody would see her.

Here, she thought, I shall be safe. She pushed open the door and entered.

A great wave of heat struck down at her from the tiles, constricting her temples, suffocating her. She dragged herself across to the shuttered window and drew the bolts. A dazzle of light leapt straight at her.

Beyond the opposite roofs spread the open country as far as the eye could reach. Below was the village square. There was not a soul about. The pebbles of the footpath glittered: the wind-vanes on the houses stood motionless. At the corner of the street a sort of moaning sound with occasional strident modulations, was issuing from one of the lower floors. It was Binet working at his lathe.

She leaned against the embrasure of the window and read the letter with little harsh bursts of angry laughter. But the more she concentrated her attention on its contents, the more muddled did her mind become. She felt as though she could see his face, hear his voice, hold him in her arms. The irregular beating of her heart, which was like a battering-ram within her bosom, grew quicker. She stared about her wishing that the earth would open. Why not have done with it all? Who could stop her? She was free.

She went closer to the window and stared down at the paved roadway.

'I'll do it!' she said to herself.

The light striking up at her from below seemed to draw the weight of her body down into the great empty space. She felt as though the surface of the square were spinning before her eyes, climbing up the walls to meet her. The floor of the room was tilting like the deck of a pitching ship. She stood there, almost hanging over its edge. All round her was nothing but vacant space. The blue of the sky enveloped her, the air eddied in her empty skull. She had only to let herself go, only to let that nothingness receive her body. The buzzing of the lathe went on and on, like some angry voice calling to her.

'Emma!' cried Charles: 'Emma!' She stopped.

'Where on earth are you? Come down!'

The thought that she had just escaped from death made her almost faint with terror. She closed her eyes. Then, at the touch of a hand upon her sleeve, she gave a start. It was Félicité.

'Master's waiting for you, ma'am. The soup is served.'

And she had to go down! To join him at table!

She tried to eat, but the mouthfuls of food choked her. She spread her napkin as though to examine the darns, and felt a sudden desire to count the threads in the linen. Suddenly she remembered the letter. Had she lost it? Where could it be? But her mind felt so tired that she could not even invent an excuse to leave the table. She realized that she was being a coward. She was frightened of Charles and felt quite convinced that he knew everything. There was, indeed, a strange note in his voice when next he spoke.

'I gather we're not likely to see much more of Monsieur Rodolphe.'

'Who told you that?' she said with a start.

'Who told me?' he replied, somewhat surprised by the sharpness in her voice: 'why, Girard, whom I ran into just now outside the Café Français. He's gone on a journey, or is just about to go.'

She uttered a sob.

'What is there so surprising about that? He frequently goes away on pleasure trips, and I must say I don't blame him. When a man's rich and unattached . . . Our friend's a great one for pleasure, quite the lad. Monsieur Langlois told me . . .'

He stopped because the servant, who had just come into the room, was busy putting back into the basket the apricots which lay scattered all over the sideboard. Charles, without noticing his wife's high colour, asked that they should be handed to him. He took one from the basket and bit into it.

'First rate!' he said: 'here, have one.'

He held out the basket, but she pushed it away calmly.

'Just smell! What an aroma!' he said, moving the fruit to and fro beneath his nose.

'I'm stifling!' she exclaimed, jumping up. She made an effort of will and the spasm passed. Then:

'It's nothing,' she said: 'nothing at all, just nerves. Do sit down and go on with your meal!'

She was afraid lest he should start questioning her, fussing over her, refusing to leave her alone.

He had sat down again in obedience to her wish, and was spitting the apricot kernels in his hands, putting them in his plate.

Suddenly, a blue tilbury drove across the square at a brisk trot. Emma uttered a cry and fell to the floor on her back. She lay there quite rigid.*

The fact was that Rodolphe, after much careful thought, had decided to leave for Rouen. Now, since the only road from La Huchette to Buchy goes by way of Yonville, he had been compelled to drive through the village, and Emma had recognized him by the glow of his lamps which cut through the dusk like a flash of lightning.

Hearing a sudden uproar in the house, the chemist ran across the road. The table, with all the plates on it, had been overturned. Gravy, meat, knives, the salt-cellar and the cruet-stand, lay scattered about the floor. Charles was calling for help. Berthe was crying from fright, and Félicité, with trembling hands, was unlacing her mistress who was shaking with convulsive jerks.

'I'll run back to the laboratory for some aromatic vinegar,' said the apothecary.

After sniffing at the bottle, she opened her eyes.

'I knew that would do it,' he said: 'that stuff would wake the dead!'

'Speak to us!' said Charles: 'speak to us! Everything's all right. It's I, your own Charles who loves you! Don't you recognize me? See, here's our little girl: take her.'

The child was tottering forward with arms outstretched to hang about her mother's neck. But Emma, turning away her face, said abruptly:

'No . . . no . . . nobody!'

She fainted away again. They carried her to her bed.

She lay there, her mouth open, her eyes fast shut, her hands flat on the sheet, motionless and white as a waxen figure. Two tears trickled slowly from her eyes on to the pillow.

Charles remained standing within the alcove, while the chemist, close beside him, maintained that meditative silence which is called for in the more serious moments of human life.

'Don't worry,' he said, nudging Charles with his elbow. 'I think the paroxysm has passed.'

'Yes, she's resting a little now,' replied Charles, whose eyes were on her sleeping face. 'Poor woman . . . poor woman . . . another relapse!'

Then Homais asked how the accident had occurred. The doctor answered that she had had a sudden seizure while she was eating some apricots.

'Extraordinary!' was the chemist's comment. 'Still, it is quite possible that the apricots were the cause of the syncope. Some temperaments, you know, are strangely susceptible to certain smells. The problem would well repay study, both from the pathological and the physiological aspects. Priests are well aware of the importance of *odours* and have always made use of aromatic gums in their rites, with the object of numbing the rational faculties and provoking a state of ecstasy, which is easily achieved with women who are more highly strung than men. I have heard cases of women fainting at the smell of burnt horn or new bread.'

'Take care not to wake her,' said Bovary in a low voice.

'Nor is it only human beings', went on the apothecary, 'in whom such anomalies are to be found. You will see the same thing even in animals. You can scarcely be unaware, for instance, of the aphrodisiac effect produced by *nepeta cataria*, commonly known as catmint, on the feline species. To take another example, for which I can vouch, Bridoux (once a colleague of mine who now has a business of his own in the rue Malpalu) owns a dog which falls into convulsions whenever anyone holds out a snuff-box. Bridoux will often make the experiment in front of his friends, at the little country-place he has at Le Bois-Guillaume. Who would believe that a simple sternutatory* could produce such ravages in the organism of a quadruped? Curious, isn't it?'

'Yes,' said Charles, who was not listening.

'But it only goes to prove', continued the other with an air of benign self-satisfaction, 'how numberless are the irregularities of the nervous system. To return to the case of your good lady. I have always, I confess, regarded her as an excessively sensitive subject. If you take my advice, my friend, you will avoid all those so-called remedies which undermine the constitution under pretext of attacking the symptoms. No superfluous medicaments! A regular dietary

treatment is the only thing that will do any good—sedatives, emol-
lients, dulcificants. Don't you think, also, that it might be as well to
work on the imagination?'

'In what way? How do you mean?' asked Bovary.

'That is precisely what we have to decide. *That is the question,** to
quote a phrase which I read recently in some paper.'

But at this point, Emma, struggling back to consciousness,
exclaimed:

'The letter! . . . where is the letter?'

They thought she was delirious, and, soon after midnight, she
actually became so. Brain-fever had set in.

For forty-three days Charles never left her. He entirely neglected
his patients. Not once did he go to bed, but was always at her side,
feeling her pulse, applying mustard poultices and cold compresses.
He sent Justin as far as Neufchâtel for ice, but it melted on the way
back, and he sent him for more. He called in Monsieur Canivet for
a consultation, and got Dr Larivière, under whom he had once
studied, to come over from Rouen. He was in despair. What frightened him most was her state of utter prostration. She said nothing,
heard nothing, and even seemed to feel nothing. It was as though
both body and soul were at last freed from the turmoil in which for
so long they had been living.

Towards the middle of October she was able to sit propped up
with pillows in her bed. Charles wept the first time that he saw her
eat a piece of bread and butter and jam. She began to regain her
strength, and got up for a few hours each afternoon. One day, when
she was feeling better, he tried to make her take a walk round the
garden, leaning on his arm. The gravel of the paths was barely
visible under the drifts of dead leaves. She moved one step at a time,
shuffling along in her slippers, Charles supporting her shoulders.
And all the while there was a smile on her lips.

Walking thus, they reached the bottom of the garden where they
were close to the terrace. Very slowly she straightened herself, shad-
ing her eyes with her hands, the better to see the view. She stared
into the distance, the far, far distance. But the only thing to be seen
on the horizon was the smoke of extensive grass fires rising from the
hills.

'You'll tire yourself, darling,' said Bovary. He propelled her gently
towards the arbour.

'Sit down on this bench. You will be comfortable there.'

'No—oh no!' she replied in faltering tones.

She had an attack of giddiness, and that evening there was a relapse. This time, though the violence of her illness seemed to have diminished, its characteristics appeared to be more complex. At times the pain would be in her heart, at others in her chest, her head, her limbs. There was a recurrence of nausea, and Charles feared that this might be an early symptom of cancer.

As though all this were not enough, the poor man was worried about money.

CHAPTER XIV

IN the first place, he did not know how he could repay Monsieur Homais for all the medicaments he had had from the shop, for though, as a doctor, he was entitled to be supplied free of charge, the thought of being under such an obligation made him almost blush. Then, the household expenses, now that everything was left in the cook's hands, were terrifying. Bills were pouring in on him, and the tradesmen were beginning to murmur. Monsieur Lheureux was especially exigent. Indeed, profiting by the circumstances of Emma's illness, and choosing the moment when she was in her most critical state, he deliberately added to the amount of her bill, and, without waiting for further instructions, delivered the travelling cloak, the hand-bag, two trunks instead of one, and a number of other items as well. It was no use for Charles to say that he did not need the things. The draper merely answered, in a very arrogant tone, that they had been ordered and that he would not take them back. Besides, he said, if he did, that might merely have the effect of delaying Madame's convalescence. He advised Monsieur to think very seriously before he did anything rash, and added that he would take him to court rather than be done out of his due or have the goods back. Charles gave orders that the various items should be returned to his shop. Félicité forgot to carry out his instructions, however, and because he had other matters to worry him, he thought no more about what he had said. Monsieur Lheureux returned to the charge and, alternately threatening and whining, manoeuvred in such a way that Bovary finally gave him a bill at six months. But scarcely had he signed the paper than a reckless thought came to him. He would borrow a thousand francs from Monsieur Lheureux. With considerable embarrassment, he asked whether they could not come to a satisfactory arrangement. He would pay back the principal, he said, in a year's time, plus any interest the other might like to fix. Lheureux hurried to his shop, returned with the money, and dictated a second bill which stipulated that Bovary would, on the 1st September following, pay to his order the sum of one thousand and seventy francs which, with the one hundred and eighty already owing, made a round total of twelve hundred and fifty. Thus, since he was lending at six per cent, was taking a one and a half per cent commission, and had made a good thirty-three and a third profit on the goods supplied, the whole transaction would represent a net gain of one hundred and thirty francs,* over a period of twelve months. He had hopes, too, that the business would not end there: that the doctor, finding himself unable to settle, would renew his bill, and that his own poor little bit of capital, fed on as fattening a diet as any patient in a hospital, would return to him one day considerably plumper than it had left him, and in sufficient quantity to burst his money-bags.

Everything to which he had set his hand was turning out well. He held a contract for the supply of cider to the Neufchâtel hospital: Maître Guillaumin had promised him shares in the Grumesnil peat-bogs, and he was thinking of starting a new road-service between Argueil and Rouen which would soon, no doubt, spell ruin for the rickety old diligence belonging to the Golden Lion, and, being quicker, cheaper and capable of carrying larger loads, would give him control of all the local trade.

Charles continually asked himself by what possible means he could pay back such a large sum during the next twelve months. He cudgelled his brain to find a way, and played with the idea of having recourse to his father, or of selling something. But his father might be deaf to his appeal, and there was nothing he *could* sell. He decided that he was so deeply involved that to brood upon the disagreeable subject was useless. He suffered pangs of self-reproach at the thought that he was forgetting all about Emma. His whole mind, he felt, ought to be given to her. If she were not his prime concern, he must be guilty of depriving her of something that was her due.

The winter was hard. Emma's convalescence was slow. When the weather was fine he had her chair moved to the window—the one which commanded a view of the square, for she had taken a dislike to the garden, and the blinds on that side of the house were kept permanently drawn. She wanted him to sell her horse. Everything she had once loved now displeased her. She seemed to have no thoughts for anything other than her own health. She stayed in bed, having light meals, and rang for the servant to bring her various infusions, or merely to chat with her. The snow on the roof of the market-hall filled the room with a still, white, reflected radiance. Later, the rain began to fall. She spent her days nervously anticipating the inevitable return of all the trivial events of her existence, which now counted as less than nothing for her. The most important was the arrival, each evening, of the Swallow. Whenever that event occurred, she could hear the raised voice of the landlady, and other voices answering her, while Hippolyte's lantern, as he hunted in the boot for the various packages, showed like a star in the darkness. At noon Charles came home, and, later, went out again. Then she would take some broth. At five o'clock, just as the daylight was fading, the children, shuffling along the pavement in their clogs on their way home from school, would rattle the latches of the lean-to sheds, one after the other, with their rulers.

This was Monsieur Bournisien's favourite hour for paying her a visit. He inquired after her health, brought her items of news, and mingled religious exhortation with sly pieces of gossip in a way that she found far from unattractive. The mere sight of his soutane brought her a sense of comfort.

One day, at the crisis of her illness, when she had really thought that she was dying, she had asked him to administer communion. While her room was being prepared for the sacrament, the chest-of-drawers, with its litter of medicine bottles, arranged as an altar, and dahlia blossoms strewn on the floor by Félicité, she felt some powerful influence pass over her which seemed to rid her of all pain, to kill in her all faculty of perception, all ability to feel. Her body, lightened of its burden, had ceased to think. A new life was beginning. She felt as though her being would mount to God and disintegrate in his love, as incense dissipates in vapour. The sheets of her bed were sprinkled with holy water. The priest took the white Host from the sacred pyx, and, in an almost swooning condition, so great was her joy, she advanced her lips to take the body of her Saviour which he held out for her acceptance. The curtains of the alcove swelled and bellied gently about her like clouds, and the rays of the two candles burning on the chest-of-drawers appeared to her eyes like sunbursts of glory. The ceremony over, she let her head fall back on the pillows, quite convinced that the air was filled with the music of angelic harps, and that she could see, mounted on a golden throne within a sky of blue, and surrounded by saints with green palms in their hands, God the Father shining in majesty, at a sign from whom angels would wing to earth on flaming pinions to take her in their arms upon her final journey.

So tenaciously did this vision of splendour linger in her mind as the most beautiful dream it was possible to have, that she struggled to recover the sensation. In a way it did continue. Its impact was less intense, but the sweetness that it shed was no less profound. Her soul, bruised by pride, rested at length in Christian humility, and, relishing this pleasing visitation of weakness, she contemplated within herself that destruction of self-will which should open a breach to the invasion of grace. She realized that worldly happiness might yield its place to still greater felicities: that above all other loves was another love which dwindled not neither did it end, but would grow greater through all eternity. Amid the illusions of her hope she caught a glimpse of a state of purity which floated above the earth, and merged with that heaven where she aspired to be. She wanted to become a saint. She bought rosaries and wore sacred medals. She longed to have beside her pillow a reliquary encrusted with emeralds, which she could kiss every night.

The curé marvelled at her mood, though he feared that her religion, by reason of its very ardour, might end by coming within measurable distance of heresy, and even of fanaticism. But, since he was not deeply versed in such matters beyond a certain point, he wrote to Monsieur Boulard, bookseller to the archbishop, asking him to send 'some treatise of repute suitable for a lady of intelligence'.

The bookseller, with as much indifference as he would have shown had he been despatching a consignment of hardware to negroes, usually replied to such inquiries by making up an assorted package of any religious books which happened to be in demand at the moment. There would be little manuals composed on the method of question and answer, pamphlets written in the stiff, pompous style associated with Monsieur de Maistre,* and various rather sugary novels, bound in pink boards and turned out wholesale by troubadour seminarists or penitent blue-stockings.* In this particular lot there was *Take it to Heart; The Man of the World at the Feet of Mary*, by Monsieur de ——, Knight of this, that or the other Order, and *Some Errors of Voltaire, designed for the Instruction of the Young.*

Madame Bovary had not yet sufficiently recovered to be able to apply her mind seriously to anything, and she embarked upon this course of reading in far too headlong a fashion. The narrowness of the religious mind got on her nerves, and she heartily disliked the polemical volumes because of the violence with which their writers insisted on attacking persons of whom she knew nothing. The secular stories, tricked out with odds and ends of piety, seemed to her to show such complete ignorance of the world, that they insensibly alienated her from those very truths she was seeking. Nevertheless, she persisted, and when at last the particular book she was reading fell from her hands, she was convinced that she was a victim of the most subtle form of Catholic melancholy that an ethereal soul could imagine.

As to Rodolphe, she had sunk the memory of him deep in her heart, where it remained more solemn and more motionless than the mummy of a king in an underground tomb. A faint exhalation from this great embalmed devotion permeated everything about her, giving an odour of tenderness to the immaculate climate in which she wished to live henceforward. When she knelt at her gothic prie-dieu she addressed the Lord in the same sweet words which once she had murmured to her lover in the ecstatic transports of adultery. This she did in the hope of finding faith. But no delectation of the soul descended on her from on high, and she would get to her feet with a sense of physical exhaustion, and a vague feeling that she had been cheated. This search was, she thought, but an added merit. In the pride of her devotion, Emma compared herself to those great ladies of the past whose glory had formed the substance of her dreams when she used to look at the portrait of La Vallière:* majestically they had swept the long trains of their lace-trimmed robes into lonely retreats, there to lay at the feet of Christ the tears which were the tribute of hearts wounded by the world.

Next, she expended herself in works of extravagant charity. She made clothes for the poor, and sent loads of wood to women in childbed. One day, when Charles came home, he found three good-for-nothing tramps seated in the kitchen guzzling soup. She summoned home her small daughter whom, during the period of her illness, her husband had boarded out with her former nurse. She wanted to teach her to read, and, no matter how often Berthe flew into tantrums of tears, refused to be irritated as once she had been. She was fully determined to adopt an attitude of resignation and universal indulgence. Her speech for ever moved in the regions of the ideal. She would say to the child:

'Has your tummy-ache gone, my angel?'

Madame Bovary the elder could find nothing in all this to criticize adversely except, perhaps, her daughter-in-law's mania for knitting vests for orphans, instead of mending her own dusters. But the good lady, harassed by domestic quarrels, was happy enough in the quiet atmosphere of the house, and stayed on until after Easter in order to avoid the sarcasms of old Bovary, who made a point of sitting down to a good meat meal every Friday.

Emma found a certain amount of spiritual support in the stern principles and grave manners of her mother-in-law. But she was not wholly dependent on her company, and, on most days, enjoyed the society of other ladies. There was Madame Langlois, Madame Caron, Madame Dubreuil, Madame Tuvache, and always, between two o'clock and five, the excellent Madame Homais, who had resolutely refused to give credence to the gossip which was going the rounds about her neighbour. The Homais children, too, paid her frequent visits, accompanied by Justin. He would go upstairs with them to her room and stay there, standing by the door quite motionless, saying nothing. Madame Bovary would frequently begin her morning toilet without paying the slightest attention to him, first taking out her comb and shaking down her hair with a vigorous movement of her head. The first time he saw it fall to her ankles in a cascade of black waves, the poor fellow felt as though he had been made suddenly free of some extraordinary and novel region the splendours of which filled him with terror.

Probably Emma did not notice either his silent attentions or his shyness. It did not occur to her that the love which had vanished from her own life might be throbbing close to her beneath a coarse cotton shirt, in the heart of an adolescent who was only too susceptible to the power of her beauty. However that might be, she was so indifferent now to everything, used such emotional language, wore so haughty an expression, and assumed for the world at large such a variety of manners, that it was no longer possible, where she was concerned, to distinguish selfishness from charity or corruption from virtue. One evening, for instance, she lost her temper with the servant who had asked to be allowed to go out, and was stammeringly seeking some plausible excuse. Suddenly:

'I suppose you're in love, eh?' Emma had asked, and, without waiting for the blushing Félicité to reply, had added in tones of melancholy:

'Off with you, then! Go and enjoy yourself.'

At the beginning of spring, she had the whole garden rearranged from end to end, in spite of Bovary's protests. Not but what he was delighted to see her interest revive in something. This new mood of hers developed still further with her returning strength. In the first place she managed to get rid of Madame Rollet, the former foster-mother, who, during her convalescence, had fallen into the habit of paying rather too many visits to the kitchen, always bringing with her the two children who were out at nurse with her, as well as her regular boarder, who had an appetite more voracious than a cannibal's. Next, she freed herself from the importunities of the Homais family, discouraged, one by one, her various other visitors, and even took to going rather less regularly to church, much to the satisfaction of the apothecary, who said jokingly:

'You *were* getting in rather deep with the dog-collars, weren't you?'

Monsieur Bournisien continued to pay her daily visits after his catechism class. He liked to sit outside, taking the air in 'the grove', as he called her garden arbour. It was the time of day at which Charles usually came home. They both felt the heat, and sweet cider was always brought out, in which they drank to Madame's complete recovery.

Binet usually contrived to be there—or rather, a little further down the river, fishing for crayfish below the terrace wall. Bovary would invite him to take a little refreshment. He was a great hand at uncorking stone bottles.

'You must hold them firmly on the table,' he said, glancing round him at the view with an air of great self-satisfaction—'cut the wire, and then push the cork up little by little, very gently, as they do with soda-water in restaurants.'

But very often, in the middle of his demonstration, the cider would spurt in their faces, and this inevitably led the gentleman of the cloth to indulge in the same witticism, which he brought out with a throaty laugh:

'Its excellence hits you in the eye!'

The priest was, as a matter of fact, a thoroughly good fellow, and was not at all outraged when, one day, the chemist advised Charles to take his wife to hear the famous tenor Lagardy at the Rouen theatre. It would, he said, be a change for her. Astonished at the curé's failure to react, he set himself to elicit his views, and was told for his pains that the other considered music to be far less demoralizing than literature.

The chemist at once set about championing the cause of letters. The theatre, he maintained, was an admirable challenge to prejudice, and, under the guise of entertainment, served to inculcate virtue.

'*Castigat ridendo mores*,* Monsieur Bournisien. Take, for instance, most of Voltaire's tragedies,* which are skilfully diversified with philosophical reflections, and form a positive school of morals and diplomacy for the people.'

'I once saw a piece called *Le Gamin de Paris*,'* put in Binet, 'in which one of the characters was an old general hit off to the life. He rebuked a young man of good family who had seduced a working-girl, and at the end she . . .'

'Of course,' went on Homais, 'there is bad literature, just as there is bad chemistry. But I hold that to condemn without exception the most important of the fine arts is sheer stupidity, a gothic attitude worthy of the abominable times in which Galileo was imprisoned.'

The priest began to argue. 'I know', he said, 'that there are admirable works and admirable authors, but the mere fact of persons of both sexes sitting together in a hall adorned with worldly extravagance and deliberately designed to charm the senses, to say nothing of all the pagan make-believe, the rouge, the candles, the effeminate voices—all these things cannot, in the long run, but engender a sort of dissolute mood in the audience and assail its members with indelicate thoughts and impure temptations. That, at any rate, is the view taken by all the Fathers of the Church.* If'—he concluded, in a voice which had suddenly assumed a note of rapt ecstasy, while he rolled a pinch of snuff on his thumb, 'if the church has condemned theatrical displays, it is because she has good reason to do so. It is for us to submit to her decrees.'

'But why', asked the apothecary, 'does she excommunicate the players?—for there was a time when they openly took part in the Christian ceremonies. Yes, they used to play in the very choirs of our churches. They produced a species of farces called "Mysteries" in which very often the laws of decency were set at defiance.'

The churchman took refuge in a groan, while the chemist continued:

'Besides, look at the Bible, which contains, as you must know, a number of very spicy details, and several passages which are, to say the least, extremely free!'

Monsieur Bournisien made a gesture of annoyance, and he went on:

'I think you'll agree that it is hardly a work which should be placed in the hands of young persons. I should be sorry if I thought that Athalie. . . .'

'It is the Protestants, not we'—broke in the other, now out of all patience—'who recommend the general reading of the Bible!'

'No matter'—said Homais—'I am really amazed that in these days and in this enlightened country, there should be found people set on proscribing a form of intellectual relaxation which is inoffensive, thoroughly moral, and sometimes positively beneficial to health. Don't you agree, Doctor?'

'Most certainly,' replied Bovary. He spoke rather nonchalantly, either because, sharing the other's views, he did not wish to offend any of those present, or because he had no views at all.

The discussion seemed to have died down, when the chemist saw fit to discharge a final shaft.

'I have known priests in my time who put on ordinary clothes so as to see dancers doing the high-kick!'

'Oh, come now . . .!' said the curé.

'But—I—have.'

'Well, then, they were in the wrong,' said Bournisien, by this time resigned to anything the other might say.

'And that's not the only thing they do, either!' exclaimed the apothecary.

'Sir!' said the churchman, with so fierce a look that his antagonist was intimidated.

'All I meant to say', he replied in a less truculent tone, 'was that tolerance is the surest way of drawing men's hearts to religion.'

'There I agree with you,' admitted the good man resuming his seat: 'there I agree with you.'

But he stayed only two minutes longer, and as soon as he had gone Monsieur Homais said to the doctor:

'Well, that's what you might call getting down to it hammer and tongs . . . and I think I pretty well wiped the floor with him, didn't I? . . . You take my advice and go to the theatre with your wife, if only for the satisfaction of annoying one of those black crows for once in your life. Great heavens! if there was anybody who could take my place in the shop, I'd come along with you myself. Don't waste any time. Lagardy's making only one appearance. He's under contract to go to England at a very high salary. Knows which side his bread is buttered, if all I hear is true. Fairly rolls in money—takes three mistresses and a cook with him wherever he goes. These great artists all burn the candle at both ends. They feel the need of a wild kind of existence—it helps to stimulate their imagination. But they invariably die in the workhouse, because they're never sensible enough to save money when they're young. Well, so long, see you again soon!'

This idea of going to the theatre quickly bore fruit in Bovary's mind. He lost no time in mentioning it to his wife, who at first refused on the grounds of fatigue, trouble and expense. But Charles, unlike his usual self, did not give up the struggle. He had got it firmly fixed in his head that the excursion would be beneficial, and he saw no reason at all why it should not take place. His mother had sent him three hundred francs on which he had long since ceased to count, his outstanding debts did not amount to a very serious total, and the date on which the bill he had given to the great Lheureux would fall due was still so far off that there was no real need to think about it at all. He insisted, therefore, in what he thought was the most tactful manner imaginable, until finally she was nagged into saying 'yes'.

At eight o'clock next morning they set off in the Swallow.

The apothecary, whom nothing, in fact, kept at Yonville, although he was convinced that he could not budge from his shop, sighed as he bade them farewell.

'A comfortable journey to you,' he said, 'you most fortunate of mortals!'

Then, turning to Emma, who was wearing a blue silk dress with four flounces, he added:

'You look as pretty as a cupid! I prophesy a terrific success in Rouen!'

The diligence set down its passengers at the Red Cross Hotel, on the place Beauvoisine, just such an inn as is to be found on the outskirts of any provincial city: a place of large stables and small bedrooms, with hens in the yard pecking at corn beneath the mud-caked gigs of commercial travellers—a sound old caravanserai with balconies whose worm-eaten wood creaked in the wind on winter nights, filled with people, noise and food, where the black table-tops were sticky with spilt coffee and brandy, the thick window panes yellow with flies, and the damp cloths stained with absinthe. Since there is always something of the village about such places—as there is about the farm-labourer in his Sunday best—a café inevitably forms part of their accommodation, opening on to the street, with a kitchen-garden at the back facing the open country.

Charles immediately started off on a number of errands. He got the stage-box mixed up with the gallery, the pit with the dress circle, asked for explanations which he failed to understand, was referred by the box-office attendant to the manager, went back to the inn, paid another visit to the box-office, and, in this way, walked the whole length and breadth of the town more than once, from the theatre to the boulevard.

His wife bought herself a hat, a pair of gloves and a bouquet. He was continually fidgeting lest they miss the rise of the curtain, with the result that they had no time to swallow so much as a mouthful of soup, and turned up at the entrance to the theatre* before the doors were open.

CHAPTER XV

THE waiting crowd was neatly drawn up along the wall of the theatre in a series of queues separated by rails. At the corners of the near-by streets huge posters, printed in florid type, repeated the same announcement over and over again: *'Lucie de Lammermoor'**
. . . Lagardy . . . Opera. . . . etc. It was a fine evening. Those waiting for the doors to open were feeling hot. Sweat ran into carefully

curled hair; there was much mopping of red faces with pocket-handkerchiefs, and, now and again, a warm breeze from across the river faintly agitated the edges of the canvas awnings drawn down over tavern doors. But a little further off a welcome coolness was to be found where an icy draught, smelling of tallow, leather and oil, exuded into the street. This was the peculiar exhalation given off by the rue des Charrettes, a thoroughfare full of black warehouses in and out of which barrels were being constantly rolled.

Afraid of looking ridiculous, Emma said that she would like to take a turn round the quays before going into the theatre, and Bovary, though he was prepared to humour her, kept his tickets in his hand, and his hand in his trouser pocket, pressed against his stomach, just to be on the safe side.

As soon as she got back into the foyer, Emma was conscious that her heart was beating more quickly. Involuntarily, a little smile of vanity curled her lips as she saw the crowd surging to the right down a corridor, while she went up the stairs leading to the dress circle. She took a childish pleasure in pushing the large curtained doors open with her fingers. She breathed in the dusty smell of the passages with delight, and, as soon as she was seated in their box, began to preen herself with the easy unconcern of a duchess.

The house began to fill. There was much extracting of opera-glasses from cases. The regular subscribers recognized one another from afar and exchanged greetings. They had come here to forget the anxieties of commerce in the atmosphere of the fine arts, but, since they could never wholly forget 'business', their talk was of cotton, spirits and indigo. Some of the older men, resigned and inexpressive, with whitish hair and whitish faces, looked like silver medals which had been tarnished by exposure to lead fumes. The young bucks-about-town strutted in the stalls, displaying a great expanse of pink or apple-green cravat in the openings of their waistcoats. Looking down on them from above, Madame Bovary admired the way in which they rested the palms of their hands in their tight yellow gloves on the gold knobs of elegant dress canes.

The candles in the orchestra were being lit: the great crystal chandelier was let down from the roof, scattering a sudden gaiety from its sparkling lustres. Then the musicians came in, one by one. At first there was a discordant hubbub of sonorous bass, scraping fiddles, blaring cornets and whimpering flutes and flageolets. At long

last came the three knocks on the stage, there was a roll of side-
drums, a crash of chords from the brass, and the curtain rose revealing a country scene.

It represented a clearing in a wood, with a little stream on the left,
purling away in the shade of an oak-tree. Peasants and lords, with
plaids on their shoulders, sang a hunting chorus. This was followed
by an invocation to the Spirit of Evil, sung by a captain who raised
both his arms to heaven. To him there entered another, and they left
the stage together, after which the huntsmen began again.

Emma, remembering her early reading,* found herself caught up
into the very heart of Sir Walter Scott. It was as though she could
hear through the mist the sound of Scottish bagpipes echoing in the
undergrowth. Her recollection of the novel made it easy for her to
follow the libretto; and she traced the movement of the story, phrase
by phrase, while the vague thoughts thronging her mind vanished,
almost as soon as formed, beneath the gusts of music. She let herself
be lulled by the melodies, and felt her whole being vibrate as though
the bows of the violins were being drawn across her own taut nerves.
Her two eyes were not adequate to take in the costumes, the scenery,
the characters, the painted trees which trembled whenever anyone
walked across the stage, the velvet bonnets, the cloaks, the swords
and all the paraphernalia of fancy, quivering in the harmony of
sound as in the atmosphere of a strange new world.

A young woman advanced to the front of the stage, throwing a
purse to a groom dressed in green. She was left alone, and gradually
the listening ear became aware of a flute, the notes of which might
have been the murmuring of a stream or the twittering of a bird.

Lucie, with a look of extreme seriousness, began her aria in G
major. She bewailed her love, she begged for wings. Emma, too,
would have liked to escape from life and fly away in an embrace.

Suddenly Edgar Lagardy appeared.* His face had that magnificent pallor which imparts something of the majesty of antique
marble to the ardent races of the South. His virile figure was clad in a
brown doublet. A little dagger with a chased hilt swung against his
left thigh, and he gazed languorously about him, showing his white
teeth.

The story went that a Polish princess, hearing him one evening
singing on the beach at Biarritz, where he was busily at work mending boats, had, there and then, fallen in love. She had ruined herself

for his sake, but he had abandoned her for other women, and his reputation as a lover had enhanced his fame as an artist. The astute little mummer was always careful to insert in his bills some poetically worded phrase, descriptive of his fascinating person and sensitive nature. A fine natural organ, sublime self-assurance, more temperament than intelligence, and a larger dose of pomposity than of poetry, gave the finishing touch to this admirable example of the charlatan, with its mixture of the barber and the toreador.

From his very first entrance he enraptured the audience. He clasped Lucie in his arms, left her, then returned, always, apparently, in a state of despair. Bursts of anger alternated with quavering passages of the sweetest grief. The notes which issued from his uncovered throat were eloquent of sighs and kisses.

Emma leaned forward, the better to see him, scraping the velvet of the box with her fingernails. Her heart drank its fill of his melodious lamentations which were drawn out to an accompaniment of passages on the double-bass and resembled the cries of shipwrecked mariners in the tumult of a storm. She recognized all the intoxicating delights, all the agonies, of which she herself had almost died. The voice of the singing heroine seemed but the echo of her own consciousness, the illusions which haunted her, part of her own experience. But no one in the world had ever loved like this! had ever wept like Edgar, when, on the night of their parting, they sang to one another beneath the moon— '*A demain! à demain!*' The house rocked with applause. The finale had to be given again from the beginning. The lovers spoke of the flowers upon their graves, of oaths and exile, of fate and hope, and when the last words of leave-taking had been sung, Emma uttered a piercing cry which merged into the overtones of the closing bars.

'Why', asked Bovary, 'is this lord so intent on persecuting her?'

'But he isn't,' she replied, 'he is her lover.'

'But he keeps on swearing that he will be revenged on her family. Besides, that other man, the one who was on the stage a moment or so back, said "I love Lucie and believe she loves me too," and then went off arm in arm with her father. That *is* her father, isn't it, the ugly little man with a cock's feather in his cap?'

As soon as Charles caught sight of the false wedding-ring which is meant to deceive Lucie, and makes its appearance after the piece of recitative dialogue in which Gilbert exposes his abominable schemings to his master, Ashton, he was convinced, in spite of Emma's explanation, that it was a love-token sent by Edgar. He confessed, furthermore, that he was losing track of the story, because the music made it very difficult to hear the words.

'What does that matter?' said Emma: 'do be quiet.'

'But I like to understand what is going on, as you very well know,' he replied, leaning over her shoulder.

'Oh, please stop talking!' she said, having by this time come to the end of her patience.

Lucie advanced to the front of the stage, half supported by her women. There was a wreath of orange-blossom in her hair, and she looked paler than her white satin dress. Emma thought of her own wedding-day, and saw again in imagination the long procession moving churchwards through the corn-fields, with herself in its midst. Why had she not, like this other, resisted and implored? Far from doing that, she had actually rejoiced in the event, not realizing into what an abyss she was about to fall. . . . If only, in the full bloom of her beauty, before it had become smirched by marriage and the disenchantments of adultery, she could have anchored her life to the solid rock of a loving heart! Had virtuous sentiment, the delights of the body and the duties of her station been fused and melted into one another, she would never have fallen from so lofty a pinnacle of happiness! But such ecstasies, no doubt, are but lies imagined by the hungry heart when it despairs of love! She knew now the triviality of those passions which art paints so much larger than life. She forced herself not to think of these things, and tried to see in the stage representation of her agonies nothing but a moving fantasy designed for no purpose but to amuse the eye. She even smiled to herself in a mood of contemptuous pity, when a man wrapped in a black cloak appeared between the velvet curtains at the back of the scene.

He made a gesture, and his great Spanish hat fell to the ground. Immediately, the instruments of the orchestra and the singers struck up the sextet. Edgar, his eyes blazing with anger, dominated all the others. His tenor voice soared over theirs. Ashton, in deep and solemn tones, egged him on to commit murder. Lucie voiced her shrill sorrow. Arthur, standing apart, sang modulations in a middle register, while the bass of the parson pealed like an organ note, and the women, repeating his words, supplied a charming chorus. All the singers stood in a row, and emotions of anger, jealousy, terror, pity and amazement found simultaneous expression. The outraged lover brandished his naked sword. His lace collar jerked in response to the movements of his breast. This way and that way he strode, the silver-gilt spurs on the soft leather boots which fell to his ankles sounding as he stamped the stage. Such love, thought she, must be proof against time and use if he could pour it in such copious streams upon the crowd. Her desire to mock was powerless against the impact of the role's poetic appeal. She was drawn to the man by the illusion of the part he played. She tried to imagine life as she might have known it, had fate been kind. A glamorous, an amazing and splendid life. If only they could have met and loved! With him she would have travelled through all the kingdoms of Europe, moving from capital to capital, sharing his weariness and his triumphs, gathering in armfuls the bouquets showered upon him. With her own fingers she would have embroidered his stage costumes, and every evening, seated at the back of her box, behind a grill of gilded trellis-work, would have listened open-mouthed to the voice of that great soul singing for her alone. Even in the fervour of his playing he would have spared her a look from his place upon the stage. A sudden madness seized her. He *was* looking at her! There could be no doubt about it. She longed to rush into his arms, to take refuge in his strength as in the incarnation of perfect love, to cry aloud to him—'Take me away! Oh, take me away! . . . Let us go. My love, my dreams, all, all are yours!'

The curtain fell.

The mingled smell of gas and human breath, the movement of the air set up by the ladies' fans, served but to make the atmosphere more stifling. Emma wanted to go out, but a crowd blocked the corridors, and she fell back in her chair, her heart palpitating so violently that she found it difficult to breathe. Charles, fearing she might faint, ran to the buffet to get her a glass of barley-water.

He found it far from easy to get back to his seat, because he was holding the glass in his two hands, and at every step he took somebody jolted his elbow. As it was, for all his care, he spilled about three-quarters of its contents over the shoulders of a Rouen lady in a short-sleeved gown. Feeling the cold liquid trickling down her back, she set up such a screeching that the bystanders might have been forgiven for thinking that she was having her throat cut. Her husband, a mill-owner, started abusing the clumsy perpetrator of the crime, while he mopped away with his handkerchief at the stains on the pink silk taffeta, muttering all the time about compensation, costs and damages.

At last Charles succeeded in reaching his wife, completely out of breath.

'Thought I should never get here,' he panted: 'such a crowd: never seen so many people. . . .'

A moment later he added:

'Guess whom I ran into?* . . . Monsieur Léon . . .'

'Léon?'

'As large as life. He's coming along to pay his respects.'

He had scarcely finished speaking than the former lawyer's clerk of Yonville entered the box. He held out his hand with the casual ease of one accustomed to move in high society, and Madame Bovary mechanically extended her own, yielding, no doubt, to the attraction of a will stronger than her own. The last time she had felt its influence was on that spring evening, with the rain pattering on the green leaves, when they had stood by the window, saying good-bye.

Quickly recalling herself to an awareness of the conventions, she made a violent effort to throw off this mood of lethargy induced by the remembered past, and began to stammer a few hurried phrases.

'Why, how *are* you? . . . What a surprise to see you here!'

'Quiet!' cried a voice from the pit, for the third act was just beginning.

'Are you living in Rouen?'

'Yes.'

'How long have you been here?'

'Chuck 'em out!'

People were turning to look at them. They stopped talking.

But she was no longer listening to the stage. The chorus of guests, the scene between Ashton and his servant, the great duet in D major—everything, so it seemed to her, was going on at a vast distance. She was remembering the card-parties at the chemist's, their walk together when she had been to see her child's foster-mother, the way he had read aloud to her in the arbour, the intimate talks they had had by the fire—all the trivial incidents of that poor little love-affair which had pursued its long and uneventful course in an atmosphere of discreet sentiment, and which, till this moment, she had completely forgotten. Why was it all coming back to her? What combination of events had brought it once more into her life?

He stood behind her, leaning his shoulder against the partition, and now and again she shivered a little as she felt his warm breath on her hair.

'Do you find this entertaining?' he asked, leaning so close that the point of his moustache touched her cheek.

She replied with a nonchalant air: 'Not particularly . . .'

He suggested that they leave the theatre and go somewhere for ices.

'Oh, not yet,' said Bovary; 'do let's stay. Her hair is coming down,* and I think that means it's going to be tragic!'

But Emma found no interest in the mad scene. Lucie's acting seemed to her to be exaggerated.

'She screams too loudly,' she said, turning to Charles who was busy listening.

'Maybe . . . a little too loudly . . .' he answered, torn between his frank enjoyment of the play and the respect he felt for his wife's judgement.

Léon sighed noisily.

'The heat in here is . . .'

'Quite intolerable! You're perfectly right.'

'Does it worry you?' asked Bovary.

'Yes. I can't breathe. Do let's go.'

Monsieur Léon draped her long lace shawl lightly across her shoulders, and all three of them went down to the quay and sat outside a café. The conversation at first turned on the subject of her illness, though Emma kept on interrupting Charles, fearing, she said, that Monsieur Léon might be bored. He, on his side, explained that he had come back to Rouen for two years, and was working in a first-rate practice with the object of making himself familiar with the kind of business which came the way of an ordinary Normandy lawyer, since it was very different from the work to which he had grown accustomed in Paris. He asked for news of Berthe, of the Homais family and of old Madame Lefrançois. There was nothing more they could talk about with her husband there, and the conversation soon flagged.

People from the theatre began passing along the pavement, humming or shouting at the tops of their voices *'Oh bel ange, ma Lucie!'** Léon, anxious to show how well up he was in the arts, began to talk about music. He had heard Tamburini, Rubini, Persiani,

Grisi.* Compared to them, Lagardy, for all his success, was very small beer.

'Still,' interrupted Charles, who was pecking at his rum sorbet, 'I'm told he's really wonderful in the last act. I'm sorry we left before the end. I was just beginning to enjoy myself.'

'Oh, well,' said the lawyer's clerk, 'he'll be giving another performance before very long.'

But Charles replied that they were going home the next day.

'Unless', he added, turning to his wife, 'you'd like to stay on alone, darling.'

Faced by such an unexpected chance of seeing his hopes realized, the young man hurriedly changed his tactics. He waxed eloquent in praise of Lagardy in the final scene. It really was magnificent, sublime!

Hearing this, Charles insisted.

'You can come back on Sunday. Make up your mind. It would be wrong to miss such a chance, if you think it would do you even the least little bit of good.'

The nearby tables were emptying. A waiter very discreetly posted himself within call. Charles, understanding the hint, took out his purse, but the lawyer's clerk restrained him with a touch on the arm, and was careful to leave two silver coins over and above the amount of the bill, dropping them on the marble table-top so that they rang.

'I really am very distressed', murmured Bovary, 'at your paying like this. . . .'

The other made a gesture expressive of both carelessness and cordiality. As he took his hat, he said:

'Then it's all settled, isn't it? — tomorrow, six o'clock?'

Charles protested once more that he could not stay away longer, but that there was no reason whatever why Emma should not. . . .

'I don't quite know what to say,' she stammered with a rather curious smile.

'Well, think it over. Sleep on it, and we can decide tomorrow.'

To Léon, who was walking with them, he remarked:

'Now that you are back in this part of the world, I hope you'll come and take a bite with us now and again.'

The lawyer's clerk promised that he would not fail to do so, especially since he had got to go to Yonville on business connected with his law work.

They parted at the passage Saint-Herbland,* just as the cathedral clock was striking half-past eleven.

PART THREE

CHAPTER I

MONSIEUR LÉON, during his time as a law student, had managed to go a good deal to La Chaumière,* and had even succeeded in cutting rather a dash among the *grisettes*,* who decided that he looked very 'distinguished'. He was in every way a model student, wearing his hair neither too long nor too short, and being careful not to spend the whole of his quarter's allowance on the first of the month. He kept on good terms with his teachers. From excesses he had always held aloof, as much from timidity as fastidiousness.

Often, when reading in his room, or sitting beneath the lime-trees in the Luxembourg Gardens, he would let his copy of the Code* fall to the ground, and give himself up to memories of Emma. But, little by little, his feeling for her grew less, smothered under an accumulated load of other desires. Not that it ever vanished altogether, for he still had hopes, and could indulge his imagination with the vaguest of vague promises which shone in his future like a golden apple glowing amidst the foliage of some fantastic tree.

When, after three years of absence, he saw her again, the old passion awoke once more. He must, he decided, make up his mind once and for all whether or not he really wanted to possess her. His natural shyness had been worn down as the result of contact with gay companions, and he returned to the provinces full of contempt for those who had never trod the asphalt of the boulevards in varnished boots. Faced by the billowing laces of a Parisian lady encountered in the drawing-room of some illustrious doctor covered with decorations and boasting his own carriage, the poor young man would, no doubt, have trembled like a schoolboy; but here, in Rouen, walking along the quay with the wife of a petty country practitioner, he felt wholly at his ease, and was convinced from the first that he would dazzle her. Self-assurance depends upon environment. One does not speak the same language in a drawing-room as in the attics, and the virtue of the rich lady is protected by the knowledge of all the bank-notes which she wears, like a cuirass, in the lining of her stays.

When, on this particular evening, Léon took his leave of Monsieur and Madame Bovary, he followed them along the street at a safe distance. Having seen them stop at the Red Cross, he turned on his heel and spent the rest of the night concocting a plan of action.

At about five o'clock the next afternoon, he entered the kitchen of the inn with a tight feeling in his throat, and cheeks from which every vestige of colour had vanished. He was urged on by that species of determination, common in cowards, which sticks at nothing.

'Monsieur is not in,' he was informed by one of the hotel servants.

This he took to be a good omen, and went upstairs.

Emma was in no way disconcerted by his coming: in fact, she apologized for having forgotten to tell him where they were staying.

'I guessed,' said Léon.

'But how?'

He pretended that chance had led him to her, a sort of instinct. She began to smile. At once, to make good his blunder, Léon explained that he had spent the morning inquiring for her at every hotel in Rouen.

'Am I to take it that you have decided to stay on?' he asked.

'Yes,' she said, 'though it was foolish of me to do so. One should not let oneself get the habit of playing with the idea of impracticable pleasures when one is hedged in, as I am, with a thousand claims. . . .'

'Oh, I thought . . .'

'But then, you are not a woman. . . .'

Men, however, are not without their sorrows, and the conversation took a philosophic turn. Emma had a great deal to say about the misery attendant on earthly affections, and about the eternal loneliness in which the human heart must live. To make himself more interesting in her eyes, or ingenuously copying her melancholy, which had infected him, the young man declared that he had been hideously bored all the time he had been pursuing his law studies. The procedure of the courts irritated him, he had begun to feel the attraction of other professions, and his mother nagged at him in every letter she wrote. The more they talked, the more did each define the causes of his and her unhappiness, finding, by the mere process of confession, a sort of stimulus to their growing intimacy. But they stopped abruptly, sometimes on the very threshold of complete confidence, in the very act of seeking some phrase which might bring the necessary illumination. She did not admit her passion for another, nor he the fact that he had forgotten her.

Perhaps he no longer remembered those suppers enjoyed after nights spent in dancing with women of the town, and she, doubtless, had no recollection of the trysts she had kept when she used to run to her lover's house through the morning grasses. The sounds of the city reached them scarcely at all, and the room seemed tiny, as though it had deliberately contracted in order to press into closer proximity the loneliness of their two hearts. Emma, dressed in a dimity négligé, sat with the weight of her hair supported by the back of an old armchair. The yellow wallpaper was like a golden ground for the portrait of her head which, bare of scarf or hat, was duplicated by the mirror, with its white central parting, and the lobes of her ears peeping from under the waves of her hair.

'Forgive me', she said, 'for talking like this. You must find the eternal tale of my grievances excessively boring.'

'Far, far from it!'

'If you only knew!' she went on, raising her lovely, tear-brimmed eyes to the ceiling—'all that I have dreamed!'

'I, too . . . I have suffered terribly! Often I would leave my lodging, and tramp the city, aimlessly walking along the river so as to numb my senses with the noise of the crowded streets, yet never succeeding in banishing the obsession which haunted me. There is a print-seller's shop on one of the boulevards, and, in the window, an Italian engraving which depicts one of the Muses. She is wearing a tunic, and stands looking at the moon, with twined forget-me-nots upon her loosened hair. Something always drove me to that spot, and I would stay there for hours together.'

Then, in a trembling voice—

'She was a little like you,' he added.

Madame Bovary turned away her head that he might not see the smile which shaped itself irresistibly upon her lips.

'Often', he continued, 'I wrote you letters, but always tore them up.'

She did not answer, and he went on:

'I imagined at times that some stroke of fortune might bring you to me. I thought, sometimes, that I had caught sight of you at the corner of a street, and would run after every cab I saw with a

veil blowing from the window—a veil like the one you used to
wear. . . .'

She seemed determined to let him talk without any interruption
from her. Crossing her arms and lowering her eyes, she sat gazing at
the rosettes on her slippers, wriggling her toes within their satin
sheaths.

But then she gave a sigh.

'What more lamentable than, like me, to drag out a useless existence? If only our sorrows could help others, we might find consolation in the thought of sacrifice!'

Then he would sing the praises of virtue, duty and silent self-
immolation. For he was obsessed to an extraordinary degree by a
need for devotion which nothing could satisfy.

'I should dearly love,' said she, 'to be a nursing sister. . . .'

'Such saintly tasks do not, alas, fall to the lot of us men, and I can
see for myself no profession . . . save, perhaps, that of a doctor. . . .'

Emma interrupted him with a silent shrug, and entered upon a
complaining account of the illness in which she had all but lost her
life. If only she had done so, she would not be suffering now. At once,
Léon expressed himself as being envious of the *peace of the tomb.*
One evening, he said, he had actually written a will in which he
directed that he should be buried wrapped in the handsome rug with
velvet bands that she had given him.

For it was thus they would have wished to be, each setting up an
ideal to which they now adjusted their past lives. And besides, feelings are endlessly extended by language, as though forced through a
metal-press.

At this story of the rug, however, she said: 'Why?'

'Why?'—he hesitated, and then added—'It was because I loved
you very dearly.'

Congratulating himself on having got over the difficult part, Léon
watched her face out of the corner of his eye.

It was like a sky swept clean of cloud by the wind. The weight of
gloomy thoughts which had darkened her blue eyes, seemed now to
have been withdrawn. Her expression was wholly radiant.

'I always thought you did. . . .'

Together they went over the trivial events of that distant time, the
sorrows and happiness of which they had just evoked by the magic of
a single word. He reminded her of the clematis arbour, of the clothes

she had worn, of the furniture that used to stand in her room, of the white house as he recalled it.

'And our poor cactus plants? What has happened to them?'

'The cold killed them last winter.'

'Do you know, I used to think of them such a lot. Often I would see them in imagination, as once I had seen them with my eyes, when, on summer mornings the sun shone on your Venetian blinds . . . and between their leaves I used to get a glimpse of your bare arms.'

'Ah, my poor friend,' she said, and held out her hand.

Quickly, Léon pressed it to his lips. He breathed deeply, and——

'You exercised over me in those days', he said, 'a power which I could not have explained, but which held me captive. Once, for instance, I came to your house—but I don't expect you remember the occasion to which I am referring. . . .'

'Yes, I do,' she said—'go on.'

'You were downstairs, in the hall, just preparing to go out. You were standing on the bottom step of the stairs—I even remember the hat you were wearing—it had a trimming of blue flowers. Without any invitation from you, and in spite of my better judgement, I went out when you went out. Each moment I grew more and more aware of my foolishness. I continued to walk close to you, not quite daring to follow you, yet not wishing to go away. Whenever you went into a shop, I stayed in the street with my nose glued to the window, watching you take your gloves off as you laid down your money on the counter. A little later, you rang the bell at Madame Tuvache's house, and when the servant had admitted you, I stood there like an idiot as the heavy door slammed to behind you.'

As she listened to his account of the incident, Madame Bovary was astonished to think how old she was. All these emanations from the past seemed to extend the bounds of her existence, to open up great vistas of sentiment down which she wandered in imagination. Every now and again, with eyes half closed, she murmured gently:

'Ah yes . . . how true . . . how true. . . .'

They heard eight o'clock chime from the many belfries of the Beauvoisine quarter which is full of boarding-schools, churches and huge, empty mansions. They said no more, but felt, as they looked at one another, a sort of murmuring in their heads, as though there were something audible in the mutual encounter of their glance.

They were holding hands, and all the past and all the future, all their memories and all their dreams, were caught up, and mingled in the sweetness of an ecstasy. The darkness deepened on the walls, but still they could see the crude colours of four prints representing the *Tour de Nesle*,* with lettering beneath them in Spanish and French. Through the sash-window a corner of the darkened sky showed between pointed roofs.

She got up, lit two candles on the chest-of-drawers, and then sat down again.

'Well? . . .' said Léon.

'Well? . . .' she echoed him.

He was wondering how he could resume their interrupted dialogue, when she remarked:

'How is it that no one has ever before said things like that to me?'

He explained that lofty natures were difficult to understand. He had loved her at first sight, and despair filled his heart when he thought what happiness might have been theirs had good fortune thrown them together earlier; had they been able to link their lives in bonds that nothing could have broken.

'I, too, have thought like that at times . . .' she said.

'What an exquisite dream!' murmured Léon.

Lightly fingering the blue border of her long white sash, he added: 'Why should we not begin again?'

'No, no, my friend,' she answered: 'I am too old, you are too young . . . Forget me. There will be other women to love you . . . and for you to love.'

'But not like you!'

'What a child you are! Come, let us be sensible; we *must* be sensible!'

She set herself to explain how impossible was any such passionate love between them. They must, she said, as heretofore, confine their love to that of brother and sister.

Was she serious in this?—all one can say with certainty is that she did not know herself the answer to that question, so immersed was she in the charm of his seduction, so determined that she would not yield. She looked on him with eyes of tenderness, yet gently fended off the shy caresses of his trembling hands.

'Ah, forgive me!' he exclaimed, drawing back.

Emma was seized by a vague disquiet. Such half-hearted advances seemed to her more dangerous than ever Rodolphe's brazenness had been when he had pounced on her with open arms. No man had seemed, in all her life, so handsome. His whole manner was eloquent of an exquisite frankness. He lowered his long, silky lashes which curled at the ends. His smooth cheek reddened—or so she thought—with the desire to possess her, and she felt an almost irresistible longing to touch it with her lips. Leaning towards the clock, as though to see what time it was –

'Heavens! how late it is!' she said: 'what a pair of gossips we are!'

He took her meaning, and felt for his hat.

'I had quite forgotten the theatre! My poor husband let me stay for the sole purpose of going there again. Monsieur Lormeaux, who lives in the rue Grand-Pont, is taking me, with his wife.'

His last chance had gone, for she was leaving for home next morning.

'Is that true?' he asked.

'Yes.'

'But I *must* see you again,' he went on. 'There are things I've got to tell you. . . .'

'What things?'

'One in particular . . . something important . . . something serious. . . . No, no, you mustn't go away. . . . Don't you understand even now? Can't you guess?'

'I ought to . . . for you are a skilled talker!'

'Ah! don't make a jest of it. . . . For pity's sake let me see you again . . . once . . . just once. . . .'

'Well, then . . .'

She stopped, as though she had suddenly changed her mind:

'But not here. . . .'

'Anywhere you say. . . .'

'Would you . . .'

She seemed to be turning something over in her mind, then finished her sentence with a business-like brevity—

'. . . meet me tomorrow at eleven in the cathedral?'

'I will be there!' he cried, and seized her hands: but she withdrew them.

Both were standing now. He was behind her, and, as she bent her head, he leaned forward and imprinted a long kiss on the back of her neck.

'You are mad!' she said with a little ripple of laughter: 'quite, quite mad!'

He redoubled his kisses.

Pressing forward above her shoulder, he seemed to be seeking in her eyes some sign of consent, but the glance she gave him was full of an icy majesty.

He took three steps backward to the door, but halted on the threshold. In a trembling voice he whispered:

'Till tomorrow!'

She answered with an inclination of the head, and vanished into the next room like a bird.

That evening she wrote him an interminable letter cancelling the arrangement for their meeting. All was over between them. Their happiness depended on their never seeing one another again. But, having sealed her missive, she remembered that she did not know his address, and was at a loss to know how to get it delivered. 'I will give it to him myself,' she decided. 'He is sure to keep the appointment.'

Next morning, Léon flung his window wide open and, going out on to the balcony, hummed to himself as he polished his dress-pumps till they shone and shone again. He put on a pair of white trousers, the thinnest of thin socks, and a green coat. He drenched his handkerchief with all the essences upon his dressing-table, paid a visit to the hairdresser, and then undid all the work put in by that artist in the matter of curling and singeing, so as to impart to his appearance a more natural elegance.

'It's still too early,' he thought, looking at the cuckoo-clock which hung in the shop, and noticing that it marked only nine o'clock.

He dawdled over an old fashion-paper, went out, smoked a cigar, walked the length of three streets, decided that it must be almost time for their meeting, and sauntered slowly in the direction of the wide open space in front of Notre-Dame.

It was a lovely summer's morning. Silver knick-knacks glittered in the jewellers' windows, and the light, falling obliquely on the walls of the cathedral, seemed to strike sparks from the cracks in the grey stones. A flock of birds was pirouetting against a blue sky round the Gothic pinnacles of the bell-towers. The great square, echoing to the voices of the thronging crowds, was filled with the scent of the masses of flowers which stood banked along the pavements—roses, jasmine, carnations, narcissi and tuberoses irregularly interspersed with quantities of damp greenery—catmint and groundsel for the birds. The fountain in the middle plashed and gurgled, and beneath large umbrellas, flanked by high pyramids of melons, the bare-headed market-women sat making up little bouquets of violets in twists of paper.

The young man bought one. It was the first time that he had ever bought flowers for a woman, and, as he sniffed their scent, his heart swelled with pride, as though this act of homage intended for another were being rendered to him.

All the same, he felt nervous lest he be seen and recognized: but he set his teeth and walked resolutely into the church.

The verger was standing on the threshold in the middle of the left-hand door of the main entrance, beneath the figure of the *Dancing Marianne*.* He wore a plume in his hat, a sword on his thigh, and carried a staff of office in his hand. He looked more dignified than any cardinal, and shone resplendent as a sacred pyx.

He advanced towards Léon and, with one of those smiles expressing a certain sly benignity which ecclesiastics assume when they question the young, said:

'No doubt, sir, you are a stranger here, and would wish to see the curiosities of the Sacred Fabric?'

'No,' said Léon.

He began by making the round of the aisles, then, returning to the entrance, contemplated the square. There was no sign of Emma, and he retraced his steps to the choir.

The lower portion of the pointed arches of the nave was reflected in the brimming holy-water stoups* with sections of the stained glass, but the marble rim of the basins broke the replica which, at a lower level, lay on the flagstones like a rug of many colours. The sunlight from outside struck deep into the building through the triple entry in three enormous rays. Now and again, at the far end of the church, a sacristan would hurry by, making, as he passed the altar, that casual genuflexion which is the common property of all pious folk who are pressed for time. The crystal lustres of the chandeliers hung motionless. In the choir a silver lamp was burning, and, from the side chapels—the darkest part of the interior—came an occasional ghostly sigh, or the sound of a slammed grill which reverberated beneath the soaring traceries.

Léon moved with solemn steps, keeping close to the walls. Never had he found life so good. In a moment now she would come, charming, excited, glancing over her shoulder to see whether she were being followed—with her flounced dress, her gold lorgnon, her dainty boots, and other touches of elegance which as yet he had not sampled. There would be about her that aura, so irresistibly seductive, yet so impossible to describe, of virtue on the point of surrender. The church, like some gigantic boudoir, would spread around, the vaulted ceiling bending forward to catch within its sanctuary of shadows the whispered confession of her love. The windows cast their resplendent light for her face alone; the censer was emitting wreaths of smoke that she might stand there like an angel misted about with clouds of perfume.

But still she did not come. He sat down on a chair, and his wandering attention was caught by a window of blue glass on which a number of boatmen were depicted, carrying baskets.* He looked at it long and earnestly, counting the scales on the fish and the buttonholes in the men's doublets. But his thoughts were elsewhere, trying to account for Emma's continued absence. Nearby, the verger was indulging in a good deal of private indignation at the expense of this stranger who dared to admire the cathedral without assistance. Such conduct he regarded as monstrous, tantamount to theft and not far removed from sacrilege.

There was a swish of silk on the flagstones, the glimpse of a hatbrim, of a black hood. . . . It was she! Léon jumped up and ran to meet her.

Emma looked pale: she was walking quickly.

'Read this,' she said, holding out a sheet of paper—'No, don't'—and she snatched her hand from his. Then she went into the Lady Chapel,* knelt down, leaned her head against the back of the chair in front, and started to pray.

This pious whim irritated the young man, though he found a certain charm in seeing her thus lost in her devotions in the very middle of a lover's tryst, like some great lady of Spain. But when there seemed likely to be no end to her preoccupation, he soon grew bored.

Emma was praying, or, rather, forcing herself to pray, hoping that heaven might grant her strength of mind. The more surely to attract divine intervention, she feasted her eyes on the glories of the Tabernacle,* breathed in the perfume of the white wild-flowers blooming in the great vases, and listened to the silence of the church, though it had but the effect of increasing the turmoil of her heart.

She got up, and they were about to leave the building when the verger hurried forward:

'No doubt, ma'am, you are a stranger here and would like to see the curiosities of the Sacred Fabric?'

'No!' exclaimed the lawyer's clerk.

'Why not?' said she, for her tottering virtue was clinging to the Virgin, to the sculptured effigies, to the tombs, to everything, in fact, which might afford her a refuge.

That his conducted tour might proceed in its due and proper sequence, the verger led them as far back as the main entrance, where he pointed with his staff to a great circle of black stones set in the floor without carving or inscription of any kind.*

'That', he said pompously, 'represents the circumference of Amboise's great bell.* It weighed forty thousand pounds, and there was none to match it in Europe. The workman who cast it died of joy. . . .'

'Let us get away from here,' said Léon.

Their guide moved on. When he had once more reached the Lady Chapel he spread his arms in an inclusive gesture of demonstration, and his voice expressed more pride than that of a landed proprietor displaying the fruit-trees in his walled garden.

'This simple stone covers the mortal remains of Pierre de Brézé,* Lord of Varennes and Brissac, Grand Marshal of Poitou and Governor of Normandy, slain at the Battle of Montlhéry,* 16th July, 1465.'

Léon bit his lip and tapped impatiently with his foot.

'The horseman to his right, armed cap-à-pie and mounted on a rearing charger, is his grandson, Louis de Brézé, Lord of Bréval and Montchauvet, Count of Maulévrier, Baron de Mauny, Chamberlain to the King, Knight of the Order, and, like his grandsire, Governor of Normandy—died 23rd July, 1531, it being a Sunday, as the inscription states. The figure seen below, on the point of entering a tomb, is another representation of the same. It would be impossible, as I think you'll agree, to see a better visual expression of the act of death.'

Madame Bovary raised her lorgnon. Léon stood motionless, looking at her. He made no attempt to move or to speak, so discouraged was he by this joint display of volubility and indifference.

The guide, who seemed destined to be with them through eternity, continued:

'The female figure shown in tears in his close proximity, is his wife, Diane de Poitiers,* Countess of Brézé, Duchess of Valentinois, born 1499, died 1566. The figure to her right is that of the Holy Virgin. And now, if you will come this way, you will see the Amboise tombs,* both being cardinals and archbishops of Rouen. That one over there was Minister to King Louis XII,* and a generous patron of the cathedral. His will contained a legacy of three thousand golden crowns to the poor of the city.'

Talking all the while he pushed them into a chapel cumbered with balustrades.* Some of these he moved, thus revealing a block of stone which might well have been a badly carved statue.

'This', he said with a deep sigh, 'formerly adorned the tomb of Richard Coeur de Lion, King of England and Duke of Normandy. It was the Calvinists, sir, who reduced it to its present state.* With deliberate malice they buried it in the earth beneath the bishop's throne. Note the door by which Monsignor has access to his palace. Follow me, *if* you please, and we will pay a visit to the stained glass of La Gargouille.'*

Monsieur Léon hurriedly took a silver coin from his pocket, and seized Emma by the arm. The verger stood dumbfounded. He could not understand such untimely munificence, there being so many things for the visitors still to see.

He called after them:

'But the spire, sir—the spire!'

'No thanks,' said Léon.

'You'll be making a great mistake, sir, if you miss it. Four hundred and forty feet high, only nine less than the Great Pyramid of Egypt, and constructed *entirely* of cast iron, it . . .'

Léon fled, for it seemed to him that his love which, for the past two hours, had been immobilized in the church as though it had formed part of the fabric, was now on the point of evaporating like smoke up the species of truncated funnel, oblong cage or filigree chimney which so perilously, so fantastically, crowns the cathedral, for all the world like an eccentric fantasy of some whimsical tinker.*

'Where are you taking me?' she asked. He made no reply, but continued to walk quickly on. Madame Bovary had just dipped her finger in the holy water stoup when they heard behind them a sound of heavy breathing broken by the regular tap-tapping of a stick. Léon turned his head.

'Sir!'

'What's the matter now?'

He recognized the verger and saw that he was carrying under one arm a pile of twenty large paper-bound books, which he was clasping to his stomach in an effort to keep them from falling. They were, all of them, works dealing with the cathedral.

'The fool!' muttered Léon, and flung out of the church.

A small street-urchin was loitering in front of the building.

'Run and fetch me a cab!'

The boy shot off like a bullet down the rue des Quatre-Vents. For some minutes they stood there, quite alone, face to face and slightly embarrassed.

'Oh, Léon . . . really . . . I don't know whether I ought . . .'

She spoke with a simpering air, but added on a more serious note: 'I suppose you realize that all this is highly improper?'

'What d'you mean, improper?' replied the young man. 'People do it every day in Paris.'

Those words decided her as though they were an irrefutable argument.

No cab, however, appeared. Léon was afraid she might go back into the church. But at last it turned up.

'Oh, but do, please, at least leave the building by the North Door!'* cried the verger, who had remained standing on the threshold – 'just so as to see *The Resurrection, The Last Judgement, Paradise, King David*, and *The Damned Souls in Hell Fire*!'

'Where does Monsieur wish to go?' inquired the driver.

'Anywhere you like!' said Léon, pushing Emma into the vehicle.

It lumbered off.

Down the rue Grand-Pont they went, crossed the place des Arts, the quai Napoléon, the Pont Neuf, and stopped short in front of the statue of Pierre Corneille.*

'Drive on!' said a voice from within.

The cab set off again, and, gathering speed on the slope which leads down from the place La Fayette, swung into the station yard at a hand-gallop.

'No, straight on!' cried the same voice.

It passed through the city gates, and once on the public promenade, trotted gently between the rows of great elms. The driver mopped his forehead, put his leather hat between his legs, and, cutting across the side-walk, took a course along the river, skirting the turf. He followed the tow-path with its surface of dry pebbles, and drove on a long way towards Oyssel, beyond the islands.

But suddenly he increased his speed, dashed through Quatre-mares, Sotteville, La Grande Chaussée and the rue d'Elbeouf, stop-ping for the third time in front of the Zoological Gardens.

'Get on, will you!' cried the voice more angrily than ever.

Resuming its journey, the cab went by Saint-Sever, the quai des Curandiers, the quai aux Meules, crossed the bridge again into the place Champ-de-Mars, rumbling past the gardens of the hospital where old men in black coats were sunning themselves, and along a terrace green with ivy. It went back up the boulevard Bouvreuil, on along the boulevard Cauchoise, and up Mont-Riboudet and so to the hill of Deville.

There it turned, and aimlessly, without taking any definite direc-tion, drove on at random. It was seen at Saint-Pol, at Lescure, at Mont Gargan, at Rouge-Mare, in the place du Gaillard-bois: it was seen in the rue Maladrerie and the rue Dinanderie, in front of Saint-Romain, of Saint-Vivien, of Saint-Maclou and Sainte-Nicaise, in front of the Customs House, at the Vieille-Tour, at Trois Pipes and the cemetery. From time to time the driver cast despairing glances from his box at the taverns he was passing. It was beyond his com-prehension what frenzy of locomotion forbad his fares to stop. Occasionally he attempted to draw up, only to hear behind him exclamations of fury. Then he lashed more vigorously than ever at his sweating jades; heedless of jolts he pursued his career, bumping into various obstacles, but not caring; demoralized and almost in tears from thirst, fatigue and misery.

Down at the harbour, in a hurly-burly of wagons and casks, along the streets, at various milestones, the citizens stared wide-eyed at that most extraordinary of all sights in a provincial town—a carriage with drawn blinds, constantly reappearing, more secret than a tomb and bucketing like a ship at sea.

Once, about midday,* out in the open country, with the sun strik-ing full on the plated lamps, a bare hand emerged from behind the little curtains of yellow canvas, and scattered some scraps of paper which eddied in the wind and settled afar off, like so many white butterflies, on a field of red flowering clover.

At last, about six o'clock, the cab stopped* in a lane of the Beauvoisine quarter, and a woman got out. She walked away with her veil lowered, and did not once turn her head.

CHAPTER II

ON arriving at the inn, Madame Bovary was surprised to find that the diligence was no longer there. Hivert had waited for fifty-three minutes, at the end of which time he had started without her.

There was no compulsion on her to leave, but she had given her word that she would be home that evening. Besides, Charles would be waiting for her, and she was already conscious of that feeling of apathetic docility which, for many women, is at once the penalty of adultery and its atonement. She hurriedly packed her trunks, paid her bill, took a cab which was standing in the yard, and, by dint of pestering the driver with protests, encouragement and inquiries about what the time was and how far they had gone, managed to overtake the Swallow just as it was passing the first houses of Quincampoix.

Scarcely had she sat down in her corner than she closed her eyes, and did not open them again until they were at the bottom of the hill, where she saw Félicité in the distance standing in front of the forge, on the lookout for her. Hivert reined in his horses, and the cook, hoisting herself up to the level of the window, said, with an air of mystery:

'Please go at once to Monsieur Homais's, ma'am, it's very urgent.'

Silence, as usual, brooded over the village. At every corner of every street were little reddish heaps from which steam rose into the air, for it was the jam-making season, and in Yonville all the housewives chose the same day for the boiling of their fruit. But the particular heap which stood in front of the chemist's shop was large enough to attract general attention, and could claim over its competitors that superiority which belongs of right to a laboratory in comparison with mere private stoves, to something which proceeds from a general need and not simply and solely from a private whim.

She entered. The large armchair was overturned, and even the

Fanal de Rouen lay spread out on the floor between two pestles. She pushed open the door of the passage, and there, in the middle of the kitchen, amid brown jars filled with red-currants stripped from their stalks, sugar grated and sugar in lumps, scales on the table and copper pans on the fire, saw the whole muster of the Homais family, old and young alike, with aprons up to their chins and forks in their hands. Justin was hanging his head and the chemist was shouting:

'Who told you to look in the Den?'

'What has happened? what is the matter?'

'What is the matter?' replied the apothecary; 'I'll tell you what's the matter. There's jam-making going on. The women are doing the cooking, but the mixture had too big a head on it, and was on the point of boiling over, so I sent for another pan. And what must this lout do through sheer laziness or apathy, but take down the key of the Den from where it hangs in my laboratory!'

This was the name he gave to an attic under the roof which was full of household utensils and stocks of various commodities used in the business. He would often pass long hours there alone, labelling, decanting, repacking. In his eyes it was far more than a simple store-room. It held for him the dignity of a sanctum whence would emerge, decked out elaborately by himself, all sorts of pills, boluses, infusions, lotions and potions destined to spread his fame through all the surrounding countryside. No one was allowed to set foot in it, and such importance did he attach to the place, that he swept it out with his own hands. If the shop, open to all-comers, was the spot in which he proudly exhibited his skill, the Den was an asylum of refuge where, with self-centred concentration, he found pleasure in the work of his choice. He regarded Justin's thoughtlessness as a monstrous piece of irreverence. With his face redder than the cur-rants, he repeated—

'Yes, of the Den: the key which locks up the acids and the caustic alkalis. He must needs go and take one of the spare pans! a pan with a lid! I might never have wanted to use it, but no matter: everything employed in the delicate operations of my art is an object of import-ance! Devil take it! one must draw the line somewhere and not utilize in quasi-domestic activities things intended for pharmaceutical pur-poses! It is as though someone were to set about carving a chicken with a scalpel, as though a magistrate . . .'

'Don't get so excited,' said Madame Homais, and Athalie, tugging at his coat-tails, set up a cry of 'Papa! papa!'

'Leave me alone!' went on the apothecary: 'leave me alone! Good Lord, I might as well be in the grocery business! Go ahead, the lot of you! Show no respect for anything! Break! smash! let the leeches loose! burn the mallow! Use the retorts for pickling gherkins! Tear up the bandages! . . .'

'But you had . . .' Emma began.

'Just a moment! . . . Do you realize the risks you were running? Did you notice nothing—in the left-hand corner of the third shelf? Speak! answer! say something!'

'I . . . d–don't know . . .' stuttered the lad.

'Ah, so you don't know? Well, I do! What you saw was a blue glass bottle, sealed with yellow wax. It contains a white powder, and I put a label on it myself, with the word *Dangerous*! D'you know what's in that bottle! Arsenic! You must needs go and meddle with *that*, take a pan standing beside *that*!'

'Beside it!' exclaimed Madame Homais, clasping her hands. 'Arsenic! why, you might have poisoned all of us!'

The children began to scream as though they already felt the most appalling agonies within them.

'Or a patient,' went on the apothecary. 'I suppose it would have afforded you pleasure to see me in the dock at the next assizes, and later dragged to the scaffold? Don't you know how careful I always am when I dispense prescriptions, even though I *have* been at it for years? I am often quite unmanned with terror when I think of the responsibility which devolves upon me. For the government never tires of persecuting us, and the absurd laws under which we live are a veritable sword of Damocles suspended over our heads!'

Emma no longer thought of asking what she was wanted for, and the chemist drove full speed ahead into his breathless tirade.

'This is how you repay the kindness which has been lavished on you. This is the reward I get for watching over your interests like a father! Where would you be now but for me? How would you have been fed, educated, clothed and given an opportunity to take an honoured place, some day, in the ranks of society? But before you can do that you have got to sweat at the oar and grow a tough skin on your hands, as they say. *Fabricando fit faber, age quod agis.*'*

He quoted Latin in his exasperation. He would have quoted

Chinese or the language of Greenland, had he known them. For he was at one of those crises in which the mind pours out, muddled and jumbled, everything that is in it, like the ocean when, swept by tempest, it tosses to the surface weed and sand alike.

He went on:

'I am beginning to regret that I ever saddled myself with you! I should have done better to let you wallow in the miser- able squalor of your origins! You will never be good for any thing but tending horned beasts! You have no aptitude for the sciences! You barely know how to stick on a label, and here you live in my house like a cathedral canon, like a gorged cock, stuffing yourself sick!'

But Emma, turning to Madame Homais, said:

'I was told to come. . . .'

'Heavens above!' broke in the good woman with an air of tragedy—'how am I to break it to you? . . . Such terrible news!'

She got no further. The apothecary thundered on.

'Empty it! scour it! take it back!—hurry, hurry!'

He shook Justin by the collar of his smock so violently that a book tumbled out of the lad's pocket.

Justin bent to pick it up, but Homais was quicker, and, having seized the volume, stared at it, his eyes starting from his head, his mouth hanging open.

'*Conjugal . . . Love*,'* he said slowly, separating the two words. 'Oh admirable! admirable indeed . . . quite charming . . . illustrated, too . . . This is the last straw !'

Madame Homais stepped forward:

'No! don't touch it!'

The children wanted to look at the pictures.

'Leave the room!' said their father with all the authority of a despot.

They went out.

At first Homais paced up and down the room with long strides, holding the book open in his hands, rolling his eyes, fighting for breath, his neck swelling, on the verge of an apoplectic fit. Then he went straight across to his apprentice and confronted him with folded arms.

'So, you are replete with all the vices, wretched youth! . . . You didn't stop to think, I suppose, that this infamous work might have fallen into the hands of my children, might have struck a spark in their minds, might have tarnished Athalie's purity, corrupted Napoleon—who is already a man in all but age! Are you sure they have not read it? Are you prepared to swear? . . .'

'There's something you want to tell me, I believe,' said Emma.

'Oh yes, ma'am . . . your father-in-law's dead!'

Bovary the elder had, in fact, passed away the evening before, quite suddenly, as the result of an apoplectic seizure, after leaving the table. Charles, from an excessive concern for her feelings, had asked Monsieur Homais to break the sad news gently.

He had turned over in his mind what he should say, had rounded, polished, balanced the necessary phrases, and had achieved a master-piece of tact and indirection, of subtle nuances and delicate hints. But anger had swept oratory to the winds.

Emma, despairing of any more detailed account, left the shop. For Monsieur Homais had resumed the course of his vituperation. But he was calmer now, and grumbled away in paternal fashion, fanning himself the while with his skull-cap.

'It is not that I wholly disapprove of the work. Its author was a doctor. It contains certain items of scientific information which it is well that a man should have—which, I will go so far as to say, a man *must* have. But later, later . . . wait until you are grown up and your character is fully formed.'

At the sound of Emma's knock, Charles, who had been waiting for her, came forward with his arms open, and said, with tears in his voice:

'My dear, dear wife. . . .'

Very gently he leaned forward to kiss her. But at the touch of his lips, the memory of the man she had left took hold on her, and she passed her hand over her face with a shudder.

But she managed to say:

'I know . . . I know. . . .'

He showed her the letter in which his mother told of what had happened without any sentimental hypocrisy. The only thing she regretted was that her husband had been deprived of the comforts of religion, having died at Doudeville,* in the street, just outside a café, after a patriotic dinner at which he had been present with a number of former officers.

Emma handed back the letter. At dinner, from a sense of what was due, she pretended that she did not want any food. But he pressed her, and she set herself resolutely to eat, while Charles, opposite, sat motionless in an attitude of dejection.

From time to time he raised his head and gave her a long look eloquent of distress. Once he sighed.

'If only I could have seen him again!'

She said nothing. Then, realizing that some comment was expected of her:

'How old was your father?'

'Fifty-eight.'

'Ah!'

And that was all.

A quarter of an hour later, he added: 'My poor mother! what will become of her?'

She made a gesture expressive of ignorance. Seeing her so taciturn, Charles assumed that her mood was the result of sorrow, and forced himself to say nothing lest he add to the pain which was afflicting her. Throwing off his own melancholy:

'Did you enjoy yourself yesterday?' he asked.

'Yes.'

When the cloth had been removed, Charles remained seated. So did she, and, as she watched him, the monotonous sameness of what she saw gradually drove all pity from her heart. He seemed to her to be in every way a sickly, weak, negative, poor creature. How could she get rid of him? What an interminable evening! Something stupefying, like opium fumes, numbed her faculties.

They heard the tap-tap of a stick on the wooden floor of the hall. It was Hippolyte bringing in her luggage.

In order to set it down he had to make a painful half-circle with his wooden leg.

'He doesn't even think of it any more!' she said to herself, watching the poor devil whose coarse red hair was dripping with sweat.

Bovary felt in his purse for a farthing. He did not seem to realize how humiliating for him was the mere presence of this man, who stood there a living reproach to his incurable incompetence.

'That's a pretty bouquet,' he said, noticing Léon's violets on the mantelpiece.

'Yes,' she replied without interest, 'I bought it from a woman who was begging in the street.'

Charles took the violets. Their freshness cooled his eyes which were red from weeping. He sniffed them delicately. Hurriedly she took them from him and put them in a bowl of water.

Next day, Madame Bovary the elder arrived. She and her son cried a good deal, and Emma, saying that she had a number of orders to give, disappeared.

On the morrow, there were details of mourning to be discussed. The two women took their work-baskets and sat in the arbour by the river-side.

Charles was thinking about his father. He was surprised at the amount of affection he felt for a man whom, till then, he had thought he loved only in a very half-hearted fashion. Old Madame Bovary was thinking about her husband. The worst times of her past now seemed enviable to her. All grievances were washed away by her instinctive regret for old habits of living now gone for ever. From time to time, while she plied her needle, a large tear slid down her nose and hung for a moment suspended at its tip.

Emma was thinking that scarcely forty-eight hours ago *they* had been together, shut away from the world, drunk with passion, unable to take their eyes from one another. She tried to recapture every tiny detail of the day just gone, but the presence of her mother-in-law and of her husband made her feel awkward. She would have liked to hear nothing, see nothing, that she might not disturb the vivid memory of her love which, do what she would, was slipping away from her under the pressure of external sensations.

She was unpicking the lining of a dress, and odds and ends of material lay scattered round her. Old Madame Bovary, without raising her eyes, was using her scissors, which squeaked, and Charles, in his list slippers and the old brown overcoat which he had adopted as a dressing-gown, was sitting with his hands in his pockets, maintaining the general silence. Close to them, Berthe, in her little white apron, was scraping up the gravel on the garden path with her spade.

Suddenly Monsieur Lheureux came in by the gate.

He had called to offer his services '*in view of the melancholy circumstances.*' Emma replied that they thought they could do without his assistance. But he refused to take no for an answer.

'A thousand pardons,' he said: 'but I should very much like a word with you in private:' and he added in a lower voice: '. . . about you know what.'

Charles went red to the tips of his ears. 'Ah yes . . . of course, and, turning in his embarrassment to his wife, said:

'I wonder, my dear, whether you'd mind . . .'

She seemed to understand what he meant, for she got up.

'It's nothing,' Charles reassured his mother: 'probably some trivial matter connected with the house.'

He did not want her to know about the bill, for fear of what she might say.

As soon as they were alone, Monsieur Lheureux proceeded, without further beating about the bush, to congratulate Emma on coming into money. This done, he led the conversation on to such indifferent topics as fruit-trees, the harvest, and the state of his own health, which was only so-so, now up, now down. The truth of the matter was, he explained, that he slaved like five thousand devils, though, in spite of what people said, he didn't make enough to allow him butter with his bread.

Emma let him talk. For the last two days she had been prodigiously bored.

'And you, I hope, are quite well again?' he went on: 'my word, but your husband was in a terrible state! He's a decent enough chap, though he and I haven't always seen eye to eye.'

She asked what had been the trouble between them, for Charles had said nothing to her about the argument over her purchases.

'You're not going to tell me you don't know?' said Lheureux. 'It was over those fancies of yours—the travelling trunks.'

He had pulled his hat down over his eyes and, with his hands behind his back, smiling and whistling, stood intently staring at her. Did he suspect anything? Emma felt lost in the onset of her fears. At length, however, he said:

'We've made it up now. I came here today to propose . . . an arrangement.'

This was that Bovary should renew the bill. He must, of course, do as he thought fit. He mustn't worry about it, especially not now, when he must have troubles enough on his hands.

'He'd much better shift the whole responsibility on to some one else—you, for instance. It would be quite easy with a power of attorney,* and then you and I could do business. . . .'

She did not understand, and said nothing. Turning next to his own concerns, Lheureux remarked that she could hardly refuse to buy something from him. He would send her over some black silk, twelve yards, enough for a dress.

'The one you have on is good enough for wearing about the house, but you need something better for visits. I noticed that as soon as I came in. I've got as keen an eye as any American!'

But he did not send the material: instead, he brought it in person. Then he paid another visit in order to take her measurements, and several more on various pretexts, doing his best on each occasion to be friendly and useful, to '*ingratiate*' himself, as Homais would have said, and always managing to slip in a few words of advice about the power of attorney. He never once mentioned the bill, and she ceased to think of it. In the early stages of her convalescence, Charles certainly had said something to her, but she had had so many worries, that she had forgotten all about it. Besides, she was careful to avoid starting any argument about money, an attitude which surprised the old lady, who attributed her change of temper to the religious sentiments which she had contracted during her illness.

But as soon as she had left them, Emma surprised Bovary with evidence of her practical good sense. They would have, she said, to go into the whole position very carefully, check up on their mortgages, and decide whether they had better sell everything at auction or go into voluntary liquidation.

She employed technical terms at random, used a great many big-sounding words, such as order, the future, foresight—and was for ever exaggerating the complexities of his father's estate. This went on until one day she showed him the rough draft of a document authorizing her to 'direct and administer his affairs, negotiate loans, sign and endorse bills, pay out moneys' etc. . . . She had profited from Lheureux's lessons.

Charles innocently inquired where the document came from.

'From Maître Guillaumin.'

And, cool as a cucumber, she added:

'I haven't any great confidence in it. Lawyers have a very bad reputation. I think we ought to take advice . . . but there's nobody we know except . . . no, there isn't anybody at all.'

'How about Léon?' suggested Charles, who was thinking.

But it would be difficult to explain matters by letter. She offered, therefore, to make the necessary journey. He thanked her, but refused to entertain the idea. She insisted. They engaged in a duel of mutual courtesies. At last, in a burst of carefully assumed roguishness:

'No, *please*,' she protested: 'I *will* go!'

'How good you are!' he said, kissing her on the forehead.

Next day she took her seat in the Swallow for the trip to Rouen, where she was to ask counsel of Monsieur Léon.

She stayed there for three days.

CHAPTER III

THEY were three full, exquisite and splendid days, a true honeymoon.

They stayed at the Hôtel de Boulogne, down on the quay. They spent the whole time there, with shutters and doors closed, with flowers scattered on the carpet. Iced drinks were brought up at intervals from the morning onwards.

When evening came they took a boat with an awning and went out to one of the islands for dinner.

It was the hour of the day when from every shipyard came the sound of caulking hammers working on the hulls. The smoke of burning pitch drifted up between the trees, and the surface of the river showed patches of oil heaving unevenly in the red light of the setting sun, like floating plates of Florentine bronze.

They went downstream through a medley of moored vessels, whose long, slanting cables grazed the top of their little craft.

Gradually the sounds of the town grew fainter, the rumbling of carts, the hubbub of voices, the barking of dogs on the decks of ships. Emma took off her hat. They landed on their island, and sat in the low-ceiled public room of a tavern, which had black nets hanging round its door. They ate fried smelts, cream and cherries. They lay on the grass and embraced under the poplars, in a quiet place. They longed to live like a couple of Robinson Crusoes, for ever in this tiny spot which seemed to them, in their mood of bliss, to be the loveliest in all the world. It was not the first time that they had seen trees, blue sky and green turf, or heard the lapping of water and the moaning of the breeze through the leaves, but it is doubtful whether they had ever before known the wonder of these things. It was as though nature had never before existed, or had taken on its full beauty only now that their desires were gratified.

At night they went back. The boat skirted the islands. They sat in the darkness of the stern, saying nothing. The square-cut oars creaked in the metal rowlocks, and the rhythmical sound was like that of a metronome in the silence, while the painter trailing behind them kept up a gentle rippling in the water.

Once, when they were thus bound for home, the moon rose, and they greeted it with no lack of phrases, finding the planet melancholy and full of poetry. Emma even began to sing:

'*Un soir, t'en souvient-il? nous voguions*,'* etc.

Her weak, melodious voice was lost over the waters and the wind blew her trilling notes into nothingness. Léon listened to them as they went by him like the fluttering of wings in the surrounding air.

She sat facing him, leaning against the bulkhead where an open shutter let in the moon. Her black dress, billowing out in a great fan of draperies, made her look slimmer and taller. Her head was raised, her hands clasped, and her eyes were fixed upon the heavens. At times the willow shadows blotted her out entirely, but the next moment she would reappear, like a vision, in the light of the moon.

Léon, lying beside her in the bottom of the boat, found a piece of flame-coloured silk ribbon beneath his hand.

The boatman examined it. After a while he said:

'Probably belongs to a party I took for a row the other day. A gay lot, they was, gentlemen and ladies, with cakes and champagne and cornets—the whole bag of tricks! There was one of 'em in particular, good-looking, tall gent he was, with a little bit of a moustache. Make 'em laugh!—I should say he did! They kept on saying something like:

'Tell us a story . . . Adolphe . . . Dodolphe . . . some name like that.'

She shivered.

'Don't you feel well?' asked Léon, edging closer to her.

'It's nothing . . . just the chill of the night air, I expect.'

'Don't suppose *'e's* ever short of women,' went on the old salt in a quiet voice, doubtless imagining that he was giving an exhibition of good manners to the strangers. Then, spitting on his palms, he resumed his oars.

But the time came at last when they had to part. Their good-byes were sad. He agreed to write under cover to Madame Rollet, and such minute instructions did she give him in the matter of double envelopes, that he was filled with admiration of her amorous cunning.

'Everything is really all right, isn't it?' she said as she kissed him for the last time.

'Of course it is!'—But why, he wondered, as he took his lonely way back through the streets, was she so anxious to get that power of attorney?

CHAPTER IV

LÉON began very soon to assume an air of superiority in the presence of his companions. He saw less of them than he had done, and was neglecting his work.

He waited for her letters and read them over and over again. He wrote to her. He conjured up her image with the full force of his desires and memories. His longing to see her again, instead of diminishing with absence, increased to such an extent that one Saturday morning he played truant from his office.

When, from the top of the hill, he saw the church-tower below him in the valley, with its tin weather-vane turning in the breeze, he felt the same sort of pleasure compounded of triumphant vanity and egotistical sentiment as must come over a millionaire returning to his native village.

He prowled round her house. A light was shining in the kitchen. He watched her shadow on the blind. No one appeared.

When old Madame Lefrançois saw him, she became very talkative. He was 'taller and thinner' than he used to be, she said. Artémise, on the other hand, thought him 'stockier and more tanned'.

He dined, as of old, in the small parlour, but without a companion, for Binet, sick of waiting for the Swallow, had now advanced the time of his meal by an hour, and sat down at five o'clock punctually, though he still quite often asserted that the *old ticker* was slow.

Plucking up courage, Léon went across and knocked at the doctor's door. Madame was in her room, and it was a quarter of an hour before she came down. Monsieur seemed to be delighted to see him again, but did not stir from the house all that evening or the next day.

Léon saw her alone late that evening, behind the garden, in the lane—that same lane where she had been wont to meet another! The weather was stormy. They talked under the shelter of an umbrella by the glare of lightning flashes.

Their periods of separation were becoming intolerable.

'Death would be preferable!' said Emma. She writhed in his arms, weeping.

'Good-bye!—good-bye! when shall I see you again?'

They ran back for one last kiss, and it was then that she promised, by hook or by crook, to discover some way in which she might always be free to see him at least once a week. She was sure this could be managed. She was full of hope. There was some money coming to her.

She bought for her room a pair of yellow curtains with broad stripes, which Monsieur Lheureux said he was letting her have dirt cheap. She dreamed of a carpet, and Lheureux, saying that 'there wouldn't be much difficulty about that', obligingly undertook to get one for her. She could no longer do without his help. Twenty times a day she would send for him, and he would put aside anything he happened to be doing, without so much as a sigh. No one could understand either why it was that Madame Rollet lunched every day at Emma's house, and even paid her visits in private.

It was about this time, that is to say early in the winter, that Madame Bovary seemed to have been taken with a great passion for music.

One evening, while Charles was listening to her, she began the same piece over again four separate times. She made no concealment of her vexation, but he, not noticing the difference, exclaimed:

'Bravo! . . . First rate! . . . you mustn't stop . . . go on.'

'No, it's terrible: my fingers are all thumbs!'

Next day he begged her to play to him again.

'All right, if it pleases you.'

Charles had to admit that she had lost something of her skill. She confused her keys, stumbled over her notes, and finally broke down altogether.

'It's no use! I ought to take lessons, but . . .'

She bit her lips and added:

'Twenty francs a time: that's too dear.'

'It certainly is rather a lot,' said Charles with a foolish giggle. 'Still, I think we might find someone who would teach you for less. There are lots of musicians who have not made a reputation as yet but who are often worth more than the celebrities.'

'I don't know where you're going to find them.'

Next day, when he came home, he gave her a sly look. For a while he said nothing, but at last could contain himself no longer:

'How obstinate you can be sometimes! I was over at Barfeuchères today, and Madame Liégeard assured me that her three daughters at the convent school are taking lessons at two francs an hour from quite a well-known teacher.'

She shrugged her shoulders, but made no attempt to open her instrument.

Whenever she passed close to it, however (and if Bovary was within earshot) she sighed:

'Ah, my poor piano!'

When anyone came to the house she invariably remarked that she had entirely given up her music and that there were very good reasons why she could not start studying again. Much sympathy was expressed on her account. What a pity it was that someone with so much talent should talk like that! The visitors even went so far as to take up the question with Bovary. He was made to feel that he was in some way responsible. The chemist, in particular, was very outspoken.

'You're making a great mistake. Natural talents should never be allowed to lie fallow. Besides, don't you realize, my dear friend, that by encouraging your wife to study you would save a lot of money in the long run on your daughter's musical education. I am strongly of the opinion that a child's natural teacher is its mother. It was one of Rousseau's favourite ideas.* No doubt it is still regarded as being somewhat revolutionary, but I am quite sure that, ultimately, it will carry the day over all opposition, just as has happened in the matter of suckling babies,* and of vaccination.'*

Charles returned to the question of piano-playing. Emma replied bitterly that they had much better sell the instrument. But the thought of seeing the poor piano, which had been a source of so much self-congratulation, moved from the house, was more than he could bear. It would be tantamount, in some indefinable way, to the suicide of one whole part of himself.

'If,' he said, 'you'd like an occasional lesson, I think it could be managed without ruining me.'

'But it's no good taking lessons unless one means to go on with them,' she replied.

In this way she managed to get his consent to her going to town once a week to see her lover.

After only a month she was indeed found to have made considerable progress.

CHAPTER V

IT was on Thursdays that she went into Rouen. On these occasions, she got up and dressed quietly so as not to wake Charles who might have made some comment about the time.

She would pace to and fro, stopping in front of the windows and looking down into the square. The early day would be filtering between the pillars of the market-hall, and in the pale light of dawn the capital letters which adorned the front of the chemist's shop (where all the shutters were closed) could be plainly seen.

When the clock marked a quarter-past seven, she would walk across to the Golden Lion. Artémise yawned as she unbolted the front-door and raked up the hot embers from under the ashes for her visitor's benefit. There was no one in the kitchen but Emma. From time to time she went out into the street. Hivert was harnessing the horses in leisurely fashion, listening the while to Madame Lefrançois who, with her night-capped head projecting from an upper window, was giving him a number of instructions and explanations which would have completely confused anybody else. Emma tapped with her foot on the flagstones of the yard. At last, having drunk a bowl of soup, he put on his driving coat, lit his pipe, grasped his whip, and took his seat on the box without any sign of hurry.

The Swallow started off at a hand-trot. In the course of the first quarter of a mile it made a succession of stops for the purpose of picking up passengers who were waiting at their garden gates. Those who had booked their places the night before kept it waiting. Some were still in bed. Hivert called to them by name, swore loudly, and finally, dismounting from his box, thundered on the panels of the door. The wind blew through the cracked screens of the diligence. At last, however, the four benches had their full complement, the vehicle rumbled off, and the long line of apple-trees slid slowly past. The road, flanked by ditches filled with yellow water, dwindled away to the distant horizon.

Emma was familiar with every inch of it. She knew that after the
pasture-land there was first a post, then an elm, a barn or roadman's
cabin. Sometimes, to give herself surprises, she would close her eyes.
But she never lost her sense of the mileage to be covered.

Gradually the brick houses grew more frequent, the earth gave
out a harder note beneath the wheels, the Swallow glided between
gardens in which, through the lattice-work of iron gates, the eye
caught a glimpse of statues, of an occasional hillock crowned with a
trellised arbour, clipped yews or children's swings.

Suddenly the whole city lay spread below them.* Tiered like an
amphitheatre and drowned in mist, it overflowed into a confused
huddle of houses out beyond the bridges. In the distance the open
country began again, climbing the further slopes in a dull monotony
until it seemed actually to touch the low, grey sky. Seen thus from
above, the whole landscape had the motionless appearance of a picture. The ships at anchor were crowded together in one corner. The
river swept round the foot of green-clad hills, and the oblong islands
had the appearance of large black fish lying on the surface of the
water. The factory chimneys belched huge brown plumes of smoke
shredded at their extremities by the breeze. She could hear the roar
of the foundries and the thin carillons of churches whose towers
pierced through the mist. The leafless trees along the boulevards
showed as patches of violet between the houses. Roofs, shining with
moisture, glittered in a broken line that rose and fell with the height
of the buildings in different parts of the town. An occasional puff of
wind blew the clouds towards Saint-Catherine's hill like aerial waves
breaking silently against a cliff.

The sense of crowded lives made her feel almost giddy. Her heart
swelled with awareness of them, as though the hundred and twenty
thousand souls quivering down there before her eyes were, at one
and the same moment, discharging in the form of a vapour all the
passions with which she supposed them to be torn. Her love swelled
as she looked on the wide spaces of the scene before her, and took to
itself some of the vague tumult that rose from the valley. She poured
it out again on the spreading panorama, over the squares, the prom-
enades, the streets. The old Norman city looked to her eyes like a
gigantic metropolis, a Babylon, which she was on the point of entering. She leaned through the curtains of the diligence, both hands
upon the ledge, drinking in the breeze. The three horses broke into a

gallop. The stones grated in the mud, the vehicle swayed from side to side. Hivert hailed the wagons he passed long before he had come up with them, and several groups of towns-folk, who had been spending the night in Le Bois-Guillaume, drove quietly down the hill in their little family equipages.

They drew up at the city bounds. Emma took off her over-shoes, changed her gloves, readjusted her shawl. Twenty yards further on she said good-bye to the Swallow.

The town was waking up. Assistants in skull-caps were washing down the shop windows, and women with baskets on their hips were crying their wares at the corners of the streets. She walked with her eyes cast down, brushing the walls and smiling with pleasure behind her lowered black veil.

From fear of being seen she did not, as a rule, take the shortest route, but plunged into the gloomy lanes, and emerged, sweating with nervousness, at the far end of the rue Nationale, close to the fountain. It is the district given over to the life of the theatre, to low taverns and prostitutes. Frequently a cart would pass her loaded with pieces of scenery which trembled to the movement of the wheels. Aproned waiters were busy scattering sand on the pavement between the tubs of evergreen. The air was filled with the smell of absinthe, cigar-smoke and oysters.*

She would turn a street corner and recognize him by the curly hair escaping from under his hat. Léon, keeping to the pavement, would walk on, and she would follow till they reached his hotel. He would go upstairs, open the door, enter the room . . . and then, what an embrace!

After the kisses came a flood of words. They told one another all the tiresome happenings of the week, their forebodings, their hunger for letters. But for the moment all these things were forgotten, and they gazed at one another with little bursts of delighted laughter and a wealth of lovers' epithets.

The bed was a large affair of mahogany made in the shape of a boat. The curtains, of red material, hanging from near the ceiling, were looped back over the recessed pillow—and there was no lovelier sight than her dark hair and white skin seen in relief against the wine-red background when, with a gesture of modesty, she clasped her two bare arms across her breast, and hid her face in her hands.

The warm room with its carpet that deadened every sound, its gay ornaments and tranquil light, seemed just made for the intimacies of passion. The uprights of the canopy ended in arrow-points. The brass curtain-rings and the great balls on the andirons glittered suddenly in a fitful burst of sunshine. On the mantelpiece, flanked by candlesticks, were two of those big pink shells which echo the sound of the sea when held to the ear.

How dearly they loved that pleasant room which was so full of gaiety in spite of its rather faded splendours. Each time they came, the furniture was in its accustomed place, and sometimes they would find a few hairpins, which she had forgotten on the previous Thursday, beneath the pedestal of the clock. They took their meal by the fire on a small table inlaid with rosewood. Emma carved, loading his plate to an accompaniment of lovers' talk; and when the champagne overflowed the delicate glass and ran down over her rings, her laughter was loud and wanton. So utterly lost to all else were they in their possession of one another, that they felt as though the house was theirs, that they would live in it, as husband and wife gifted with eternal youth, till death should come for them. They talked of 'our room', 'our carpet', 'our chairs'. She even spoke of 'my slippers'— they had been a present from Léon in response to one of her sudden whims. They were of pink satin trimmed with swansdown. When she sat on his knee her leg, too short to reach the ground, hung suspended in the air, and the dainty little shoe—which had no back—dangled from her bare toes.

He savoured for the first time the indescribable delicacy of feminine elegance. Never before had he come across such grace of language, such quietness in dress, such poses as of a weary dove. He admired the exaltation of her spirit and the lace of her petticoat. Was she not *a woman of the world* and a married woman, the perfection, in short, of what a mistress should be?

By the vacillation of her moods, in turn mystical and joyous, talkative and silent, ardent and casual, she woke in him a thousand wild desires, evoking natural instincts and forgotten memories. She was the 'beloved' of all the novels that ever had been written, the heroine of all the plays, the vague 'she' of all the many volumes of poetry. On her shoulders he recognized the golden bloom of the *Bathing Odalisque*:* she had the elongated body of some medieval maiden, and resembled, too, the *Pale Woman of Barcelona*.* But more than anything else, she was an angel.

Often, as he looked at her, it seemed to him as though his soul, freed from the body and seeking to embrace her, broke like a wave about the sleek curves of her head, and sought, by an irresistible attraction, to attain the whiteness of her bosom. He would sit on the ground at her feet, and, with his elbows on his knees, would look at her with straining eyes and a smile upon his lips. And she would lean towards him, murmuring, as though choked with the rapture of her passion.

'Don't move, don't speak! Just look at me! Such sweetness comes from your eyes, that I am better for the mere beholding of it!'

She called him 'child'. 'Child,' she would say, 'do you love me?'

And she would scarcely hear his answer in the sweet precipitancy of his kisses.

There was a little bronze cupid on the clock with a simpering smile on its lips, and its arms curved beneath a gilded wreath. Often they laughed at it, but when the time for parting came the world grew solemn.

Motionless they stood, facing one another, and:

'Till Thursday,' they said, 'till Thursday!'

Then, suddenly, she would take his head between her hands, kiss him swiftly on the forehead, murmur 'Adieu!' and hasten down the stairs.

She used to go to the hairdresser in the rue de la Comédie, to have her hair done. Dusk would be falling, and they would be lighting the gas in the shop.

She could hear the little bell which rang in the theatre to tell the performers to get ready, and across the road could see men with whitened faces and women in faded finery going into the stage-door.

It was always hot in the small room where the ceiling was too low and a stove was for ever noisily burning among the wigs and pomades. The smell of the heated tongs and the feel of plump hands massaging her head soon made her feel drowsy, and she would drop off for a while, sitting there in her dressing-gown.

The assistant who attended to her hair frequently offered her tickets for the masked ball. This interlude over, she would start on the journey home, first retracing her steps to the Red Cross where she took her overshoes from where she had hidden them under a bench, then settling into the diligence among the impatient passengers. Some of these would get out at the bottom of the hill, and she would be left alone.

At each bend of the homeward road she got a more extensive view of the city lights which showed as a spreading luminous mist above the huddled houses. Emma would kneel on the cushioned seat and let her gaze stray at random about the dazzling scene. Softly she would stifle her sobs, would murmur Léon's name and blow him tender words and kisses which the wind scattered.

There was a well-known local figure, a poor tramp, who used to wander with his stick amidst the traffic on the road. His body was a mass of rags, and an old, shapeless beaver, which he wore pulled down over his brow like an inverted basin, hid his face. When he took it off he revealed, where the eyelids should have been, two gaping, bleeding holes. The flesh was flaking away in scarlet tatters, and pus oozed from the sockets, congealing into greenish scabs which extended as far as his nose, the black nostrils of which twitched in a series of convulsive sniffs. Whenever he spoke to anybody he threw back his head with a sort of imbecile giggle, exhibiting bluish pupils which rolled continually with an outward movement which brought them in contact with the open sore.

He sang a little song as he followed along behind the carriages:

> Souvent la chaleur d'un beau jour
> Fait rêver fillette à l'amour*

it ran, with a lot else about birds, sunlight and green leaves.

Sometimes Emma would turn and find him unexpectedly standing bareheaded behind her. When that happened she would start back with a cry. Hivert made frequent jokes at his expense, suggesting, for instance, that he should rent a booth at St Romain's Fair, and show himself off, or asking him how his sweetheart was. It was no infrequent occurrence for his hat to appear abruptly in the diligence through the open side curtains in the course of one of their trips, while he hung outside, clinging to the running-board between the mudguards with his free arm. His voice, at first feeble and whining, rose to a shriller note, and trailed off into the night like the wordless lamentation of some vague distress. Heard through the tinkling of bells, the whispering of trees and the rumbling of the empty vehicle, it held a suggestion of the far-away which Emma found very upsetting. It struck to the bottom of her soul, like the tail of a whirlpool into an abyss, and seemed to sweep her out into the empty spaces of an illimitable melancholy. But Hivert, feeling the balance of the diligence disturbed, would stretch his arm and strike at the blind man with his whip. The lash caught the sore place on his head, and he would drop off into the mud with a howl.

Sooner or later the passengers in the Swallow dozed off, some with their mouths open, others with their chins sunk on their chests, leaning on their neighbour's shoulder, or jolting to the uneasy rhythm of their movement, with one arm through the strap. The light of the lanterns which swung above the cruppers of the horses seeped through the chocolate-coloured curtains of coarse linen and threw blood-red shadows on the motionless travellers. Emma, in a frenzy of sadness, sat shivering in her clothes, feeling her feet growing colder, and the touch of death in her heart.

Charles was waiting for her at home. The Swallow was always late on Thursdays. But at last Emma appeared. She scarcely so much as gave her little girl a kiss. Dinner was not yet ready, but she seemed not to mind, and found excuses for the cook. Félicité, nowadays, could do almost anything with impunity.

Often, noticing her pallor, he would ask whether she were feeling unwell.

'No,' she said.

'But you seem so strange this evening.'

'It's nothing—nothing at all.'

There were days when she went straight upstairs almost as soon as she got in, and Justin, who happened to be there, would move about noiselessly, finding ways of making himself useful to her which were more ingenious than any maid could have thought of, however excellent. He would put the matches and the candle where she could find them, see that a book was within her reach, lay her nightdress ready for her, and turn down the bed.

'That will do,' she would say: 'now run along.'

For he had a way of standing there, his arms hanging and his eyes staring, as though caught in the web of a sudden dream.

The next day was always dreadful, and the days that followed still more intolerable by reason of her impatient longing for the renewal of her happiness—a sharp craving which familiar memories woke to fever-pitch, which could find its natural outlet only in Léon's arms seven days later. *His* ardours were concealed beneath expressions of wonder and of gratitude. Emma savoured this love of his in a rapt, shy way. She fed it with every artifice of sentiment, and was faintly fearful lest a time might come when she would lose it.

Often she said to him in accents of gentle melancholy:

'You, too, will leave me . . . you will marry . . . . you will be like all the others.'

'What others?' he asked.

'Oh, just men,' she answered.

Then, repulsing him with a gesture of weariness, she would add:

'You're all beasts, all of you!'

One day when they were discoursing philosophically on the dis-illusionments of earthly life, she said (to test his jealousy, or, maybe, because she felt an irresistible desire to unbosom herself) that once, long ago, before he had come into her life, she had loved somebody—'somebody not at all like you', she added quickly, and swore by her daughter's life that *nothing had happened*.

The young man believed her, but plagued her with questions all the same, asking what sort of person this other man had been.

'He was a ship's captain, darling.'

This she said to discourage him from any attempt to discover more, and to heighten her value in his eyes by giving him to believe that she had exercised a fatal fascination on one who must have been by nature a fighter, and a man accustomed to adoration.

The lawyer's clerk felt then the lowliness of his own position. He was envious of epaulettes and stars and titles. Such things must needs be pleasing to one of her expensive tastes.

She did, all the same, keep silent about many of her extravagant thoughts, about her longing, for instance, to have a blue tilbury drawn by an English horse and driven by a groom in top-boots, in which she might go into Rouen. It was Justin who had fired her with this particular whim, when he begged to be taken into her service as a footman. Not that the absence of this luxury in any way lessened the pleasure of her arrival at their weekly trysts, though it certainly did sharpen the bitterness of the return journeys.

Often, when they had been speaking together of Paris, she would conclude with the same murmured words:

'How lovely it would be if we could live there!'

'Are we not happy as we are?' the young man would tenderly reply, stroking her hair.

'Of course we are—it's just that I'm a mad, mad creature!— Kiss me!'

During all this time she was more charming to her husband than ever before, making pistachio cream for his delectation, and playing waltzes to him after dinner. He thought himself the luckiest of mortals, and she was basking in her freedom from anxiety, when suddenly, one evening:

'It *is*', he asked, 'Mademoiselle Lempereur who is giving you lessons, isn't it?'

'Yes.'

'That's odd, because I saw her recently at Madame Liégeard's, and mentioned you. She said she did not know you.'

It was like a thunder-clap. Emma managed, however, to answer him quite naturally.

'I expect she's forgotten my name.'

'Or there may be more than one Mademoiselle Lempereur in Rouen who teaches the piano,' he suggested.

'That's perfectly possible.'

Then, hurriedly, she added:

'I have her receipts,' she said: 'wait, I'll show them to you.'

She went over to her desk, fumbled in the drawers, got all her papers mixed up, and at last so completely lost her head that Charles begged her not to go to so much trouble for a few wretched acknowledgments.

It so happened that, on the Friday following, as Charles was putting on one of his boots in the dark little dressing-room into which all his clothes were huddled, he felt a twist of paper between the leather and his sock. He took it out and read:

Received in respect of a quarter's lessons and various goods supplied, the sum of sixty-five francs.

> Félicité Lempereur
> Professor of Music.

'I wonder how on earth that got into my boot!'

'I suppose', she answered, 'that it must have fallen out of that old cardboard box on the shelf where you keep your bills.'

From that moment life became for her a long succession of lies in which she swathed her love as in a veil, to hide it.

Lying became such a necessity of her being, such a mania, such a pleasure, that if she said she had walked the day before on the right-hand side of the street, the natural assumption was that it had been on the left.

One morning, when she had just left the house, as usual, some-what lightly dressed, there was a sudden snow-squall. Charles, look-ing out of the window at the weather, saw Monsieur Bournisien setting off for Rouen in the great Monsieur Tuvache's trap. He hurried downstairs and gave the ecclesiastic a shawl which he begged him to deliver to his wife at the Red Cross. No sooner had the priest arrived at the inn, than he asked to see the wife of the Yonville doctor. The landlord replied that she was very rarely there. That evening, running into Madame Bovary in the Swallow, the curé told her of the embarrassing position in which he had found himself, though without seeming to attach much importance to it. For he was full of the praises of a preacher who was performing miracles of eloquence at the cathedral, and causing all the ladies of the city to flock to his sermons.

Still, even if *he* had not asked her to explain the incident, others might not show a like discretion. She decided, therefore, that it would be wiser always to leave the diligence at the Red Cross, so that any good folk from her native village who happened to meet her on the stairs, would have no reason to suspect anything.

One day, however, Monsieur Lheureux met her coming out of the Hôtel de Boulogne on Léon's arm. She was terrified; he might chat-ter. But he was not such a fool as to do that.

But he came into her room three days later, closed the door, and said:

'I need some money.'

She said she had none to give him. Lheureux was loud in his complaints, and reminded her how very accommodating he had always been.

It was true that of the two bills backed by Charles, Emma had so far paid off only one. She had begged him, and he had consented, to substitute for the second, two others, and these had actually been renewed at a very long date. He then took from his pocket a list of articles supplied and still not paid for—curtains, a carpet, material for covering the chairs, several dresses and various toilet articles, totalling, in all, about two thousand francs.

She hung her head, and he went on:

'If you are short of cash, you still have *real property.*'

He was referring, he said, to a wretched tumbledown house at Barneville, close to Aumale, which brought in next to nothing. It had originally formed part of a small farm which old Monsieur Bovary had sold. Lheureux knew everything there was to be known about it, even to its precise acreage and the name of its nearest neighbours.

'In your place,' he told her, 'I should get rid of it, settle for what I owed and still have a tidy sum over.'

She argued that it would be difficult to find a purchaser. He encouraged her with the hope that he might be able to dig one up. To this she replied that she did not see how she could acquire a legal right to sell.

'Haven't you a power of attorney?' he inquired.

The word came to her like a breath of fresh air.

'Leave the bill with me,' she said.

'Oh, you needn't bother your head about that!' he replied.

He returned the following week, boasting that after a great deal of searching he had discovered a certain Langlois who, for some time past, had been casting covetous glances at her property. He had not, he said, committed himself on the subject of price.

'Oh, the price doesn't matter!' she exclaimed.

Still, it would be better, he pointed out, to go carefully. The business was worth a journey, and, since she could not make it herself, he offered to go and talk things over with Langlois.

When he got back, he said the man was willing to go to four thousand francs.

Emma brightened at the news.

'And I must say', he added, 'it seems a good offer to me.'

Half the sum was paid over to her immediately, but when she wanted to settle his account, he said:

''Pon my word, it goes against the grain with me to see you shell out all that at one go. . . .'

She looked at the bank-notes. What an unlimited number of meetings she and Léon could have for two thousand francs!

'But . . .' she stammered.

'Oh, come now,' he said with a good-natured laugh, 'don't tell me that a woman can't juggle the household accounts. There are not many domestic secrets *I* don't know!'

He looked at her fixedly, playing the while with two long strips of paper which he was holding in his hands. At last, opening his pocket-book, he laid on the table four promissory notes of a thousand francs each.

'Just sign these,' he said, 'and keep the money.'

She felt shocked by the suggestion and protested loudly.

'But if I hand over the surplus to you,' said he as bold as brass, 'aren't I doing you a service?'

Taking a pen, he scribbled at the foot of the account— 'Received of Madame Bovary, the sum of four thousand francs.'

'What are you worrying about? In six months' time you'll get the balance due on that old house of yours, and I've dated the last of the bills not to fall due until after that.'

Emma was a bit confused in her calculations,* and there was a sound of chinking in her ears, as though a number of gold pieces were spilling from their bags on to the floor about her. Lheureux went on to explain that he had a friend called Vinçart, a Rouen banker, who would discount the four bills, and that when that was done, he would himself give her back any balance over and above the sum owing to him.

Actually, however, he gave her only eighteen hundred francs, instead of two thousand, since his friend Vinçart ('as is only fair') had deducted two hundred for commission and expenses in con-nexion with his discounting activities.

Then he mentioned casually that he would like a receipt.

'You see . . . in business . . . sometimes . . . and please be sure to date it.'

A vista of all the whims she would now be able to gratify opened before Emma. She had enough good sense left to lay aside a thousand crowns to be used when the first three bills fell due. By ill luck, the fourth was delivered at the house on a Thursday, and Charles, thor-oughly upset by the incident, waited for his wife to explain matters to him when she came back.

She had not told him about this bill, she said, because she wanted to spare him all domestic worries. She sat on his knee, kissed him, and cooed at him. She gave him a long list of all the household articles she had bought on credit.

'You must admit', she finished up, 'that the total is not really very high, considering how many items there are.'

Charles, by now at his wits' end, had recourse, shortly after this, to the ever-present Lheureux who promised to straighten things out if he would sign two further bills, one being for seven hundred francs at three months. In order to meet it, the wretched man wrote a pathetic letter to his mother. Instead of answering it, she turned up in person, and in reply to Emma's question, whether he had got anything out of her, he replied:

'Yes, but she insists on seeing the accounts.'

Very early next morning Emma ran across to Monsieur Lheureux's and begged him to make out another invoice showing a total of not more than a thousand francs. For, had she shown old Madame Bovary the one for four thousand she would have had to explain that she had paid two thirds of it already, and this would have compelled her to admit that she had sold the house. That transaction had been successfully carried through by the draper, and did not, in fact, come out until later.

In spite of the fact that the items, taken separately, were not extravagant, her mother-in-law was quick to condemn such expenditure as excessive.

'Surely you could have done without a carpet? Why did you have the armchairs recovered? When I was your age, one armchair in a house was thought sufficient, and was used only by the elderly—at least, that was how things were in my mother's house, and you can take my word for it that *she* knew what was expected of her. We can't all be rich, and no fortune will last for long if it is squandered away in dribs and drabs. I should blush at such self-indulgence, old as I am and needing all the little comforts I can get . . . Dresses, indeed! . . . gewgaws! . . . . Silk lining at two francs a yard—when you can get the same thing in cotton for ten sous!—or even eight!'

Emma, lying sprawled on the sofa, tried hard to keep her temper.

'Please don't go on like that!'

But the other continued to lecture her, prophesying that she and her husband would end in the workhouse. It was all Bovary's fault, of course. The only good thing to be said was that he had, at least, promised to cancel the power of attorney.

'What!'

'Yes, he has sworn to do that,' replied the dame.

Emma opened the window and called to Charles. The poor fellow had to confess that his mother had forced him to give her his word.

Emma left the room and came back a few minutes later holding, with an air of outraged dignity, a large sheet of paper.

'I am deeply beholden to you,' said the old lady and threw the power of attorney into the fire.

Her daughter-in-law broke into loud and strident laughter which was the forerunner to a fit of hysterics.

'Great heavens!' exclaimed Charles. 'You're just as much to blame as she is, coming here and making scenes!'

His mother remarked, with a shrug, that it was all a 'put-up job'.

But Charles, revolting for the first time in his life against maternal authority, put up so forceful a defence of his wife, that the elder woman announced her own imminent departure. And leave she did, the very next day. At the last moment he tried to make her change her mind, but she was adamant.

'No,' she said, 'you love her more than you love me, which, no doubt, is perfectly right and proper and all in the order of nature. But just you wait and see! Good luck to you! . . . It will be a long time before I come here again . . . making scenes, as you call it!'

Charles, however, remained just as sheepish as ever in his wife's presence, and Emma made no attempt to conceal the rancour she felt against him for his lack of confidence. He had to go down on his knees to her before she would consent to a renewal of the power of attorney, but finally they went together to Maître Guillaumin and got him to draw up a second document in all respects like the first.

'I quite understand', said the lawyer, 'that a man engaged, as you are, in the pursuit of science, cannot be bothered with the practical details of everyday life.'

Charles felt much relieved by this tactful remark, which gave to his weakness the flattering appearance of preoccupation with higher things.

In what an orgy of emotion did Emma indulge with Léon, the Thursday following, in their hotel bedroom! She laughed, she wept, she sang, she danced, she rang for ices and wanted to smoke cigarettes. Extravagant though he thought this display, he found her adorable, superb.

He knew nothing of the reaction which drove her on to snatch avidly at all the pleasures of life. She became irritable, greedy, voluptuous. She walked with him in the streets with head held high, not caring, she said, whether or not she ran the risk of compromising herself. But there were times when she trembled at the sudden thought that she might run into Rodolphe. They had, of course, parted for ever, but she could not feel perfectly sure that the bond between them had been completely severed.

One evening she did not return to Yonville. Charles completely lost his head, and little Berthe sobbed as though her heart would break and refused to go to bed unless her mamma was there. Justin went along the road in the hope of meeting her.

Monsieur Homais left his shop.

Finally, at eleven o'clock, Charles, unable to stand the strain any longer, harnessed the trap, jumped into it, lashed the horse into a gallop, and arrived at the Red Cross about two o'clock in the morning. There was no one about. It occurred to him that the lawyer's clerk might have seen her, but he did not know where he lived. Fortunately, he remembered the name of his employer, and hurried to his house.

Dawn was breaking, and he could just make out the escutcheon over the lintel. He knocked. Somebody shouted down the information he sought, though without opening the door, adding a deal of abuse of people who came knocking up honest folk in the middle of the night.

The house in which the lawyer's clerk lived had neither bell nor knocker, and there was no concierge. Charles thundered on the shutters with his fist. At the sight of a police constable he became frightened and went away.

'I'm mad,' he told himself: 'I expect Monsieur Lormeaux asked her to stay to dinner.'

But the Lormeaux family no longer lived in Rouen.

'Perhaps she stayed to look after Madame Dubreuil . . . but no, it can't be that. Madame Dubreuil died six months ago . . . Where *can* she be?'

An idea occurred to him. He went into a café, asked for the *Directory* and hurriedly looked through it for the name of Mademoiselle Lempereur. He found that she lived in the rue de la Renelle-des-Maroquiniers—No 74.

As he turned into the street, Emma appeared at its further end. He did not so much embrace, as hurl himself upon her, crying:

'Who was it kept you here last night?'

'I was feeling unwell.'

'What was the matter with you? . . . Where were you? . . . How exactly do you mean, unwell?'

She passed one hand over her forehead and replied:

'At Mademoiselle Lempereur's.'

'I was sure that was where I should find you. I was on my way there.'

'There's no point in your going further,' said Emma, 'she went out a few moments ago. But, do, please, not get into a state when something of this kind happens again. How can I feel free if I know how terribly upset you feel whenever I'm just a few minutes late!'

This was her way of reassuring herself that she need not worry about him when she was off on one of her escapades. Nor did she fail to take full advantage of the situation thus established. Whenever she was seized with a sudden desire to see Léon, she would set out, with no matter how flimsy an excuse, and, since he would not be expecting her that day, would seek him out in his employer's chambers.

The first few times this happened, it brought them both a special kind of happiness. But a moment soon came when he could no longer conceal the truth from her, namely, that his employer had made a very vigorous protest about his being disturbed in this way.

'Oh, why bother about him!' she said: 'come along!'

And out he slipped.

She wanted him to dress entirely in black and to grow a little chin-tuft, so as to resemble the portraits of Louis XIII. She insisted on being shown where he lived, and declared that his room was squalid. He felt ashamed of it, and blushed. But she took no notice and advised him to buy some curtains like the ones she had. He protested that this would involve him in a deal of expense.

'So you're penny-wise, are you?' she said with a laugh.

Each time they met nothing would satisfy her but that Léon should give her a full account of all he had been doing since their last meeting. She asked him to write some verses, just for her, a love-poem in her honour. But he never succeeded in rhyming the second line, and was driven to copy out a sonnet which he found in a *keepsake*.

This he did, not from any motive of vanity, but simply and solely with the object of humouring her. He never argued over her fancies, and accepted all her tastes. He became her mistress far more completely than she was ever his. Her kisses and her tender words stole away his heart. Where had she learned the arts of a power to corrupt which was so profound, yet so well disguised, that it appeared to be almost disembodied?

CHAPTER VI

OFTEN, when Léon had travelled to Yonville to see her, he had been the chemist's guest at dinner, and felt in honour bound to ask him back.

'With the greatest pleasure,' Monsieur Homais replied. 'It'll do me good to take a plunge into the great world, because I'm getting into a rut here. We'll go to the theatre, dine in a restaurant, and behave like a couple of madcaps!'

'Oh, my dear, do be careful!' murmured Madame Homais in an access of tender concern, terrified by the very vagueness of her idea of the perils to which he seemed ready to expose himself.

'What are you worrying about? Don't you think I'm ruining my health enough, living as I do in a continual atmosphere of drugs? But women are all the same—jealous of science, yet up in arms as soon as one proposes to indulge in a little innocent distraction. But never mind her: I'm your man. One of these fine days you'll see me turn up in Rouen, and then we'll make the money fly!'

Time was when the apothecary would have shunned such an expression: but he had recently become addicted to a playful and Parisian style of speech which he regarded as being the last word in good taste. Like his neighbour, Madame Bovary, he eagerly questioned the young man about the manners of the capital, and went so far as to talk slang in the hope of shocking his respectable fellow-citizens, using words like *turne, bazar, chicard, chicandard, Breda-street*, and saying *Je me la casse*, instead of *Je m'en vais.**

Thus it happened that Emma, on one of her Thursdays, was surprised to find Monsieur Homais in the kitchen of the Golden Lion, dressed as for a journey. That is to say, he was wearing an old top-coat which nobody had ever seen, and was carrying a bag in one hand and in the other, a foot-warmer which he used in the shop. He had not mentioned his plan to a soul, fearing lest he create a feeling of public disquiet by his absence.

No doubt he was excited at the idea of seeing once again the scenes in which his youth had been passed, for he never ceased talking all the way to Rouen. As soon as they arrived, he jumped nimbly from the diligence and went in search of Léon.

In spite of all the objections raised by the lawyer's clerk, he dragged him off to the big Café de la Normandie, into which he made a state entry with his hat on his head, thinking that to uncover in a public place was a sure sign of provincialism.

Emma waited three-quarters of an hour for Léon. At the end of that time she hurried along to his place of business. Lost in all sorts of conjectures, accusing him of indifference, and reproaching herself for her weakness, she spent the afternoon with her face glued to the window.

At two o'clock Homais and Léon were still facing one another across a café table. The large room was emptying. The flue of the stove, which was shaped like a palm-tree, unfolded its golden crown on to the white ceiling. Close to where they were sitting, outside the window in the sunshine, a little jet of water was plashing into a marble basin where, amid cress and asparagus fronds, three torpid lobsters lay outstretched. Near them, on the fountain's rim, was a pile of quails.

Homais was enjoying himself. Though his head was swimming more as a result of the general air of luxury than from the effects of good food and drink, the Pommard had, to some extent, stimulated his faculties, and when a rum omelette appeared he began to advance a number of highly immoral theories on the general subject of women. 'Smartness' was what fascinated him more than any other quality. What he really adored was an elegant *toilette* seen in a setting of rich furniture. In the matter of physical attributes, he liked a 'nice little piece'.

Léon glanced despairingly at the clock. The apothecary went on eating, drinking and talking.

'You must feel very shut away here in Rouen,' he said suddenly: 'not but what the object of your affections lives reasonably near.'

The other blushed, and he added: 'Come on, out with it. . . . You're not going to deny that at Yonville . . .'

(The young man began to stammer.)

'. . . you've done a good deal of courting under the Bovarys' roof?'

'Courting? Who with?'

'Why, the maid, to be sure!'

He meant this perfectly seriously, but Léon, whose vanity had got the better of his prudence, protested in spite of himself. Besides, he said, he didn't like women unless they were dark.

'I approve your taste,' said the chemist: 'they've got more temperament.'

Leaning across, and speaking in his friend's ear, he detailed the various symptoms by which a woman of temperament may be recognized. He even launched into a disquisition on the subject of ethnographic variations. The women of Germany, he maintained, are dreamy, those of France wanton, Italians passionate.

'What about negresses?' asked the lawyer's clerk.

'A taste for negresses is confined to artists,'* said Homais: 'waiter! two coffees.'

'Oughtn't we to be moving?' said Léon at last impatiently.

'*Yes* . . .' replied the other in English. But he insisted on seeing the proprietor before they left, and, on the latter's appearance, began to load him with compliments.

At this point in the proceedings the young man, in an effort to shake his friend off, said that he had a business visit to make.

'In that case, I'll go along with you,' said Homais.

As they took their way through the streets, he talked to him of his wife, his children, their future and the future of the business, explaining at considerable length in what a state of disintegration he had found it, and to what a level of perfection he had raised it.

When they reached the Hôtel de Boulogne, Léon left him abruptly, rushed upstairs, and found his mistress in a great state.

At mention of the chemist she flared up. Her lover produced a number of explanations of what had happened, each sounder than the last. It really wasn't his fault! She knew, didn't she, what Monsieur Homais was like? How could she possibly suggest that he preferred his company to hers? But she turned away and made as though to leave him. He held her back, fell on his knees and put his arms round her waist, assuming a languorous expression, eloquent at once of supplication and desire.

She stood there with a serious, an almost frightened expression on her face. Her eyes were swollen with weeping and brimming over with tears. She dropped her reddened lids and gave him her hands. He was just raising them to his lips when a servant appeared with a message to the effect that someone was waiting for him.

'You'll come back?' she said.

'Of course.'

'But when?'

'At once.'

'Just a little trick of mine,' said the chemist, as soon as he saw Léon. 'I knew you were annoyed at having to make this visit so I thought I'd interrupt it. Let's go along to Bridoux's for a drink.'

Léon swore that he must be getting back to his work, at which the apothecary made a number of jokes about bundles of old papers and legal procedure in general.

'Why not give Cujas and Bartolo* a miss for this once? What's to stop you? Come, be a good fellow. Bridoux's got a very curious dog— well worth looking at.'

But the lawyer's clerk remained obdurate.

'Well, then. I'll come with you and wait until you've finished. I can read the paper, or glance through the Code.'

Léon, feeling a bit dazed by his scene with Emma, by the ceaseless flow of Monsieur Homais's talk, and, perhaps, as a result of all the food he had eaten, showed signs of indecision. It was as though the chemist exercised a sort of fascination over him.

'Let's be getting along to Bridoux's,' said the latter: 'it's only just round the corner, in the rue Malpalu.'

From sheer cowardice, foolishness, and that indefinable feeling which so often involves us in actions against our will, Léon let himself be diverted to Bridoux's. They found him in his little yard superintending the activities of three waiters who were sweating and straining at the wheel of a seltzer-water machine.* Homais gave them much good advice and embraced Bridoux. They had a drink. Twenty times at least did Léon try to break away, but his companion held him back with a restraining hand.

'Just a minute,' he said, 'and I'll be with you. We'll run along and see the boys at the *Fanal de Rouen*. I'll introduce you to Thomassin.'

At last, however, Léon managed to free himself. He rushed back to the hotel, but Emma was no longer there.

She had just left in a state of high dudgeon. Her feeling for him at the moment was one of hatred. His failure to keep the promise he had given when they met seemed to her an outrage, and she sought in her mind for other reasons which might justify a break with him. He was incapable of heroic conduct: he was weak, common, less strong-minded than a woman, stingy, too, and mean-spirited.

After a while she grew calmer, and decided, at length, that she had probably been too hard on him. But the denigration of those we love always has the effect of weakening, to some extent, the bonds of affection. One should never touch idols: the gilt may come off on one's hands.

More and more did they get into the habit of talking about things that had nothing to do with their love. Emma's letters were full of passages about flowers, poetry, the moon and the stars, poor make-shifts of a dying passion which is trying hard to find nourishment in external things. On the eve of each of their meetings she told herself that *this* time their happiness would be unclouded, only to confess, after the event, that she had felt no emotions out of the ordinary. Such recurrent disappointments were always swept away by a renewed surge of hope, and when next she saw him, she was more on fire, more exigent, than ever. She flung off her clothes with a sort of brutal violence, tearing at her thin stay-lace so that it hissed about her hips like a slithering snake. She tiptoed across the room on her bare feet to make sure that the door was really locked, and then, with a single gesture, let her things fall to the floor. Pale, speechless, solemn, she threw herself into his arms with a long shudder.

But on her brow, pearled with cold sweat, on her stammering lips, in her wild eyes and in the fierce clasp of her arms, there was some-thing at once exaggerated, undefined and gloomy. Her mood seemed to Léon to slip between them and keep them apart.

He dared not question her, but, finding her so adept in the arts of love, told himself that she must surely have experienced every shade of suffering and delight. What once he had found charming now faintly frightened him. Moreover, he began to rebel against her ever-growing desire to absorb him utterly. He resented a victory which would hold him permanently in subjection, and fought against his own infatuation. But the mere sound of her footstep made his cour-age ooze away. He was like a drunkard when he sees strong drink.

True, she let no opportunity slip of showering attentions on him, ranging from exotic meals to coquetries in dress and melting glances. She brought roses from Yonville in her bosom and threw them in his face. She expressed anxiety about his health: she gave him advice about the conduct of his daily life, to increase her hold on him, and hoping, perhaps, to enlist the powers of heaven on her side, she hung round his neck a little medal stamped with the image of the Virgin. Like a fond mother, she asked him about the company he kept. She said:

'You're not to see them, you're not to go out, you're to think only of us. Love me!'

She would have liked to watch over his every movement, and even thought of having him followed in the streets. There was a sort of tramp for ever hanging about his hotel who would have suited her purpose . . . but her pride revolted at the idea.

'It can't be helped: what does it matter if he *does* deceive me? *I* don't care!'

One day, when they had parted early, and she was walking back alone along the boulevard, she recognized the wall of her old convent. She sat down on a bench in the shade of an elm. What peace of mind she had known in those far-off days! How she longed to feel once again the ineffable yearnings which once she had sought in books.

She saw in imagination the early months of her marriage, her days of riding through the woods; she saw the Vicomte waltzing and Lagardy singing . . . and suddenly, she saw Léon, too, diminished in the same perspective of time.

'But I *do* love him!' she said to herself.

But what good did that do? She was not happy; she never had been happy. Why had her life been such a failure? Why did everything on which she leaned crumble immediately to dust? If only somewhere there had been for her somebody strong and handsome, some man of valour, ardent and tender with the heart of a poet and the body of an angel, a lyre with strings of brass, striking to heaven a note of elegiac passion. . . . Might she not, even now, find such a one? No, it was impossible. Besides, nothing was worth the trouble of a search. Life was one great lie! Every smile concealed a yawn of boredom, every joy a curse, every pleasure a feeling of disgust! The wildest kisses left upon her lips nothing but a craving for still greater ecstasies which never could be realized. There came a noise of long-drawn metallic rattling, and four strokes sounded from the convent clock. Only four o'clock! It seemed to her that she had been sitting on this bench from all eternity. But an infinity of passion may be compressed into a minute, like a crowd of persons in a narrow space.

Emma lived with no thought for anything but her own feelings, and worried about money less than would an arch-duchess. One day, however, a little weakling of a fellow, red of face and bald of head, paid her a call. He said he had been sent by Monsieur Vinçart of Rouen. He removed the pins which secured the side-pocket of his long green overcoat, stuck them in his sleeve, and politely held out a paper.

It was a bill for seven hundred francs, endorsed by her, and made over by Lheureux to Vinçart, in spite of the promise he had given.

Hastily, she sent her servant across to his house, but he could not come.

The stranger, who had remained standing, and looking about him with curious glances which were, to some extent, concealed by his heavy, fair eyebrows, now asked with an innocent air:

'What answer am I to give Monsieur Vinçart?'

'Oh, tell him', replied Emma, 'that I have not got the money by me. I will settle with him next week . . . ask him to be good enough to wait . . . It shall be next week without fail.'

At that he said nothing more, but left her.

But next day at noon, she was served with a legal demand. The sight of the stamped paper, with, on it, in large letters, the words— 'Maître Hareng, Sheriff's Officer of Buchy' repeated more than once, so frightened her that she hurried across to the draper.

She found him in his shop in the act of tying up a parcel.

'Your very humble servant!' he said: 'just excuse me for a moment, please.'

He made no attempt to leave off what he was doing. There was a young girl of about thirteen helping him; she was slightly hump-backed and combined in his establishment the duties of cook and shop-assistant.

At last, making a great clatter with his clogs on the floor of the shop, he led the way upstairs to the first landing, where he showed her into a poky little office. It contained a large deal desk, on which were a number of ledgers secured by padlocked metal straps. Against the wall, beneath several samples of Indian calico, was a safe of so large a size that it must have contained much more than merely notes and coin. The fact was that Lheureux issued loans on security. Into that very safe he had put Madame Bovary's gold chain, as well as some earrings belonging to poor old Tellier, who, having been forced at long last to sell out, had bought a wretched grocery business at Quincampoix, where he was slowly dying of asthma surrounded by candles which looked a good deal less yellow than his face.

Lheureux sat down in a large wicker armchair.

'Well, and what's the news with you?' he asked.

'Look!'

She showed him the paper.

'I don't see what I can do about it.'

At that she flew into a rage, reminding him of his promise not to put her bills into circulation.

This he admitted.

'But my hand was forced. The knife was at my own throat.'

'And what's going to happen now?' she demanded.

'That's easy to answer—a judgement in the courts, and then the bailiffs . . . quite a simple little matter!'

It was with the greatest difficulty that Emma kept herself from striking him. She asked, quite calmly, whether there wasn't any way of keeping Monsieur Vinçart quiet.

'Keeping Monsieur Vinçart quiet! You don't know him. He's got the temper of a dancing dervish!'

Then *he* must do something, she said.

'Now, just you listen to me. Up to now I should say I'd treated you pretty decently.'

He opened one of the ledgers:

'Look at this.' He ran his finger up and down the page:

'Let's see . . . let's see . . . 3rd August, two hundred francs . . . 17th June, hundred and fifty . . . 23rd March, forty-six . . . April . . .'

He stopped, as though afraid that he might commit some foolishness.

'And that's not counting the bills backed by your husband, one for seven hundred francs, the other for three. As to your own little account, with the accrued interest . . . well, there's no end to *that*. . . . The whole thing's a proper mess, and I wash my hands of it!'

She cried. She even went so far as to call him her 'kind Monsieur Lheureux'. But he threw all the blame on 'that swine Vinçart'. Besides, he said, he was completely cleaned out. All his accounts were outstanding. The very clothes were being torn from his body. A poor shopkeeper like him couldn't afford to make loans.

Emma said no more. Monsieur Lheureux, nibbling the end of a pen, seemed uneasy at her silence, for he continued:

'If I could count on some of the money due to me coming in, I might . . .'

'Well,' she pointed out, 'there's still the balance on the Barneville sale owing. . . .'

'What d'you mean?'

When he heard that Langlois had not yet completed his payment, he seemed mightily surprised. Then, in honeyed tones:

'So, we're in complete agreement, eh?'

'Arrange things in any way you like!'

He closed his eyes in deep thought, jotted down some figures, and then, declaring that he was going to find it all very difficult, that he was taking big risks and 'bleeding himself white', dictated four bills of two hundred and fifty francs each, so dated as to fall due at a month's interval from one another.

'If only Vinçart'll listen to me! Well now, that's all signed and sealed between us. There's no shilly-shallying about me. Sound as a pippin, that's what I am!'

A little later he casually exhibited a few of his more recent purchases, none of which was, in his opinion, worth her attention.

'Take this dress material, for instance, at seven sous the yard, guaranteed fast colours—folk just gobble it down, though you realize, of course, that I don't let them in on the secret'—this he said so that admitting sharp practice in his dealings with others, he might convince her that in *their* dealings he was honest.

Just as she was going, he called her back, in order to show her three lengths of trimming which he had picked up recently at a bankrupt sale.

'Lovely stuff!' he said, 'and very much sought after just now— excellent for antimacassars.'

More dexterously than any juggler, he wrapped the trimming up in a piece of blue paper and put it into Emma's hands.

'But do at least tell me how much. . . .'

'We'll talk about that later . . .' was his comment as he turned on his heel.

That evening she urged Bovary to write to his mother, asking her to send them as soon as possible what was still due under his father's will. This he did, only to be told in reply that he need expect nothing further. The estate had now been wound up, and all that they could look forward to, apart from the house at Barneville, was an annual income of six hundred francs, which they could be sure she would pay over regularly.

Emma hurriedly sent out accounts to two or three of her husband's patients, and, finding this method of raising money successful, began to make use of it more and more frequently. She was always careful, when she did so, to add as a postscript the words: 'Please say nothing about this to my husband. You know how proud he is. I trust that you will forgive me for having bothered you, and remain, your obedient servant . . .'

One or two of the recipients sent back letters of protest, but these she intercepted.

Another thing she did was to sell her old gloves and hats and any odds and ends of scrap metal on which she could lay her hands. She drove a hard bargain—the peasant strain in her invariably demanding a handsome profit on any transaction. On her trips, too, to the city she would pick up various second-hand objects, which, failing other customers, she could always dispose of to Monsieur Lheureux. In this way she bought ostrich feathers, Chinese porcelain and old chests. She borrowed from Félicité, from Madame Lefrançois, from the landlord of the Red Cross: in fact, from any and everybody. With the money which ultimately came to her from the Barneville sale, she paid off two of the bills. The fifteen hundred francs left to her just dribbled through her fingers. She ran still further into debt—and so it went on.

At times, it is true, she did try to keep some sort of account, but, on looking into her affairs, she found evidence of a situation so appalling that she could scarcely believe her eyes. She would begin her calculations all over again, but quickly becoming confused, would give up the struggle and think no more about her finances.

Home, these days, was a very melancholy place. Tradesmen could be seen emerging from the front-door looking furious. Handkerchiefs lay about on the stoves, and little Berthe had holes in her stockings—much to the horror of Madame Homais. When Charles, from time to time, nervously hazarded an observation, Emma replied rudely that *she* wasn't to blame.

Why these outbursts of temper? He attributed them to her old complaint, and blamed himself for regarding as faults what really were the effects of illness. He accused himself of egotism, and felt like giving her a good hug.

'But she'd only find me a bore, if I did,' he reflected, and made no move.

He got into the habit of going for a lonely stroll after dinner, and, on his return, would perch little Berthe on his knee and try to teach her to read with the help of his medical journal. But the child, who was never given any regular lessons, soon opened her great mournful eyes in a solemn stare and started to cry. He did everything he could to comfort her, fetching water in one of the garden cans so that she could make rivers in the sand, or breaking twigs off the privet hedge for her to use when she played at planting trees in the flower-beds. This did not much injure the garden which was, in any case, over-grown with long grass as a result of their being so behindhand with Lestiboudois's wages. But the child soon felt cold and began to cry for its mother.

'Much better call nanny, darling,' he said: 'you know how mummy hates being disturbed.'

It was now early autumn, and the leaves were already falling—just as they had done two years before, during her illness. When would all this end?—he wondered, and continued his walk with his hands clasped behind his back.

His wife was in her room. No one went up to her. She spent most of her time, now, shut away up there, mentally numbed and only half dressed. Occasionally she would burn Oriental pastilles which she had bought from an Algerian who kept a shop in Rouen. To avoid having to put up with her husband's presence beside her all night she had persuaded him, after a lot of humbug, to sleep on the second floor. Left alone, she would lie all night long, till dawn broke, reading books of extravagant fantasy filled with descriptions of orgies and sadistic adventures. Often a sudden panic would seize her so that she cried aloud. Charles would run downstairs.

'Oh, go away!' she would exclaim.

At other times, increasingly consumed by that secret flame which drew its nourishment from her adulterous abandonment, panting, shaken and tormented by desire, she would fling her window open, breathe in the cold air, shake out the heavy weight of her hair, look at the stars, and dream of princely lovers. Léon was ever in her mind. She would have given all she had at such moments for a single one of those meetings which had been lately breeding in her a sense of satiety.

They were her gala days, those meetings. She wanted them to be gloriously caparisoned, and, when he could not afford to pay for them unaided—which was almost always—came liberally to his assistance. He tried to persuade her that they would be just as well off in some more modest hotel, but she always found objections to advance against any change in their habitual arrangements. One day she took from her bag six little silver-gilt spoons (they had been her father's wedding-present to her) and asked him to pledge them for her at a pawnbroker's. Léon obeyed, though he disliked the whole business. He was afraid of being compromised.

Thinking the matter over afterwards, he decided that his mistress was beginning to act very strangely, and that perhaps his friends were not altogether wrong in wishing to get him away from her. Somebody, as it happened, had sent his mother a long anonymous letter with the object of warning her that he was ruining himself with a married woman. The good lady, scenting that threat to all respectable families, the vaguely defined but always pernicious female, the siren, the monster, the fantastic denizen of love's lower depths, had at once communicated her fears to Maître Dubocage, his employer, who promptly set himself to do all that the most exigent of parents could possibly expect. For three-quarters of an hour he talked to the young man, striving to open his eyes and keep him from the abyss that lay ahead. An intrigue of this kind, he pointed out, must in the long run do harm to his practice, and he begged Léon to break with his charmer, if not for his own sake, at least for his master's.

Léon was driven at length to promise that he would not see Emma again, and he reproached himself now for not having kept his word. He realized all the difficulties which might beset him in the days to come, all the sermonizing that she might draw down upon his head, to say nothing of the jokes of his companions in the course of their daily sessions round the office stove. Besides, he was about to be promoted senior clerk, and now, if ever, was the time for him to take his career seriously. He gave up playing the flute because it stimulated his imagination to indulge in sentimental reveries—for every middle-class young man thinks, some time or other, in the heat of adolescence, if only for a day, if only for a minute, that he is cut out for the rôle of lover or of hero. The most squalid little philanderer has, at moments, dreamed of dusky princesses, and every lawyer carries within him the broken remnants of a poet.

Whenever, now, Emma flung herself on his bosom and burst into tears, he was merely bored. His heart, like those people who can stand only a certain limited quantity of music, grew indifferent to the clamour of a love whose delicate undertones he could no longer distinguish.

They knew one another too well to experience, in the act of pos-session, that sense of wonder which multiplies its joys a hundred-fold. She was as wholeheartedly sick of him as he was weary of her. Emma found in adultery nothing but the platitudes of marriage.*

But how was she to shake him off? Humiliated though she might feel by the squalor of a happiness bought at such a price, she still clung to it from habit, or, perhaps, from some perversity of her nature. Each day that passed she pursued him with unrelenting ardour, spoiling what delights she might have found by setting her hopes too high, and then, when they were disappointed, accusing him as though he had been guilty of betrayal. She even longed for some catastrophe, so that it might force them apart, since she herself lacked courage to engineer a break. She still wrote him love-letters, because of a notion she had that a woman should always write to her lover.

But as soon as she took a pen in her hand, the Léon she saw in imagination became a totally different being from the Léon whom she knew—a synthetic figure compounded of things remembered, things read and loved in books and the images created by her own insatiable passion. This shadowy creature became at last so real to her, so accessible, that her heart beat faster even though she could not see him clearly, so completely was his person (like that of a god) lost in the multiplicity of his attributes. He dwelt in that azure land where silken ladders swayed from balconies in a scent of flowers and the radiance of moonlight. She felt him close to her. In a moment he would be at her side, would sweep her out of herself in the rapture of a kiss. But a moment later she felt bruised and beaten, as though she had been dropped from a great height. For these visionary ecstasies of love left her more exhausted than whole nights of dissipation.

She experienced now a general sense of fatigue from which she was never wholly free. Writs began to rain on her, pieces of stamped paper at which she scarcely looked. She wished she were dead, or that she could go on sleeping without ever having to wake up.

On the day of the mid-Lent festivities she did not go back to Yonville, but spent the evening at a masked ball. She wore velvet breeches and red stockings, a wig knotted at the nape of her neck, and a cocked hat. She danced all night to the wild music of trombones, the centre of a whirl of merrymakers. In the morning she found herself under the portico of the theatre, in the company of five or six people dressed up as longshoremen and sailors, all of them friends of Léon's, who talked about going on somewhere for supper.

All the cafés in the neighbourhood were full. Down by the harbour they found a third-rate restaurant where the proprietor gave them a small room on the fourth floor.

The men whispered together in a corner, no doubt discussing what their entertainment was going to cost. The company consisted of a clerk, two medical students and a shop-assistant. Fine companions for her! As to the women, she quickly realized from the sound of their voices that almost all of them must come from the very lowest class. She felt frightened, pushed back her hair, and sat with lowered eyes.

The others began to eat, but she took nothing. Her forehead felt burning hot. There was a pricking sensation in her eyelids and her skin was icy cold. Her head still throbbed with the noise made by a thousand dancing feet on the wooden floor of the dance-hall. The smell of the punch and the smoke of cigars made her dizzy. She was beginning to faint. The others carried her to the window.

Day was just breaking, and a great red patch was spreading across the pale sky towards St Catherine's hill. There was a ruffle of wind on the livid surface of the river. The bridges were empty of life. The street lamps were being extinguished.

At last she came to herself. She thought of Berthe fast asleep yonder in her nurse's room. But a cart full of long iron strips drove past, making the walls of the house vibrate to the accompaniment of a deafening metallic rattle.

On a sudden impulse she left the place, took off her fancy-dress, told Léon she must go home, and remained all alone at the Hôtel de Boulogne. She hated everything and everyone, including herself. She longed to be able to fly out of the window like a bird, to find renewed youth in some place far away in the stainless spaces of the sky.

She went out, crossed the boulevard and the place Cauchoise, wandered for a while in the suburbs and, at last, reached a wide street overlooking the gardens.* She walked quickly. The fresh air calmed her, and, little by little, the memory of the crowds, of the masks, of the dances and the crystal chandeliers, of the supper and the women, all drained away like thinning mist. When she got back to the Red Cross, she flung herself on her bed in her small, second-floor room with its pictures of the *Tour de Nesle*.

At four o'clock that afternoon she was woken by Hivert.

As soon as she reached home Félicité showed her a greyish sheet of paper stuck behind the clock. She read:

'Be it known by these Presents that in due and legal Execution of the Judgement of the Court. . . .'

What judgement? True, she had been given another paper the evening before, but had been able to make nothing of it. She read on, and was appalled when she came to these words:

'Madame Bovary is hereby, in the Name of His Majesty the King, of the Law, and in the interests of Justice, ordered and enjoined . . .'

She skipped the next few lines, and, a little further on, saw:

'within the next twenty-four hours, unfailingly . . .'

What was it all about?

'. . . to pay the total amount of eight thousand francs . . .' and then, lower still:

'. . . This she shall do or suffer the full rigours of the Law, and, in especial, the Seizure by Officers of all Furniture and Effects . . .'

What was she to do? . . . Twenty-four hours! Why, that meant tomorrow! This, she thought, was another of Lheureux's tricks designed to frighten her. It was borne in on her suddenly what he was after, what all his seeming kindness had amounted to. The only reassuring element in the situation was that the figure mentioned was a gross exaggeration. But the truth was that, as a result of buying and never paying, of borrowing, of backing bills which grew larger and larger with each renewal, she had finally piled up a nice little capital sum for the great Lheureux, of which he now stood urgently in need for purposes of speculation.

She paid a call on him in his shop, doing her best to make it appear casual.

'I suppose you know what has happened? I can only suppose that it is some kind of a joke. . . .'

'Oh, dear me, no . . .'

'What do you mean?'

Slowly he turned to face her, folded his arms and said:

'Did you really think, my fine lady, that I should go on being your banker and provider till the end of time, just out of Christian charity? You can't deny that I have a perfect right to recover my outlay?'

She exclaimed at the amount of the debt.

'I can't help that. The court has made its award: judgement has been given, and you have been duly notified. Besides, it's Vinçart, not me, who's concerned.'

'But couldn't you? . . .'

'I can do nothing at all.'

'At least let us talk it over. . . .'

She was playing for time. She hadn't realized, she said, how bad things were. Everything had happened so quickly.

'And who's fault is that?' said Lheureux with an ironical bow. 'While I was slaving away like a nigger, you were having a good time.'

'Oh, for heaven's sake, don't start preaching at me!'

'A little preaching hurts no one,' he replied.

All her courage had ebbed away. She begged him to help her. She even touched his knee with a pretty, delicate white hand.

'Keep your distance! Anyone'd think you were trying to seduce me!'

'You beast!' she cried.

'Dear me, what a little fire-eater we've become!' he said with a laugh.

'I'll tell everyone about you . . . I'll let my husband know. . . .'

'If it comes to that, there are one or two little things *I* could show your husband!'

He took from the safe her receipt for eight hundred francs given at the time of Vinçart's discounting operations.

'I suppose you think,' he went on, 'that the poor dear fellow won't jump to the fact that you've been robbing him?'

She crumpled up, more completely stunned than if she had been struck to the ground with a club. He was pacing between the window and his desk, saying over and over again:

'I'll show it him, don't make any mistake about that. I'll show it him!' Then, going close to her, he said in a gentler tone:

'It's not very amusing for you, I know, but, after all, it might be worse. Nobody's dead, and, since the only course open to you is to pay me my money . . .'

'But how am I to find it?' said Emma wringing her hands.

'Bah! a woman who's got as many friends as you have . . .'

The look he gave her was so knowing, so terrifying that she was shaken with a convulsive shudder.

'I give you my word . . .' she said: 'I'll sign. . . .'

'I've had enough of your signatures.'

'I can still sell . . .'

'Talk sense!' said he with a shrug: 'there's nothing left you *can* sell.'

He looked through the peephole which gave into the shop, and said:

'Annette—don't forget the three remnants of No. 14.'

The servant appeared. Emma understood what he meant, and asked how much money he would need to stop proceedings.

'It's too late now. . . .'

'But suppose I brought you several thousand francs—a quarter of the sum—a third—almost all of it?'

'No, quite useless.'

He pushed her gently towards the stairs.

'I implore you, monsieur Lheureux!—just a few more days!'

She began to sob.

'Oho! so it's to be tears now!'

'You'll drive me to do something desperate!'

'A fat lot I care!' he said, and shut the door.

CHAPTER VII

She put up a fine show of stoicism next day when Maître Hareng, accompanied by two witnesses, arrived at the house to give legal notice of seizure.

They began with Bovary's consulting room. They omitted the phrenological head as constituting a 'tool of his trade'. But in the kitchen they noted down the dishes, pots, chairs and candlesticks, and, in the bedroom, all the odds and ends of ornaments. They examined her clothes, her linen and the contents of her dressing-room. Her whole domestic existence, down to its most intimate details, was exposed to the gaze of the three men like a corpse laid out for a post-mortem.

Maître Hareng, buttoned up in a close-fitting frock-coat, with a white cravat and very tight trouser-straps, kept saying from time to time:

'With your permission, Madame . . . with your permission. . . .'

He frequently emitted little ejaculations of delight.

'Charming . . . *v-e-r-y* pretty.'

Then he would resume his writing, dipping his pen in the inkhorn which he carried in his left hand.

When they had finished with the bedrooms, they went up to the attics.

She had stowed away up there a desk containing Rodolphe's letters. It had to be opened.

'Ah, a correspondence!' said Maître Hareng, smiling discreetly. 'With your permission, Madame, I will see whether the box contains anything else.'

He up-ended the letters very gently as though to shake out any napoleons which might be concealed in the pages. She was seized with indignation at the sight of his coarse hands, with their soft, pink, slug-like fingers pawing the papers which had made her heart beat so violently.

They went away at last. Félicité came back. Emma had put her on guard so as to keep Bovary out of the way. Together, they hurriedly installed the 'man in possession' under the tiles. He gave them his word that he would stay there.

All that evening, Charles seemed to wear a worried look. She scrutinized his face anxiously, imagining that she could detect accusation in the deep-etched lines. Whenever her eyes wandered to the mantelpiece adorned with Chinese hand-screens, to the big curtains, to the armchairs, to all those things which had sweetened the bitterness of her life, she was seized with remorse, or, rather, with a feeling of immense regret that, so far from killing her passion, merely stimulated it. Charles kept quietly poking the fire, his two feet stretched on the fender.

At one moment, the bailiff, tired, no doubt, of his long imprisonment, made a slight noise.

'Is that somebody walking about upstairs?' asked Charles.

'No,' she replied, 'it's an open casement banging in the wind.'

The day following was Sunday, and she set off for Rouen with the intention of calling on all the bankers whose names she knew. They were away in the country, or travelling. But she would not accept defeat, and the few she did find she asked for money, protesting that her need was urgent, and promising to repay the debt. Some of them laughed in her face. All of them refused.

At two o'clock she hurried to Léon's lodgings. Nobody answered her knock. At last, however, he appeared.

'What brings you here?'

'I'm disturbing you!'

'No . . but . . . .'

He confessed that his landlord did not much like his having 'lady visitors'.

'There's something I must talk to you about.'

He took down his key, but she stopped him.

'Oh no, not here . . . let us go to *our* place.'

They went to their room at the Hôtel de Boulogne.

As soon as she got there, she drank a large glass of water. She was very pale. She said:

'Léon, will you do something for me?' She held both his hands hard and shook them.

'Listen,' she went on, 'I need eight thousand francs.'

'You must be mad!'

'Not yet.'

She told him about the seizure, and poured out all her misery. Charles knew nothing. Her mother-in-law hated her, her own father could do nothing. Surely, he, Léon, would set about finding the absolutely essential sum.

'But what d'you think I can do?'

'What a coward you are!'

'You are exaggerating this crisis,' he said stupidly. 'Maybe a thousand crowns would keep this fellow quiet.'

All the more reason for making an effort. One *must* be able to raise three thousand francs somehow. . . . Besides, Léon could stand guarantee for her. . . .

'Try!' she said . . . 'you must *do* something. . . . Oh, please, *try*!— I'll be so . . . so loving to you!'

He went out, came back in an hour's time, and said, looking very solemn:

'I've seen three people . . . nothing doing.'

They sat facing one another, on either side of the fireplace, motionless, saying nothing. Emma shrugged and stamped her foot. He heard her mutter under her breath.

'If I were in your place, *I'd* find it all right!'

'Where?—can you tell me that?'

'Where you work.'

She gave him a meaning look.

The expression of her flashing eyes was brazen, devilish; the way in which she kept her lids half closed lascivious and provocative. So irresistible was the effect on the young man, that he felt himself grow weak before the silent concentration of her will. She was urging him to commit a crime, and he was terrified. To avoid bringing the matter into the open, he beat his forehead with his fists and exclaimed:

'Morel's due back tonight, and I'm sure he won't refuse me—at least, I hope he won't.' (Morel was one of his best friends, the son of a rich merchant.) 'I'll bring you the money tomorrow,' he added.

Emma received this optimistic suggestion with less joy than he had expected. Could it be that she suspected him of lying? He grew very red, and went on:

'But if I don't turn up by three, darling, don't wait for me. . . . And now I really must go: please forgive me: good-bye. . . .'

He grasped her hand, but it lay limp in his. Emma was by this time too weak to feel anything.

Four o'clock struck. She got up, preparatory to returning to Yonville. She followed the routine of habit with no more life in her than there is in a mechanical toy.

It was a fine day, one of those March days when the air is limpid but strikes chill, and the sun shines in a pale and colourless sky. Many of the good people of Rouen were strolling about the streets in their Sunday best, with happy expressions on their faces. She reached the open space in front of the cathedral. The congregation was just coming out from vespers. A crowd of worshippers was flowing through the three doors like a river running beneath the triple arches of a bridge. In the middle, motionless as a rock, stood the verger.

She remembered the day when, nervous but filled with hope, she had penetrated into the great nave. How much less deep and mysterious it had seemed then than her love.

She walked on, weeping behind her veil, aimless and so shaken that she felt like fainting.

'Look out!' cried a voice from within a carriage-entry, the doors of which were just swinging open.

She stopped to give passage to a tilbury drawn by a prancing black horse, and driven by a gentleman in a sable coat. Who was it? She knew him. . . . The vehicle dashed out and disappeared.

It was the Vicomte! She turned her head, but the street was deserted. So overcome did she feel by the encounter, so sad, that she had to lean against a wall to keep herself from falling.

She might have been mistaken, but couldn't feel sure. Everything, within and without, was abandoning her. She had the sensation of being lost, of rolling, beyond control, in limitless gulfs. It was almost with joy that, when she reached the Red Cross, she saw the excellent Homais, who was superintending the loading on to the Swallow of a large box filled with medicaments. He was holding, wrapped in a silk handkerchief, six of the little rolls known locally as *cheminots*.*

Madame Homais was very fond of these heavy little buns, shaped like turbans, which are eaten in Lent with salted butter, the last remaining relics of medieval fare—dating perhaps from the Crusades—on which the hardy Normans of old were wont to gorge themselves, fancying that they saw before them on the table, lit by yellow torch-flames, and flanked by pitchers of mulled wine and huge sides of pork, the heads of Saracens waiting to be devoured. The apothecary's wife munched them as they did, heroically, in spite of her appalling teeth. Consequently, whenever Monsieur Homais went to town, he invariably brought some back, always buying them at the shop of their famous maker in the rue Massacre.

'Delighted to see you,' he said, stretching out a hand to help her into the Swallow.

He put the *cheminots* into the net rack, and sat bare-headed and with folded arms in a pensive and Napoleonic attitude.

But when the blind beggar, as usual, appeared at the foot of the hill, he exclaimed:

'I can't understand how it is that the authorities still tolerate such anti-social activities! These miserable creatures ought to be shut up and made to work. 'Pon my word, progress moves at a snail's pace. We are plunged in barbarism!'

The blind man held out his hat, which bobbed about at the door like a part of the hangings that had broken loose.

'A case', said the chemist, 'of scrofulous infection.'

Although he was perfectly familiar with the poor fellow, he pretended that he was seeing him for the first time, murmured a number of medical terms,* such as *cornea*, *opaque cornea*, *sclerotic*, *facies*, and finally asked, in a paternal tone:

'For how long, my man, have you suffered from this terrible affliction? It would be much better for you to follow a strict diet than to go drinking yourself silly in taverns.'

He recommended him to confine his potations to sound wine and to eat only roasted meat.* The beggar went on with his song. He seemed to be almost imbecile. At last, Monsieur Homais opened his purse.

'Here is a ha'penny for you: give me back a farthing change, and don't forget what I told you. You'll feel all the better for it.'

Hivert permitted himself an audible doubt on the efficacy of the prescription. But the apothecary guaranteed to cure the man himself with an antiphlogistic ointment of his own concoction, and gave him his address.

'Monsieur Homais, hard by the market-hall: known all over the town.'

'Well, at least we shall have had a good laugh!' said Hivert.

The blind man squatted down on his haunches, threw back his head, rolled his glaucous eyes, stuck out his tongue, rubbed his stomach with both hands, and emitted a sort of low howl like a starving dog. Emma, in a spasm of disgust, threw him a five-franc piece over her shoulder. It was all the money she had left. She thought it a fine gesture to squander it in this way.

The conveyance had started again, when suddenly Monsieur Homais leaned out of the window and exclaimed:

'No farinaceous or milk foods! Wear wool next to the skin, and expose the affected parts to the smoke of juniper berries!'

The sight of well-known objects slowly passing before her eyes distracted Emma from her present woes. She felt herself overwhelmed by an intolerable fatigue, and arrived home numbed, discouraged and half asleep.

'What's to come will come,' she said to herself.

After all, something extraordinary might happen at any moment. Lheureux might even die!

She was awakened at nine o'clock next morning by the sound of voices in the square. A crowd had gathered round the market-hall to read a large poster stuck on one of the pillars. She saw Justin clamber on to a mounting-stone and start to tear it down. But at that moment the village constable came up and seized him by the collar. Monsieur Homais came out of his shop, and Madame Lefrançois, in the middle of the crowd, looked as though she were about to make a speech.

'Oh, ma'am, ma'am!' cried Félicité, running in. 'There's terrible things going on!'

The poor girl, trembling with agitation, held out a yellow paper which she had just torn from the door. Emma saw at a glance what it contained. It announced that everything in the house was for sale.

The two women looked at one another in silence. There was no secret at that moment between servant and mistress. At last Félicité heaved a sigh:

'If I were you, ma'am, I should go straight to lawyer Guillaumin.'

'D'you really think I ought to? . . .' The unexpressed meaning of the question was—

'You know the lawyer's house from the servants' side. Has the old man ever spoken about me?'

'Oh do go, ma'am: I do feel sure it'll be for the best.'

Emma dressed, putting on her black gown and her cloak trimmed with jet beads. So as to avoid notice (there were still many people in the square), she kept away from the village, taking the path by the river.

She arrived quite out of breath at the lawyer's gate. The sky was overcast and a little snow was falling.

At the sound of the bell Théodore appeared on the steps in his red waistcoat. There was something familiar in the way he opened the gate to her, as to an old friend. He showed her into the dining-room.

A large porcelain stove was roaring beneath a cactus plant which filled the alcove. Framed in black wood against the dark green wall-paper were the *Esmeralda* by Steuben* and Schopin's *Potiphar*.* The table was laid. Two silver chafing-dishes, the crystal door-knobs, the hardwood floor, the furniture— everything in the room shone with a meticulous English cleanliness. The windows were decorated with pieces of coloured glass in each corner.

'This', thought Emma, 'is how a dining-room ought to look.'

The lawyer entered, clutching his palm-embroidered dressing-gown to his side with his left hand, while, with his right, he kept on taking off and quickly replacing his purple velvet skull-cap which was perched affectedly on the right-hand side of his head. Each time it was removed she could see three strands of fair hair caught up into a tuft on the top of his skull and carefully arranged round his bald patch.

He offered her a chair, while he himself sat down to breakfast with many apologies for his lack of manners.

'I beg you, sir . . .' she began.

'Continue, madame, I am listening. . . .'

She set about describing the situation in which she found herself, which Maître Guillaumin knew already, since he was secretly in league with the draper from whom he got the capital he needed for his various mortgages.

He was familiar, therefore (much more familiar than she was), with the long history of the bills. He knew that they had begun by being for quite small amounts, that they had passed through many hands, that they had been so arranged as to fall due at long intervals, and that they had been constantly renewed. He was well aware that the merchant, when the moment came for gathering together all the writs for non-payment, not wishing to appear in the light of a blood-sucker, had asked his friend Vinçart to initiate the necessary proceedings in his own name.

She interspersed her tale with recriminations against Lheureux, to which the lawyer, from time to time, replied with unimportant comments. Eating his cutlet and drinking his tea, he buried his chin in a sky-blue cravat secured by two diamond pins linked by a gold chain, and smiled a strange smile which was at once oleaginous and equivocal. He noticed that her feet were damp.

'Put them on the stove,' he said . . . 'higher . . . on the porcelain.'

She was afraid of making it dirty. The lawyer protested with an air of gallantry:

'Nothing is ever spoiled by beauty.'

She tried to touch his heart, and grew emotional. She told him how her home was threatened by poverty, spoke of her troubles and her needs. He fully understood, he said, how difficult it must be for so elegant a lady! Without interrupting his meal, he turned until he was facing her squarely, and drew his chair so close to hers that his knee brushed her boot, the sole of which was curling backwards and smoking from the heat of the stove.

But when she asked him for a thousand crowns he compressed his lips, and said he only wished he had had the handling of her estate, because there were a hundred ways in which even a lady might turn her money to account. She could have speculated, with practically no risk at all, either in Grumesnil peat or in Le Havre real estate. He let her eat out her heart with rage at the thought of the fantastic sums which she would almost certainly have made.

'How comes it,' he asked, 'that you never came to me?'

'I really don't know,' she replied.

'Were you frightened of me? I'm the one who ought to complain. I realize that we scarcely know one another . . . all the same, I am deeply devoted to you . . . I trust that the sincerity of my sentiments is not in question?'

He stretched out his hand, took hold of hers, covered it with greedy kisses, and kept it on his knee, toying delicately with her fingers, and murmuring sweet nothings.

His weak voice drooled on like a running brook. His eyes gleamed behind the polished glitter of his spectacles, and his fingers crept up her sleeve and fumbled at her arm. She felt horribly embarrassed.

At last she sprang up:

'I am waiting, sir!'

'For what?' asked the lawyer, who had suddenly become extremely pale.

'For the money.'

'But . . .'

Then, yielding to his overmastering desire:

'All right, you shall have it!' he said. He began shuffling towards her on his knees, taking no account of his dressing-gown.

'Stay with me, I beg! I love you!' He seized her round the waist.

A flood of scarlet surged into Madame Bovary's face. She recoiled from him, a terrible expression in her eyes.

'Sir! you are taking impudent advantage of my distress. I may be a fit object of pity, but I am not for sale!'

She left the room.

The lawyer stayed where he was in a condition of extreme astonishment and staring at his handsome carpet-slippers. They had been a love-gift, and the sight of them at last brought consolation.

Besides, it was just dawning on him that an adventure of the kind he had been contemplating might have led him into rather too deep water.

What a beast! what a cad! . . . what humiliation!

This she said to herself as she fled, trembling, beneath the aspens which lined the road. Disappointment at the failure of her overtures gave added strength to her indignant consciousness of outraged virtue. It seemed to her that providence was intent on dogging her footsteps. But pride came to her assistance. Never before had she rated herself so high or others so low. A spasm of violent aggressiveness shook her. She wanted to inflict physical injury on the whole male sex, to spit in the face of every man who came her way, to trample him under foot. She walked straight ahead at a rapid pace, pale, quivering, furious, scanning the empty horizon with tear-dimmed eyes, as though taking pleasure in the hatred which almost kept her from breathing.

As her home came in sight she felt giddy. She could scarcely move another step, yet go on she must. Where else could she go? whither could she flee?

Félicité was waiting for her on the doorstep.

'Well? . . .'

'No!' said Emma.

For the next quarter of an hour they passed in review all the possible inhabitants of Yonville who might be prepared to help her. But whenever Félicité mentioned a name, Emma replied:

'Do you really think so? That would be no good.'

'The master will be home directly. . . .'

'I know it only too well . . . leave me to myself.'

She had tried everything: there was nothing more she could do. As soon as Charles appeared she would say to him:

'Go away! The carpet you are treading on no longer belongs to us. Not a single piece of furniture, not a pin, not the smallest article in the whole house is yours now, and it is I who have ruined you, luckless creature that you are!'

He would give a great sob, his tears would flow freely, and then, the first shock over, he would forgive her.

'Yes,' she murmured, grinding her teeth, 'he will forgive me. But if he had a million to offer it would not be enough to justify him in my eyes for ever having known me. . . . Nothing can do that, nothing!'

This idea of Bovary's moral superiority exasperated her. Whether she confessed or did not confess, whether she confessed now, in a few hours' time or tomorrow, made no difference. There was no way now of preventing him from knowing the full extent of the catastrophe. She had no alternative but to wait for the horrible scene which was bound to come, to bow her shoulders beneath the load of his magnanimity. A sudden impulse seized her to go back once more to Lheureux—but what good would that do?—to write to her father, but it would be too late. Perhaps she was beginning to regret that she had not yielded to the lawyer, but before she could give much thought to the idea, she heard the sound of a horse trotting up the lane. It was Charles. He opened the gate. He looked paler than the plaster on the wall. Running downstairs, she quickly slipped out by the back-door into the square, and the Mayor's wife, who was talking to Lestiboudois in front of the church, saw her go into the tax-collector's house.

She hurried away to tell Madame Caron the news. The two ladies went up to the attic where, concealed behind some washing hanging on a line, they took up a position of vantage from which they would see everything that was going on at Binet's.

He was alone in his workroom, making a replica in wood of one of those indescribable ivories which consist of crescents and spheres, one within the other, the whole standing upright like an obelisk and serving no conceivable purpose. He was just shaping the last piece. The end was in sight! In the dark room a cloud of yellow dust flew from beneath the tool like a scatter of sparks from under the hooves of a galloping horse. The twin wheels turned and hummed. Binet was smiling, his chin down, his nostrils distended. He seemed lost in the kind of happiness which, as a rule, accompanies only those mediocre occupations that tickle the intelligence with easy difficulties, and satisfy it with a sense of achievement beyond which there is nothing left for dreams to feed on.

'There she is!' said Madame Tuvache.

But the noise of the lathe made it impossible to hear what she was saying.

After a while, the two ladies thought they heard the word *francs*, and old mother Tuvache hissed—'She's begging for time to pay her taxes!'

'That's what it looks like,' replied the other.

They saw her pacing up and down, looking at the napkin-rings ranged along the walls, the candlesticks, the baluster-knobs, while Binet stroked his beard with an air of self-satisfaction.

'Is she going to give him an order?' said Madame Tuvache.

'But his things aren't for sale'—objected her neighbour.

The collector seemed to be listening. He was blinking his eyes as though finding it difficult to grasp what was being said. Madame Bovary talked on in a gentle, supplicating manner. She went close to him, her breast rising and falling. Neither was saying anything now.

'D'you think she's making advances to him?' said Madame Tuvache.

Binet had flushed crimson to the tips of his ears. Emma took his hands.

'That really is too much!'

She must be making some abominable suggestion, because the collector—who was a good fellow, he had fought at Bautzen and at Lutzen,* had taken part in the Campaign of France,* and had even been recommended for a decoration—suddenly recoiled as though he had seen a snake, exclaiming:

'Madame, what can you be thinking of. . . .'

'Women like that ought to be whipped!' said Madame Tuvache.

'Where has she gone now?' asked Madame Caron.

For, during this brief interchange, Emma had disappeared. When next they saw her, she was going up the main street and turning to the right as though heading for the cemetery.

They lost themselves in conjectures.

'I can't breathe! Unlace me!' said Emma when she reached the former nurse's house.

She fell on the bed, shaking with sobs. Madame Rollet covered her with a petticoat, and remained standing close by. Seeing that her visitor made no response, she moved away, sat down at her wheel, and began to spin flax.

'Oh, please stop!' murmured Emma, thinking that she was still hearing Binet's lathe.

'What's the matter with her?' wondered the other: 'what's brought her here?'

Emma had run to her house, driven on by a sort of panic which made it impossible for her to stay at home.

Lying motionless on her back, with a fixed stare in her eyes, she saw everything round her as it were in a blur, though she was forcing herself, with an imbecile concentration, to focus the contents of the room. She fastened her gaze on the peeling plaster, on two sticks smouldering end to end in the grate, on a spider crawling above her head in a crack of the beam. At last she managed to collect her wits. She remembered . . . a day she had once spent with Léon . . . how long ago it seemed! . . . with the sun shining on the river, and the air sweet with the scent of clematis. . . . Then, carried away by her memories, as by a boiling torrent, she presently recalled the events of the previous day.

'What time is it?' she asked.

Madame Rollet went outside, held up the fingers of her right hand towards the point of the compass where the sky showed lightest, and, coming slowly back into the room, said:

'Just on three o'clock.'

'Thank you, thank you.'

He would come, she was sure of that. He would have found the money. But he might be at Yonville not knowing that she was here. She begged the old woman to run home and fetch him.

'But you must hurry. . . .'

'I'm going, dearie, I'm going!'

Emma was surprised now that she had not thought of him in the first place. He had given her his word yesterday and would not fail. She could see herself already, in imagination, going to Lheureux and laying the three bank-notes on his desk. But she would have to think of some story to tell Bovary. What should it be?

It was a long time, all the same, before Madame Rollet got back. But because there was no clock in the cottage, Emma was afraid that she might perhaps be exaggerating the length of her absence. She took a few turns in the garden, walking very slowly. She went a little way up the path which led along the hedge, but hurried back, thinking that the good woman might have returned by a different route. Finally, tired of waiting, a prey to suspicions which she tried to keep from her, no longer certain whether she had been there a minute or a hundred years, she sat down in a corner, closed her eyes and stopped her ears. The gate creaked. She jumped up. But before she could utter a word, Madame Rollet said:

'There's no one up at your place.'

'What!'

'Nobody at all. Your husband is crying and asking for you. They're hunting for you everywhere.'

Emma said nothing. Her eyes were rolling, her breath was coming in pants. The country-woman, frightened by the look on her face, instinctively drew back, thinking she must be mad. Suddenly, Emma struck her forehead and uttered a cry, for the thought of Rodolphe had flashed into her mind like lightning on a dark night. He was so kind, so sensitive, so generous! Besides, should he hesitate to render her this service, there were ways in which she could bring pressure to bear. One glance from her eyes would wake in him the memory of their former love. So off she hurried to La Huchette, quite oblivious of the fact that she was about to acquiesce in what, only a few hours before, had roused her indignation. It never occurred to her that what she proposed to do really amounted to prostitution.

CHAPTER VIII

SHE kept on asking herself while she walked, 'What am I going to say? How am I going to begin?' As she drew near to La Huchette she found herself recognizing the bushes, the trees, the gorse covering the hill, and, down below, she saw the château. The feelings of an earlier tenderness came flooding back, and her poor oppressed heart dilated in the atmosphere of love. A warm wind was blowing in her face. The snow was melting, falling in slow drops from the young shoots on to the grass.

She entered, as of old, by the small gate in the park wall, and reached the Court of Honour which was bordered by a double row of tufted limes. Their long branches swayed in the wind with a swishing sound. The kennel dogs all started barking, but the noise brought no one from the house.

She went up the wide, straight staircase with its wooden balusters, which led to a corridor paved with dusty tiles. On to this a succession of rooms opened as in monasteries or inns. His was at the far end, on the left. Just as she was about to take the latch in her hand, her strength suddenly failed her. She was afraid he might not be there, almost hoped he would not. Yet, this was her last hope, her last chance of salvation. She stood for a moment collecting herself.

Conjuring up the picture of her dire necessity, she forced herself to the sticking point and entered the room.

He was seated in front of the fire, his feet on the fender, smoking a pipe.

'You!' he said, springing up.

'Yes,' she said: 'Rodolphe, I want to ask your advice.'

Hard though she tried to say something more, she could not.

'You haven't changed: still as charming as ever!'

'Oh!' she replied bitterly, 'my charms can't be so very alluring. Don't forget you spurned them!'

He embarked upon an explanation of his conduct, excusing himself in vague, general terms, for want of any more convincing story.

She let herself be beguiled by his words, and, still more, by the sound of his voice and the sight of his person. So powerfully did these things affect her, that she pretended to believe, perhaps even did actually believe, in the pretexts he put forward for having broken with her. He couldn't, he said, go into details. A secret was involved on which depended the honour, nay, perhaps even the life, of a third person.

'It doesn't matter,' she said, looking at him with melancholy eyes: 'but I have suffered terribly.'

He replied with an air of philosophic detachment:

'Life is like that.'

'Have things been well with you since we parted?' asked Emma.

'Oh, neither well . . . nor ill.'

'It might have been better had we never separated.'

'It might.'

'Do you mean that?' she said, coming closer.

She sighed.

'Oh, Rodolphe, if only you had known how much I loved you!'

It was then that she took his hand. They remained for a while, their fingers interlocked, as on that first day at the show. From a feeling of pride, he strove to make no display of emotion. But letting her head fall on his breast, she said:

'You didn't *want* me to be able to live without you, did you? One can never break oneself of the habit of being happy. I was in despair! I thought I should have died! I will tell you later all about that time. And you . . . you ran away from me! . . .'

It was true that for the past three years he had studiously avoided her, actuated by that natural cowardice which characterizes the stronger sex.

With coquettish movements of the head, with little coaxing gestures like those of a sentimental kitten, she talked on.

'There have been other women in your life, admit it! Oh, I understand it well enough, and certainly don't blame *them*. I expect you fascinated them as you fascinated me. You're a man, you've got everything that makes a man attractive. But we're going to begin all over again, surely? We're going to be lovers once more! See, I am smiling, I am happy . . . say something!'

She was a sight to steal any man's heart, with a tear trembling in her eyes like a raindrop left by a storm in a flower's blue cup.

He drew her on to his knee. With the back of his hand he stroked the smooth hair in which, in the gathering dusk, a last ray of sunlight shimmered like an arrow of gold. At last, very gently, he kissed her eyelids.

'You have been crying,' he said: 'why is that?'

She broke into sobs.

Rodolphe interpreted the spasm as one of love that could no longer be controlled. She made no answer to his question, and he took her silence for modesty entrenched within its last defences.

'Forgive me!' he exclaimed. 'No other woman can delight me as you do! I have been a fool, a villain! I love you, and will love you for ever. What is the matter? tell me!'

He fell on his knees.

'It's just . . . that I am facing ruin, Rodolphe. You *will* lend me three thousand francs, won't you?'

'But . . . But . . .' he said slowly, getting to his feet, while his face assumed a serious expression.

'You know', she hurried on, 'that my husband had entrusted the whole of his fortune to a lawyer. Well, the lawyer has run away. We've borrowed. The patients weren't paying up, and we haven't been able to realize all our property. Everything will come right in the end, but for the moment we have to find three thousand francs, or we'll be sold up. We need it now, immediately, and so, counting on your friendship, I came here.'

'Ah!' thought Rodolphe, who had suddenly gone very pale, 'so *that*'s the reason for this visit!'

Without the slightest show of emotion, he said:

'Dear lady, I haven't got such a sum.'

He was not lying. Had the money been at hand, he would doubt-less have given it to her, unpleasant though such fine gestures usually are. Of all the storms that beat down love, a request for money provides the coldest douche, and strikes most deeply to the roots.

For a moment or two she just looked at him.

'You haven't got it?'

Several times she repeated the same words:

'You haven't got it! . . . I might have spared myself this final humiliation. You never really loved me! You are just like all the others!'

She was betraying herself, courting ruin. Rodolphe broke in on her, swearing that he was 'in deep water' himself.

'For that I am sorry,' said Emma: 'sincerely sorry. . . .'

She fixed her gaze on a damascened carbine which formed part of a trophy of arms.

'But a poor man like you doesn't lavish silver on the butt of a gun, or buy a clock inlaid with tortoiseshell'—she went on, pointing to a buhl timepiece—'or silver-gilt whistles for riding-crops'—she touched them as she spoke—'or trinkets for watch-chains. I notice that you want for nothing, not even for a liqueur-stand in your bedroom. The only person you love is yourself. You live well, you have a château, farms, woods. You hunt, you take trips to Paris . . . and that's not all'—she exclaimed, taking up his sleeve-links which were lying on the mantelpiece. 'Why, the smallest of these knick-knacks could be turned into money . . . Not that *I* want them . . . you can keep the lot for all I care!'

She threw the links from her so violently, that the gold chain broke against the wall.

'I would have given you everything, would have sold all I had. I would have worked with my hands, would have begged along the roads, just for a smile, a look, just to hear you say "thank you". How can you sit there calmly in your chair, as though you hadn't made me suffer enough already? But for you, as you know full well, I might have lived happily. What was it induced you to come into my life? Was it a bet? . . . But you *did* love me, you told me so in the old days . . . and again, just now. Better far for me if you had turned me out of the house! My hands are still warm with your kisses. Here is the very spot on the carpet where you swore on your knees to love me for ever! You made me believe you meant it! For two years you led me on through the most glittering dream, the sweetest dream that ever was . . . Do you remember what journeys we planned? Oh, that letter you wrote!—it tore my heart to shreds . . . and now that I come back to my rich, free, happy lover, to implore of him such help as any stranger would have given, kneeling to him with an offer of love and devotion, he pushes me away for no better reason than that it would cost him three thousand francs!'

'But I haven't got three thousand francs!' replied Rodolphe with that utter calm of manner which hides cold anger as with a shield.

She left the room. The walls seemed to have lost their fixity, and to tremble as she passed. She felt as though the ceiling would crush her. Back, down the long avenue, she went, stumbling over the piles of dead leaves which the wind was whipping into little eddies. At last she reached the ha-ha by the gate. So eager was she to get out that she broke her nails against the latch. A hundred yards further on, breathless and almost falling, she stopped. She turned and looked for the last time at the impassive bulk of the château set, with its long rows of windows and its three courtyards, in the frame of park and garden.

She remained there in a sort of a daze, conscious of herself only because of her throbbing arteries. They seemed to her to be making a deafening noise that filled the whole countryside. The ground under her feet felt more yielding than the sea, and the furrows, to her eyes, were huge brown waves curling and breaking about her. All that her mind contained of memories and thoughts suddenly flared up and burst like the thousand stars and sparkles of a rocket. She saw her father and Lheureux's office, the room where she and Léon held their tryst, a strange and different landscape. Madness seized on her and she was frightened. Somehow she managed to get control of herself, though her mind was still confused, for the root cause of her horrible state, the problem of money, was now entirely banished from her consciousness. It was only in her love that she suffered, and through this memory she felt her soul slipping away, as those on the point of death sense their life ebb through a bleeding wound.

Daylight was almost gone. The rooks were on the wing.

She had the impression, on a sudden, that the air was full of flaming globules that burst like meteors, twisting and turning as they fell, and looked like small flattened objects on the snow where they lay melting between the branches of the trees.* In the heart of each she saw Rodolphe's face. They grew in number, crowding to a point and seeming to force a way into the very substance of her body. Then suddenly they vanished, and she realized that what she had been looking at was light streaming from many windows through the mist.

The situation became crystal-clear to her. It was as though she were standing upon the brink of a deep gulf. Her panting breath tore at her lungs. In an ecstasy of heroism, which brought her a feeling that was almost happiness, she ran down the hill, crossed the cattle-bridge, continued along the path and into the lane, until finally she reached the market-hall and came to a halt outside the chemist's shop.

It was empty. Just as she was about to cross the threshold, a sudden fear made her stop. The sound of the bell might bring somebody. Slipping through the gate, therefore, holding her breath and feeling her way along the wall, she got as far as the kitchen where a candle stood burning on the range. Justin, in his shirt-sleeves, was carrying a dish.

'They're at dinner. I must wait.'

He appeared for the second time. She tapped on the window. He came out.

'The key!—the key to the room upstairs where the . . .'

'What do you mean?'

He looked at her, astonished by the pallor of her face which showed dead white in the darkness. She seemed to him to be amazingly lovely and great with majesty, like a ghost. Though he did not yet grasp what it was she wanted, he had a presentiment of terror.

She spoke again, quickly, and in a low voice, a soft voice which came meltingly to his ears.

'I want it: give it me!'

The wall was thin and she could hear through it the tinkle of plates in the dining-room.

She pretended that she was going to kill some rats which were keeping her awake.

'I'll tell the master. . . .'

'No! stay here!'

Then, with an assumption of calmness:

'It's not worth disturbing him. *I'll* tell him about it later. Just light me upstairs, please.'

She entered the passage on which the door of the laboratory opened. Hanging on the wall was a key labelled '*The Den*'.

'Justin!' called the apothecary, who was growing impatient.

'Let us go up.'

He followed her.

The key turned in the lock, and she went straight to the third shelf, so truly did her memory serve her. She lifted down the blue jar, pulled out the stopper, rummaged inside with her hand, and withdrew it filled with a white powder. This she began to eat on the spot.

'Don't do that!' he cried, flinging himself upon her.

'Ssh! someone might come.'

He was desperate, and wanted to call for help.

'Say nothing: it would be your master who would get the blame.'

She went home in a mood of sudden peace, almost like somebody with a calm sense of duty done.

When Charles, appalled by the news of the seizure, reached home, Emma had just gone out. He shouted, wept, fainted—but she did not return. Where could she be? He sent Félicité to the Homais's, to Monsieur Tuvache, to Lheureux, to the Golden Lion—to every place he could think of. In the lucid moments of his anguish he saw his reputation blasted, their fortune lost, Berthe's future ruined. But why? . . . There was no sign of her, not a word. He waited until six o'clock in the evening, and then, unable to stand the strain any longer, and thinking she might have gone to Rouen, walked half a mile up the road, saw nobody, hung about for a while, and then returned.

She had come back.

'What happened? . . . Why is all this going on? . . . Explain!'

She sat down at her desk and wrote a letter which she slowly sealed, adding the date and the hour. Then, very solemnly, she said:

'You must read this tomorrow. Till then, please don't ask me any questions—any at all!'

'But . . .'

'Oh, leave me alone!'

She lay down at full length on her bed.

She was awakened by a bitter taste in her mouth. She caught a glimpse of Charles, and shut her eyes again.

She began to observe her own reactions curiously. She wanted to make sure whether or not she was suffering. As yet she felt nothing. She could hear the ticking of the clock, the sound of the fire, and Charles's breathing as he stood by the bed.

'Death's no such great matter,' she thought. 'I'll just go to sleep, and everything will be over.'

She drank some water and turned her face to the wall.

The disgusting taste of ink persisted.

'Oh, I'm so thirsty'—she murmured—'so terribly thirsty.'

'What's wrong with you?' asked Charles, handing her a glass.

'It's nothing at all . . . *do* open the window . . . I'm stifling!'

She was caught by a sudden spasm of nausea,* and had barely time to snatch her handkerchief from under the pillow.

'Take it!' she said hastily: 'take it and throw it away!'

He questioned her but she answered nothing. She lay there not stirring a finger, fearful that the least emotion might make her sick. She was conscious of an icy chill moving upwards from her feet towards her heart.

'It's beginning now!' she whispered.

'What's that you're saying?'

She rolled her head slowly from side to side. The movement was eloquent of pain, and all the while she kept opening and shutting her mouth as though something heavy were lying on her tongue. At eight o'clock a fresh bout of nausea came on. Charles noticed a sort of white grit adhering to the side of the basin.

'Extraordinary!' he said more than once: 'really very odd!'

But in a strong voice she exclaimed:

'No, you're wrong!'

Then very gently, almost as though caressing her, he passed his hand over her stomach. She uttered a shrill scream, and he jumped back in terror.

Then she began to groan, feebly at first. A fit of trembling shook her shoulders, and she became whiter than the sheet at which her fingers were clawing. Her pulse was irregular: when he felt her wrist it was almost imperceptible.

Great beads of sweat were standing out on her face which had taken on a faint blue tinge. It was as though some metallic exhalation had turned it rigid. Her teeth were chattering, and her eyes, suddenly enlarged, gazed vaguely about her. To every question she replied only with a movement of the head. Two or three times she even smiled. By degrees the groans became louder; at times they sounded almost like suppressed screams. She pretended she was feeling better and would soon get up. But another series of convulsions gripped her.

'Oh God! this is frightful!'

He flung himself on his knees by the bed.

'What have you been eating? Tell me . . . answer, in heaven's name!'

There was a tenderness in his eyes such as she had never seen before.

'There, over there,' she moaned in a voice that was growing weaker all the time.

He rushed to the desk, broke the seal, and read aloud: 'Let no one be blamed.' . . . He stopped, passed his hand over his eyes, and then went on with the letter.

'What! . . .Oh, help . . . help!'

He could do nothing but repeat the single word 'Poisoned! . . . poisoned!' Félicité ran over to Homais who cried it aloud as he crossed the square. Madame Lefrançois heard it in the Golden Lion. Several people rose from their beds and passed it on to their neighbours. No one in the village slept a wink that night.

Distracted, stammering, almost in a state of collapse, Charles wandered about the room. He stumbled against the furniture, tore at his hair. Never had the chemist imagined so terrible a sight.

He recovered himself sufficiently to write a note to Monsieur Canivet and to Dr Larivière. He had completely lost his head, and made more than fifteen rough drafts. Hippolyte set off for Neufchâtel, and Justin spurred Bovary's horse so hard that he had to leave it foundered and three parts dead on the hill at Le Bois–Guillaume.

Charles tried to hunt through his medical dictionary, but could not see to read. The lines danced before his eyes.

'Be calm!' said the apothecary. 'A powerful antidote is all that is necessary. What poison is it?'

Charles showed him the letter. It was arsenic.

'Very well, then,' said Homais: 'we must make an analysis.'

He knew that an analysis was necessary in all cases of poisoning. But the other, who was beyond understanding anything, could only reply:

'Make it then! . . . make it . . . only save her!'

Going over to her side, he sank to the ground and stayed there sobbing, his head resting against the edge of the bed.

'Don't cry'—she said to him—'I shan't trouble you much longer.'

'But why . . . Who drove you to this?'

She replied:

'It had to be, my dear.'

'Weren't you happy? . . . Is it my fault? I did everything I could.'

'Yes indeed, that is true . . . you are a good man.'

Slowly she passed her fingers through his hair. The gentleness of the gesture added fuel to his misery. He felt his whole being crumble in despair at the thought of losing her—now, especially, just when she was showing more love for him than at any time in their life together. He could think of nothing to do, could not decide what ought to be done, dared not take any definite step. The mere thought of making up his mind completely overwhelmed him.

Now at last, she thought, she had finished with treachery, baseness and all the innumerable desires that had tormented her. She no longer felt hatred for anyone. A dark confusion fell upon her mind. Among all the sounds of the outside world she could hear only the broken sobbing of that poor soul, gentle, indistinct, like the last echo of a symphony fading into the distance.

'Bring the child to me,' she said, raising herself on her elbow.

'Has the pain stopped?' asked Charles.

'Yes . . . Yes. . . .'

The child was carried in by the nurse. She was wearing a long nightdress below which her bare feet hung down. She looked serious and only half awake, and gazed in astonishment at the disordered room, closing her eyes against the glare of the candles which stood burning on the various pieces of furniture. Probably they reminded her of those New Year's Days, or festivals of mid-Lent, when, waking thus in a candle-lit dawn, she went into her mother's bed to get her present. For suddenly she said:

'Where is it, Mummy?'

No one spoke a word, and she went on:

'I don't see my little slipper.'

Félicité held her over the bed, but the child's eyes were still fixed on the mantelpiece.

'Has nurse taken it?' she asked.

At the sound of this word, which woke in her the memory of her adulteries and misfortunes, Madame Bovary turned away her head as though in disgust at another poison far more powerful than that which was oozing up into her mouth. But Berthe stayed where she had been set upon the bed.

'How big your eyes are, Mummy: how pale you are, and how you are sweating!'

Her mother looked at her.

'I'm frightened!' said the little girl, shrinking back.

Emma took her hand to kiss it, but the child struggled.

'Enough! take her away!' cried Charles who was sobbing in the alcove.

For a moment the symptoms ceased. She seemed less agitated, and at each insignificant word, at each calmer drawing of her breath, he gained new hope. When, at last, Canivet came into the room, he flung himself weeping into his arms.

'Oh, you've come! . . . thank you, thank you . . . how good of you. But things are going better: look at her.'

His colleague did not share his opinion. Being the last man, as he said himself, to beat about the bush, he prescribed an emetic with the object of emptying the stomach.

Very soon she started to vomit blood. Her lips became more and more tightly compressed. Her limbs were rigid: brown patches showed on her body and her pulse thrilled beneath the doctor's fingers like the string of a harp just before it breaks.

Then she began to scream, horribly. She cursed the poison, abusing it, imploring it to be quick, and, with her stiff arms, pushed away everything that Charles, in an agony even greater than her own, tried to make her drink. He stood there, his handkerchief to his lips, and a hoarse rattle in his throat, weeping, choked by sobs which shook him from head to foot. Félicité was running about the room. Homais, motionless, was heaving great sighs, and Monsieur Canivet, who never for a moment lost his presence of mind, began all the same to feel distinctly worried.

'Devil take it! . . . but . . . the purge has acted . . . and as soon as the cause ceases to operate . . .'

'The effect should cease, too,' put in Homais: 'that stands to reason.'

'Oh, save her!' exclaimed Bovary.

Without listening to the chemist, who was venturing to suggest a further hypothesis—'It may be a salutary paroxysm'— Canivet was about to administer an antidote, when the crack of a whip was heard. The windows rattled, and a post-chaise, drawn at full speed by three horses muddied to the ears, dashed round the corner of the market-hall. It was Dr Larivière.*

The appearance of a god could not have caused greater excitement. Bovary raised his hands: Canivet stopped short in what he was doing, and Homais took off his skull-cap before ever the doctor entered the room.

Dr Larivière belonged to the great school of surgery which had flourished under Bichat:* to that generation, now no more, of philosophic practitioners who cherished their art with a fanatical passion and exercised it with a kind of exalted wisdom. Every single person in his hospital trembled when he flew into a rage, and so great was the veneration felt for him by his pupils, that they one and all strove to imitate him as soon as they had set up in practice for themselves. Replicas of Dr Larivière were to be found in every town for miles round: doctors wearing the same padded overall, the same loose frock-coat with unbuttoned cuffs which had a way of flapping over his plump hands—fine hands, on which he never wore gloves, as though to have them the readier to plunge into the pain and misery through which he moved. Scornful of decorations, titles and academic honours, hospitable, liberal, fatherly in his dealings with the poor, and practising a virtue in which he did not believe, he might well have passed for a saint, had not the keenness of his intelligence made him feared as a demon. His glance, sharper than his scalpel, drove straight to the soul, cutting through every excuse, every defence of modesty, and showing no mercy to lies. He lived among his fellows for ever radiating that quiet majesty which comes of the consciousness of great talents, of the security bred of great wealth, and was the result of forty years marked by hard work and an irreproachable private life.

As soon as he came into the room he frowned at the spectacle of Emma lying there on her back, hollow-cheeked, and with her mouth hanging open. All the while that he appeared to be listening to Canivet he was rubbing his finger to and fro beneath his nose, muttering—

'Good . . . good. . . .'

But he gave a slow shrug. Bovary noticed it. The two men looked at one another, and the surgeon, hardened though he was to the sight of misery, could not help letting a tear trickle on to his shirt frill.

He asked Canivet to come with him into the next room. Charles followed them.

'She's very, very ill, isn't she? Would a mustard plaster be of any use? Is there nothing you can suggest?—you *must* find some way, you who have saved so many lives!'

Charles flung both arms about his body, gazing at him with scared, imploring eyes, and half swooning as he clung to him.

'My poor fellow, you must be brave. There is nothing further we can do.'

Dr Larivière turned away.

'Are you going?'

'I will come back.'

He left the room as though to give some order to his driver. Canivet, who was no more anxious than he was to see Emma die under his hands, followed.

The chemist joined them in the square. He was temperamentally incapable of keeping away from famous men. He begged Monsieur Larivière to do him the honour of gracing his table.

A messenger was hurriedly sent across to the Golden Lion for some pigeons. All the cutlets that the butcher could provide, all the cream that could be procured from Tuvache, all the eggs from Lestiboudois, were hastily mobilized. The apothecary himself lent a hand in the kitchen, while Madame Homais, tightening the strings of her bodice, said:

'You must make allowances, sir. Unless one gives a day's notice in this wretched place. . . .'

'The wine-glasses!' hissed Homais.

'If we lived in a town we could at least fall back on stuffed trotters. . . .'

'Don't talk so much! . . . Let us begin, Doctor.'

He thought it advisable, as soon as the meal was under way, to volunteer some details about the catastrophe.

'The earliest symptom was a dryness in the pharynx, and this was followed by intolerable pain in the epigastrium, excessive vomiting, and coma.'

'How did she come to poison herself?'

'I have no idea, Doctor, nor can I tell you how she managed to procure the arsenious acid.'

At this moment, Justin, who was bringing in a pile of plates, was seized with a fit of trembling.

'What's the matter with you?' said the chemist.

At this question, the lad let the whole lot fall to the ground with a tremendous clatter.

'Fool!' shouted Homais: 'clumsy idiot! lout! stupid donkey!'

Then, quickly getting control of his temper, he went on.

'I wanted to attempt an analysis, Doctor ... And, *primo*, I very carefully introduced into a test-tube . . .'

'It would have been a good deal more useful', said the surgeon, 'if you had introduced your fingers into her throat.'

His colleague said nothing. He had just had a severe talking-to in private on the subject of his emetic. Poor Canivet, who had been so very arrogant and verbose over the incident of the club-foot, was now in a very modest mood, and sat with a fixed smile of approval on his lips.

Homais spread himself in his role of host. The painful recollection of Bovary had the effect of bolstering up his own egotism, and even contributed in a vague sort of way to his pleasure. The great doctor's presence quite transported him. He made a vast display of erudition, and trotted out a great number of learned words at random, such as cantharides, upas, the manchineel tree,* and the adder.

'I have read somewhere, Doctor, that cases have been known of people being poisoned, struck down suddenly, as it were, by partaking of black-puddings which had been exposed to an excessive degree of fumigation. I assume that the information was correct, for it was contained in an admirable report from the pen of one of our leading pharmacists, one of our masters, the illustrious Cadet de Gassicourt!'*

Madame Homais reappeared carrying one of those unreliable contraptions which have to be heated by methylated spirits, for Homais made a great point of always preparing coffee at the table, having first roasted and ground the beans with his own hands, and achieved the proper mixture.

'*Saccharum*, Doctor?' he asked, passing the sugar.

Then he sent for all his children, wishing to have the surgeon's opinion on their physical condition.

At last, just as Monsieur Larivière was on the point of taking his departure, Madame Homais insisted on asking his advice about her husband. She thought that the blood would go to his brain because of his habit of always dozing off after dinner.

'He doesn't need to worry about his brain!'

Grinning at his own joke, which had passed quite unnoticed, he opened the door. But the shop was full of people, and he had considerable difficulty in shaking off the great Tuvache who feared that his wife might be suffering from inflammation of the lungs because she was forever spitting into the fire. Next came Monsieur Binet who sometimes complained of a morbid hunger,* Madame Caron who was suffering from pins and needles, Lheureux, who was experiencing fits of dizziness, Lestiboudois, who was rheumatic, and Madame Lefrançois who wanted to be reassured about acidity of the stomach.

At last the three horses made off at a great pace, and the general feeling was that the famous man had not been very obliging.

Public attention, however, was diverted by the appearance of Monsieur Bournisien, who could be seen hurrying through the market-hall with the sanctified oils.

Homais, in deference to his principles, compared all priests to carrion-crows attracted by the smell of death. The sight of a churchman was unpleasing to him because the soutane turned his mind to the shroud, with the result that he abused the one because he was terrified of the other.

Nevertheless, refusing to abandon what he called his *mission*, he returned to Bovary's house accompanied by Canivet whom Monsieur Larivière, before leaving, had strongly urged to stay. But for his wife's protest, he would have taken his two sons with him, being of the opinion that it was good for them to become accustomed to painful situations, so that they might derive from them a lesson, an example, a solemn picture, which they would remember for the rest of their lives.

When they entered the bedroom, they found the prevailing atmosphere to be one of mournful solemnity. On the work-table, covered with a white napkin, lay five or six little balls of cotton-wool in a silver platter. Beside them stood a large crucifix flanked by two lit candelabra. Emma lay with staring eyes, her chin sunk forward on her breast. Her poor hands were wandering aimlessly over the sheet, with the hideous, weak movement of the dying which suggests that they are eager to cover themselves with the grave-clothes. Pale as a statue, his two eyes like red, smouldering coals, Charles, no longer weeping, stood facing her at the bottom of the bed, while the priest, on one knee, was murmuring words in a low voice.

Slowly she turned her face. She seemed to be irradiated with joy at sight of the purple stole, recovering, no doubt, in this moment of extraordinary peace, the lost ecstasy of her earlier mystic fits, and already glimpsing visions of eternal beatitude.

The priest rose and took the crucifix. Stretching her neck forward as if she were thirsty, she pressed her lips to the body of the man-God, and with all her dying strength kissed it more passionately than ever she had a lover. Then he recited the *Misereatur* and the *Indulgentiam*, dipped his right thumb in the oil, and began to administer extreme unction, first on the eyes which had coveted the splendours of this world; then on the nostrils greedy of sweet scents; then on the mouth which had given passage to lying words, had spoken the language of pride, and had cried aloud in the ecstasy of lust; then on the hands, so avid of soft stuffs; and finally on the soles of the feet which had once moved so swiftly when she had hastened to the satisfaction of desire, and now would never move again. He wiped his fingers, threw into the fire the scraps of wool moistened with the oil, and sat down by the dying woman, telling her that now she must make her sufferings one with Christ's, and abandon herself to the divine mercy.*

As he finished his exhortations, he tried to put into her hand a consecrated candle, the symbol of those heavenly glories with which so soon she would be surrounded. But by now she was too weak to close her fingers, and, but for Monsieur Bournisien, the candle would have fallen to the floor.

But she had lost something of her pallor, and on her face was a look of peace, as though the sacraments had cured her.

The priest did not fail to point this out, and even explained to Bovary that the Lord would sometimes prolong the existence of those whose salvation might thus be assured. Charles remembered another day when, as now, she had been at the point of death, and had taken communion.

Perhaps, he thought, they need not even yet despair.

And indeed, she was looking slowly about her, like one waking from a dream. In a clearly audible voice she asked for her mirror, and lay for a moment or two with her face bent above it, until two large tears trickled from her eyes. Then she threw back her head with a sigh, and collapsed on to the pillow.

At once her breath began to come in pants. Her tongue protruded from her mouth to its full length. Her eyes rolled wildly and grew pale like two lamp globes which have just been extinguished. She might have been thought already dead, had it not been that her ribs were agitated by a terrifying spasm of quick breathing, as though her soul were struggling for freedom. Félicité knelt before the crucifix, and even the chemist was a little unsteady on his legs, while Monsieur Canivet gazed with unseeing eyes into the square.

Monsieur Bournisien had returned once more to his prayers, his forehead resting on the edge of the bed, his long black soutane trailing behind him on the floor. Charles, kneeling at the opposite side, stretched out his arms to Emma. He had taken her hands and was pressing them, trembling at each beat of her heart, as at the thundering fall of stones from a doomed ruin. As the death-rattle became more marked, the churchman hastened his prayers. They mingled with Bovary's stifled sobs, and at times all other sounds seemed to vanish in the low murmur of the Latin syllables which rang out like a passing-bell.

Suddenly there was a noise of heavy clogs from the street, and the tap-tapping of a stick. A voice rose high and distinct, a hoarse voice, singing:

> Souvent la chaleur d'un beau jour
> Fait rêver fillette à l'amour.

Emma raised herself like a galvanized corpse, her hair in disorder, her eyes fixed and staring.

> Pour amasser diligemment
> Les épis que la faux moissonne,
> Ma Nanette va s'inclinant
> Vers le sillon qui nous les donne.

'The blind man!' she cried.

And she started to laugh in a fit of horrible, wild, despairing mirth. She thought she saw the hideous face of the beggar standing out from the eternal darkness like a symbol of terror.

Il souffla bien fort ce jour là
Et le jupon court s'envola!

She fell back on the mattress in a convulsion. All in the room drew close. She was no more.

CHAPTER IX

WHEN a person dies the event is always followed by, as it were, a few moments of stupefaction. It is so hard to realize the sudden coming of a state of nothingness, to resign oneself to its actual happening.

When he saw, however, that his wife lay there motionless, Charles flung himself upon her, crying:

'Good-bye Good-bye!'

Homais and Canivet led him from the room.

'You must control yourself.'

He struggled to throw off their restraining hands. 'I will be sensible,' he said, 'I won't do any harm. But let me go! I want to see her, she is my wife!'

He burst into tears.

'Weep on,' said the chemist. 'Let nature have her way. You will feel the better for it.'

Charles had become as weak as a child. He let them take him downstairs into the dining-room. Shortly afterwards, Monsieur Homais went home.

While crossing the square, he was accosted by the blind man who, having dragged himself all the way to Yonville in the hope of getting the promised antiphlogistic ointment, was asking everyone he met where the apothecary lived.

'As though I hadn't enough on my hands as it is! I can't attend to you now: come back another day!'

He hurried into his shop.

He had two letters to write, a sedative to make up for Bovary, some plausible story to invent which he could embody in an article for the *Fanal* in such a way as to conceal the fact of the poisoning, to say nothing of dealing with all the people who were waiting for him to give them the latest news. As soon as he had explained to the good folk of Yonville that Madame Bovary had used arsenic in mistake for sugar while making some vanilla custard, he went back to the doc-tor's house.

He found Charles alone (Monsieur Canivet had just left), seated in an armchair close to the window, his eyes fixed on the floor in a vacant stare.

'You should be thinking about when the ceremony is to take place,' he said.

'Why? what ceremony?'

In an uncertain, frightened voice, the poor fellow added:

'No! no! I want to keep her here!'

To keep himself from breaking down, Homais took a jug from the sideboard and started to water the geraniums.

'Thank you,' said Charles, 'that is very kind of you.'

Overwhelmed by a flood of memories which the chemist's action had let loose, he could say no more.

Homais attempted to distract his attention by embarking on a horticultural disquisition. Plants, he said, require moisture. Charles nodded his head in agreement.

'Not but what the fine weather will soon be back.'

'Ah!' breathed Bovary.

The apothecary could think of nothing else to say, and drew aside the half-curtains.

'There's Monsieur Tuvache down in the square.'

Charles repeated the words mechanically: 'Monsieur Tuvache down in the square.'

Homais had not the heart to re-open the question of the funeral arrangements. It was the priest who finally prevailed upon Bovary to give the necessary instructions.

Charles shut himself up in his consulting-room, took a pen, and after some time spent in sobbing, wrote:

I wish her to be buried in her wedding-dress, with white shoes and a wreath. Her hair is to be arranged on her shoulders. There are to be three coffins, one of oak, one of mahogany, one of lead. It is my wish that no one should speak to me. I shall be strong enough to go through with the ceremony. Over the bier a pall is to be laid, of green velvet. These are my instructions. I expect them to be carried out.

His friends were much surprised by these romantic instructions, and the chemist at once went to him and said:

'I should have thought that the velvet was something of a super-fetation. Just consider the expense.'

'What business is that of yours!' cried Charles. 'You did not love her! Go away! . . .'

The churchman took him by the arm and led him into the garden, discoursing the while on the vanity of earthly things. God, he said, was all-mighty and all-good. We must submit to his decrees without murmuring. Indeed, we should be grateful to him.

Charles broke out into a stream of blasphemies.

'I hate and detest your God!'

'The spirit of rebellion is still active in you,' sighed the priest.

But Bovary was far away. He walked with great strides along the wall on which his fruit-trees had been trained. He ground his teeth and looked unuttered curses at the sky. But not a leaf stirred.

A thin rain was falling. His chest was uncovered and he began to shiver. He went back into the house and sat in the kitchen.

At six o'clock a metallic clatter was heard coming from the square, and heralding the arrival of the Swallow. He sat, with his forehead pressed to the glass, watching the passengers get out. Félicité made up a mattress for him in the drawing-room. He threw himself down on it and fell asleep.

Philosopher though he was, Monsieur Homais respected the dead. Consequently, bearing no grudge against Charles, he came back in the evening to watch by the body, bringing with him three books and a writing-case, intending to take notes.

Monsieur Bournisien was there too, and two large candles were burning at the head of the bed which had been moved out from the alcove.

The apothecary, oppressed by the silence, began very soon to voice his sympathy for the 'unfortunate young woman'. The priest replied that nothing could now be done save pray for her.

'Still, you must admit', said Homais, that of two alternatives, one must be true. Either she is dead and in a state of grace (to use the language of the church), in which case there is no need of prayers, or she died impenitent (that, I believe, is the ecclesiastical phrase), and, if that is so . . .'

Bournisien interrupted in a churlish tone that even were that true, it would still be necessary to pray.

'But', objected the chemist, 'since God knows all our needs, what good can prayer do?'

'If you can speak of prayer in those terms, I can only assume that you are no Christian'—said the priest.

'I beg your pardon!' answered Homais: 'I have a high regard for Christianity. In the first place, it abolished slavery and gave the world a code of lofty morals. . . .'

'That is not the question! All the texts. . . .'

'Oh, texts! Read your history. It is well known that the Jesuits falsified the lot of them.'

Charles entered the room, walked across to the bed, and drew back the curtains.

Emma was lying with her head on her right shoulder. The corner of her open mouth formed, as it were, a black hole in the lower part of her face. Her two thumbs were flexed inwards towards the palms of the hands. There was a powdering of what looked like white dust on her lashes, and her eyes were beginning to disappear in a viscous pallor which gave the impression that spiders had been spinning a delicate web over their surface. The sheet sagged between her breast and her knees, rising, further down, to a peak above her toes. It seemed to Charles as though some great weight, some mass of infinity, were lying upon her.

The church clock struck two. They could hear the sluggish murmur of the river flowing past the terrace in the darkness. Now and again, Monsieur Bournisien blew his nose noisily, and Homais scratched with his pen on the paper.

'Why not go away, my friend?' he said: 'the sight tears at your heart.'

As soon as Charles had left them, the chemist and the curé embarked once more upon their argument.

'Read Voltaire,' said the one: 'read d'Holbach, read the *Encyclopaedia*!'*

'Read *Les Lettres de quelques juifs portuguais*!'* said the other: 'read *La Raison du christianisme*, by Nicolas* who was once a magistrate!'

They grew heated: their faces were flushed, they both spoke at once without listening to one another. Bournisien was scandalized at such an exhibition of effrontery: Homais marvelled at such stupidity. They were within measurable distance of exchanging insults, when

Charles suddenly reappeared. A sort of fascination drew him back. He was continually coming upstairs.

He stood immediately opposite the dead woman, that he might see her more clearly, and lost himself in a contemplation so profound that it ceased to be painful.

He remembered stories he had heard of cataleptic trances, of the miracles achieved by magnetism. He told himself that if only he wanted her badly enough he might, perhaps, succeed in bringing her back to life. Once he leaned towards her and cried in a low voice— 'Emma! Emma!' The force of his breath set the candle flames flickering against the wall.

In the early hours of the next day old Madame Bovary arrived. As Charles embraced her he fell into a fresh fit of weeping. She tried, as the chemist had done, to say something to him about the cost of the funeral, but he grew so angry that she relapsed into silence. He even told her to go at once into town to buy what was needed.

He remained alone all that afternoon. Berthe had been taken across to Madame Homais. Félicité stayed upstairs in the bedroom with Madame Lefrançois.

In the evening there were visitors. Charles got up, shook hands without uttering a word, and the newcomers sat down with those already there, ranged in a semi-circle in front of the fire. They sat swinging their crossed legs, and occasionally sighing deeply. All were immeasurably bored, but none would be the first to go.

When Homais returned at nine o'clock (for two days now it had been impossible to look into the square without seeing him), he brought a provision of camphor, benzoin and aromatic herbs, as well as a jar full of chlorine to counter any noxious gases. At the moment of his arrival the servant, Madame Lefrançois and the elder Madame Bovary were circling about the bed, putting the final touches to Emma's funeral apparel. They lowered the long, stiff veil which covered her completely to her feet in their satin slippers.

Félicité was sobbing.

'Oh, my poor mistress! my poor mistress!'

'Just take a look at her,' sighed the landlady of the Golden Lion: 'still as pretty as ever. One could almost swear she was just going to get up!'

Then they leaned over the bed in order to arrange her wreath. To do this, it was necessary to raise her head slightly, and as they did so a flood of black liquid came from her mouth, as though she were vomiting.

'Oh, heavens!' exclaimed Madame Lefrançois: 'take care of the dress! Give us a hand, you,' she added, turning to the chemist: 'or are you afraid?'

'Afraid, I?' he answered, with a shrug. 'She's not the first dead person I have seen. I had plenty to do with corpses when I was walking the hospital in my student days. We used to brew punch in the lecture-room while we were doing dissections. Death holds no terrors for a philosopher. Why, as I have often said, I have made arrangements to leave my body to the faculty so that it may serve the cause of science!'

As soon as the curé turned up, he asked how Monsieur Bovary was feeling, and, on hearing the apothecary's answer, said:

'The blow is still very recent: you must remember that.'

Whereupon Homais congratulated him on the fact that, unlike the general run of mankind, he was not exposed to the grief of losing a dearly loved life-companion. This remark at once led to an argument on the celibacy of the clergy.

'It is not natural for a man to live without a woman,' said Homais: 'there have been crimes. . . .'

'But, *sabre de Dieu*!' cried the churchman, 'how do you expect a man who is tangled in the toils of matrimony to keep, for instance, the secrets of the confessional?'

Homais proceeded to attack the institution of confession, and Bournisien to defend it, the latter dwelling more particularly upon acts of reparation which had been, and could be, brought about by its means. He quoted a number of anecdotes designed to prove that thieves had, quite suddenly, become honest men. There were cases, he said, of soldiers who, on approaching the seat of penitence, had felt the scales fall from their eyes. Finally, there was the incident of the Minister at Fribourg. . . .

His companion was by this time fast asleep, and, finding the air of the room rather oppressive, he opened the window. The noise he made in doing so wakened the chemist.

'Here, take a pinch of snuff,' said the curé; 'it clears the brain.'

There was a sound of long-drawn-out barking in the distance.

'Can you hear a dog howling?' asked the chemist.

'There is a popular belief that dogs can smell the presence of

death,' replied the priest. 'Something similar is said about bees—
that they leave the hive when people die.'

Homais refrained from criticizing these superstitions, for he had
fallen asleep again.

Monsieur Bournisien was made of sterner stuff and continued for
a while to move his lips in silent prayer. But gradually he let his chin
drop on to his chest; his fat black book slipped to the floor, and he
began to snore.

There they sat, facing one another, with protruding stomachs,
puffy faces and scowling expressions, united, after all their arguments, in an identical weakness of the flesh. They were as motionless
as the corpse which looked, for all the world, as though it were
sharing their slumbers.

When Charles came into the room he did not wake them. This
was his final visit. He had come to say farewell.

The aromatic herbs were still smouldering, the clouds of blue
vapour mingling with the fog which was creeping in through the
window. A few stars were showing and the night was mild.

Great drops of candle-wax were falling on to the sheets. Charles
gazed at the yellow flames, watching them burn until his eyes ached.
The satin of her dress was pale as moonlight, and the watered texture gave the illusion of faint movement. Emma had disappeared in
the elaboration of her attire. It seemed to him as though she had left
her body and had got lost in a confusion of many objects, of the
silence and the darkness, of the passing breeze and of the smell of
damp slowly rising from the earth.

Suddenly he had a vision of her in the garden at Tostes, seated on
the bench against the thorn-hedge—walking the Rouen streets—
standing in the doorway of their home—in the farmyard at Les
Bertaux. He could hear again the laughter of the small boys dancing
beneath the apple-trees. The room was filled with the scent of her
hair, and her dress rustled and crackled as he touched it. It was the
same dress that she was wearing now!

He stood there a long while remembering his past happiness, the
way she had held herself, her gestures, the tones of her voice. Wave
after wave of despair surged over him unceasingly like the waters of a
flooding tide.

He was moved by a terrible curiosity. Slowly, with thumping
heart, he lifted her veil with the tips of his fingers. His cry of horror

woke the two sleepers. They led him downstairs to the dining-room.

Félicité came to say that he had asked for a piece of her hair.

'Cut some off,' said the apothecary.

She was too frightened to obey, and, taking a pair of scissors, he approached the bed. He was shaking so violently that he pricked the skin of her temples more than once. Finally, fighting down his emotion, he made two or three great snips at random. They left white scars among the beautiful black tresses.

Then he and the curé returned to their several occupations, dozing off from time to time, and accusing one another when they woke. Monsieur Bournisien sprinkled the room with holy water, and Homais threw a little chlorine on the floor.

Félicité was careful to set a bottle of brandy for them on the sideboard, some cheese and a large cake.

About four o'clock in the morning, the apothecary, by now completely worn out, sighed deeply and said:

'I could do with a little nourishment.'

The man of religion did not need to be asked twice. He went out to say his mass, and then returned. They ate and drank, both chuckling from time to time without quite knowing why, a prey to that sort of aimless gaiety which attacks us all after a mournful vigil. As the priest drained his last glass, he slapped the apothecary on the back and said:

'Given long enough, we shall agree!'

Downstairs, in the hall, they met the undertaker's men. For two hours Charles had to endure the torture of hearing hammers resounding on wood. At last they brought Emma down in her oaken coffin and enclosed it in the other two. But the outer one was too large, and they had to fill up the spaces with wool taken from the mattress. Finally, when the three lids had been polished, screwed down, and soldered, the bier was exposed to public view in front of the house. The front-door was thrown open, and the people of Yonville began to flock in.

Old Rouault arrived. When he saw the black pall, he fainted dead away in the square.

CHAPTER X

THE chemist's letter had not reached him until thirty-six hours after the event, and, in any case, Monsieur Homais, out of consideration for his sensibility, had so phrased it that he could not know what to expect.

His first reaction had been to collapse as though struck down by apoplexy; his second, to grasp that she had not actually died. But by now she might have. . . . Finally, he had put on his smock, taken his hat, strapped on his spurs and ridden off hell for leather. During the whole of his journey he had been breathing hard and suffering agonies of uncertainty. Once, indeed, he was driven to dismount. He could no longer see anything, thought he heard voices all round him, and felt that he was going mad.

Dawn broke. He noticed three black hens roosting in a tree. He started back in terror from the terrible omen. Then he promised the Virgin three chasubles for the church, and vowed that he would make a pilgrimage, barefooted, from the cemetery of Les Bertaux to the chapel of Vassonville.

He rode into Maromme and shouted for the ostler at the inn. He thrust the stable door open with his shoulder, pounced on a sack of oats, poured a bottle of sweet cider into the manger, and once again leapt on to his mare who set off with a shower of sparks from her hooves.

He told himself that of course they would save his daughter. The doctors would discover some remedy, of that he was sure. He recalled all the miraculous cures of which he had heard.

Then he had a vision of her dead. She lay there on her back in the middle of the road. He drew rein and the hallucination vanished.

At Quincampoix he drank three cups of coffee in quick succession, to give himself courage.

It occurred to him that the writer of the letter might have made a mistake in the name. He felt for it in his pocket, but dared not open it.

He played with the idea that the whole thing might be a practical joke on the part of someone who owed him a grudge—a grim sort of joke. Besides, if she were dead, wouldn't everybody know? But there was nothing out of the ordinary about the look of the country through which he was riding. The sky was blue, the trees were swaying in the breeze. A flock of sheep passed him. The village came in sight. People along the road saw him galloping along, bunched over his saddle, flogging his mount to ever greater efforts, so that the girths dripped blood.

As soon as he recovered consciousness, he flung himself weeping into Bovary's arms.

'My daughter!—Emma!—My child! Tell me what happened!'

The other answered in a voice broken by sobs.

'I don't know—I don't know—it is the curse of heaven!'

The apothecary separated them.

'These horrible details are useless. I will tell Monsieur all he wants to know. The whole village is here! For God's sake show a little dignity, assume the aspect of the philosopher!'

The poor fellow wanted to appear strong-minded, and kept on saying:

'You are right . . . I must be brave! *Nom d'un tonnerre de Dieu*!' shouted the old man, '*I'll* show them. I will go with her to the very end.'

The bell began to toll. Everything was ready. It was time for the procession to move off.*

Seated together in one of the stalls of the choir, the two men watched the three choristers pass to and fro before them, chanting. The serpent-player* blew with all his might. Monsieur Bournisien, in full canonicals, intoned in a thin voice. He genuflected to the Tabernacle, raised his hands, spread his arms. Lestiboudois moved about the church with his whalebone wand. The coffin had been placed close to the lectern, between four rows of candles. Charles wanted to get up and blow them out.

He tried, however, to work himself into the proper mood of devotion, to lose himself in the hope of a future life in which he would see her again. He tried to imagine that she had gone off on a long journey many days ago. But when he reflected that she was underneath all *that*, that all was over, that she was to be put into the earth, he fell into a wild, black, despairing fury. At moments he thought that he could feel no more, and took comfort in this mitigation of his pain, though all the time reproaching himself as an insensitive wretch. What sounded like the sharp tap of an iron-shod stick, striking at regular intervals on the flags, reached their ears. It came from the far end of the church. It drew closer and stopped abruptly in the aisle. A man in a coarse brown jacket painfully lowered himself on to his knees. It was Hippolyte, from the Golden Lion. He had put on his new leg for the occasion.

One of the choirmen made the round of the nave, collecting. The heavy copper coins fell one after the other, with a rattle, into the silver dish.

'Hurry up! I can't stand much more of this!' exclaimed Bovary, angrily tossing him a five-franc piece.

The man thanked him with a low bow.

They sang, they knelt, they got up again. Would the business never end! He remembered how, once, in the early days of their marriage, they had gone to mass together. They had sat on the other side, to the right, against the wall.

The bell resumed its tolling. There was a great scraping of chairs. The bearers slipped their three poles beneath the bier, and the procession left the church.

At that moment Justin appeared on the threshold of the shop, but hurried in again, pale and trembling.

People were at their windows watching the *cortège* pass. Charles walked in front, holding himself very erect. He assumed a courageous expression, and made little signs of greeting to acquaintances issuing from lanes and doorways to join the crowd. The six bearers, three on each side, moved slowly, panting a little. The priest, the choirmen and the two acolytes recited the *De Profundis*, their voices rising and falling rhythmically as they moved across the fields. From time to time they disappeared from view round a corner of the winding path, but the great silver cross was all the while visible, erect among the trees.

The women followed, draped in black mantles with the hoods lowered. They carried large lit candles. The endless prayers, the lights, the stale smell of wax and soutanes, made Charles feel faint. There was a fresh breeze. The fields of rye and colza were turning green. Drops of dew were trembling on the thorn-hedge which grew along the path. The air was filled with a medley of happy sounds— the distant rattle of a cart in a rutted lane, the crowing of a cock, the hoofbeats of a colt galloping away among the apple-trees. The clear sky was speckled with pink clouds. The flower-smothered cottages

were suffused in a bluish light. Charles recognized every yard he
passed, and remembered how, on just such a morning as this, he
had emerged from them on his way home to *her* after visiting some
of his patients. The black pall, embroidered with white tear-
drops, occasionally billowed up and revealed the bier. The tired
bearers slackened their pace, and it moved on jerkily like a pitching
boat.

They arrived.

The men went on to the far end, to a spot on the turf where the
grave had been dug.

They took up their positions round it. While the priest droned on,
the red earth, piled along the edge, kept trickling from the corners in
a noiseless cascade.

The four ropes were adjusted, the coffin placed in position. He
watched them lower it. Down it went, down.

At last there was a thudding sound. The ropes grated as they were
pulled up again. Bournisien took the spade which Lestiboudois
passed to him with his left hand. Still sprinkling holy water with his
right, he gave a vigorous push to a large shovelful of earth. The wood
of the coffin gave out, beneath the shower of stones, that terrible
noise which strikes on the listening ear like the hollow echo of
eternity.

The priest handed the sprinkler to the man beside him who happened to be Monsieur Homais. The latter gave it a solemn shake and
passed it on to Charles who sank to his knees in the loose earth and
threw great handfuls into the grave, crying—'Farewell!' He blew her
kisses through the empty air, and dragged himself to the brink of the
hole that he might be swallowed up with her.

They led him away, and soon he grew calmer, feeling, perhaps, like
everybody else, a vague sense of relief that the ceremony was over
and done with.

On the way back, old Rouault began quite calmly to smoke his
pipe, a proceeding which Homais, in his heart of hearts, thought to
be sadly lacking in taste.* He noticed, too, that Binet had not put in
an appearance at all, that Tuvache had 'slipped away' as soon as the
mass was over, and that Théodore, the lawyer's servant, was wearing
a blue coat, 'as though they couldn't find him a black one which is
the usual thing on such occasions. A pretty state of affairs!' He went
from group to group, voicing his views. Everyone was expressing

deep sorrow at Emma's death, none more so than Lheureux, who had made a point of coming to the funeral.

'Poor young lady! What a terrible thing for her husband!'

The apothecary chattered on.

'If it hadn't been for me, you know, he would have done something desperate.'

'Such a good, kind soul! And to think that only last Saturday I was talking to her in my shop!'

'I should have liked to speak a few words over her grave, but I had no time in which to prepare anything.'

When they got back to the house, Charles took off his funeral clothes and old Rouault resumed his smock. It was new, and because, in the course of his morning's ride, he had several times wiped his eyes on his sleeve, the dye had come off on his face, where tears had traced long lines in the dust that covered it.

Madame Bovary the elder was with them. All three were silent. At last the old man heaved a sigh.

'D'you recollect that time I came to Tostes just after you'd lost your first? I was able to console you then; I knew what to say—but today . . .'

He groaned with the full force of his lungs. 'This means the end for me! . . . I've seen my wife go . . . and my son: now it's my daughter!'

He decided to return at once to Les Bertaux, saying he couldn't sleep in a strange house. He even refused to see his granddaughter.

'No, no. It would be too painful. But give her a hug from me. Good-bye! . . . you're a fine chap. I shall never forget this'—and he slapped his thigh. 'Don't worry! I'll see as you get your turkey just the same.'

But when he had reached the top of the hill, he turned, as always in the old days on the Saint-Victor road whenever he parted from her. The windows of the village were all ablaze with the level sun which was sinking behind the meadows. He put his hand over his eyes and looked towards the horizon to where he could see a walled enclosure with here and there the black tuft of a tree between the white stones. Then he resumed his journey at a slow pace, for his mare had gone lame.

Charles and his mother, for all their weariness, spent a long time that evening, talking. They discussed the past and the future. She would come and settle down in Yonville. She would look after his house and never leave him again. She was tactful and kind, and secretly rejoiced at the prospect of winning back an affection which, for so many years, had been withdrawn from her. Midnight struck. The village, as usual, was plunged in silence, and Charles, lying wakeful in his bed, thought all the time of *her*.

Rodolphe, who had been tramping the woods all day in an attempt to distract his mind, was sleeping peacefully in his château. Léon, too, in Rouen, was fast asleep.

But someone else there was who could not sleep.

Between the pines a lad was kneeling on her grave and weeping. There, in the shadows, he sobbed brokenly under the weight of an immense sorrow, a sorrow softer than the moonlight, deeper than the darkness. Suddenly the gate creaked. It was Lestiboudois who had come to look for the spade which he had left behind that afternoon. He saw that the figure climbing the wall was Justin.

At last he knew who the young rascal was who had been making off with his potatoes!

CHAPTER XI

CHARLES had the child brought back next day. She asked for her mummy, but was told that she was away and would bring some toys with her when she returned. Berthe spoke of her several times again after this, but a day came eventually when she passed entirely out of her mind. Charles found the little girl's gaiety quite heartbreaking. He had, as well, to endure the chemist's intolerable consolations.

His money troubles soon began again. Lheureux once more egged on his friend Vinçart, and Charles entered into a number of exorbitant commitments, since he was determined never to sell a single stick of the furniture that had belonged to *her*. His mother lost all patience, but his anger was more formidable than hers. He was a completely changed man. She left his house.

Then everybody began to exact their pound of flesh. Mademoiselle Lempereur sent in an account for six months' lessons, not one of which Emma had had (in spite of the receipts that she had shown her husband!). The whole arrangement had been the result of a plot between the two of them.

The proprietor of the lending-library put in a claim for three years' subscriptions.

Madame Rollet submitted a bill for the delivery of some twenty or so letters, but when Charles demanded an explanation, had the decency to reply:

'I know nothing about 'em. Business things they were.'

He thought that each debt he paid would be the last, but the flow never ceased.

He sent out accounts for arrears of professional fees, only to be shown the letters written by his wife. He had to apologize.

Félicité took to wearing her mistress's clothes—not all of them, for some he had kept, and would lock himself in her dressing-room to gaze at them. The two women had been much of a size, and more than once, catching a back view of the servant, he would be the victim of a momentary illusion and cry out:

'Oh, stay, stay!'

But at Whitsun she shook the dust of Yonville from her feet, and left in the company of Théodore, taking all that remained of Emma's wardrobe.

At about the same time the widow Dupuis had the honour to announce the forthcoming marriage of her son, Monsieur Léon Dupuis, solicitor, of Yvetot, to Mademoiselle Léocadie Leboeuf, of Bondeville. In the letter of congratulation which Charles sent, there occurred this phrase:

'How happy my poor wife would have been!'

One day, wandering aimlessly about the house, he went up into the attic. He felt a ball of thin paper under the sole of his slipper, straightened it out, and read: 'Be brave, Emma, be brave. I don't want to be the cause of your life's unhappiness.'

It was Rodolphe's letter which had fallen down between two boxes. There it had remained until a gust from the window had blown it towards the door.

He stood motionless, with his mouth hanging open, on the very same spot on which once Emma, paler than he was now, and over-whelmed by despair, had longed for death.

At last he deciphered a small R at the foot of the second page. What did it mean? He remembered how assiduous Rodolphe had been, and how, all of a sudden, he had vanished. He remembered his air of constraint on the two or three occasions when he had met him since. But the respectful tone of the letter kept him from guessing the truth.

'Maybe', he reflected, 'they had a platonic affection for one another.'

He was not the sort of man to go very deeply into things. He recoiled from proofs, and the vague feeling of jealousy which came over him was lost in the immensity of his sorrow.

No one, he thought, could help but adore her. No man, to be sure, but must have desired her. This realization made her seem still more beautiful in his eyes. He conceived a mad, a permanent, yearning for her, which inflamed his despair still further. It knew no limits, for the very reason that it could never, now, be satisfied.

To please her, as though she were still living, he set himself to like what she had liked, to think as she had thought. He bought himself a pair of varnished boots, and took to wearing white cravats. He put pomade on his moustache, and followed her example in the matter of signing bearer bills. She was corrupting him from beyond the grave.

He had to sell the table-silver, piece by piece, and then the drawing-room furniture. Every room in the house was stripped bare, except only her bedroom which he kept as it had always been. After dinner, he would go to it, push the round table in front of the fire, pull up *her* chair, and sit down facing it. A candle burned in one of the candlesticks, and Berthe, beside him, would be busy colouring a print.

The poor man suffered to see the child so badly clothed, with no laces in her boots, and the armholes of her blouses torn to the waist for the charwoman bothered little about such things. But she was so gentle, so pretty, there was such grace in the way she shook her lovely golden hair over her pink cheeks, that he was filled with a sense of infinite delight, mixed though it was with bitterness, like an ill-made wine which tastes of resin. He mended her toys, cut out cardboard puppets for her, or sewed up her dolls when their stomachs gaped. And if, while he was engaged on this latter task, he caught sight of his wife's work-box, of a trailing ribbon or even of a pin stuck in one of the cracks of the table, he would fall into a daydream and look so sad that Berthe, to keep him company, looked sad too.

No one came to see them, for Justin had fled to Rouen where he had become a grocer's assistant, and the chemist's children saw less and less of Berthe, their father not wishing to encourage an intimacy where there was such social inequality.

The blind beggar, whom he had failed utterly to cure with his ointment, returned to his old pitch on the Bois-Guillaume hill, where he entertained travellers with an account of the chemist's fruitless attempts at treatment, and this new departure of his became so embarrassing to Homais that whenever he went into town he hid behind the curtains of the Swallow so as to avoid having to meet the living evidence of his failure. He abused the man violently, and, wishing, in the interests of his own reputation, to be quit of him entirely, opened up with a masked battery the use of which revealed the keenness of his intelligence and the unscrupulousness of his vanity. For six consecutive months the readers of the *Fanal de Rouen* were liable to come across paragraphs couched in the following terms:

Travellers bound for the fertile lands of Picardy must surely have noticed on the hill at Le Bois-Guillaume a wretched creature afflicted by a terrible facial disfigurement. He pesters and persecutes all who use the road, and levies what amounts to a regular tribute on passer-by. Are we still living in those barbarous times of the Middle Ages when homeless men were allowed to display in our public places the leprous and scrofulous diseases which they had brought back with them from the Crusades?

or:

Notwithstanding the laws against vagrancy, the approaches to our great cities continue to be infested by bands of paupers. Some of them, and not, perhaps, the least dangerous, move about singly. Of what can our Aediles be thinking?

At a later stage he began to invent anecdotes:

Yesterday, on the hill at Le Bois-Guillaume, a nervous horse . . .

—and went on to describe an accident occasioned by the presence of the blind beggar. So well did he do his work that eventually the man was thrown into gaol. On his release, however, he resumed his former habits— and so did Homais. A regular battle ensued from which the chemist emerged victorious, and his enemy was sentenced to detention for life in the poor-house. This success emboldened Homais to still further efforts, and from then on not a dog could be run over, not a barn burned down, not a woman beaten, but he immediately made the fact known to the public, his guiding principle always being a love of progress and a hatred of all priests. He drew comparisons between the primary schools* and the Ignorantine Friars,* always to the detriment of the latter; made reference to the Saint-Bartholomew massacre on the occasion of a grant of a hundred francs to the church; denounced abuses, and launched virulent attacks. He was—to use his own phrase—'sapping the foundations'. In short, he was becoming dangerous.

But he felt stifled within the narrow limits of journalism, and soon decided that he must produce a book, a great work. He began, therefore, to compose a *General Statistical Survey of the Canton of Yonville—Together with Certain Climatological Observations*, and this led him to turn his attention to philosophy. He became preoccupied with 'major problems'—social reform, the morals of the lower classes, fish-breeding, rubber, railways, etc.* He blushed to think of himself as a member of the bourgeoisie, and adopted the manners and appearance of an artist. He took to smoking, and bought two fashionable Pompadour-style statuettes for his drawing-room.

Not that he gave up his work as a pharmaceutical chemist—far from it! He kept himself abreast of the latest discoveries, followed the great chocolate mania, and was the first man to make *cho-ca** and *revalentia** known in the Department of Seine-Inférieure. He took up Pulvermacher electric belts* with enthusiasm, and even wore one himself. Each night, when he took off his flannel waistcoat, Madame Homais was overcome with amazement at sight of the golden spirals which almost hid him from view, and felt her passion renewed for this man who was more swathed and girdled than a Scythian, more glorious than one of the Magi.

He had some charming ideas about the form to be taken by Emma's grave. His first suggestion was a broken column with drapery, but he changed this successively into an obelisk, a temple of Vesta, and some species of rotunda . . . even into 'an arrangement of ruins'. In all his schemes he included a weeping willow which he regarded as an obligatory emblem of mourning.

Charles accompanied him to Rouen in order to inspect the stock held by the monumental mason. They took with them a painter named Vaufrylard,* a friend of Bridoux, who never stopped making puns. After examining a hundred different designs, asking for an estimate, and making a second trip to the city, Charles finally decided on a mausoleum, bearing upon each of its principal faces a 'tutelary genius holding an extinguished torch'. As an inscription, Homais thought it would be impossible to improve upon *Sta viator*. That was the limit of his invention. He racked his brain, saying over and over again—*Sta viator* . . . Finally he hit upon *amabilem conjugem calcas**—which was adopted.

It is worth noting one curious fact, that Bovary, though he thought continually about Emma, began to forget her living image. He was plunged in despair at the thought that, no matter what he did, the vivid sense of her was slipping from him. Nevertheless, he dreamed of her every night. It was always the same dream, in which he came close to her only to find that, just as he was stretching out his arms, she turned to dust.

For one whole week he was seen going into the church each evening. Monsieur Bournisien even visited him once or twice, after which he came no more. The old priest, according to Homais, was becoming fanatical and intolerant. He thundered against the spirit of the times, and never failed to preach a sermon once each fortnight, in which he described the passing of Voltaire, who died, as everybody knows, devouring his own excrement.*

In spite of the thrifty manner in which Bovary lived, he could not manage to pay off his old debts. Lheureux refused to renew his bills. Distraint was imminent. Then, and then only, did he have recourse to his mother, who agreed to his taking out a mortgage on her property, though with many recriminations against Emma. In return for the sacrifice she was making, she demanded a shawl which had escaped Félicités clutches. Charles refused to give it to her, and they quarrelled.

It was she who made the first moves towards a reconciliation by proposing to take the child to live with her. She would, she said, be a help to her in the house. Charles agreed. But when the moment of parting came, his courage deserted him. This time the breach was definite and complete.

In proportion as all other attachments fell away from him, his affections became more and more centred on his daughter. But he was worried about her, because she coughed occasionally and had patches of red on her cheek-bones.

On the opposite side of the square the chemist's family flourished in a state of noisy good-health. Everything was going well with Homais. Napoleon was helping him in the laboratory, Athalie worked him an embroidered skull-cap, Irma cut out paper tops for the jam-jars, and Franklin could recite the multiplication-table straight off without a break. He was the happiest of fathers, the most fortunate of men.

No, that is not altogether true. One secret ambition there was which gnawed at his heart. He longed for the Legion of Honour— and there seemed to be every good reason why he should get it. He enumerated them thus—(1) At the time of the cholera epidemic* he had behaved with outstanding devotion. (2) He had published, at his own expense, a number of works of the greatest value, to wit (and here, in forwarding his request he made mention of the Memorandum entitled—*Cider, its Manufacture and Effects*, his *Observations on the Laniferous Wood-Louse*, submitted to the Academy;* his volume of Statistics, and even the thesis he had written for his degree in pharmacy) . . to say nothing of the fact that he was a member of several learned societies (though, actually, he was a member of one only).

'If', he would say, pirouetting on his heel, 'only because it would distinguish me from the rest when I'm on fire duty.'

In pursuit of his ambition, he consented to bow the knee to authority. Unknown to anybody, he rendered the Prefect great service at election time. In short, he sold, he prostituted, himself. He even went so far as to send a petition to the Sovereign in which he asked that *justice should be done him*. He called him Our Good King, and drew a favourable comparison with Henry IV.

Each morning he would tear open the newspaper to see whether his name figured in the Recommended list. But it didn't. At last, unable to stand the strain any longer, he had a star of honour cut in his garden lawn, with two little clumps of long grass at the apex in the guise of ribbons. Round this he would walk, with folded arms, meditating on the stupidity of governments and the ingratitude of men.

From motives of respect, or from an oddly perverse sensuality which led him to pursue his investigations with a slow deliberation, Charles had so far refrained from opening the secret drawer in the rosewood desk which Emma had habitually used. At last, one day, he sat down to it, turned the key and pushed the spring. All Léon's letters were there. This time there could be no doubt at all. He devoured them to the last page, searched every corner, examined every piece of furniture and every drawer. He even looked behind the wainscot, sobbing, howling, distracted, mad. He found a box and kicked it open. Rodolphe's portrait stared him in the face from the middle of a tumbled pile of love-letters.

His gloom became a matter of public wonder. He gave up going out, admitted no visitors, and even refused to see his patients. It was said that he had taken to secret drinking.

But at times, someone more curious than his neighbours would hoist himself to the top of the garden hedge and look over. He would see, with amazement, a man with a long beard, clad in dirty clothes, wild and unkempt, who wept aloud as he walked.

On summer evenings, Bovary would take his little daughter with him on his visits to the cemetery. They would return long after darkness had fallen, when the only light in the square was what came from Binet's window.

And yet he could not fully indulge his sorrow, having no one to share it with. He took to dropping in on Madame Lefrançois so as to be able to talk about *her*. But the landlady of the Golden Lion listened with half an ear, having troubles of her own. Monsieur Lheureux had finally succeeded in establishing 'Les Favorites du Commerce',* and Hivert, who had won a great reputation in the executing of commissions, was asking for an increase of wages, and threatening to 'go over to the enemy'.

One day, when Charles had gone to Argueil market to sell his horse—his last hope of raising money—he ran across Rodolphe.

At sight of one another, both men went pale. Rodolphe, who had confined his expressions of sympathy to sending his calling-card, at first stammered excuses, but gradually grew bolder, and went so far (it was August and very hot) as to invite the doctor to drink a bottle of beer at a local tavern. There, facing him with his elbows on the table, he chewed his cigar and talked, while Charles fell to dreaming as he contemplated the face that *she* had loved so madly. He seemed to see in it something of her. He was overcome with astonishment. If only, he felt, he could have been *this* man.

The other continued to discuss farming problems, livestock and manures, stopping, with a few commonplace remarks, every conversational crevice through which some embarrassing reference might possibly slip. But Charles was not listening. Rodolphe noticed this, and could trace the passage of memories across Bovary's expressive features. The face opposite his own grew gradually redder, the nostrils quivered, the lips moved unsteadily. At one moment, Charles, caught up in an impulse of dark fury, glared at Rodolphe who, in a sudden fright, stopped short in the middle of a sentence. But the fit passed, and the old weary melancholy returned.

'I don't hold it against you,' said the doctor.

Rodolphe remained silent, and the other, his head in his hands, went on in the same dead voice and the resigned accents of an infinite sorrow.

'No, I don't hold it against you—not any longer.'

And then, for the first and last time in his life, he uttered a deep thought:

'It was the fault of destiny.'

Rodolphe, who, after all, had been the instrument of the said destiny, felt that such an attitude, in a man so placed, was good-natured to excess and, on the whole, rather despicable.

Next day, Charles went into the arbour and sat down on the bench. Daylight filtered through the trellis-work. The vine-leaves cast their shadows on the gravel. The air was full of the scent of jasmine, the sky was blue. Flies were buzzing round the flowering lilies. Like an adolescent in love, Charles was stifled by a flood of vague yearning that swelled his aching heart.

At seven o'clock, little Berthe, who had not seen him all afternoon, came to fetch him to dinner.

His head was leaning against the wall; his eyes were closed, his mouth was open, and a lock of black hair was clutched in his fingers.

'Come, papa,' she said.

Thinking that he was playing with her, she gave him a gentle push. He fell to the ground. He was dead.

Thirty-six hours later, Monsieur Canivet, summoned by the apothecary, arrived. He opened the body, but found nothing.

When everything had been sold up, there remained twelve francs and seventy-five centimes, just enough to pay for Mademoiselle Bovary's journey to the house of her grandmother. But the good lady died that same year. Old Rouault being paralysed, an aunt took charge of the child. She is poor, and has sent her to earn her living in a cotton-mill.

Since Bovary died, there have been six doctors in Yonville. None of them, however, has made a success of the practice, so violently hostile has Homais shown himself to all of them. He himself is doing extremely well. The authorities handle him with kid gloves, and he is protected by public opinion.

He has just received the Legion of Honour.

EXPLANATORY NOTES

The following abbreviations have been used:

MB n.v. *Madame Bovary*, nouvelle version, ed. Jean Pommier and Gabrielle Leleu (Paris, José Corti, 1949)

OC Flaubert, *Œuvres complètes*, 2 vols, preface by Jean Bruneau, ed. Bernard Masson (Paris, Éditions du Seuil, 1964)

DIR *Dictionnaire des idées reçues*

Translations of passages from Flaubert's letters are mostly taken from the Steegmuller edition (see Select Bibliography).

The originals of letters cited or referred to in the notes may be found, if dated up to the end of 1858, in

Flaubert, *Correspondance*, ed. Jean Bruneau, 2 vols, *1830–1851* and *1851–8* (Paris, Gallimard, 1973 and 1980)

and, if dated after 1858, in

Flaubert, *Correspondance*, nouvelle édition augmentée (Paris, Conard, 1926–33, with Supplément 1954)

Flaubert's most frequently cited correspondents are designated in references by their initials, viz.: LB Louis Bouilhet; EC Ernest Chevalier; LC Louise Colet; HT Hippolyte Taine.

PART I

xxv *dedication*: Sénard was the lawyer who conducted Flaubert's defence in the case brought against him, the publishers and the printer after *Madame Bovary* had been serialized in *La Revue de Paris*.

1 *The preparation room*: Flaubert was at the Collège royal in Rouen between 1832 and 1840, for the most part as a boarder. An almost exact contemporary there of Flaubert's elder brother, Achille, was Eugène Delamare, the principal model for Charles Bovary. The outline biography of Delamare fits reasonably neatly: he was medical officer in Ry, married a Mademoiselle Mutel five years older than he was, was soon widowed and married the seventeen-year-old Delphine Couturier who gave birth to a daughter, and died in 1848, aged twenty-six. Delamare died in 1849. However, Delamare's character was apparently that of an active local politician who was an inconstant authoritarian husband. Less is known about his second wife and there is no firm evidence that she killed herself. (See A.-M. Gossez, *Homais et Bovary hommes politiques*, Mercure de France, 15 July 1911.)

2 *Charbovari*: the name Bovary (here slurred to evoke cart and ox and with perhaps a sly reference to Ry where Delamare married and worked) may derive from Mlle de Bovery, a local squire's daughter involved in a poison and adultery trial in 1844 and from Bouvaret, the proprietor in Cairo of an hotel where Flaubert stayed in 1849 (see letter to Hortense Cornu, 20 March 1870, and *OC* II, 560).

3 *Quos ego*: a reference to Neptune's speech in *Aeneid* i. 132 ff.

6 *Rouen*: the city was then the fifth largest in France with a population of 100,000, a considerable port and commercial centre.

7 *Anacharsis*: the Abbé J.-J. Barthélemy's very successful and influential book (1788) about fourth-century BC Greek civilization.

to study medicine: possible only to a preliminary level at the School founded in 1811 by Flaubert's father, who taught anatomy and physiology and was chief surgeon at the Hôtel-Dieu hospital where Flaubert was born. To qualify fully as a doctor it was necessary to go to Paris, but students could become an 'officier de santé' (see note to p. 9).

the Eau-de-Robec: a small tributary of the Seine in Rouen, then surrounded by dye works which discoloured the water, hence 'yellow, violet or blue' (p. 8).

9 *Béranger*: extremely popular liberal poet (1780–1857) whose writings, called *chansons*, attacked the monarchy and the clergy. Flaubert included 'admiration for Béranger' in a list of things he disliked in other people (letter to LC, 1 June 1853).

Public Health Service: the position of *officier de santé* was created between 1803 and 1892 as something like the civilian equivalent of the military post held by Charles's father. No holder of this position could conduct important surgery without the attendance of a doctor nor practise medicine outside his *département*.

Tostes: now spelt Tôtes. Small town halfway between Rouen and Dieppe. Flaubert's father owned a farm at Saint-Sulpice-la-Pierre nearby between 1828 and 1839.

10 *Les Bertaux*: Eugène Delamare's second wife, Delphine Couturier (see note to page 1), lived just outside Blainville-Crevon in the ferme du Vieux-Château, now named 'ferme Madame Bovary' in certain maps. The route through Longueville and Saint-Victor is fanciful.

14 *Yvetot*: the commercial centre of the pays de Caux with a population then of about 9,000.

15 *an Ursuline convent*: there were two in Rouen belonging to this order devoted to teaching, one in the rue Coqueréaumont and the other in the rue Morant.

16 *Ingouville*: to judge by the lawyer's actions this is probably the smart suburb of Le Havre, with exceptional sea-views, which was then being built as a fashionable residential quarter, rather than the village of the same name just south-west of Saint-Valéry-en-Caux.

22 *a marriage at midnight*: a custom in some places rather than an eccentricity. Maupassant's grandfather, whom Flaubert knew, and Madame Schlésinger, whom he idolized, had both had midnight marriages in the *département* of the Eure.

28 *Dictionary of Medical Sciences*: this comprised sixty volumes (Panckoucke, Paris, 1812–22). Flaubert found in the work some fatuous assertions (which he added to his *Sottisier*, a collection of foolish comments made in learned seriousness), so it may not have been entirely to Charles's disadvantage to leave the pages uncut.

30 *busy digesting*: when *Madame Bovary* appeared in serial form in *La Revue de Paris*, its editors worried about the propriety of this passage; it was to be raised by the prosecution at the 1857 trial in which Flaubert, the editor of the *Revue* and the printer were accused of offending public and religious morality.

31 *Paul et Virginie*: this novel of 1787 by Bernardin de Saint-Pierre describes the close friendship between two French children on the Île de France (Mauritius), a friendship which grows into adolescent love in the exotic world of the Indian Ocean and which ends in tragedy. It was a highly influential work of French Pre-Romanticism. Paul is of course not the brother of Virginie, but Emma's own brother had died young (see p. 27).

    Mademoiselle de la Vallière: mistress of Louis XIV and his court favourite until 1667. She retired ultimately to a Carmelite convent.

32 *Abbé Frayssinous's Lectures*: originally given in churches on theology and religion, these reflected the religious revival during the Restoration and were available in the *Défense du christianisme* of 1825.

    the Génie du christianisme: by Chateaubriand, who published in 1802 this famous attempt to understand Christianity through aesthetics and the senses.

33 *Agnès Sorel*: Charles VII's mistress.

    La Ferronnière the beautiful: mistress of François I.

    Clémence Isaure: this legendary lady revived the Floral Games for troubadours in Toulouse in the fourteenth century.

    and his oak: Louis IX (1215–70) by tradition sat under an oak to give wise judgement.

    Bayard: c. 1473–1524. Fought bravely and chivalrously in the Italian wars of three French kings.

    Louis XI: 1423–83. Noted for his pragmatic and unscrupulous methods to retain and further his power.

    the Massacre of Saint-Bartholomew: on the night of 23 to 24 August 1572 Huguenots were slaughtered mercilessly in Paris (and elsewhere in France in various massacres which went on until October).

33 *Henry IV*: 1553–1610. His white plume is frequently mentioned as his attribute.

Louis XIV: the plates are those mentioned on p. 33. The historical figures together form a collage of piety, beauty, love, bravery and cruelty.

'*keepsakes*': (Flaubert used the English word.) These were a personal gift to demonstrate one's affections in the shape of a book or album lavishly engraved.

34 *The image revealed . . . these visions of the world*: the Romantic literature read by Emma had some roots in Northern Europe, popularized in *De la littérature* by Mme de Staël, who extolled the world of Ossian and the bards, Shakespeare, and Germanic and Scandinavian legend rather than the classical world of the Mediterranean. Byron (*Don Juan*) and Hugo (*Les Orientales*) were largely responsible for a new vision of Italy, Greece and the Near East as places of warmth and exoticism. The classical view of the Mediterranean was of a literature and culture characterized by harmony and restraint. A letter from Flaubert to his mistress Louise Golet (3 March 1852) describes his painstaking researches into some of the more ephemeral aspects of Romanticism: 'For two days now I have been trying to enter into the dreams of young girls, and for this have been navigating in the milky oceans of books about castles, and troubadours in white-plumed velvet hats.'

Lamartinian melancholy: Lamartine's poem *Le Lac* (published in 1820) regrets the passing of love, undermined by death but recalled in the beauty of natural scenery.

35 *newly-wedded bliss is spent in exquisite languor*: Flaubert's brother Achille and his sister Caroline both travelled on honeymoon to Italy. Indeed Caroline and her husband were accompanied by Flaubert and his parents. The *Dictionnaire des idées reçues* includes Italy as a honeymoon goal.

36 *a Swiss chalet*: Rousseau was perhaps the first enthusiast for the Alps (*La Nouvelle Héloïse*, 1761).

pellets of bread: for erasing charcoal lines.

41 *in the Italian style*: the visit to La Vaubyessard is based on a memory of Flaubert's visit with his parents to the Marquis de Pomereu's *fête seigneurale* in 1836. The Marquis lived at the Château du Héron (now destroyed) just east of Ry and he had been a member of the Seine-Inférieure Conseil général between 1829 and 1833. So impressive was the occasion for the 14-year-old boy that Flaubert recalled it and his subsequent dawn walk through the park in a letter written years later to his friend Louis Bouilhet from Egypt (13 March 1850). The description of a ball in chapter V of an early work, *Quidquid volueris* (1837), is a more immediate reflection of the event.

42 *Jean-Antoine . . . 1693*: the names are fictitious, the battles are historical.

43 *in their glasses*: in bourgeois circles Emma might have expected to see women refuse wine by placing a glove in their glass.

between Monsieur de Coigny and Monsieur Lauzun: both dukes, soldiers, philanderers and intimates of Marie-Antoinette.

45 *red turbans*: the mothers are to some extent still following the style of their youth. Turbans were especially fashionable about 1820.

46 *leaping a ditch in England*: a reference to steeplechasing, then less common in France.

soup à la bisque: soup made from birds, game or crayfish.

Trafalgar puddings: probably fictitious, though 'pudding à l'amiral' existed.

47 *cotillion*: the final dance of the ball, here a waltz (for couples) by contrast with the earlier quadrille (danced as a foursome). The waltz was not always considered proper at this time.

51 *Pompadour*: the Marquise de Pompadour (1721–64) was a noted patron of the arts and an intimate of Louis XV. An elaborate rococo style is implied.

the Marjolaine: a song of the watch.

Sylphe des Salons: there was a short-lived magazine *Le Sylphe: Journal des salons* (1829–30), and another, *Sylphe: Littérature, Beaux-Arts, Théâtres*, was published in Rouen from December 1845 to January 1847.

Eugène Sue: 1804–75. Popular descriptive novelist who analysed society. Best known for *Les Mystères de Paris* (1842–3). Flaubert wrote from Constantinople to Louis Bouilhet (14 Nov. 1850): 'I took Eugène Sue's *Arthur* from the reading-room. It's enough to make you vomit; there's no word to describe it.'

Balzac: 1799–1850. Much admired by Flaubert (letter to LB, 14 Nov. 1850), who saw his death as leaving a vast gap in the world of the French novel and who was influenced especially by the *Physiologie du mariage* and *La Muse du département* when he wrote *Madame Bovary*.

George Sand: 1804–76. At the time Flaubert wrote *Madame Bovary* he had not yet come to know, befriend, and admire George Sand whose early novels stressed a defiance of conventional morality.

60 *Yonville-l'Abbaye*: a fictitious name (see note to p. 61), based on the rue de la Croix d'Yonville to the west of the Hôtel-Dieu in Rouen and close to the house at Déville owned by Flaubert's father until 1844.

a Polish refugee: after the Warsaw risings of 1830–1, when Russia crushed Poland.

PART II

61 *Yonville-l'Abbaye*: 'Yonville-l'Abbaye itself is a place which doesn't exist, so too with the Rieulle [*sic*], etc.' (Letter to Émile Cailteaux, 4 June 1857.) Yonville has many of the spatial characteristics of Ry where the Delamare

family lived, but the directions given are of a journey to Forges-les-Eaux where Flaubert, his mother and his niece Caroline had stayed in 1848. They were taking refuge from Caroline's deranged widowed father Émile Hamard and they stayed with a family friend, Maître Beaufils (see letter to EC, 4 Aug. 1848). Ry is, for reasons of discretion and mystification, never mentioned in *Madame Bovary* and it is not known whether Flaubert ever went there. Some of the site characteristics of Forges (the Bray grazing district close by and the long red gashes of the iron-ore seams which help to create the spa waters) are evident.

Flaubert's imaginary Yonville lies about 32 km or 20 miles from Rouen.

In the topography of *Madame Bovary* no place-names outside Normandy are fictitious. Street and area names in Rouen also exist (or existed at the time). In Normandy, place-names exist in the given geographical context with the exception of the following: Andervilliers; Banneville; Barfeuchères; Barneville; le Bas-Diauville; Les Bertaux; La Fresnaye; Givry-Saint-Martin; hill of Leux; La Huchette; La Panville; the Rieule (river); Saint-Jean uplands; Sassetot-la-Guerrière; Thibourville; La Vaubyessard; Yonville-l'Abbaye; Yverbonville.

62 *for miles around*: Maître Beaufils's house in Forges may still be seen today at 11 avenue des Sources. It is a large, handsome, whitewashed building.

63 *the charter*: the French constitutional charter accepted by Louis-Philippe was published on 14 August 1830.

Eaux de Vichy . . .: waters from spa towns in the Massif Central, Germany and the Pyrenees respectively, though more generally eau de Seltz is soda water or artificial mineral water. *Robs dépuratifs* are purgative fruit juice extracts, *médecine Raspail* is a camphor-based cure, perhaps for worms (see *Bouvard et Pécuchet*, ch. iii). Raspail had been called to try to save Flaubert's sister in 1846 but had failed and he is mocked in Flaubert's *Sottisier*. Racahout was a food made of flour and starch introduced into France from North Africa in the nineteenth century. Pastilles Darcet are probably named after Jean-Pierre-Joseph Darcet, French chemist. Pâte Regnault was named after Victor Regnault, a French physicist. The evidence of Flaubert's early work *La Femme du monde* (1836) suggests it was a remedy for venereal disease.

64 *the cholera epidemic*: that which crossed Europe in 1832. See also p. 320.

the tin tricolour: Louis-Philippe had revived this as the national flag. It is made of tin to be visible when the wind drops.

65 *for Poland*: see note to p. 60.

the Lyons floods: of 1840.

67 *behind my ear*: 'I have never written anything more difficult than what I am writing at present, trivial dialogue' (letter to LC, 19 Sept. 1852).

68 *the Supreme Being*: a deist cult introduced by Robespierre (who was especially influenced by Rousseau) on 7 May 1794 and publicly celebrated at

the *fête de l'Être suprême* on 8 June 1794, to combat atheism and excessive dechristianization by the institution of natural religion.

and of Béranger: Socrates had been condemned in part for the worship of his own deities. Benjamin Franklin was a freemason, Voltaire a somewhat sceptical deist. For Béranger, see note to p. 9.

the Vicaire savoyard: Rousseau's defence of natural religion, the *Profession de foi du vicaire savoyard*, is to be found in Book IV of *Émile* (1762).

immortal principles of '89: to be found in the *Déclaration des droits de l'homme et du citoyen* voted by the Constituent Assembly on 27 August 1789.

71 *fifty-four Fahrenheit*: this is 12.2° Centigrade. Flaubert's notes stated 'Homais has rather a cavalier attitude to precision' (*MB* n.v., 60).

72 *Guardian Angel*: a popular *romance sentimentale* by Pauline Duchambge (1778–1858).

74 *a library subscription*: 'I am doing a conversation between a young man and a young woman about literature, the sea, the mountains, music, all the poetical subjects. It is something that could be taken seriously, and yet I fully intend it as grotesque. This will be the first time, I think, that a book makes fun of its leading lady and its leading man. The irony does not detract from the pathetic aspect, but rather intensifies it' (letter to LC, 9 Oct. 1852).

Walter Scott: Flaubert seems to have acknowledged the greatness of both Voltaire and Rousseau whilst infinitely preferring the former (letter to Mme Roger des Genettes, 1859 or 1860). He had a low opinion of Delille, who was a popular eighteenth-century nature poet (see *Hommage à Louis Bouilhet*, III). Scott was seen as the archetypal Romantic novelist (see *Bouvard et Pécuchet*, ch. v).

the Fanal de Rouen: Flaubert was asked by the *Journal de Rouen* not to use its name here, as had been his original intention.

76 *Year XI*: 10 March 1803 is the Gregorian calendar equivalent of this Revolutionary calendar date. Flaubert is accurate about article 1, though doctors and chemists were answerable to the *Préfet* and Homais might have expected a summons to the *Préfecture*.

77 *broken into a thousand pieces*: the final disintegration of the statue follows its gradual decay. It is mentioned earlier on pp. 28, 50 and 57.

79 *Atala*: probably a memory of the Indian girl in Chateaubriand's work *Atala* (1801). Certainly there is nothing Italianate about the name.

Yseult or Léocadie: Galswinthe was Queen of Neustria (*c*.540–68), Yseult was Tristan's love in Arthurian legend, and Léocadie may be a memory of the heroine in a play of that name by Scribe and Mélesville (1824).

Irma: derived from an ancient Germanic root.

Athalie: Racine's last tragedy (1691), whose religious subject-matter irritates Homais. 'Racine! Corneille! and other talents just as mortally boring' (letter to LC, 29 Jan. 1854).

80 *Le Dieu des bonnes gens*: an anti-clerical piece of verse by Béranger (1817).

barcarolle: a Venetian gondoliers' song.

La Guerre des dieux: Parny's blasphemous poem completed in 1799.

her small daughter: worries over a similarity here with Balzac's *Le Médecin de campagne* were linked with further worries over comparison of the opening of the novel with Balzac's *Louis Lambert* and Du Camp's *Livre posthume* (letter to LC, 27 Dec. 1852).

six weeks of the Virgin: from Christmas until the Purification of the Virgin (2 Feb.) is six weeks. Mothers were traditionally expected to avoid physical exertion for six weeks after giving birth.

82 *Mathieu Laensberg*: a popular almanac first published in 1636 in Liège, which finally ceased publication in the middle of the nineteenth century.

86 *osmazome*: liquid extract of meat containing its taste and smell. The name *osmazôme* was coined by the chemist Thénard (1777–1857).

89 *flax mill*: flax cultivation and spinning were much developed during the nineteenth century in Normandy.

a bundle of straw . . . with tricolour ribbons: put up to celebrate the completion of the roof timbers.

in metres: the metric system, approved after the Revolution, was spreading only slowly in the provinces.

94 *Notre-Dame de Paris*: Hugo's novel (1831) includes in it (as Esméralda's mother) Paquette-la-Chantefleurie. If Emma is doing the thinking here she is revealing a lack of accuracy while imagining herself to be sophisticated.

103 *diachylon*: a lead plaster to reduce swelling.

104 *Caribs or Botocudos*: tribes from the West Indies and from Brazil respectively.

105 *so why not go now?*: Flaubert read law in Paris in 1842–3; but his nervous illness which began dramatically on a journey to Pont-l'Évêque in January 1844 (and his failure in the second year Law Faculty exam six months earlier) made him then abandon these studies.

107 '*English fashion, then*': Emma considers the handshake too intimate initially, and then yields to the feeling that its Englishness prevents it from being a compromising action. This affair has ended platonically and without a formal declaration; Flaubert's early plans had sketched a full and passionate love.

108 *a Jesuit*: here meaning 'a hypocrite'.

112 *Emma must be prevented from reading novels*: 'Novel—novels pervert the masses' (*DIR*).

113 *La Huchette*: Louis Campion has been considered the likely model for

Rodolphe Boulanger. He lived at Villiers, 2 km south of Ry, in a house which has since become known on I.g.n. maps as La Huchette. His relationship with Delphine Delamare remains mysterious but suggestive. (See Gossez's article (note to p. 1 above), and *OC* 1, 26.)

117 *the famous show*: this chapter set at the *comices agricoles* is the longest in the novel and took nearly five months to complete between July and December 1853. Flaubert had visited a *comice agricole* at Grand-Couronne, a little downstream from Croisset in July 1852, which he described as 'one of those inept rustic ceremonies' (letter to LC, 18 July 1852). The record of the *Nouvelliste de Rouen* of 19 and 20 July 1852 shows that Flaubert drew much material from what he had witnessed. The *comice agricole* was instituted in the late eighteenth century as a free association for the improvement of agriculture. The term became transferred to the shows, which proliferated after 1830, and *comices agricoles* (covering either a *canton*, an *arrondissement* or even a *département*) offered prizes for good use and development of agricultural implements, for breeding and cross-breeding, for soil use and for pasture development, for irrigation and for upkeep of agricultural buildings. Hard-working and long-serving farmhands, shepherds, and farm servants could receive awards.

119 *the rat in the cheese*: a reference to La Fontaine's fable *Le Rat qui s'est retiré du monde* (Fables, vii. 3).

120 *Agronomical Society of Rouen*: fictitious, but Rouen was the seat of the Seine-Inférieure Agricultural Society (see also p. 138).

125 *unable to come*: this had been the case at the 1852 Grand-Couronne comice.

133 *Cincinnatus*: fifth-century BC Roman dictator to whom the lictors brought the insignia of office while he was guiding his plough.

Diocletian: abdicated as Roman emperor in AD 305, traditionally in order to cultivate his lettuces.

emperors of China: they took part in person in the sowing season.

134 *Leroux*: the *Nouvelliste de Rouen* recorded the award of a medal and sixty francs to a farm servant who had served for forty-five years. Flaubert is happy to exaggerate the evidence of hard-won reward.

138 *followers of Loyola*: i.e. Jesuits. They had been re-established in France in 1814.

147 *on the bed-table*: Flaubert himself kept a pipe and a glass of water by his bedside. See the *Souvenirs* of his niece, Caroline Commanville (Paris, Ferraud, 1895).

150 *jujube paste*: a cough medicine.

157 *Dr Duval's book*: this is the *Traité pratique du pied-bot* by Vincent Duval published in 1839. One patient, Cécile Martin, had been successfully cured by Duval after Flaubert's father, using irons, had failed over a

period of nine months to effect a cure. It is interesting to note that the next case in the book involves a patient whose first name was Hippolyte. Flaubert had consulted his brother Achille, a surgeon, about club-foot surgery (letter to LC, 18 April 1854). Charles as an *officier de santé* should have performed a club-foot operation only in the presence of a fully qualified doctor.

157 *the equine . . . valgine forms*: respectively a club-foot taking the weight on the tip of the toe, an inward-turning club-foot, and an outward-turning club-foot.

159 *Ambroise Paré . . . Celsus . . . Dupuytren . . . Gensoul*: respectively famous French surgeon (1517–90), Roman doctor (25 BC to AD 50), French surgeon (1777–1835) for whom Flaubert's father had been anatomy demonstrator, and French surgeon (1797–1858).

tenotome: small scalpel.

161 *ecchymosis*: blotchiness caused by bleeding beneath the skin.

163 *Bon-Secours*: a pilgrimage basilica overlooking the Seine on the south-east of Rouen, consecrated in 1842.

twig of boxwood: it would have been blessed on Palm Sunday.

164 *strabism . . . lithotropy*: (an operation to correct) squinting; an operation for removing gallstones.

172 *napoleons*: gold coins each worth 20 francs.

Amor nel cor: probably a quotation from Dante, *Vita Nuova* xxiii, 31, which reads 'piansemi Amor nel core, ove dimora' ('Love wept in my heart where he abides'). Louise Colet had given Flaubert a seal with the identical motto. When she had read the novel, and because Flaubert had at his insistence ended their affair in 1854, she felt herself mocked. Presumably the wound smarted, for in 1859 she wrote a poem called *Amor nel cor* in which she half-openly derided Flaubert.

174 *a brown beard*: in French, *un collier brun*. Beards of this type, following the line of the jaw, were among Flaubert's aversions as listed to Louise Colet (1 June 1852). Cf. note to p. 9.

179 *as far as Genoa*: in 1845 Flaubert and his parents accompanied his sister Caroline and her husband Émile Hamard on their honeymoon through Paris and Marseilles to Genoa. It was in Genoa that Flaubert saw in the Balbi Palace the *Temptation of St. Antony*, which helped to inspire him to write his own versions of the work of that name. It was then attributed to Pieter Brueghel the Younger, but is now thought to have been painted by Jan Mandyn.

Monday, the 4th September: this may be a key to a possible chronology of *Madame Bovary* and would imply that we are now in 1843. This fits well with the other rather vague indications of time. But it may not be intentional and Flaubert is not always accurate about such details.

184 *the manchineel tree*: a tree found in the West Indies and South America

which has a poisonous sap and whose shadow was popularly supposed to be deadly.

188 *quite rigid*: Flaubert may be remembering his own epileptic seizure when in a cab near Pont-l'Évêque in January 1844.

189 *sternutatory*: (agent) causing sneezing.

190 *That is the question*: the English phrase (*Hamlet*, III. i) has become a fairly commonplace foreign phrase in France.

192 *one hundred and thirty francs*: seventy francs from the loan to Charles and sixty francs profit ('a good thirty-three and a third profit on the goods supplied', i.e. 'the travelling cloak, the hand-bag, two trunks instead of one, and a number of other items as well') which are valued at 'the one hundred and eighty already owing'.

195 *Monsieur de Maistre*: Joseph de Maistre (1753–1821). Flaubert in letters to Mme Roger des Genettes of 1859 or 1860 and of September 1873 scorned the writing of de Maistre's counter-attacks on the influence of the eighteenth-century *philosophes* and on scientific progress and scientific values.

penitent blue-stockings: i.e. who have turned their backs on free-thinking.

La Vallière: see p. 33 and note.

198 *Castigat ridendo mores*: 'It corrects morals by laughter', the motto composed by Santeuil for the harlequin Dominique (1637–88) to use in his theatre.

Voltaire's tragedies: there are some seventeen of these. Flaubert was scathing in his criticism of them (letter to LC, 2 July 1853).

Le Gamin de Paris: a light comedy by Bayard and Vanderbuch (1836).

the Fathers of the Church: the early Christian writers (first to sixth centuries).

201 *the theatre*: this is the *Théâtre des Arts*, built in 1775 and destroyed by fire in 1876, facing the river opposite the suspension bridge. It had a capacity of two thousand. It even had a motto based on the words *Castigat ridendo mores*. (See G. Daniels, 'Emma Bovary's Opera', *French Studies*, July 1978, for a very sensitive and informative article on Emma's visit to the opera.)

Lucie de Lammermoor: Walter Scott's *The Bride of Lammermoor* (1819) had been adapted by Donizetti for his opera *Lucia di Lammermoor*. The French version referred to in this chapter had a libretto by Alphonse Royer and Gustave Vaëz with additional music by Donizetti. Flaubert had seen the original Italian version in Constantinople (letter to Mme Flaubert, 14 Nov. 1850).

203 *remembering her early reading*: see p. 33. The plot follows that of *The Bride of Lammermoor*, but is much reduced. Henri Ashton wishes his sister Lucie to marry Sir Arthur Bucklaw. Lucie has pledged herself to Edgar Ravenswood, with whom her family has quarrelled. Ashton,

helped by Gilbert his evil henchman, convinces Lucie that Edgar has abandoned her. The wretched girl consents to marry Sir Arthur, when Edgar appears. Ashton's plot is revealed to Lucie. Edgar thinks Lucie is unfaithful and she, marrying Arthur, becomes mad and stabs him on her wedding night. Edgar challenges Ashton to a duel but he attends to his dying sister instead. Edgar learns the whole truth and kills himself in front of Ashton, who is now racked by remorse.

203 *Edgar Lagardy appeared*: Flaubert gives him the same first name as that of his role. Traditionally the model for Lagardy is the tenor G.-H. Roger.

207 *Guess whom I ran into?*: originally Flaubert had planned that Léon and Emma should meet again in Paris but 'at the theatre' (*MB* n.v. 17).

208 *Her hair is coming down*: the famous mad scene (III. vi).

'*Oh bel ange, ma Lucie!*' song by the dying Edgar (IV. vi).

209 *Tamburini, Rubini, Persiani, Grisi*: famous Italian opera singers of the early nineteenth century. Léon had intended to hear 'the Italian singers' in Paris (p. 33). Grisi was a prima donna; Persiani also composed.

210 *passage Saint-Herbland*: opposite the west front of the cathedral.

PART III

211 *La Chaumière*: famous dance-hall in Paris on the boulevard de Mont-parnasse. Founded in 1787, it was very fashionable in the first half of the nineteenth century.

grisettes: young working girls of easy virtue.

the Code: a copy of the official statute books drawn up under Napoleon I.

216 *four prints representing the Tour de Nesle*: this is a melodrama by Dumas père and Gaillardet, first performed in 1832. The play set in the early fourteenth century evokes the debauches of the three daughters-in-law of Philippe le Bel which took place, by tradition, in the tower of Nesle (on the site of the present Institut de France opposite the Louvre). The prints with Spanish and French texts, a series of scenes from the play, were four lithographs by Lordereau published in 1840.

219 *the Dancing Marianne*: this is a popular name for the thirteenth-century stone carving of Salome dancing before Herod which is on the tympanum of the Portail Saint-Jean. Flaubert's tale *Hérodias* (1877) was probably inspired in part by it

holy-water stoups: a feature not of the cathedral but of the nearby Saint-Ouen church is a 'marble holy-water stoup fixed to the first pillar on the right (on entering by the west door) in which, by a strange optical effect, part of the interior of the building is reflected' (Adolphe Joanne, *Itinéraire général de la France: Normandie*, Paris, Hachette, 1866, p. 49).

220 *boatmen . . . carrying baskets*: in the Chapelle Saint-Nicolas in the north transept a window is dedicated to the Watermen's Guild.

Lady Chapel: built between 1302 and 1320, it forms the apse of the cathedral and is noted for its fine Renaissance tombs.

the glories of the Tabernacle: there is a seventeenth-century carved wood reredos with a fine Nativity painted by Philippe de Champaigne (1629), which might have caught Emma's attention.

221 *of any kind*: this entirely unremarkable curiosity was in fact embellished with rose tracery in black flint decorated with representations of the four winds. It was destroyed in about 1883 at the time of the repaving of the square.

great bell: named after Cardinal Georges d'Amboise, Louis XII's first minister. It had formerly been hung in the Tour de Beurre, was one of the biggest bells known and was melted down in 1793 in Rémilly.

Pierre de Brézé: the de Brézés were one of the most powerful families of fifteenth-century France and their fine tombs and brief biographies are accurately described and given.

Montlhéry: the battle between the forces of Louis XI and Charles the Bold.

222 *Diane de Poitiers*: mistress of Henri II.

the Amboise tombs: Georges d'Amboise (I) who died in 1510 and after whom the bell was named and his nephew Georges d'Amboise (II), died 1550, both cardinals. Georges I is the 'generous patron'.

Louis XII: reigned from 1498 to 1515.

a chapel cumbered with balustrades: that of Saints Peter and Paul in the north ambulatory of the choir, a temporary resting place for the statue of Richard Cœur de Lion, now placed near the choir railings.

its present state: the statue had been rediscovered in 1838. The Calvinist disfigurement took place in 1562.

La Gargouille: this is at the south end of the south transept and depicts a legend of a miraculous and fantastic sort with a monster popularly thought to resemble a gargoyle.

whimsical tinker: the spire, the tallest in France, was being reconstructed in iron to replace that destroyed by fire in 1822. From 1826 to 1849 building took place. A public row over the erection suspended further work until 1875. The finishing touches took place in 1884. The spire is in fact 495 feet high, but the statistics of the Great Pyramid, climbed by Flaubert on 8 December 1849 (see letter to Mme Flaubert, 14 Dec. 1849) are correct.

223 *the North Door*: the Portail des Libraires has very beautiful carvings of the thirteenth and fourteenth centuries.

Pierre Corneille: the famous playwright (1606–84) was a native of Rouen. His statue was at this time on the western tip of the Île Lacroix. The bronze statue, 4 metres high on its plinth, was cast by David d'Angers and unveiled on 19 October 1834.

224 *about midday*: in fact the cab-ride must have begun about midday.

225 *the cab stopped*: the cab-ride may have been based in part on a scene in Chapter xi of Mérimée's *La Double Méprise* (1833). It can be followed quite clearly to 'the hill of Deville' after which it visits real places 'at random' (as the text states). The *Revue de Paris* serial publication of *Madame Bovary* in 1856 left out the cab-ride for reasons of discretion but Sénard defending Flaubert at his trial was not afraid to read it out in full.

227 *Fabricando . . . agis*: 'Whatever you do, practice makes perfect.'

228 *Conjugal . . . Love*: the French text makes it clear that this refers to the *Tableau de l'amour conjugal* by Nicolas Venette (doctor and teacher of anatomy at La Rochelle) first published in 1686 and much reprinted. To use its own words, the work is one of 'initiation sexuelle'. Flaubert claimed this 'inept production' was one of the two annual best-sellers (letter to LC, 22 Nov. 1852).

229 *Doudeville*: 25 miles north of Rouen on the road to Saint-Valéry-en-Caux.

232 *a power of attorney*: this would give Emma the right to act for her husband in financial affairs.

235 *Un soir, t'en souvient-il? nous voguions*: from verse 4 of Lamartine's *Le Lac*, first published in the *Méditations poétiques* (1820). The poet is alone in his boat and reminiscing in the imagined presence only of his love.

238 *Rousseau's favourite ideas*: in *Émile* (1762), his novel of educational theory. 'I'm now reading the *Émile* of that Rousseau. What a strange set of ideas in the book, but "it's well written", I must admit and I don't find that easy' (letter to LB, 23 May 1855).

suckling babies: see also *Émile* (Book I) and Rousseau's *Nouvelle Héloise* (1761).

vaccination: in 1796 Jenner concluded his research into how to inoculate against smallpox. Flaubert and his friends Bouilhet and Du Camp had written a parody of a tragedy by Delille (see note to p. 74), which they called *La Découverte de la vaccine* and which was probably begun in 1845 or 1846.

240 *the whole city lay spread below them*: this famous description would appear to be down the rue d'Ernemont where it reaches the route de Neufchâtel on the heights on the northern outskirts of the city.

241 *The air was filled . . . oysters*: 'I'm painting the places which were the "beloved theatre of your childhood games", that's to say: the cafés, taverns, bars and brothels which embellish the depths of the rue des Charrettes (I'm in the heart of Rouen). And I have even just left, in order to write to you, the brothels with their railings, the tubs of evergreen, the smell of absinth, of cigars and of oysters etc. The word is out: *Babylon* is there' (letter to LB, 23 May 1855).

242 *Bathing Odalisque*: an odalisque was popularly taken to mean a woman of

the sultan's harem. Odalisques figured frequently in early nineteenth-century French painting, for instance in the works of Ingres, Chassériau, and Delacroix.

Pale Woman of Barcelona: probably a romantic fantasy rather than a specific painting.

244 *Souvent la chaleur . . .*: from *L'Année des dames nationales* (1794) by Restif de la Bretonne (1734–1806).

250 *Emma was a bit confused in her calculations*: so was Flaubert. 'I'm bogged down in explanations of bills of discount, etc., which I don't really understand' (letter to LB, 27 June 1855).

255 *instead of Je m'en vais*: *turne* and *bazar* both mean 'a badly kept, dirty house', *chicard* means 'distinctive' or 'elegant', and *chicandard* is its superlative. *Je me la casse*, 'I go away', is based on the idea of bending or breaking the leg for forward movement. *Breda-street* (named after the rue Bréda—now the rue Clauzel—a centre of elegant night-life and prostitution at this time in Paris) gave its name to the slang coined by the *demimonde* who frequented the quartier Bréda, other examples of which language are quoted here by Homais. Presumably the snobbery of all things English turned the rue Bréda into *Breda-street*. In his letter of 23 May 1855 to Bouilhet written at about the time of the composition of this chapter Flaubert writes of Bouilhet's projected visit to Italy with Alfred Guerard and says: 'C'est une occâse [opportunity] (style Breda street).'

257 *confined to artists*: 'I'm getting Homais to expose some bawdy theories about women. I'm worried that it will appear too *forced*' (letter to LB, 1 Aug. 1855. See also *DIR* under 'brunes' and 'négresses').

258 *Cujas and Bartolo*: French and Italian jurists of the sixteenth and fourteenth centuries respectively. See *DIR* under their names.

a seltzer-water machine: Flaubert stayed with a chemist in Trouville who made his own seltzer water. He was something of a model for Homais (see letter to LB, 24 Aug. 1853).

267 *the platitudes of marriage*: this phrase was fiercely attacked at Flaubert's trial after the publication of the novel.

269 *the gardens*: probably the market gardens of the Prairies Saint-Gervais, a large open space west of the Hôtel-Dieu. Emma may well be in the rue du Renard running along the northern edge of the gardens.

275 *cheminots*: 'It's essential that *cheminots* find a place in *Bovary*. My book would be incomplete without the said alimentary turbans since I intend to *paint* Rouen . . . I'll see that Homais is crazy about "cheminots". It will be one of the secret reasons for his journey to Rouen, and what's more his only human weakness . . . they will come from the rue Massacre' (letter to LB, 23 May 1855). In the novel it is Mme Homais who dotes on *cheminots*. This patois word was usually spelt 'chemineau'. It is defined as 'cake of fine wheaten flour' in Henri Moisy, *Dictionnaire de patois*

normand (quoted in Flaubert, *Correspondance* 11, ed. Bruneau, Pléiade, 1980, p. 1180).

276 *murmured a number of medical terms*: 'Here now is the composition of the eye, as far as I remember it: 1st eyelids; 2nd sclerotic, or opaque cornea (it's the white); 3rd cornea proper or transparent cornea (it's the brown circle in the middle); 4th the pupil, in the centre of the cornea; 5th within, behind, the crystalline lens; 6th the optic nerve, etc. That, I think, is quite enough, beware of saying too much about it. Hommais [*sic*] is only a country chemist, he doesn't know any anatomy, he has remembered only a few words.' (Letter of 22 Sept. 1855 from LB to GF.)

roasted meat: 'And in any case: as all these ailments are the result of a scrofulous defect, he will advise him, in a kindly way, to follow a good diet, good wine, good beer, roast meat, all of this volubly, like a lesson being recited (he remembers the prescriptions which he receives daily, and which end invariably with these words: abstain from *farinaceous* and *milk* foods, and *from time to time expose the skin to the smoke of juniper berries*). I think that these pieces of advice given by a large man to this wretch who is dying of hunger would have a fairly moving effect.' (LB to GF, 18 Sept. 1855.)

277 *Esmeralda by Steuben*: i.e. a print of the painting *Esméralda et Quasimodo* (1839) (a scene based on Hugo's *Notre-Dame de Paris*) by Charles de Steuben (1788–1856).

Schopin's Potiphar: i.e. a print of a painting by Henri Frédéric Schopin (1804–80), perhaps his *Femme de Putiphar méditant sa vengeance*. Petrus Borel's *Madame Putiphar* had been published in 1839.

282 *Bautzen . . . Lutzen*: Napoleonic victories in 1813 over the Russians near Dresden and the Prussians near Leipzig.

the Campaign of France: the 'Hundred Days' between the escape from Elba and the battle of Waterloo in 1815.

289 *between the branches of the trees*: Flaubert's own hallucinations are somewhat similarly described in his letters: 'There's no day when I don't see from time to time what are like tufts of hair or Bengal lights passing before my eyes' (letter to EC, 7 June 1844).

291 *a sudden spasm of nausea*: 'When I wrote the description of the poisoning of Mme Bovary I had the taste of arsenic so much in my mouth, I had taken so much poison myself that I gave myself two bouts of indigestion one after the other—two real bouts for I threw up all my dinner' (letter to HT, Nov. 1866).

295 *It was Dr Larivière*: 'under whom he had once studied' (p. 190). He had advised the move from Tostes for the improvement of Emma's health (p. 60). In Larivière there is something of a portrait of Flaubert's father, who became a doctor in 1810 and worked at the Hôtel-Dieu in Rouen, of which he became Master in 1818. He died in office in January 1846.

Bichat: Xavier Bichat, famous French teacher of anatomy and physiology (1771–1802).

297 *cantharides, upas, the manchineel tree*: the first is a species of beetle which includes the Spanish Fly. The dried beetle was used to raise blisters on the skin or, internally, to cause a discharge of urine. The upas is a tree whose poison was used by East Indian natives on their arrows. For the manchineel tree, see note to p. 184.

Cadet de Gassicourt: Charles-Louis Cadet de Gassicourt (1769–1821), French chemist. He wrote not only on chemistry but on travel and comedy as well.

298 *morbid hunger*: Flaubert himself suffered from this.

299 *divine mercy*: the extreme unction rite had been somewhat similarly described by Sainte-Beuve in the death of Madame de Couaën in *Volupté* (1834). The defence at Flaubert's trial in 1857 linked Flaubert's description with Abbé Ambroise Guillois's *Explication historique, dogmatique, morale, liturgique et canonique du catéchisme* . . . (Le Mans, Monnoyer, 1851).

304 *read d'Holbach, read the Encyclopaedia*: the Baron d'Holbach (1723–89), philosopher and theist, author of the *Système de la Nature* (1770), was a contributor to the *Encyclopaedia* edited by Diderot and d'Alembert between 1750 and 1780, which examined the universe through the use of the reason and which attacked—often covertly—superstition and dogma.

Les Lettres de quelques juifs portuguais: by the Abbé Antoine Gunéné (1769), a reply to Voltaire's attacks on the Bible.

La Raison du christianisme by Nicolas: this defence of the Roman Catholic Church during the religious revival of the first part of the nineteenth century was by J. J. A. Nicolas. It is correctly called the *Études philosophiques sur le christianisme* (1842–5).

310 *It was time for the procession to move off*: Flaubert had been to the funeral of the wife of Dr Pouchet on 7 June 1853. He anticipated the event in a letter: 'Since I must moreover *take advantage of all I can*, I'm sure that tomorrow will be a very dark drama and that this poor man of science will be pitiable. I will find there things for my *Bovary*' (letter to LC, 6 June 1853).

serpent-player: the serpent was a musical instrument, a bass form of the cornet, shaped like a snake.

312 *a proceeding . . . sadly lacking in taste*: Flaubert, describing the funeral of his friend Alfred Le Poittevin, wrote: 'When the hole was filled in, I turned on my heels and came away, smoking, which Boivin [friend and lawyer] found lacking in taste' (letter to Maxim Du Camp, 7 April 1848).

318 *the primary schools*: instituted after Guizot's elementary education act of 1833, they multiplied slowly in the 1830s and the 1840s.

318 *Ignorantine Friars*: the monks of Saint-Jean-de-Dieu took this name out of humility. It later became a general insulting term for a Christian monk.

fish-breeding, rubber, railways, etc.: gradually we are brought up to the period of Flaubert's composition of the novel. Remy experimented with the artificial fertilization of fish spawn at La Bresse in the Vosges from 1842; Goodyear had invented vulcanization in 1837 and the uses rubber was put to multiplied subsequently in America and in Europe; the 1842 railway law had distinguished between and encouraged the coexistence and expansion of public railway companies.

cho-ca: a brand of cocoa powder.

revalentia: usually 'revalenta' or 'revalesciere'. The English industrialist Du Barry had invented this health-giving panacea made of lentils, maize, peas, beans, millet, salt, barley, and oats with cochineal colouring.

Pulvermacher electric belts: first marketed in France in 1852, this protective apparatus was worn next to the skin to cure and to ward off rheumatism, epilepsy and other afflictions.

Vaufrylard: in Madame Sabatier's salon Flaubert was known as 'le sire de Vaufrylard'. Flaubert had taken to living some of the year in Paris from 1855 onwards and he presented Madame Sabatier with a copy of *Madame Bovary* in 1857.

319 *Sta viator . . . amabilem conjugem calcas*: 'Stop, traveller . . . a wife worthy of love lies beneath your feet.'

excrement: originally he was refused burial in sanctified ground, but in 1791, thirteen years after his death, his remains were interred in the Pantheon. 'Bournisien confuses Voltaire and Rousseau—who died devouring his own excrement, as everybody knows' (note by Flaubert in *MB* n.v., 128).

320 *the cholera epidemic*: see note to p. 64.

the Academy: i.e. to the Académie des sciences, belles-lettres et arts in Rouen.

321 *'Les Favorites du Commerce'*: a 'favorite' was a small and presumably speedy cab in towns. Lheureux's service is designed as a fast coach or wagon service.